iginal · Danbi Original · Danbi Original · Danbi Original · Danbi Original · Danbi Original · D

Bring it on!

vol.3

Baek HyeKyung

ice
Kunion

Words from the Creator

It was quite difficult to work on the 3rd volume. Perhaps it's my punishment for goofing off too much while working on volume 2. I've been so on the edge, I'm afraid I've been snapping at my friends. (I'll pay you guys back with my body for being so patient with me -3-) Well, I've been thinking about what I should do for a change of pace, but I can't really come up with anything. Once the series ends, I'd like to go to Europe. One of my friends who's gone to Poland to study abroad said if I come over she'll show me around some old construction sites and pretty graveyards. Snicker. (Bring It On!) should be ending around winter so perhaps I should start planning out my trip soon. '_' I would like to thank my mom, dad, my "right-handman the blue dragon" Woo-Wun, and my "left-handman the white tiger" Jae-Eun, my drinking buddies and all those who read my books for making my daily life enjoyable. (Though I may feel unworthy of this work, I hope you all enjoy the book T.T). Everyone, thank you very very much.

Hye-Kyung Baek

Q&A

with Hae-Kyung Baek!

1. In <Bring It On!>, which character is most like yourself?
Hmmm… at first it was Yang-Ha, but now, I'm more like Ki-Ri.

2. Do you like pretty boys like Seung-Suh or Mu-Jin?
Nod nod nod nod // If they're my type and
we've got the same philosophy and they're youthful,
pretty young men, I'm willing to sell my soul
to get them... snicker.

**3. <Bring It On!> has a lot of funny plot twists,
where do you get these ideas?**
From goofing around. Dear Editor~ I get ideas from goofing around,
please give me more time to be lazy.

**4. As a manhwa artist, when are you most happy and
when are you most sad?**
I'm happy when people enjoy my work, and I'm saddest when what
I'm doing feels empty and pointless.

5. Do you have any favorite manhwa/manga artists or authors?
I have a lot but my favorite is Urasawa Naoki.

6. Last word to <Bring It On!> fans?
You'll be graced with many blessings.

Let me
goof around~.

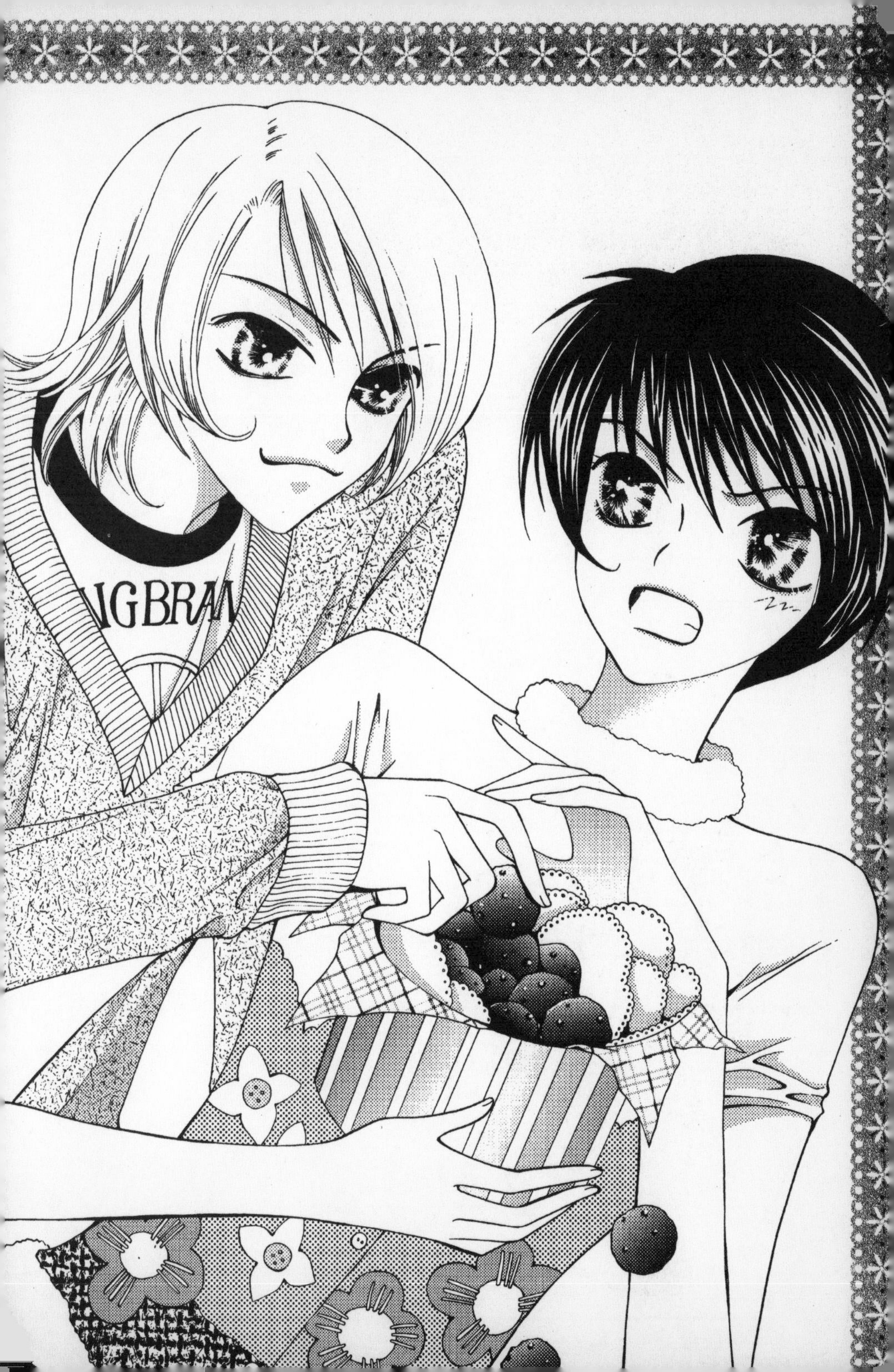

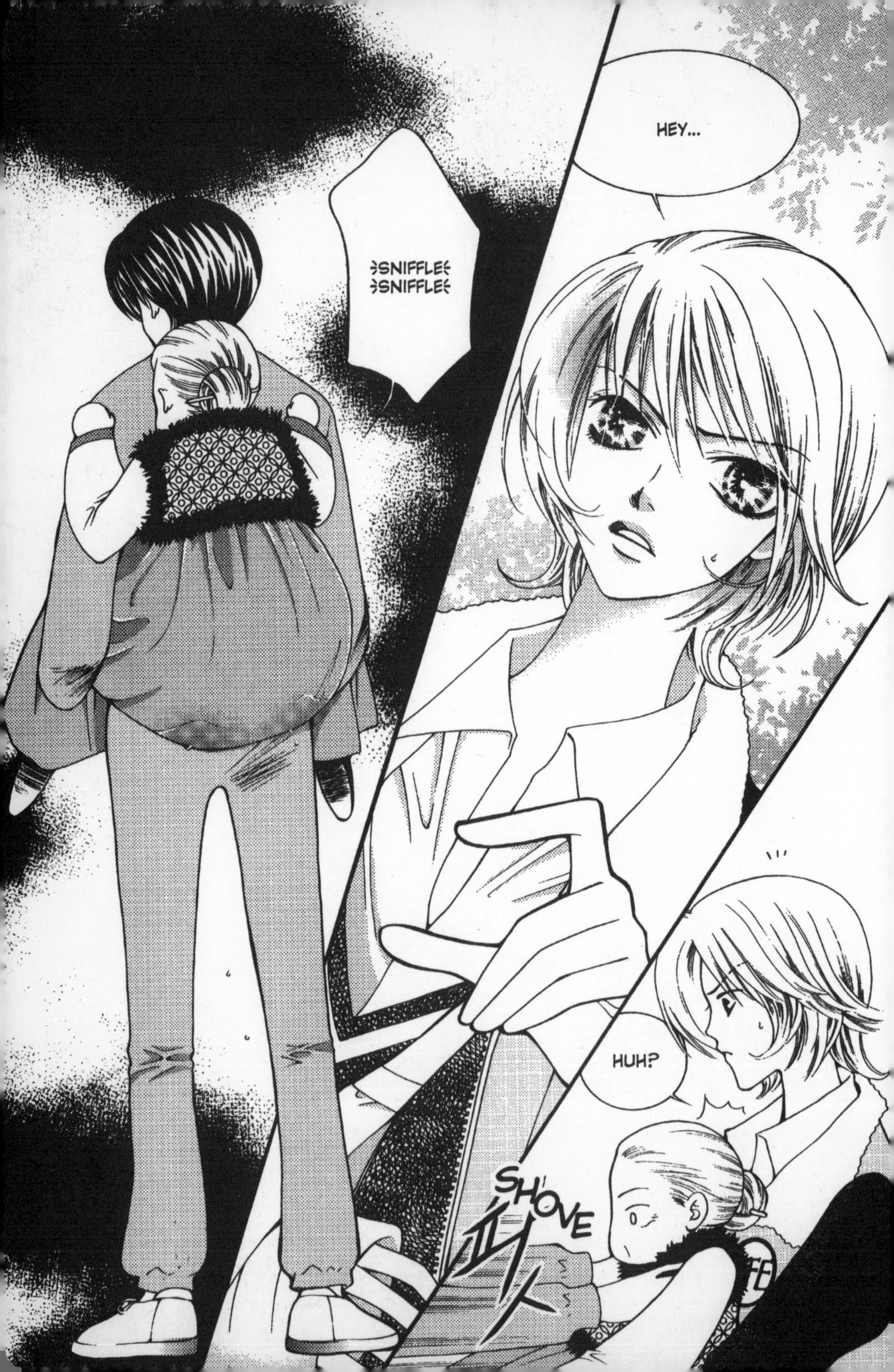
SNIFFLE SNIFFLE
HEY...
HUH?
SHOVE

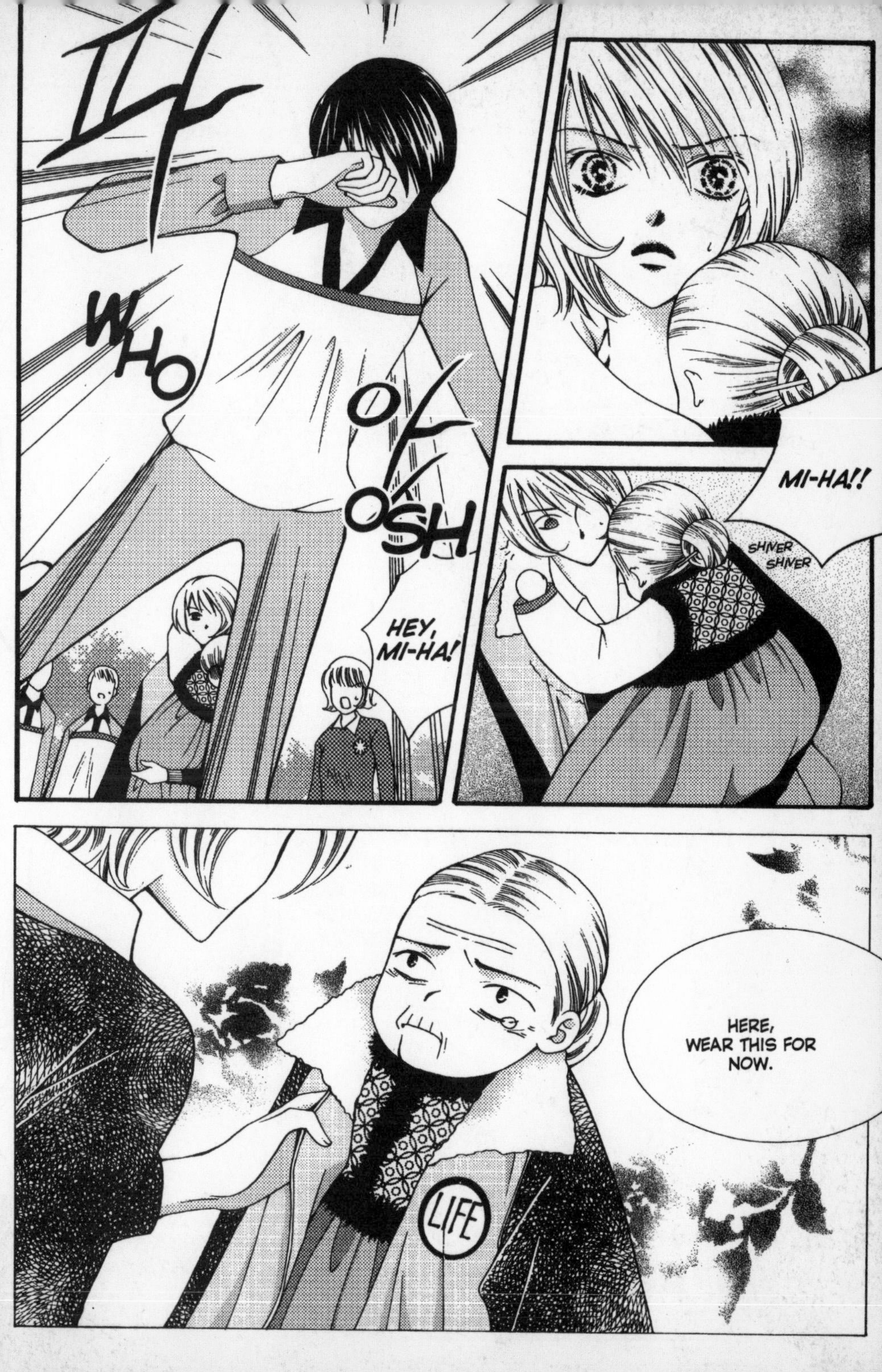
WHOOSH
HEY, MI-HA!
MI-HA!!
SHIVER SHIVER
HERE, WEAR THIS FOR NOW.
LIFE

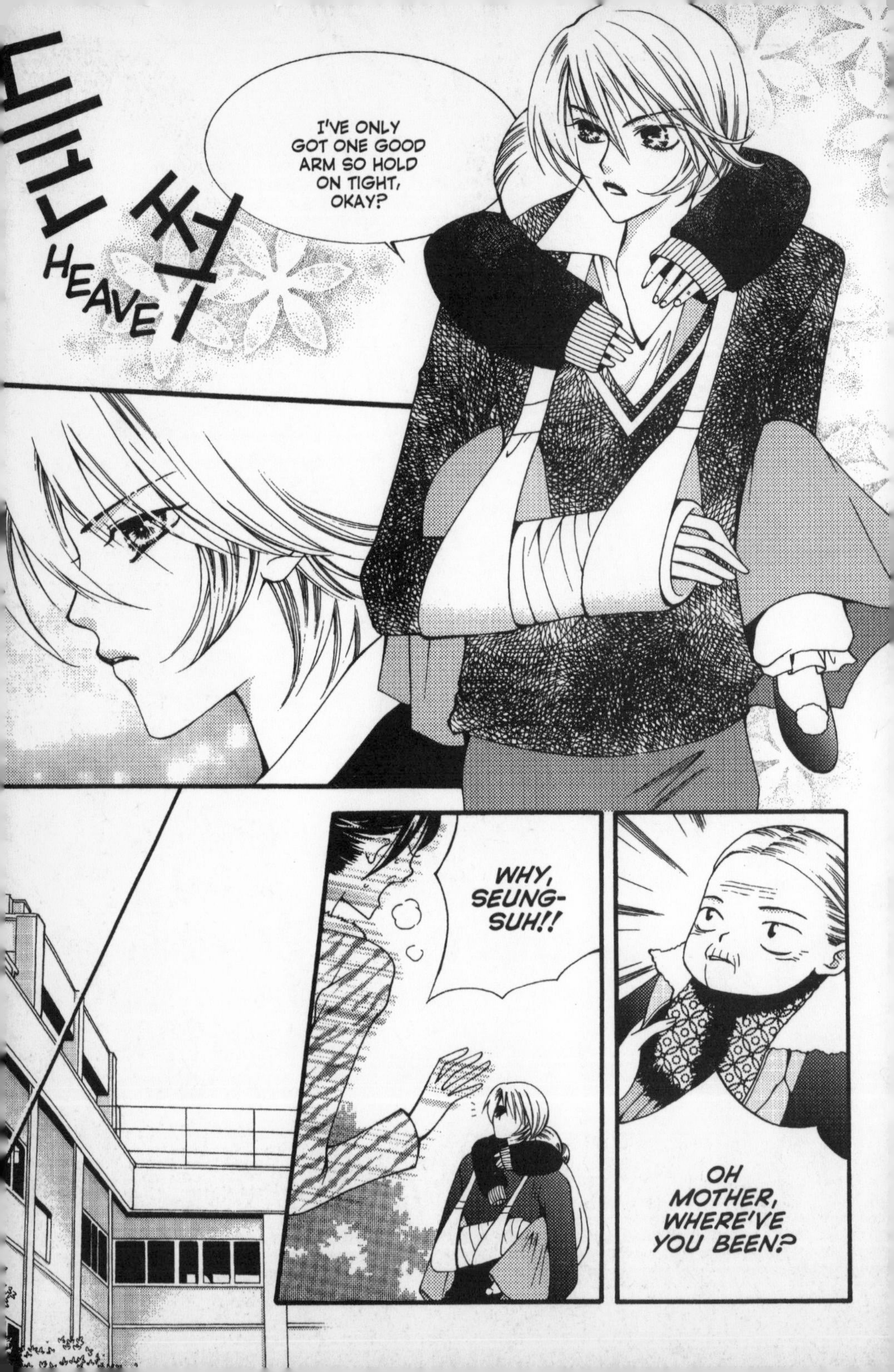
HEAVE
I'VE ONLY GOT ONE GOOD ARM SO HOLD ON TIGHT, OKAY?
WHY, SEUNG-SUH!!
OH MOTHER, WHERE'VE YOU BEEN?

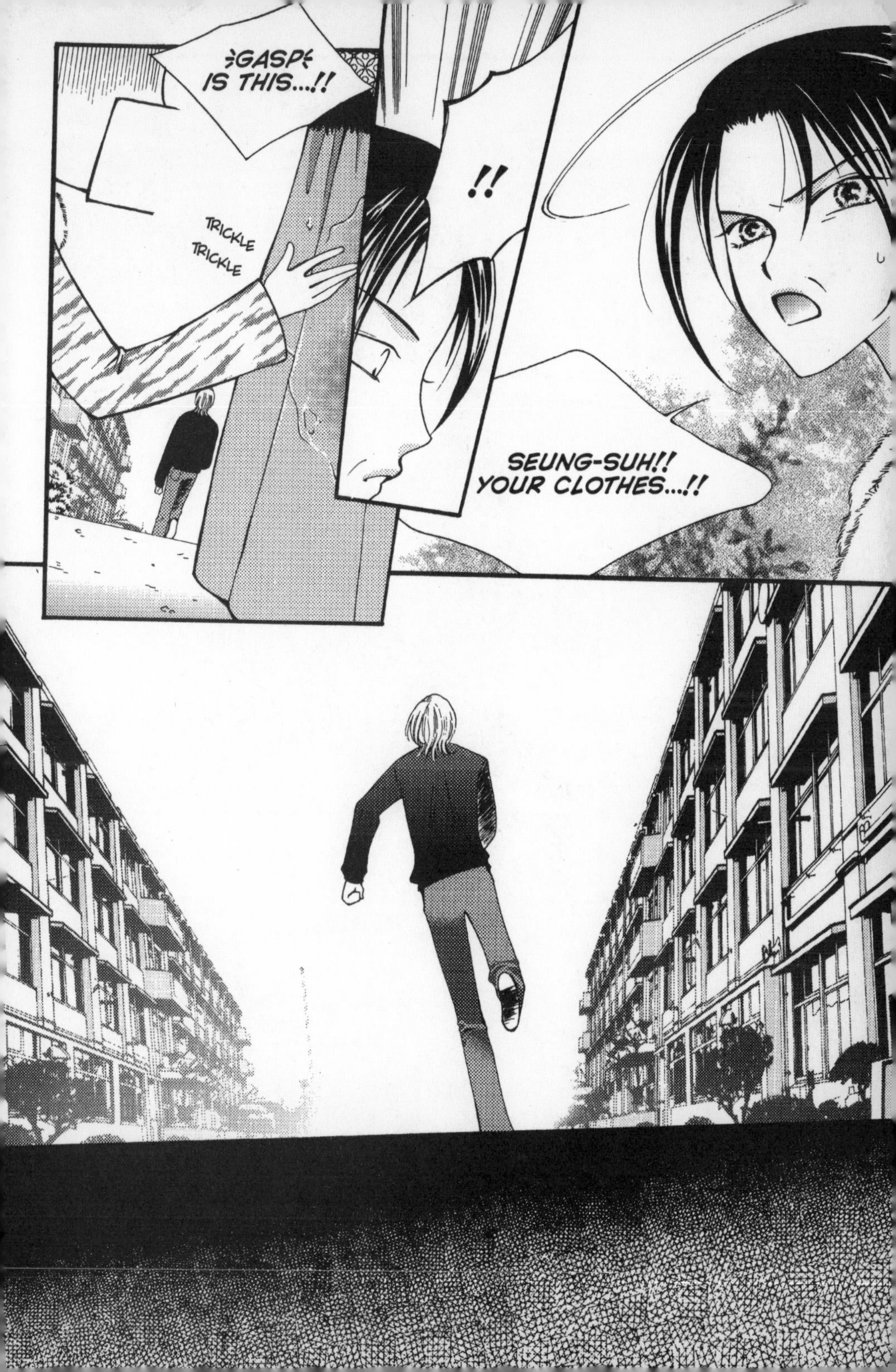

⁝GASP⁝
IS THIS...!!
TRICKLE
TRICKLE
!!
SEUNG-SUH!!
YOUR CLOTHES...!!

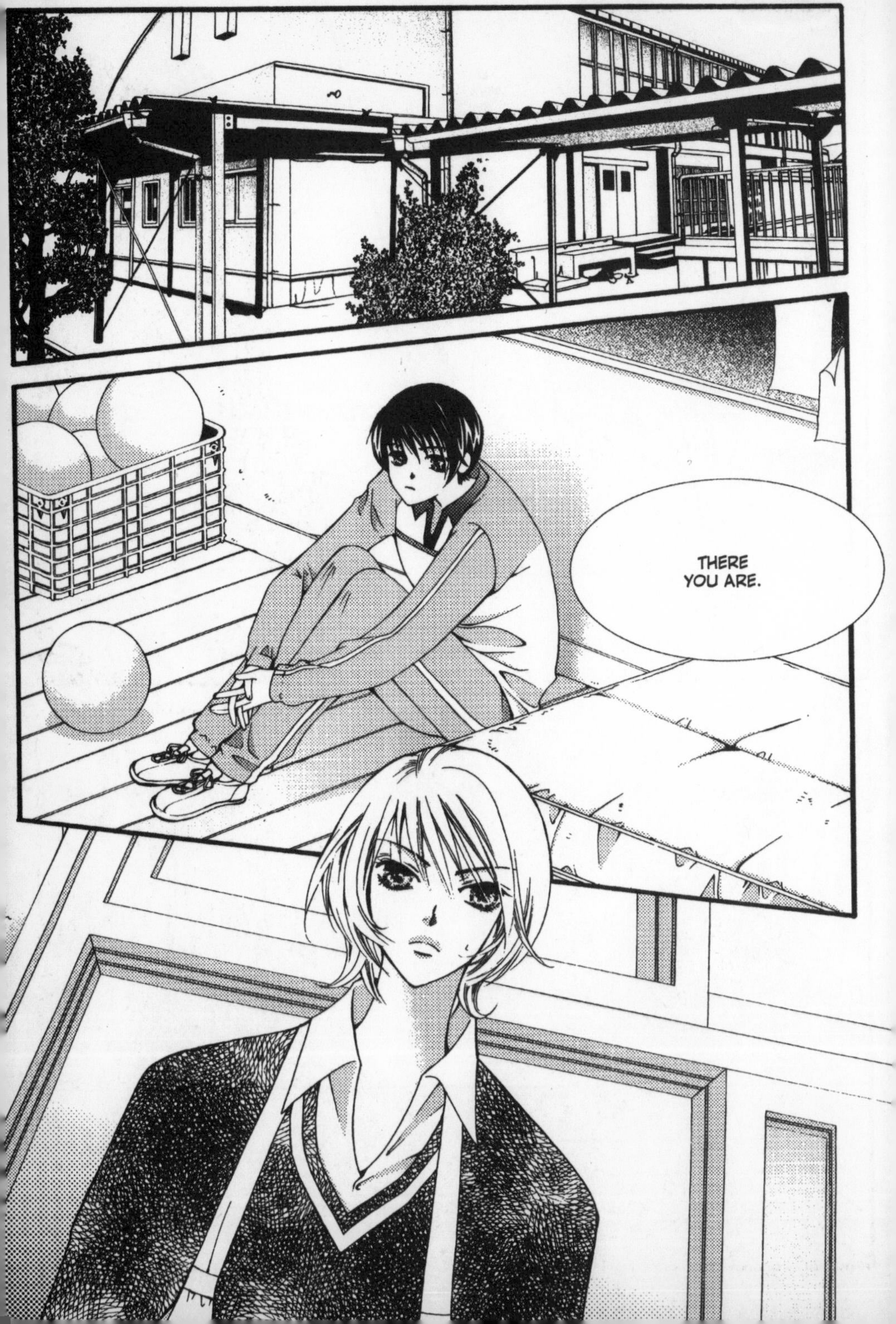
THERE YOU ARE.

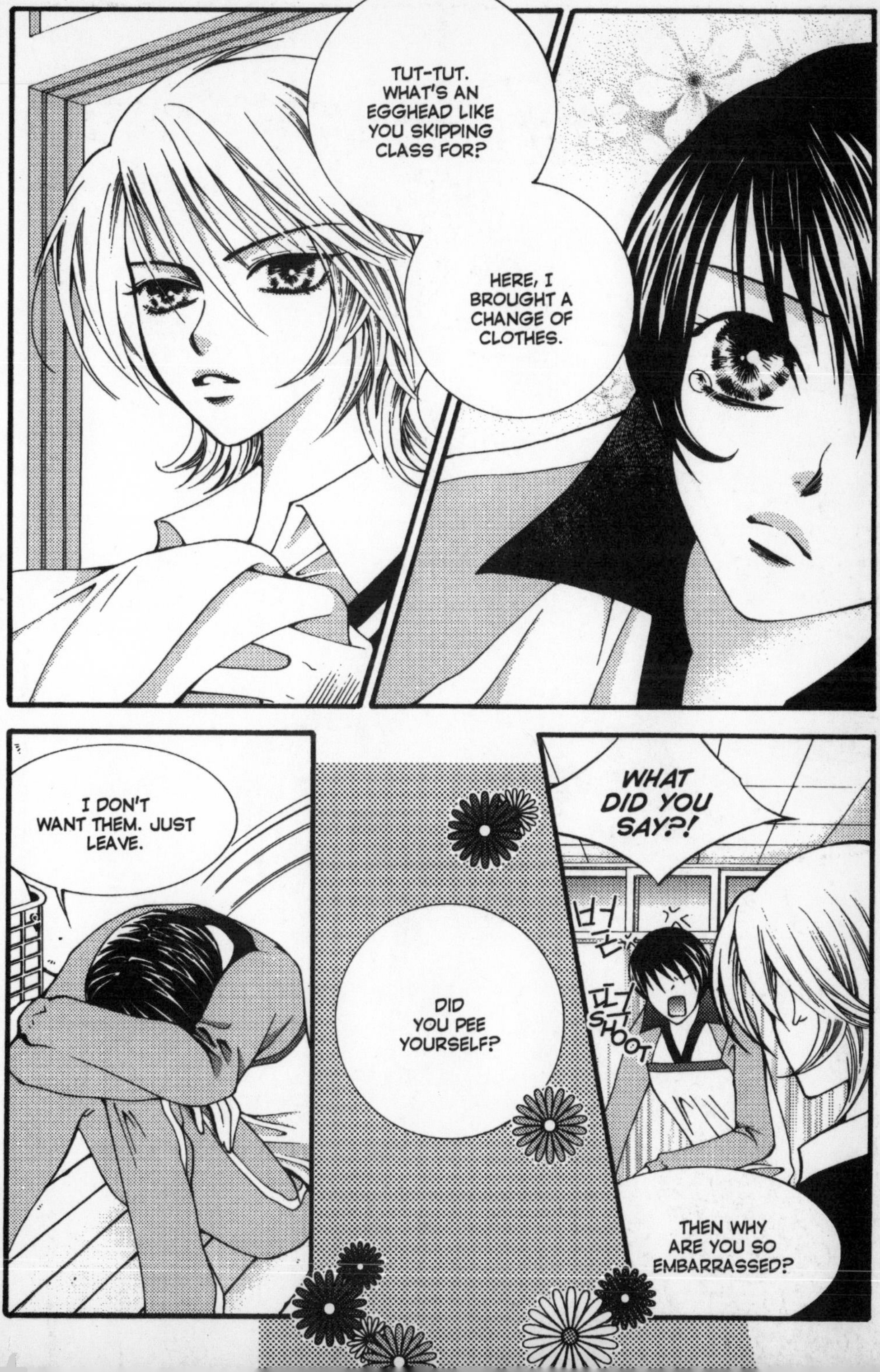
TUT-TUT. WHAT'S AN EGGHEAD LIKE YOU SKIPPING CLASS FOR?
HERE, I BROUGHT A CHANGE OF CLOTHES.
I DON'T WANT THEM. JUST LEAVE.
DID YOU PEE YOURSELF?
WHAT DID YOU SAY?!
SHOOT
THEN WHY ARE YOU SO EMBARRASSED?

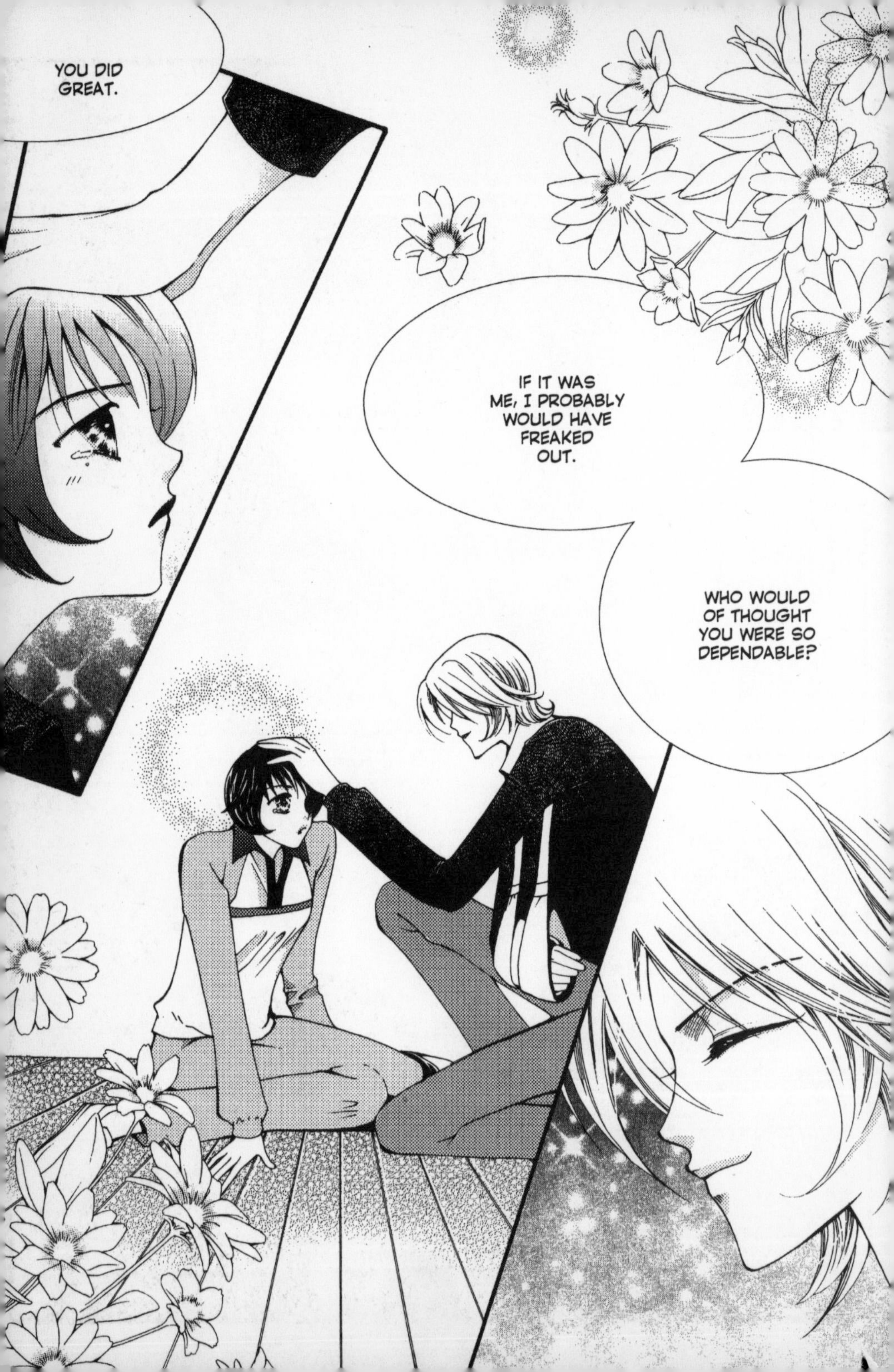
YOU DID GREAT.
IF IT WAS ME, I PROBABLY WOULD HAVE FREAKED OUT.
WHO WOULD OF THOUGHT YOU WERE SO DEPENDABLE?

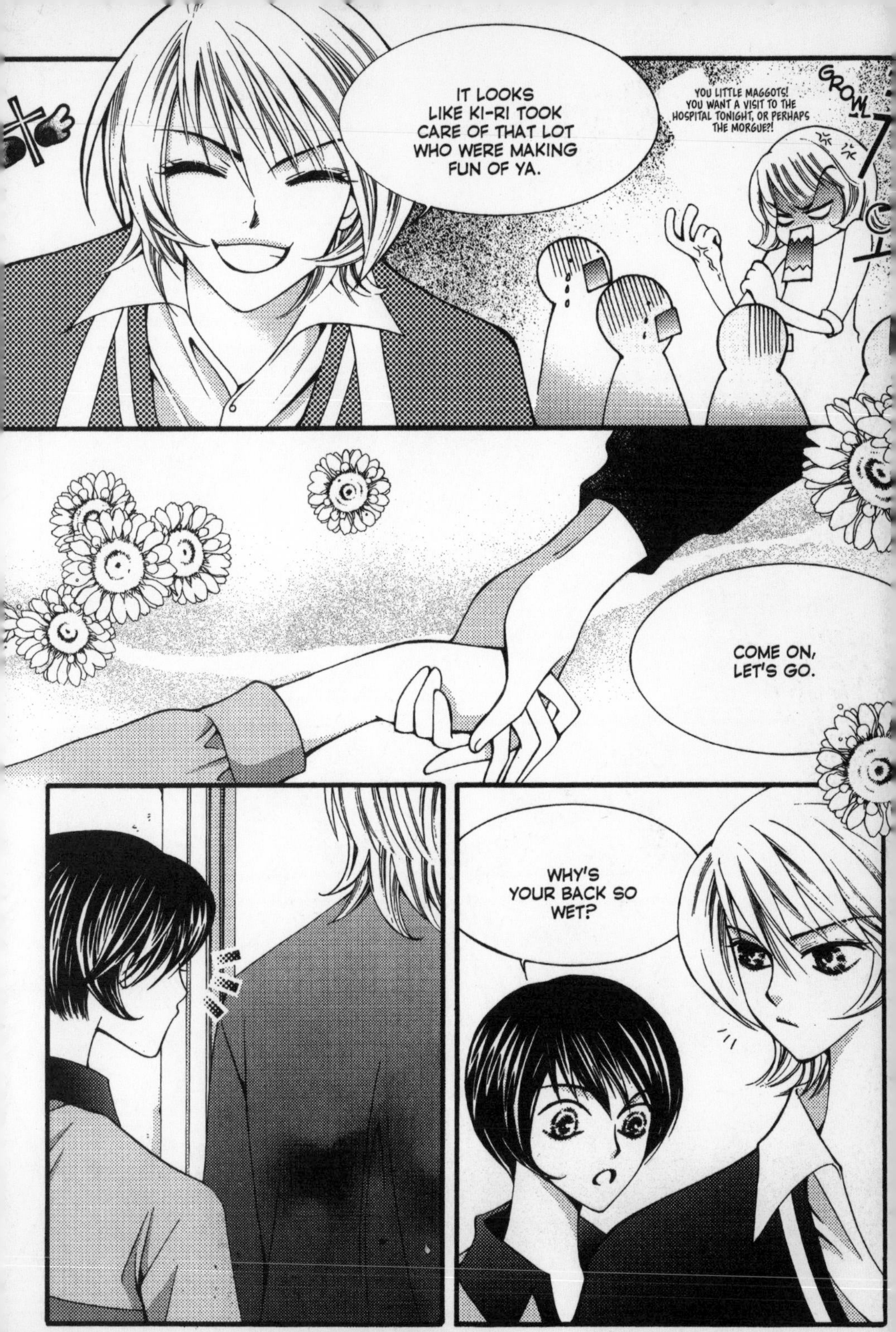
IT LOOKS LIKE KI-RI TOOK CARE OF THAT LOT WHO WERE MAKING FUN OF YA.
YOU LITTLE MAGGOTS! YOU WANT A VISIT TO THE HOSPITAL TONIGHT, OR PERHAPS THE MORGUE?!
GROWL
COME ON, LET'S GO.
WHY'S YOUR BACK SO WET?

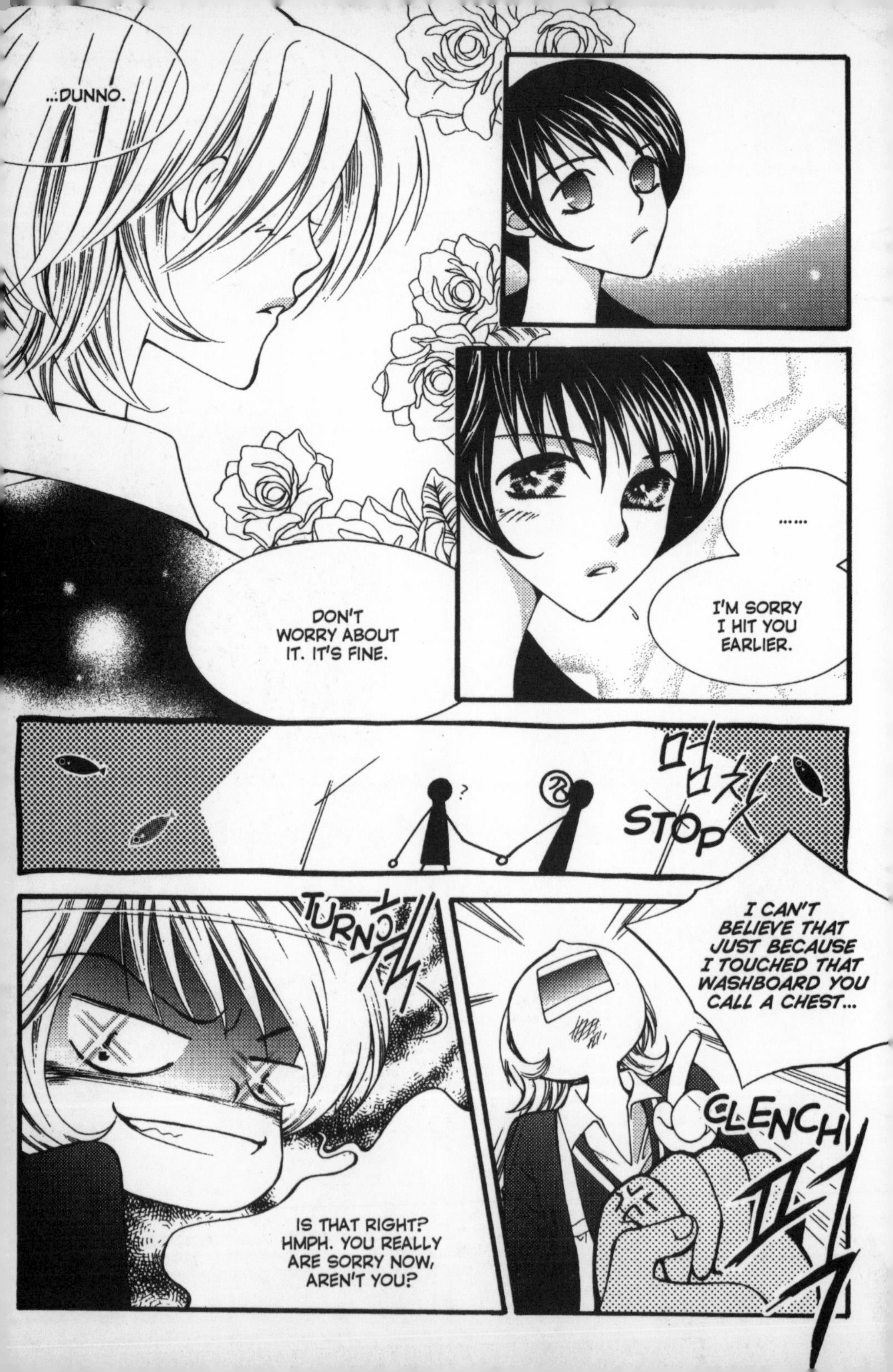
...DUNNO.
DON'T WORRY ABOUT IT. IT'S FINE.
……
I'M SORRY I HIT YOU EARLIER.
멈칫
STOP
TURN
IS THAT RIGHT? HMPH. YOU REALLY ARE SORRY NOW, AREN'T YOU?
I CAN'T BELIEVE THAT JUST BECAUSE I TOUCHED THAT WASHBOARD YOU CALL A CHEST...
CLENCH

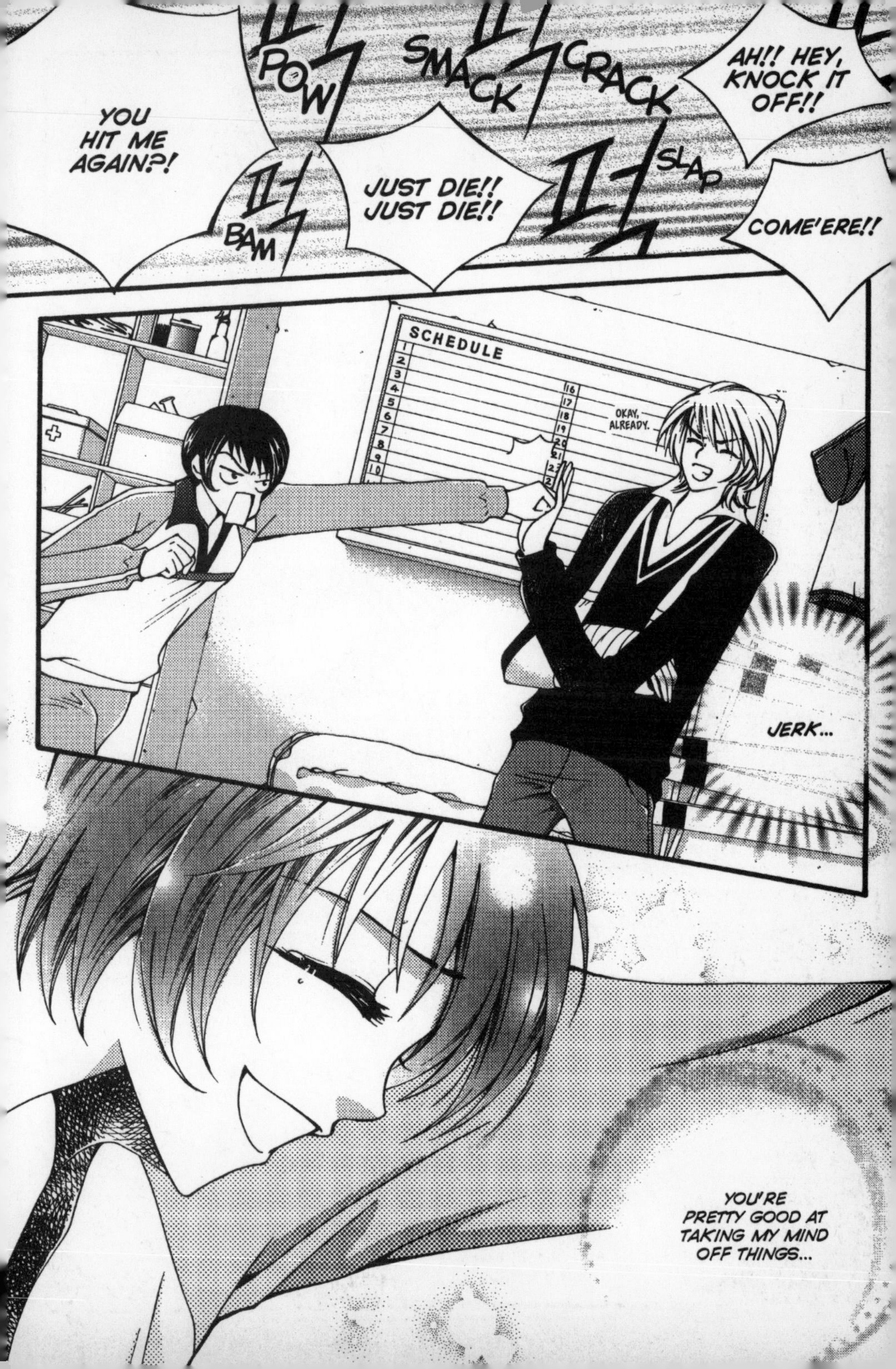
YOU HIT ME AGAIN?!
POW
BAM
SMACK
JUST DIE!! JUST DIE!!
CRACK
SLAP
AH!! HEY, KNOCK IT OFF!!
COME'ERE!!
SCHEDULE
OKAY, ALREADY.
JERK...
YOU'RE PRETTY GOOD AT TAKING MY MIND OFF THINGS...

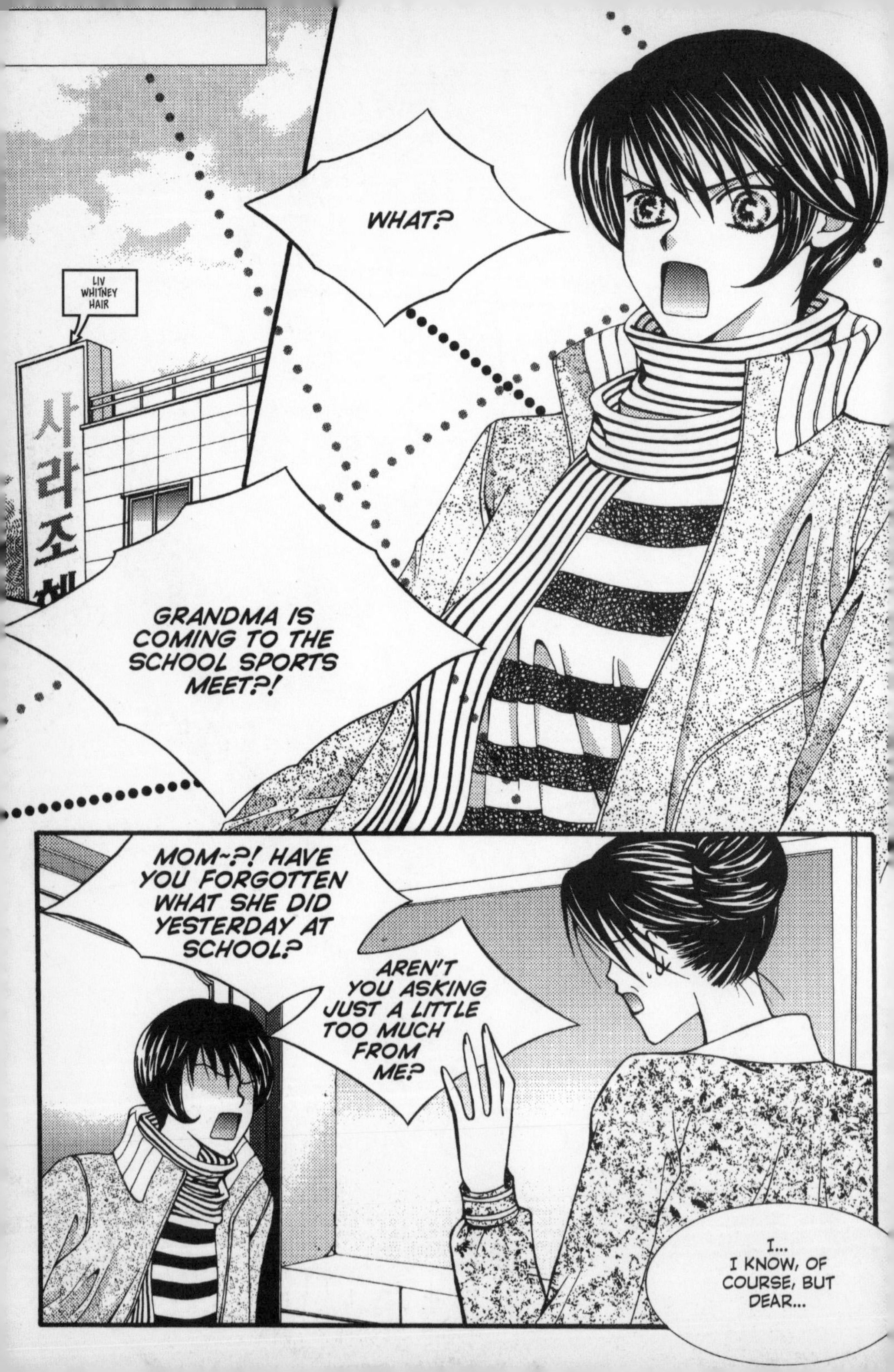
LIV WHITNEY HAIR
사라조
WHAT?
GRANDMA IS COMING TO THE SCHOOL SPORTS MEET?!
MOM~?! HAVE YOU FORGOTTEN WHAT SHE DID YESTERDAY AT SCHOOL?
AREN'T YOU ASKING JUST A LITTLE TOO MUCH FROM ME?
I... I KNOW, OF COURSE, BUT DEAR...

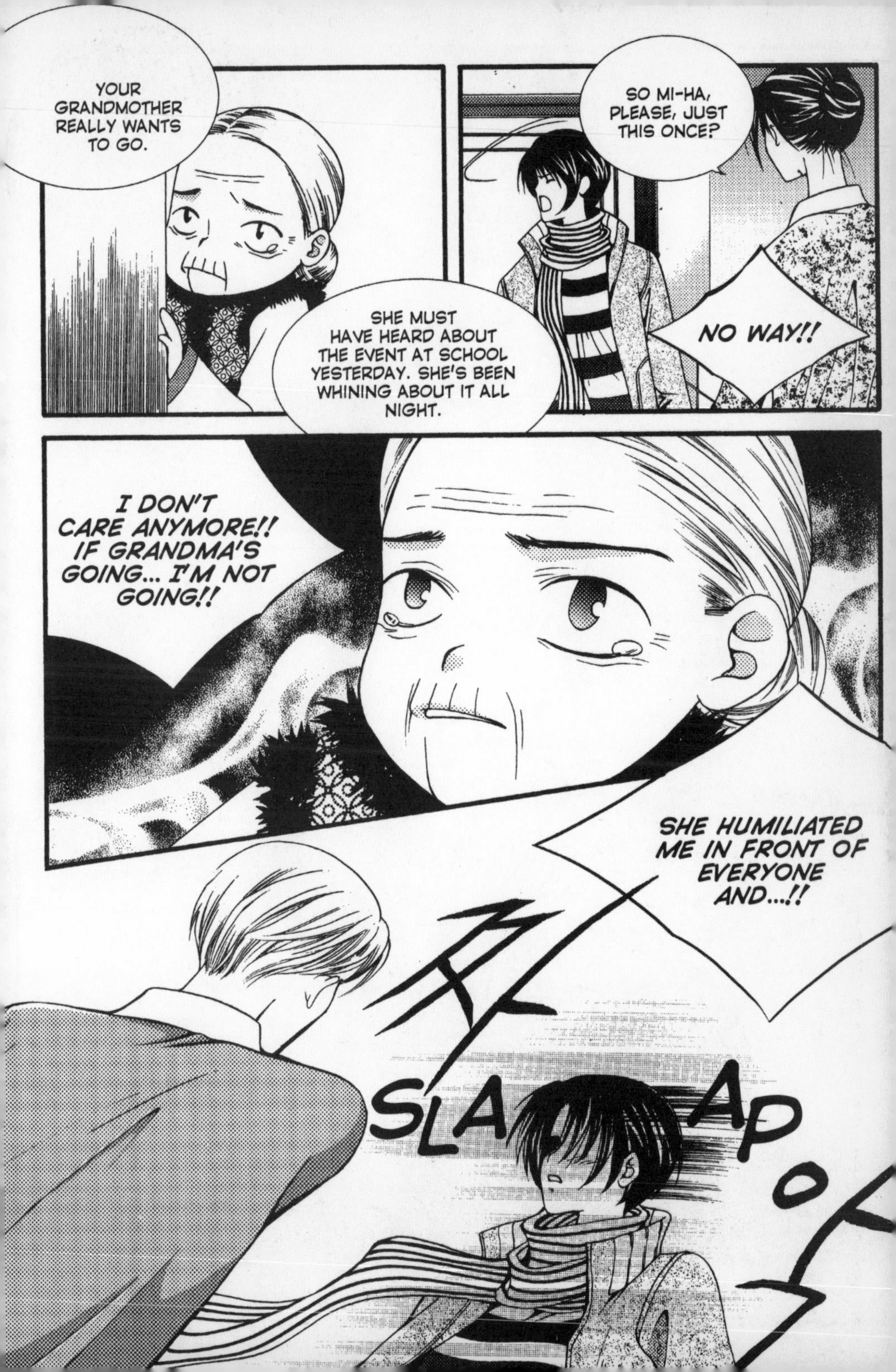
YOUR GRANDMOTHER REALLY WANTS TO GO.
SHE MUST HAVE HEARD ABOUT THE EVENT AT SCHOOL YESTERDAY. SHE'S BEEN WHINING ABOUT IT ALL NIGHT.
SO MI-HA, PLEASE, JUST THIS ONCE?
NO WAY!!
I DON'T CARE ANYMORE!! IF GRANDMA'S GOING... I'M NOT GOING!!
SHE HUMILIATED ME IN FRONT OF EVERYONE AND...!!
SLAAP

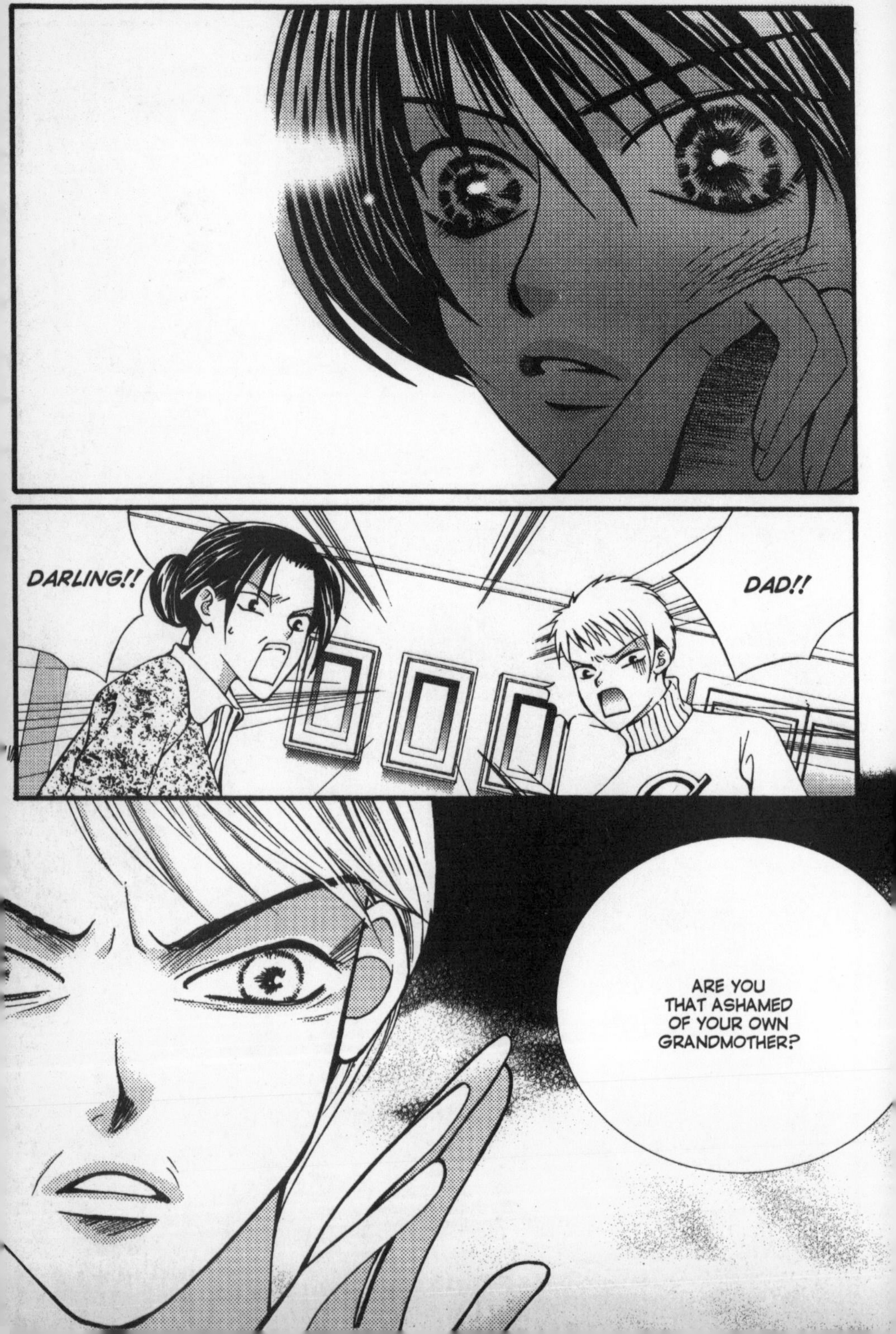
DARLING!!
DAD!!
ARE YOU THAT ASHAMED OF YOUR OWN GRANDMOTHER?

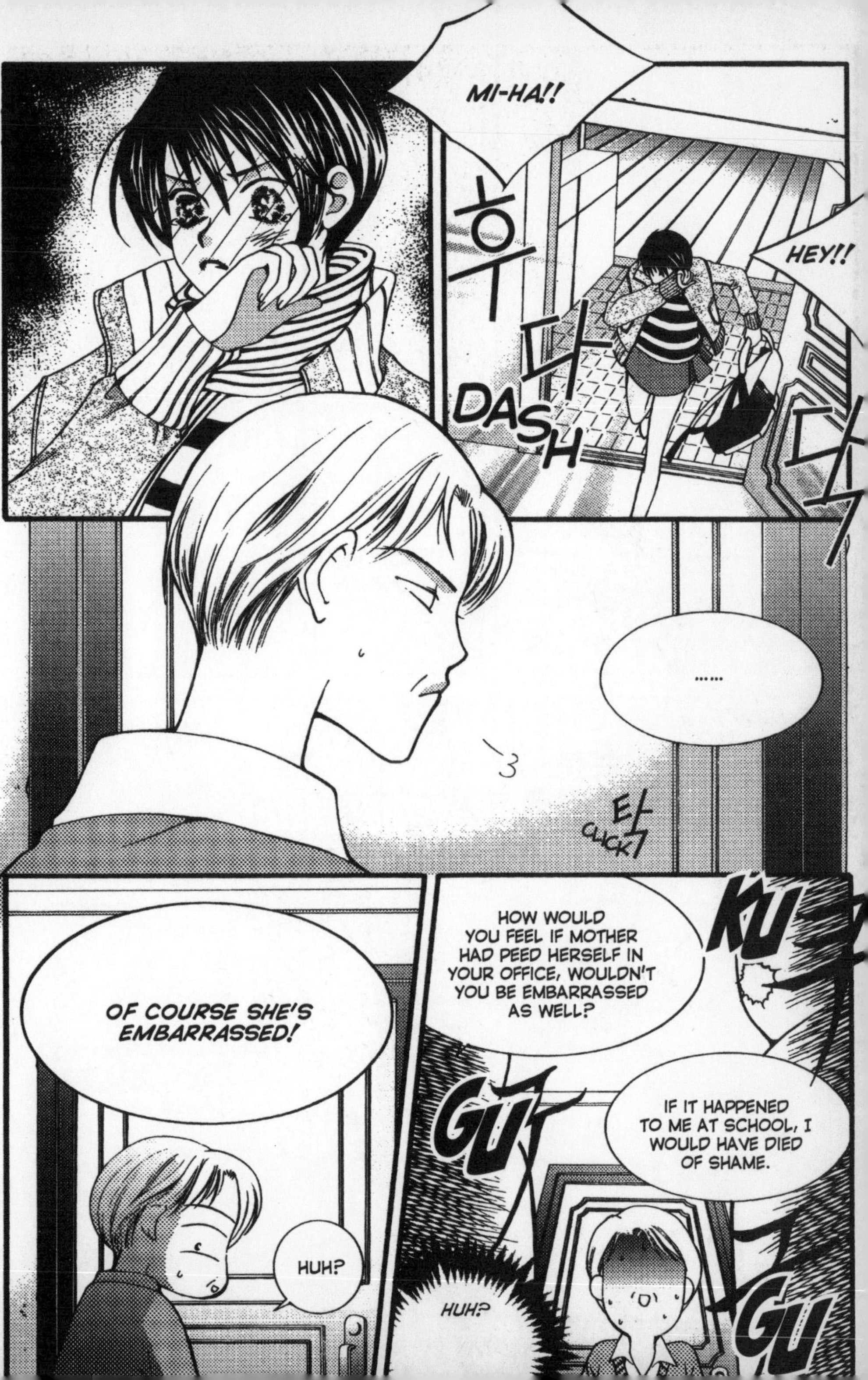
MI-HA!!
DASH
HEY!!
......
CLICK
OF COURSE SHE'S EMBARRASSED!
HUH?
HOW WOULD YOU FEEL IF MOTHER HAD PEED HERSELF IN YOUR OFFICE, WOULDN'T YOU BE EMBARRASSED AS WELL?
KU
GU
IF IT HAPPENED TO ME AT SCHOOL, I WOULD HAVE DIED OF SHAME.
HUH?
GU

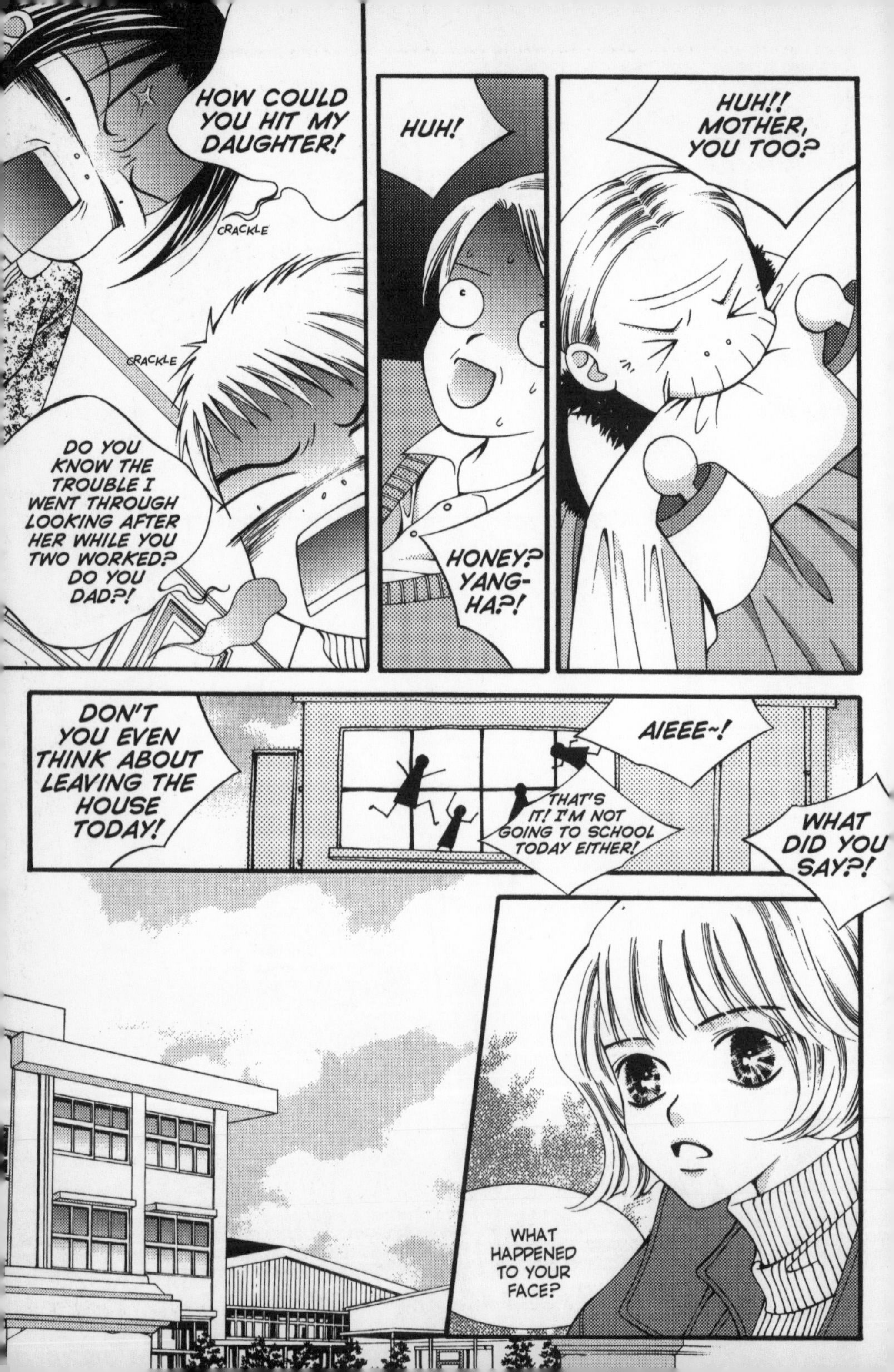
HOW COULD YOU HIT MY DAUGHTER!
CRACKLE
CRACKLE
DO YOU KNOW THE TROUBLE I WENT THROUGH LOOKING AFTER HER WHILE YOU TWO WORKED? DO YOU DAD?!
HUH!
HONEY? YANG-HA?!
HUH!! MOTHER, YOU TOO?
DON'T YOU EVEN THINK ABOUT LEAVING THE HOUSE TODAY!
AIEEE~!
THAT'S IT! I'M NOT GOING TO SCHOOL TODAY EITHER!
WHAT DID YOU SAY?!
WHAT HAPPENED TO YOUR FACE?

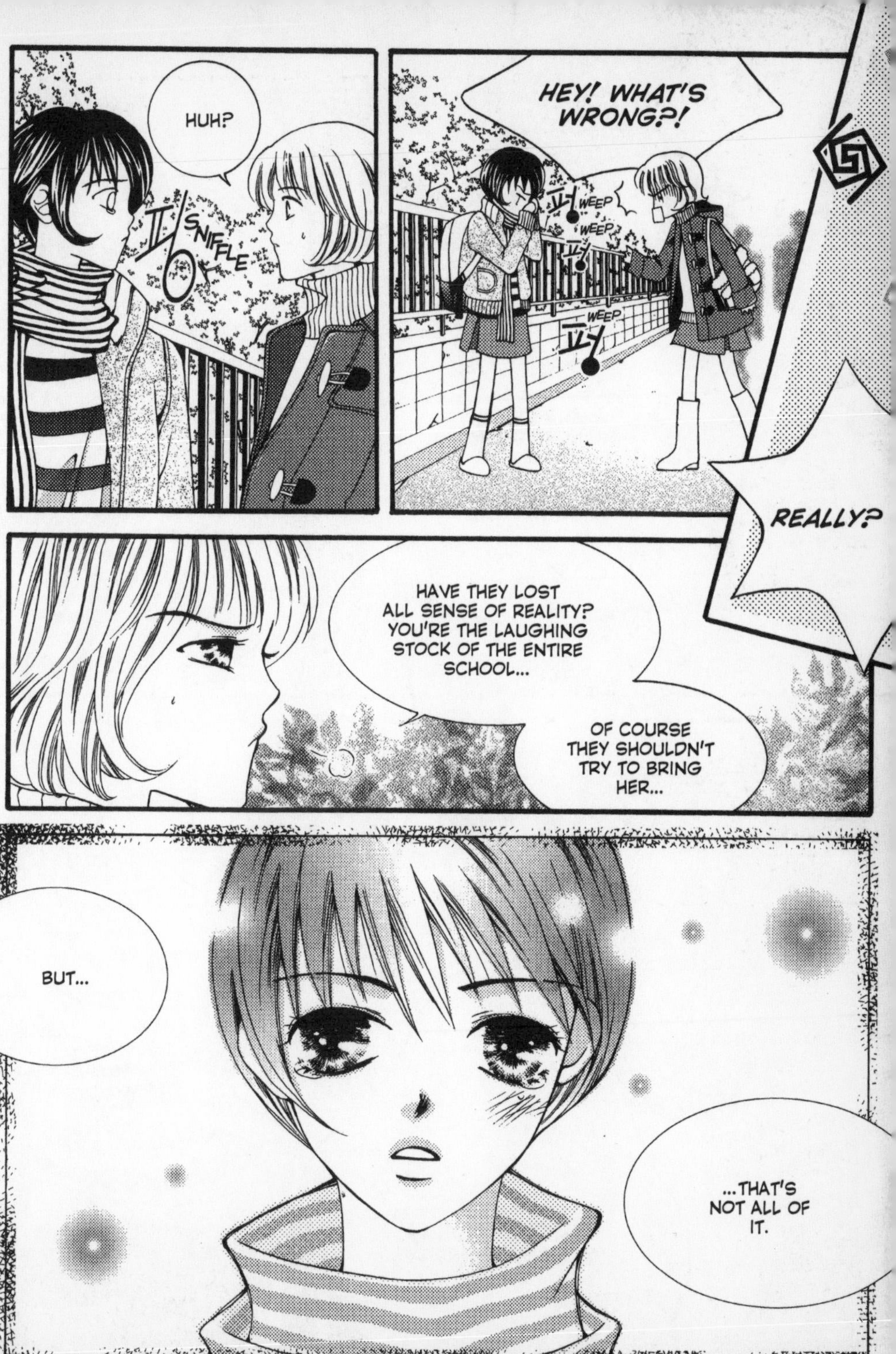

HUH?
SNIFFLE
HEY! WHAT'S WRONG?!
WEEP
WEEP
WEEP
REALLY?
HAVE THEY LOST ALL SENSE OF REALITY? YOU'RE THE LAUGHING STOCK OF THE ENTIRE SCHOOL...
OF COURSE THEY SHOULDN'T TRY TO BRING HER...
BUT...
...THAT'S NOT ALL OF IT.

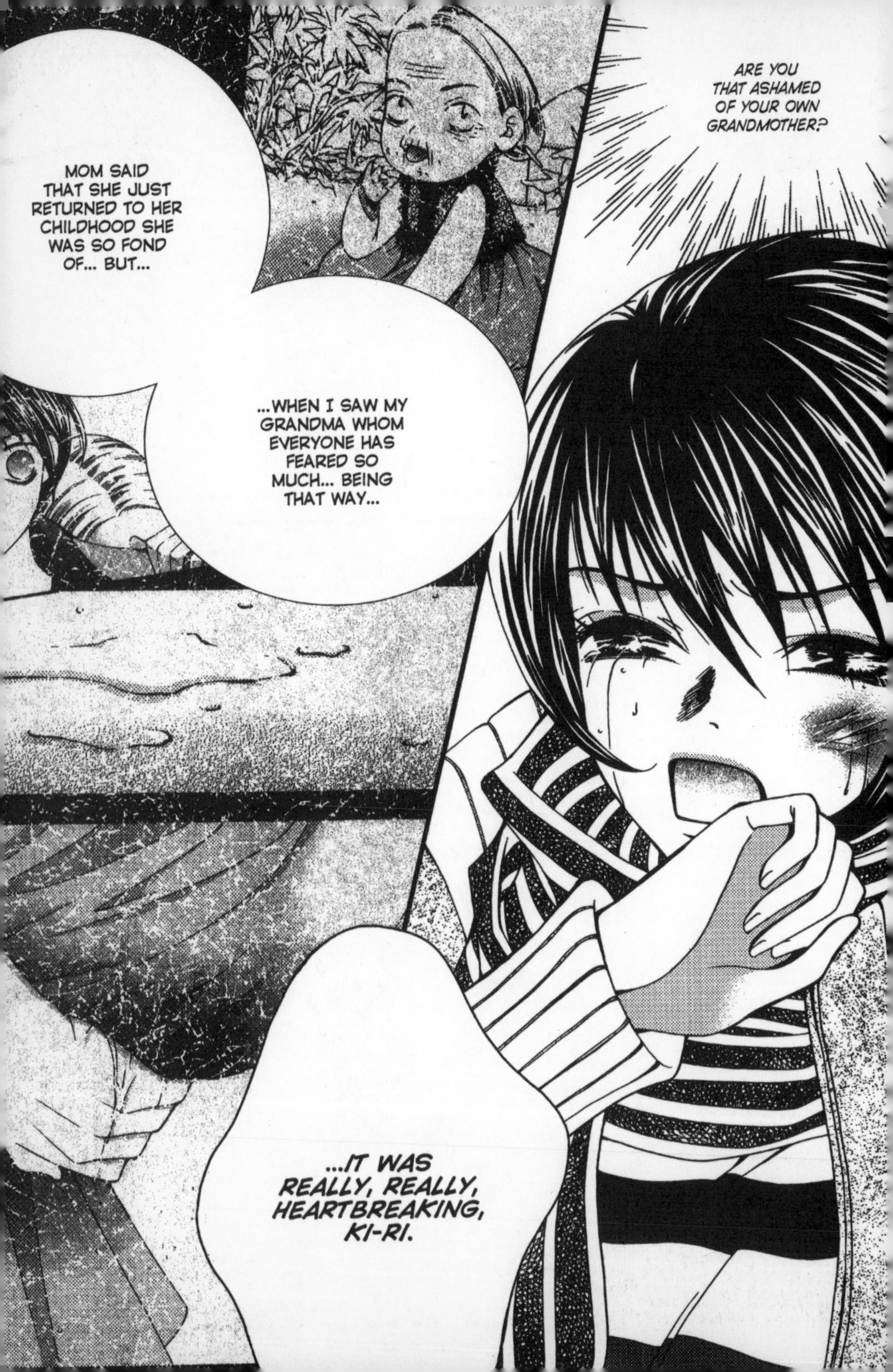
MOM SAID THAT SHE JUST RETURNED TO HER CHILDHOOD SHE WAS SO FOND OF... BUT...
...WHEN I SAW MY GRANDMA WHOM EVERYONE HAS FEARED SO MUCH... BEING THAT WAY...
...IT WAS REALLY, REALLY, HEARTBREAKING, KI-RI.
ARE YOU THAT ASHAMED OF YOUR OWN GRANDMOTHER?

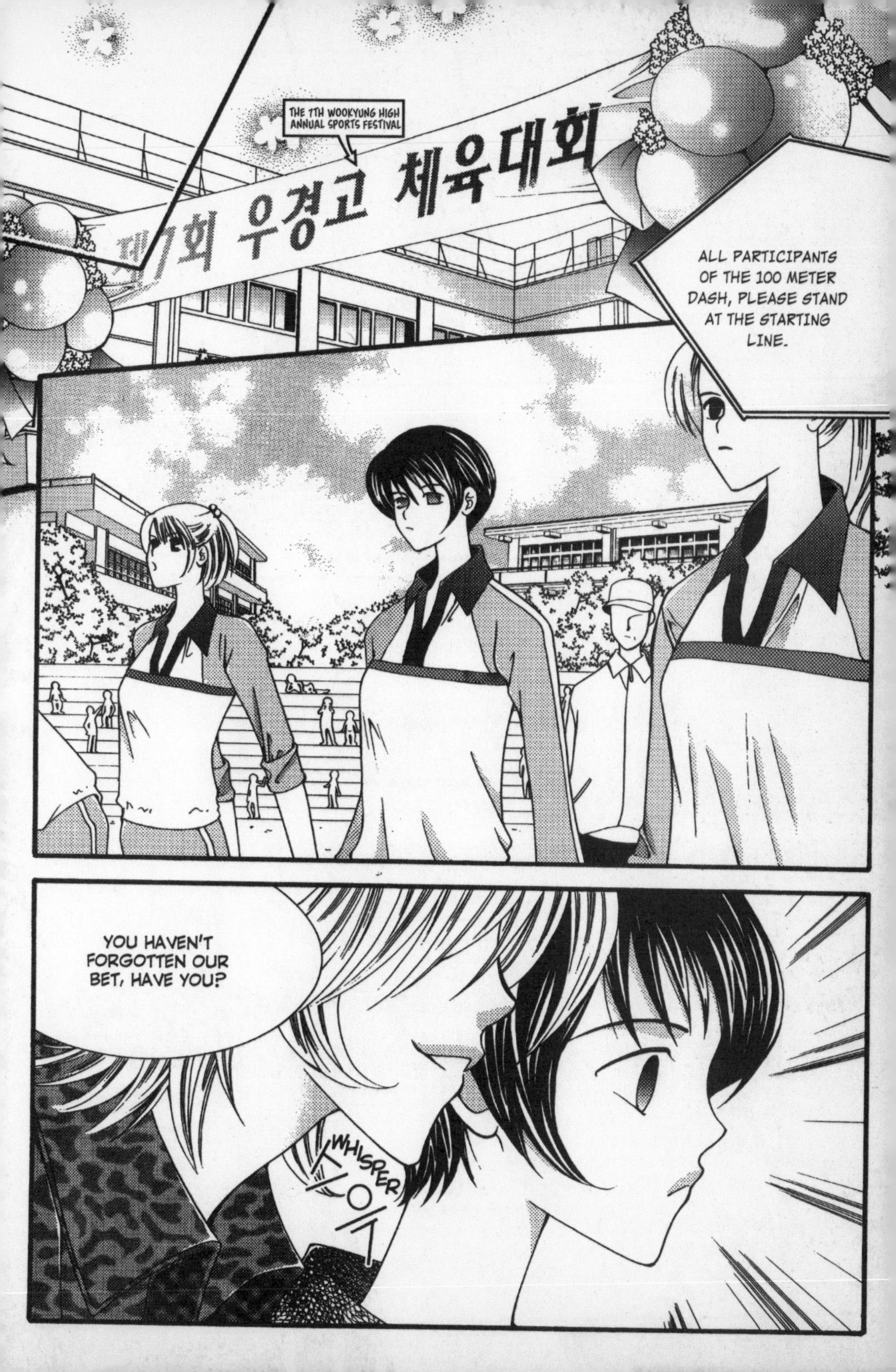

THE 7TH WOOKYUNG HIGH ANNUAL SPORTS FESTIVAL
제7회 우경고 체육대회
ALL PARTICIPANTS OF THE 100 METER DASH, PLEASE STAND AT THE STARTING LINE.
YOU HAVEN'T FORGOTTEN OUR BET, HAVE YOU?
WHISPER

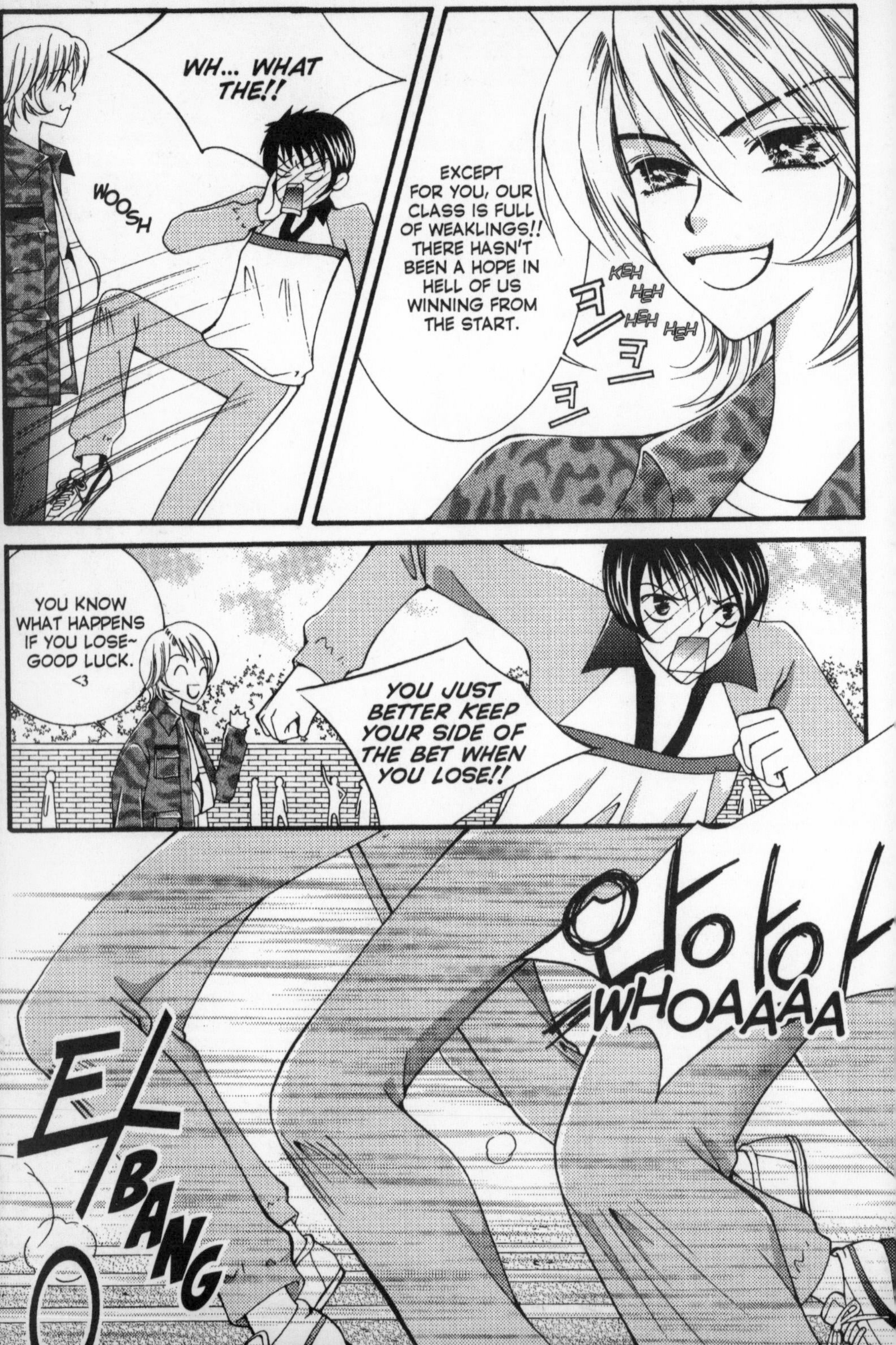
WH... WHAT THE!!
WOOSH
EXCEPT FOR YOU, OUR CLASS IS FULL OF WEAKLINGS!! THERE HASN'T BEEN A HOPE IN HELL OF US WINNING FROM THE START.
KEH HEH HEH HEH
YOU KNOW WHAT HAPPENS IF YOU LOSE~ GOOD LUCK. <3
YOU JUST BETTER KEEP YOUR SIDE OF THE BET WHEN YOU LOSE!!
WHOAAAA
BANG

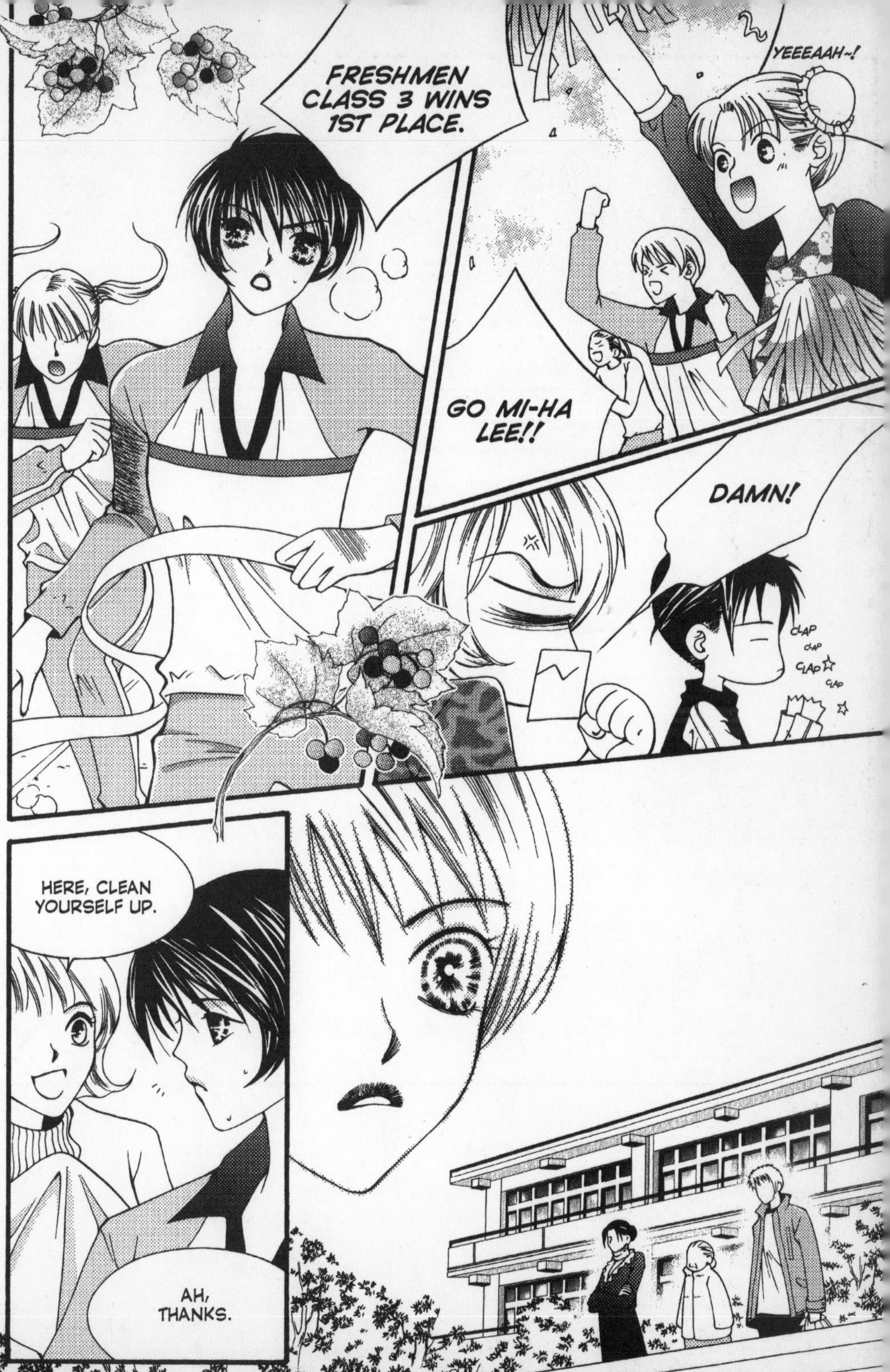
FRESHMEN CLASS 3 WINS 1ST PLACE.
YEEEAAH~!
GO MI-HA LEE!!
DAMN!
CLAP
CLAP
CLAP
CLAP
HERE, CLEAN YOURSELF UP.
AH, THANKS.

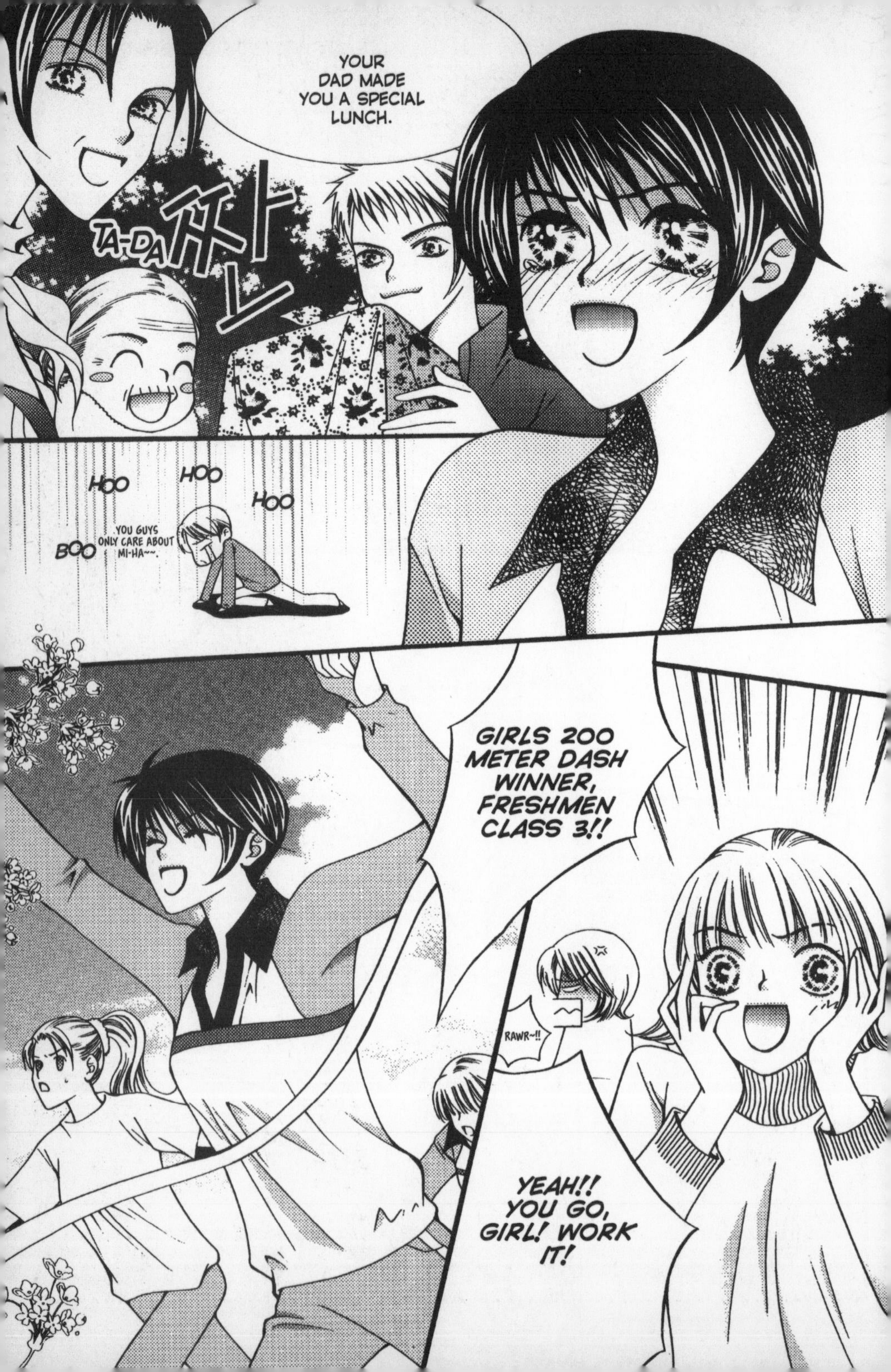
YOUR DAD MADE YOU A SPECIAL LUNCH.
TA-DA
HOO HOO HOO
BOO
YOU GUYS ONLY CARE ABOUT MI-HA~~.
GIRLS 200 METER DASH WINNER, FRESHMEN CLASS 3!!
RAWR~!!
YEAH!! YOU GO, GIRL! WORK IT!

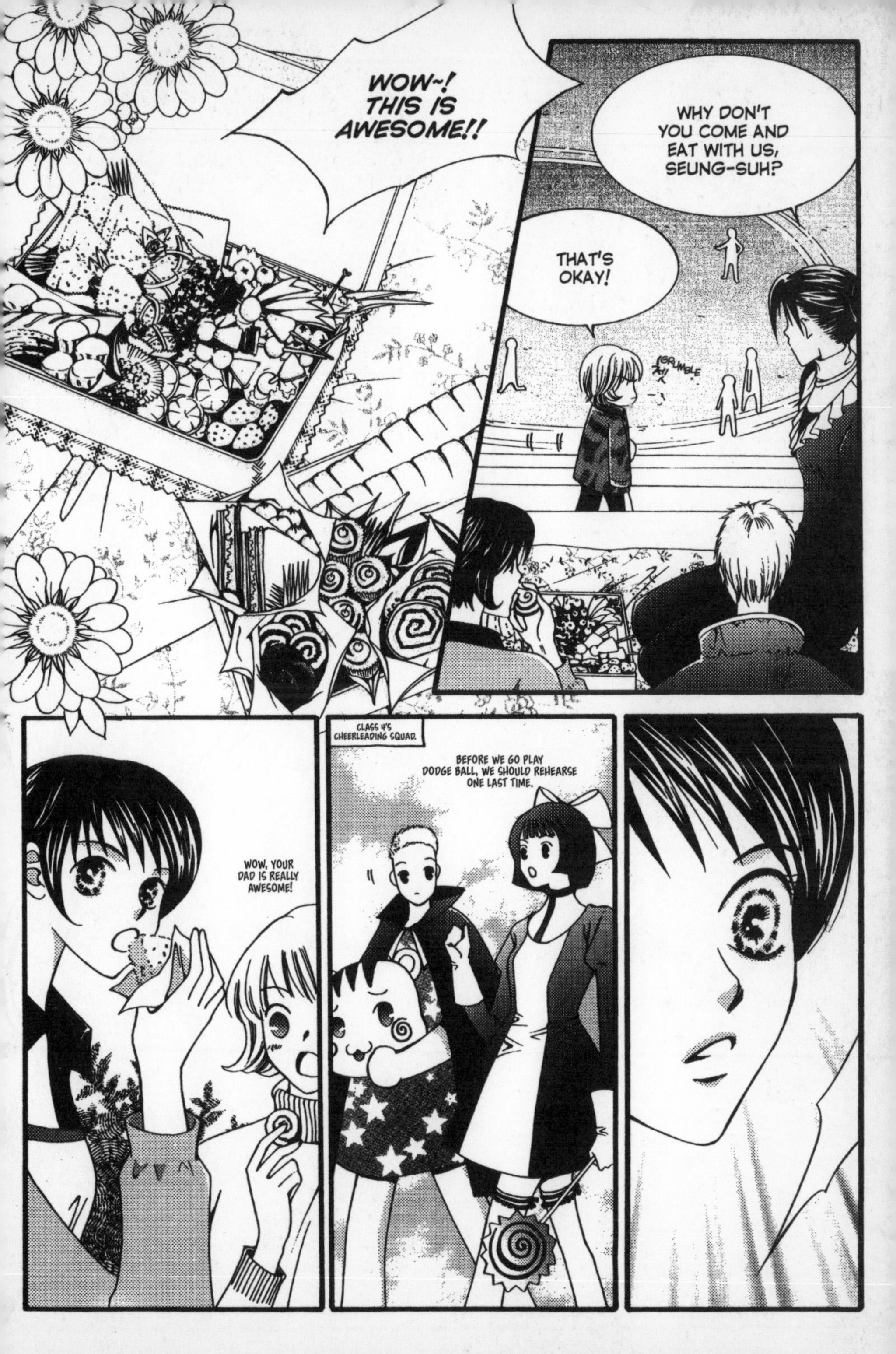
WOW~! THIS IS AWESOME!!
WHY DON'T YOU COME AND EAT WITH US, SEUNG-SUH?
THAT'S OKAY!
GRUMBLE
WOW, YOUR DAD IS REALLY AWESOME!
CLASS 4'S CHEERLEADING SQUAD.
BEFORE WE GO PLAY DODGE BALL, WE SHOULD REHEARSE ONE LAST TIME.

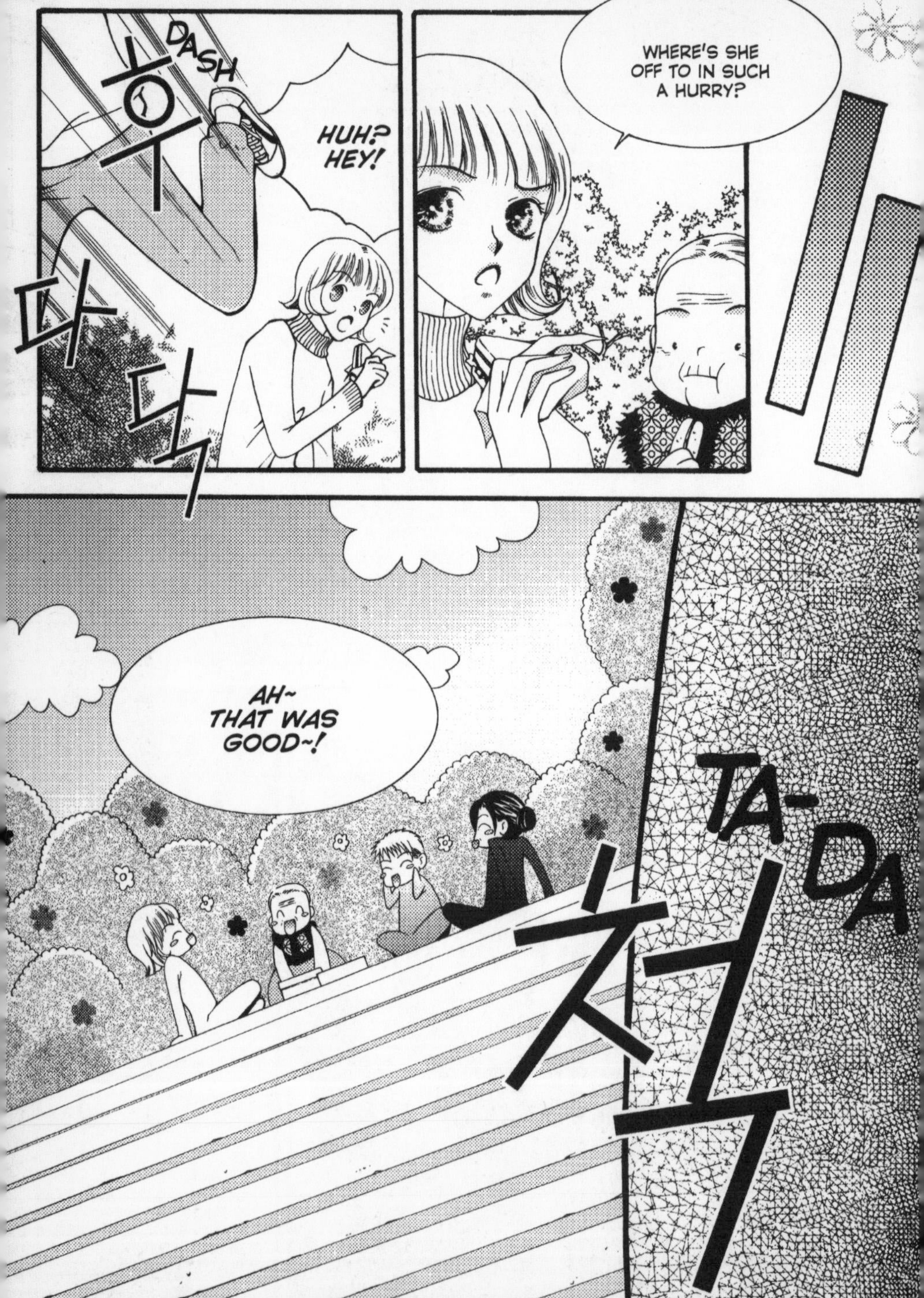
DASH
HUH? HEY!
WHERE'S SHE OFF TO IN SUCH A HURRY?
AH~ THAT WAS GOOD~!
TA-DA

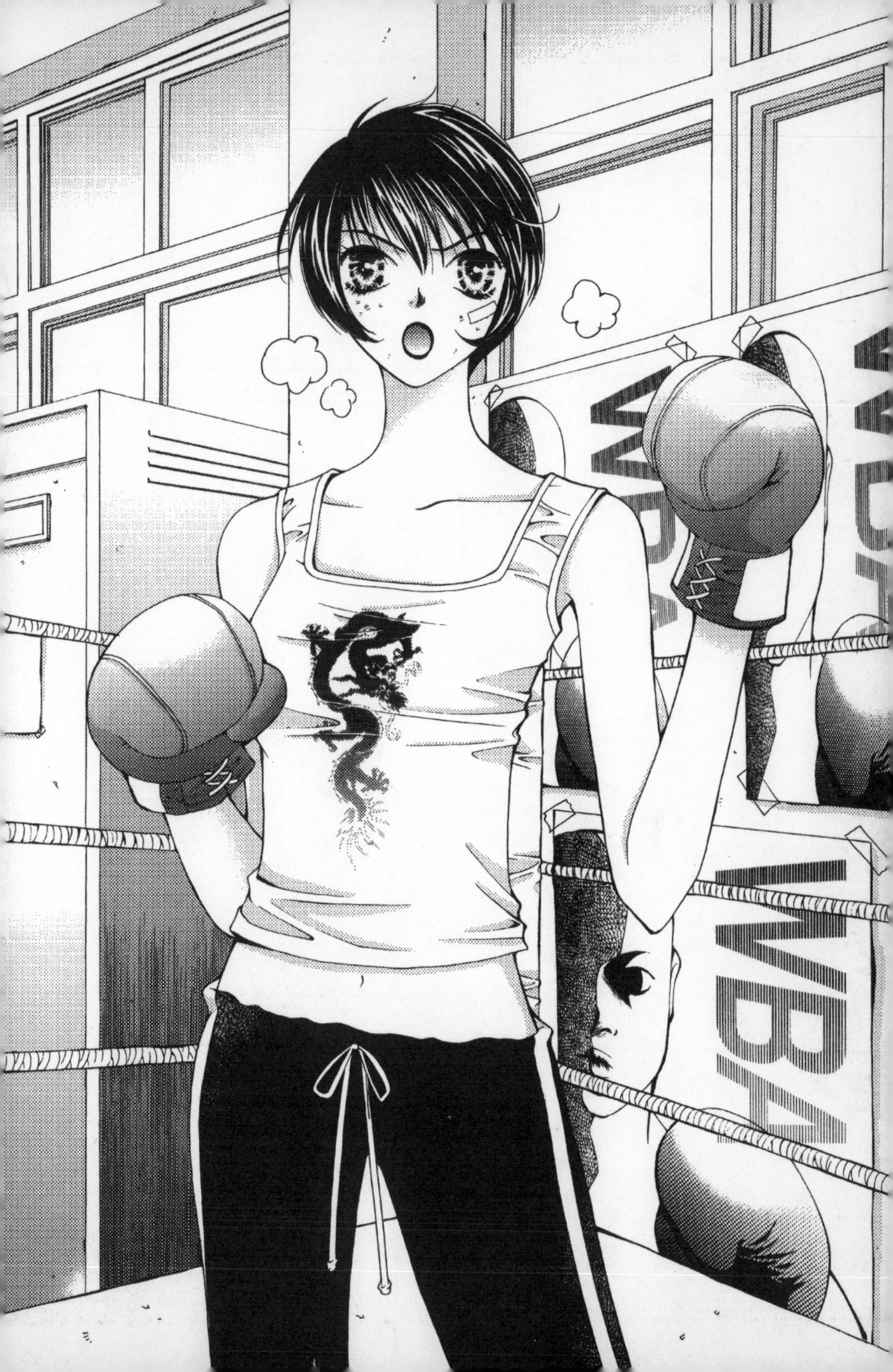
WBA

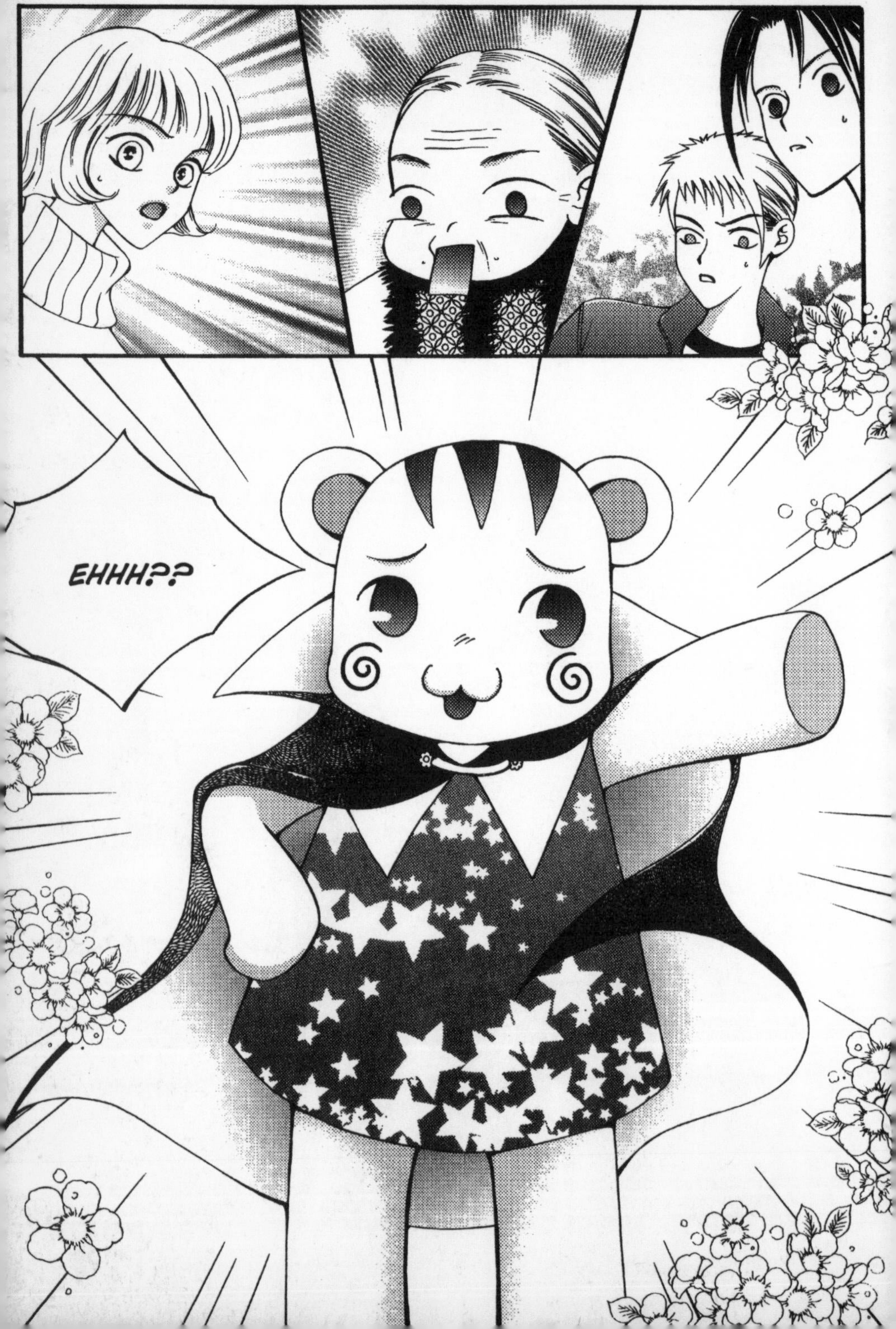
EHHH??

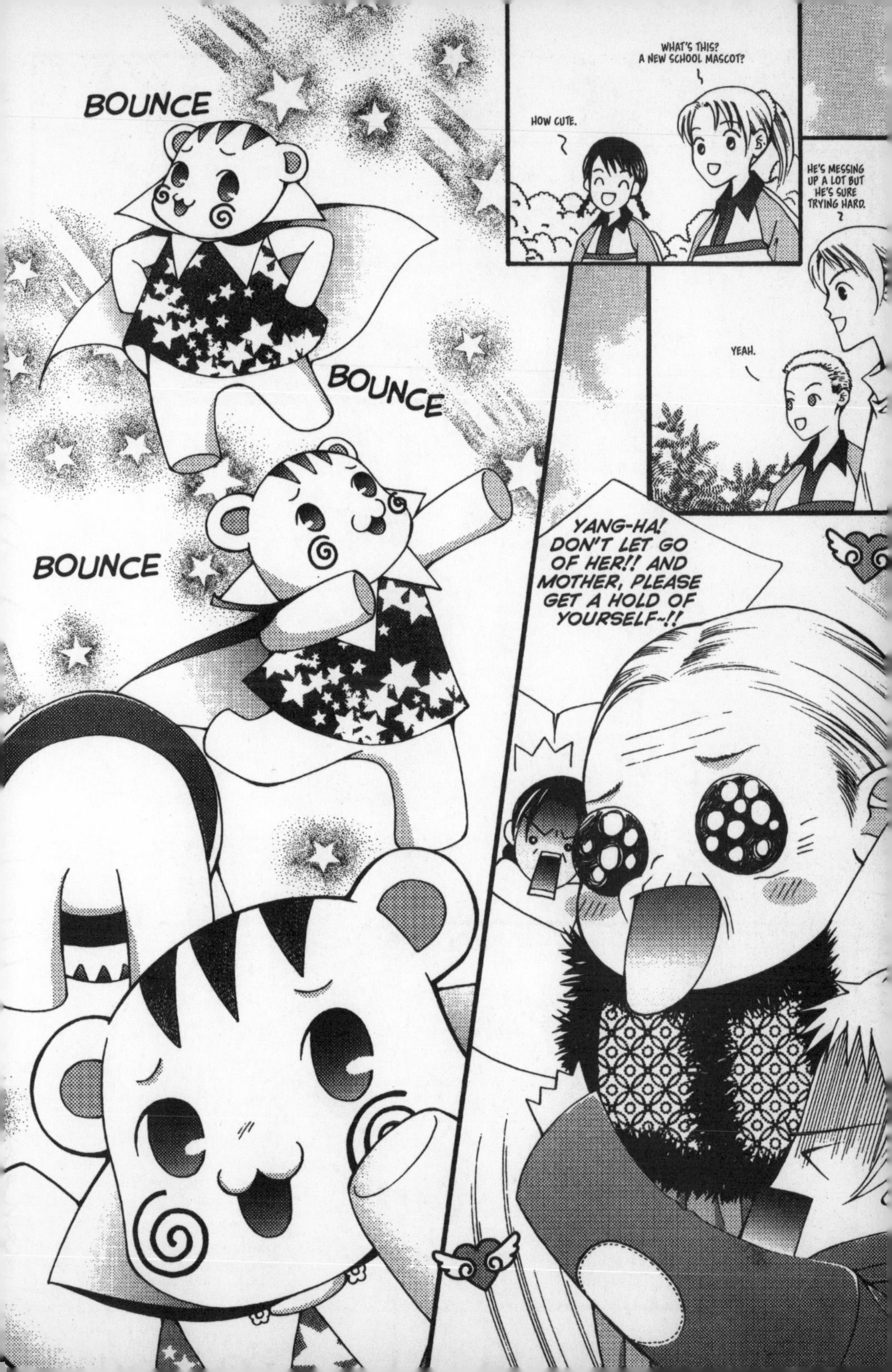
BOUNCE
BOUNCE
BOUNCE
WHAT'S THIS? A NEW SCHOOL MASCOT?
HOW CUTE.
HE'S MESSING UP A LOT BUT HE'S SURE TRYING HARD.
YEAH.
YANG-HA! DON'T LET GO OF HER!! AND MOTHER, PLEASE GET A HOLD OF YOURSELF~!!

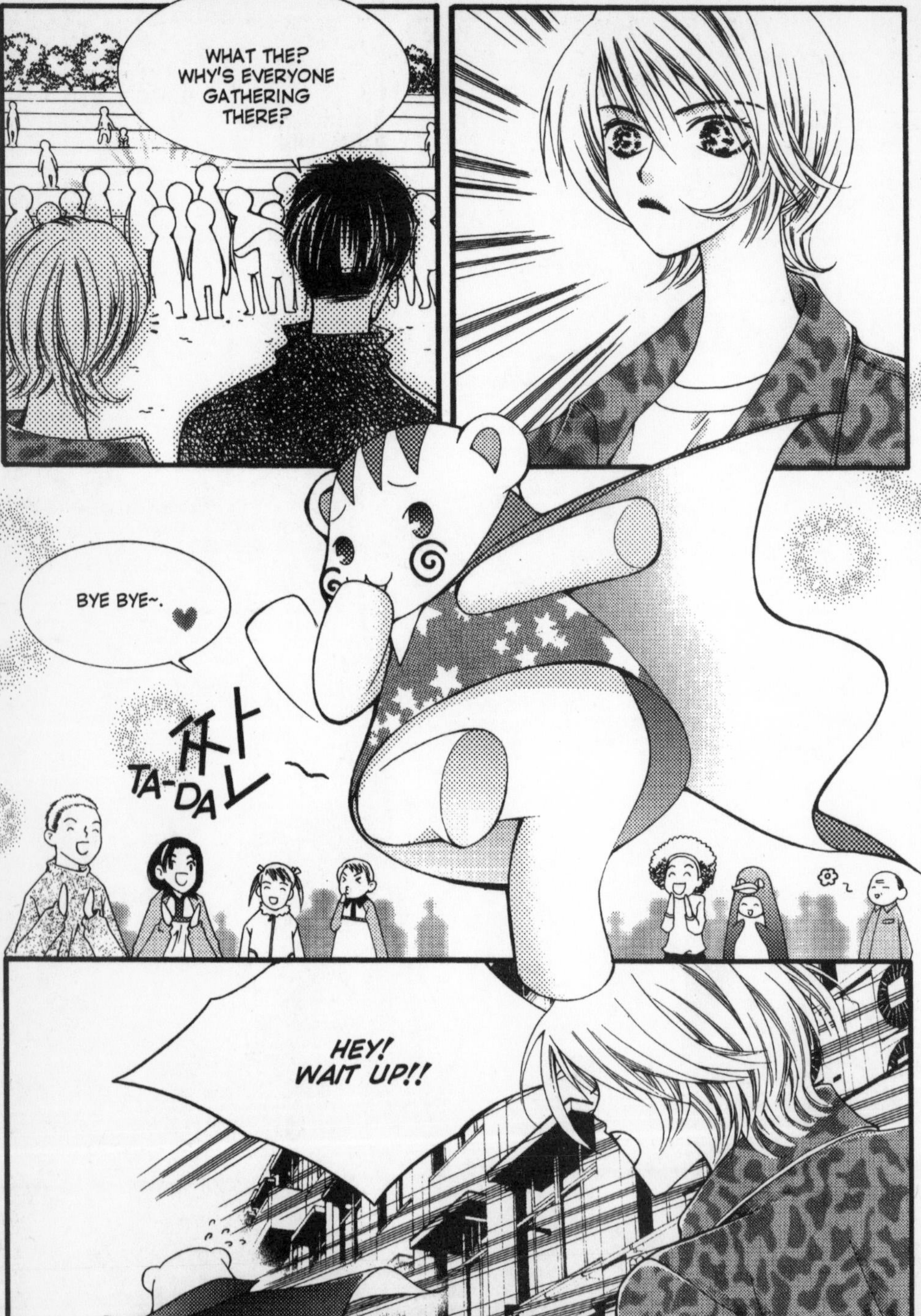

WHAT THE? WHY'S EVERYONE GATHERING THERE?
BYE BYE~.
TA-DA
HEY! WAIT UP!!

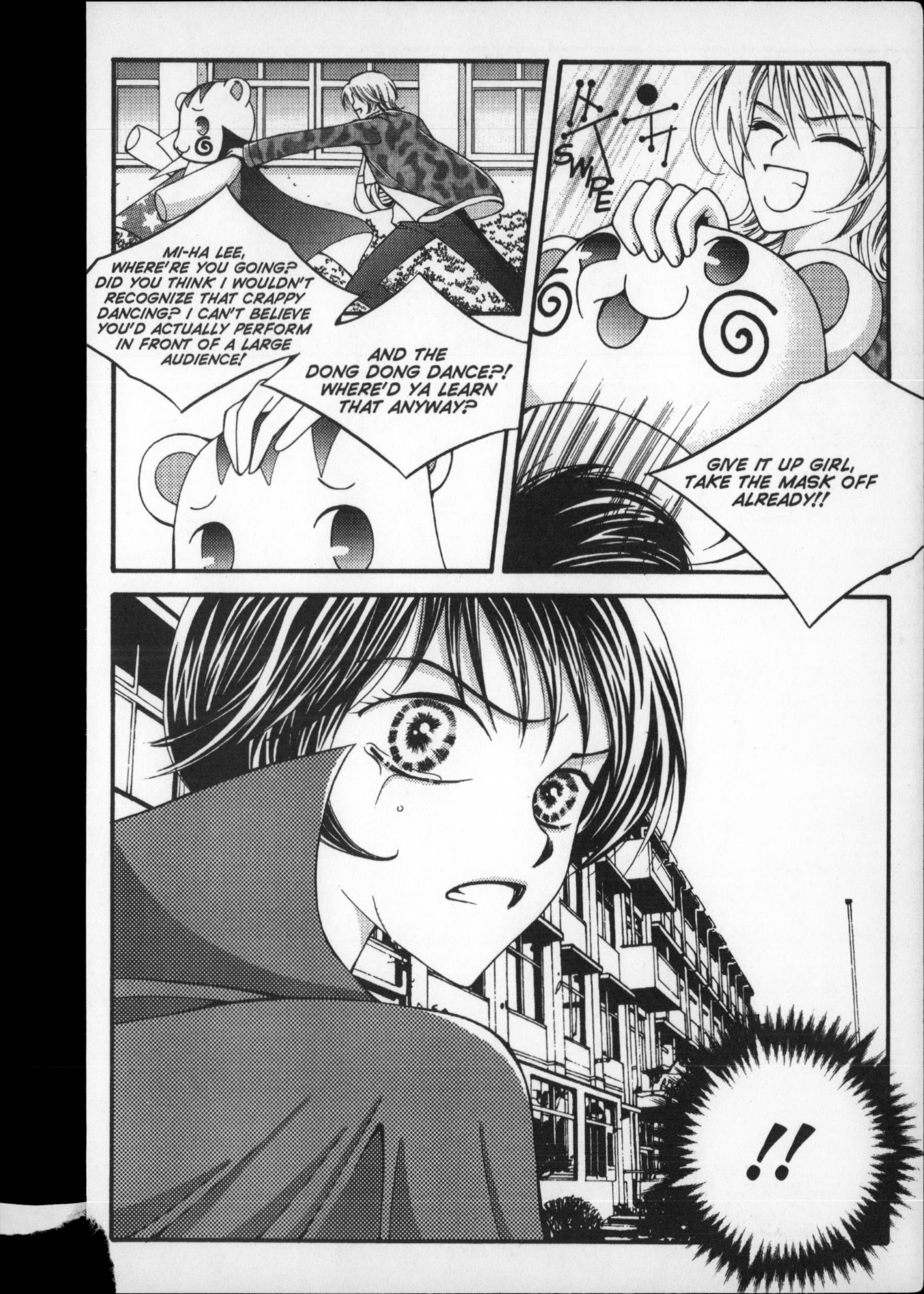
MI-HA LEE, WHERE'RE YOU GOING? DID YOU THINK I WOULDN'T RECOGNIZE THAT CRAPPY DANCING? I CAN'T BELIEVE YOU'D ACTUALLY PERFORM IN FRONT OF A LARGE AUDIENCE!
AND THE DONG DONG DANCE?! WHERE'D YA LEARN THAT ANYWAY?
SWIPE
GIVE IT UP GIRL, TAKE THE MASK OFF ALREADY!!
!!

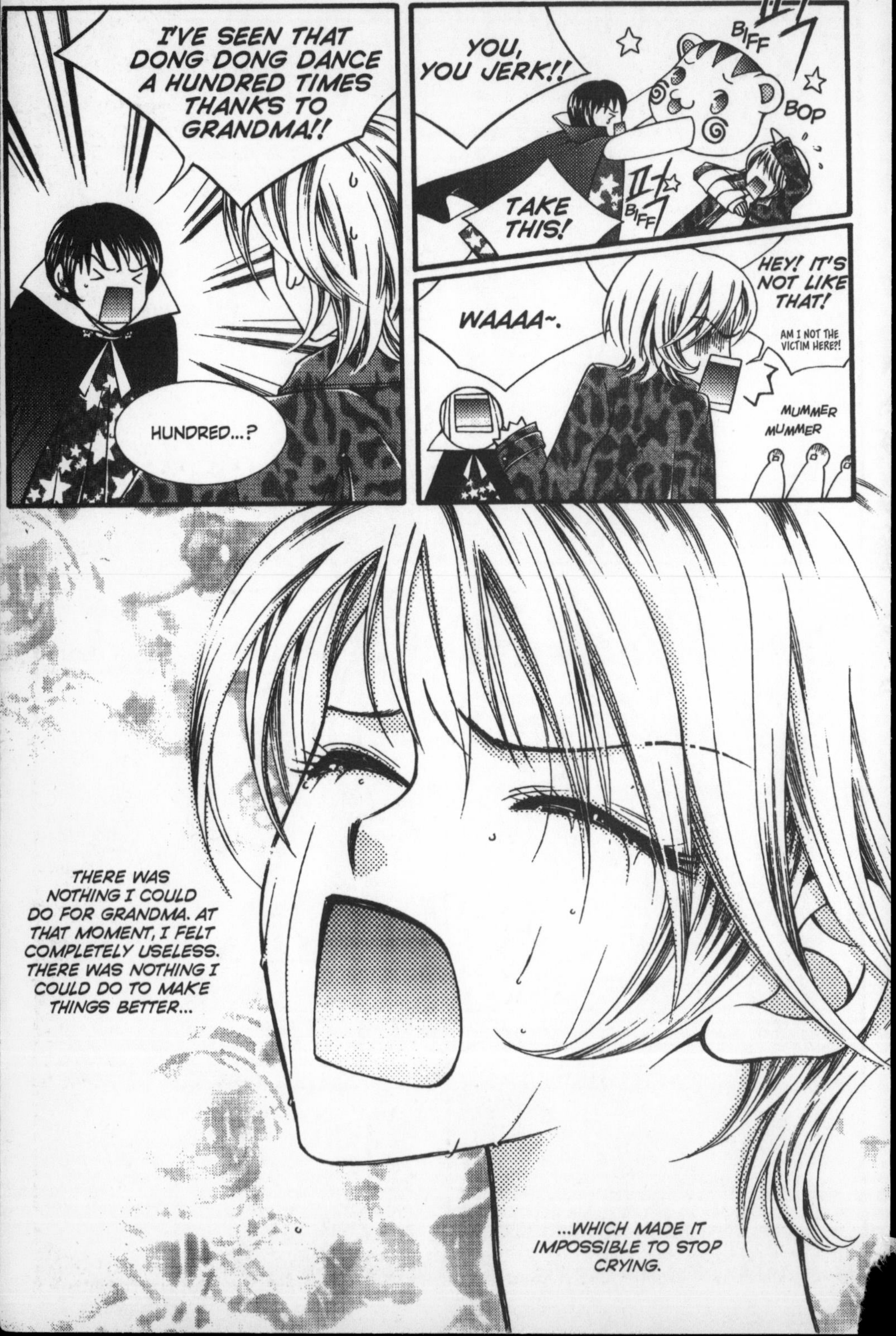
I'VE SEEN THAT DONG DONG DANCE A HUNDRED TIMES THANKS TO GRANDMA!!
HUNDRED...?
YOU, YOU JERK!!
BIFF
BOP
TAKE THIS!
BIFF
WAAAA~.
HEY! IT'S NOT LIKE THAT!
AM I NOT THE VICTIM HERE?!
MUMMER MUMMER
THERE WAS NOTHING I COULD DO FOR GRANDMA. AT THAT MOMENT, I FELT COMPLETELY USELESS. THERE WAS NOTHING I COULD DO TO MAKE THINGS BETTER...
...WHICH MADE IT IMPOSSIBLE TO STOP CRYING.

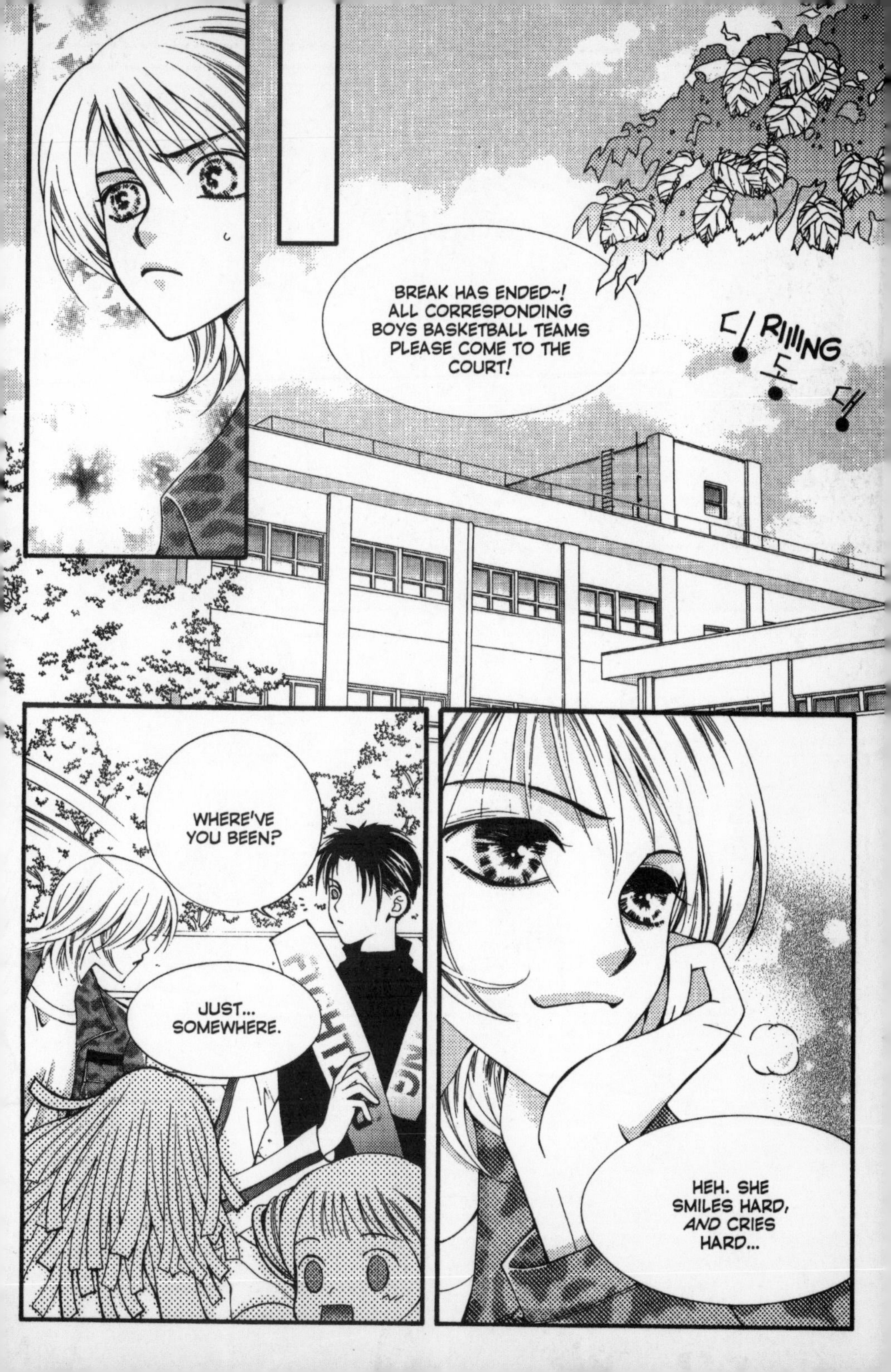
BREAK HAS ENDED~! ALL CORRESPONDING BOYS BASKETBALL TEAMS PLEASE COME TO THE COURT!
RIIIING
WHERE'VE YOU BEEN?
JUST... SOMEWHERE.
HEH. SHE SMILES HARD, *AND* CRIES HARD...

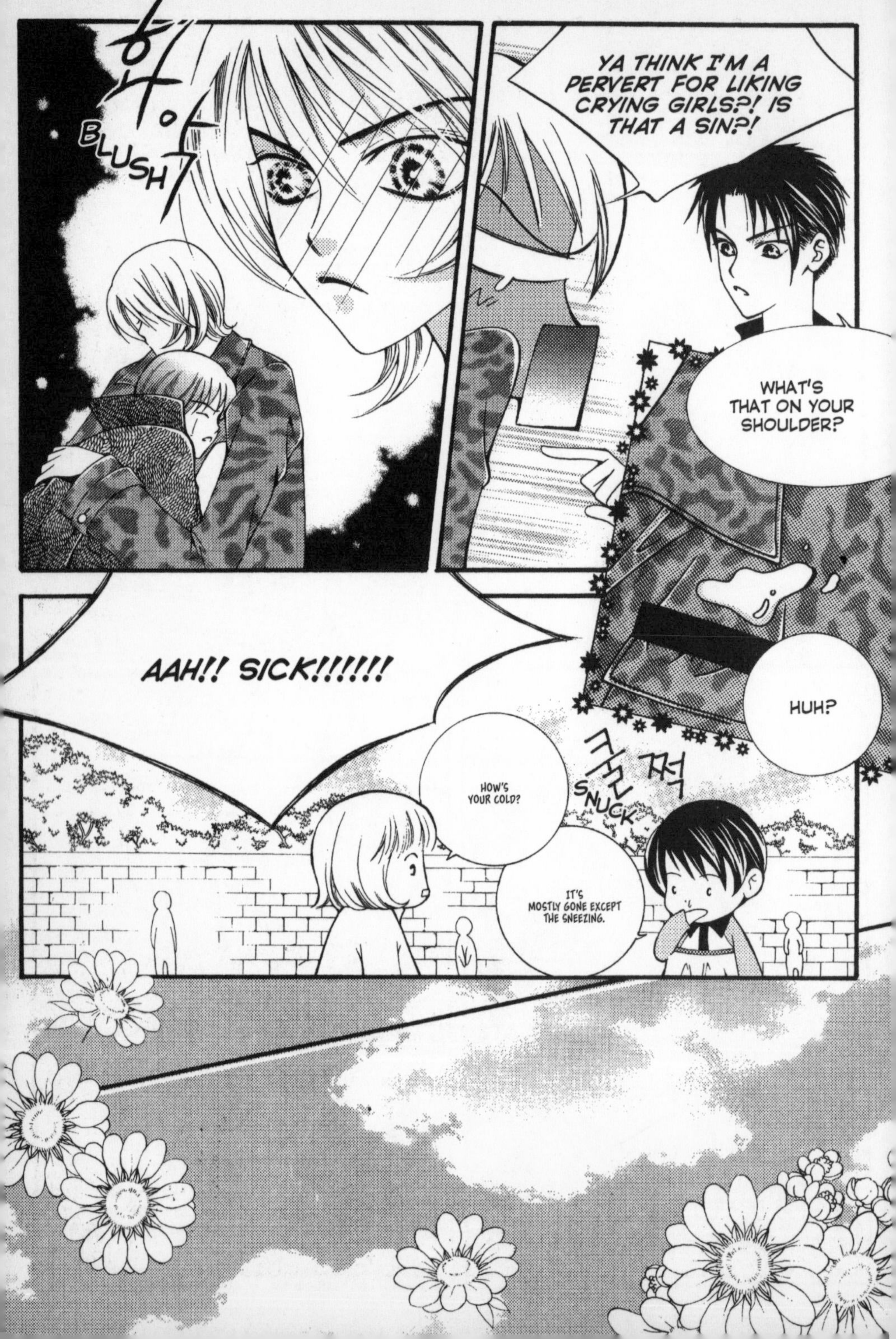
BLUSH
YA THINK I'M A PERVERT FOR LIKING CRYING GIRLS?! IS THAT A SIN?!
WHAT'S THAT ON YOUR SHOULDER?
HUH?
AAH!! SICK!!!!!!
HOW'S YOUR COLD?
SNUCK
쩍
IT'S MOSTLY GONE EXCEPT THE SNEEZING.

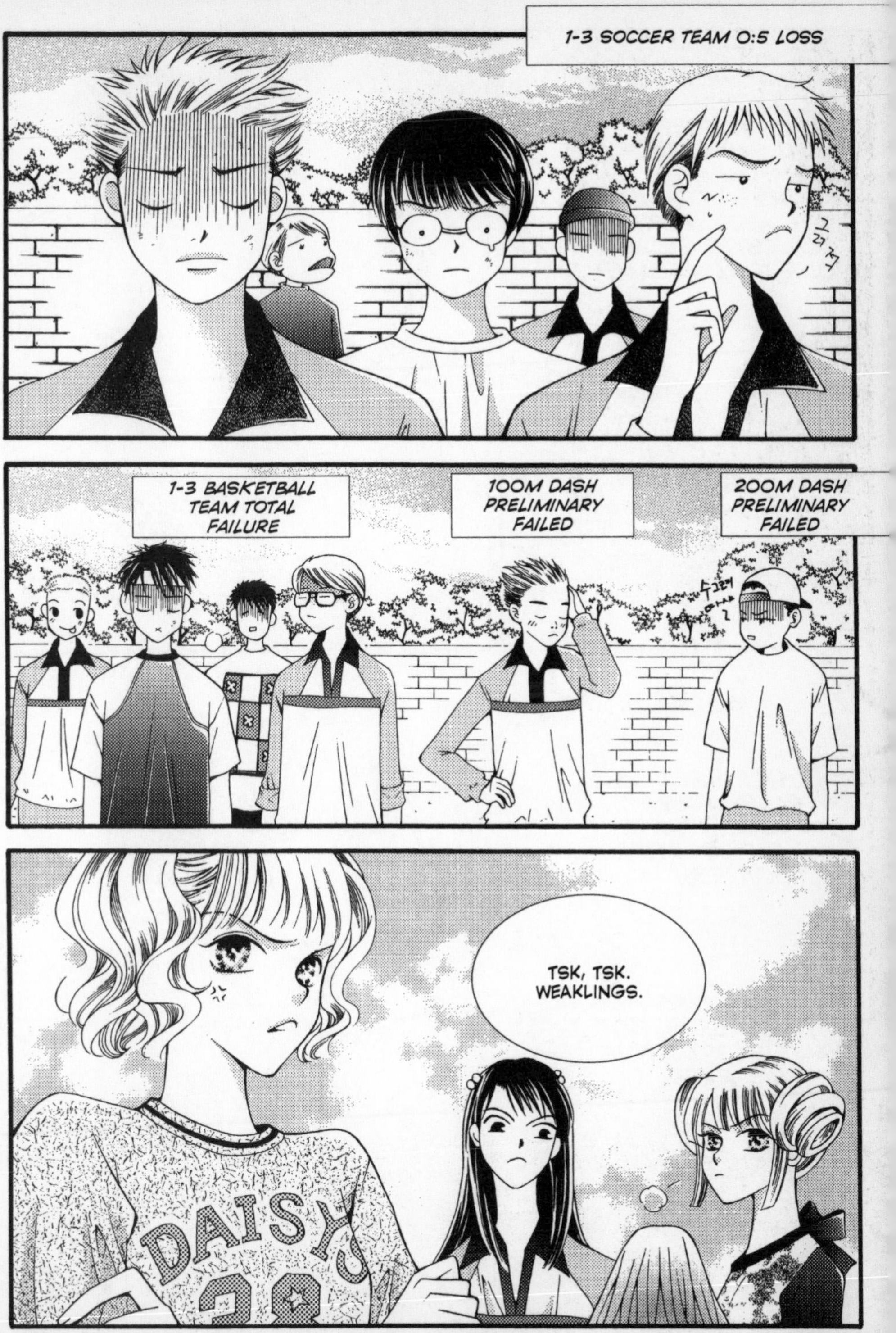
1-3 SOCCER TEAM 0:5 LOSS
1-3 BASKETBALL TEAM TOTAL FAILURE
100M DASH PRELIMINARY FAILED
200M DASH PRELIMINARY FAILED
TSK, TSK. WEAKLINGS.
DAISY

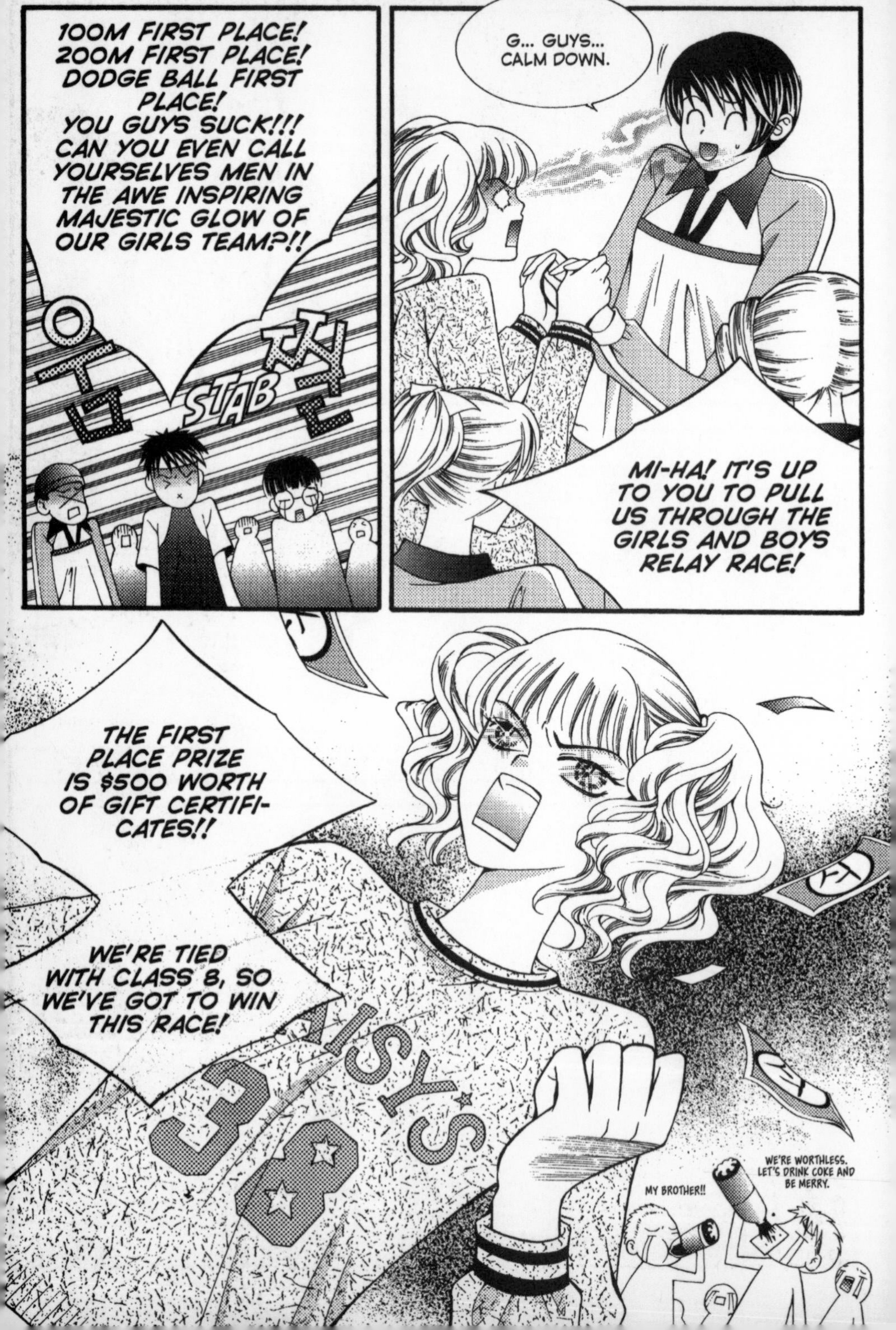
100M FIRST PLACE! 200M FIRST PLACE! DODGE BALL FIRST PLACE! YOU GUYS SUCK!!! CAN YOU EVEN CALL YOURSELVES MEN IN THE AWE INSPIRING MAJESTIC GLOW OF OUR GIRLS TEAM?!!
STAB
G... GUYS... CALM DOWN.
MI-HA! IT'S UP TO YOU TO PULL US THROUGH THE GIRLS AND BOYS RELAY RACE!
THE FIRST PLACE PRIZE IS $500 WORTH OF GIFT CERTIFICATES!!
WE'RE TIED WITH CLASS 8, SO WE'VE GOT TO WIN THIS RACE!
MY BROTHER!!
WE'RE WORTHLESS. LET'S DRINK COKE AND BE MERRY.

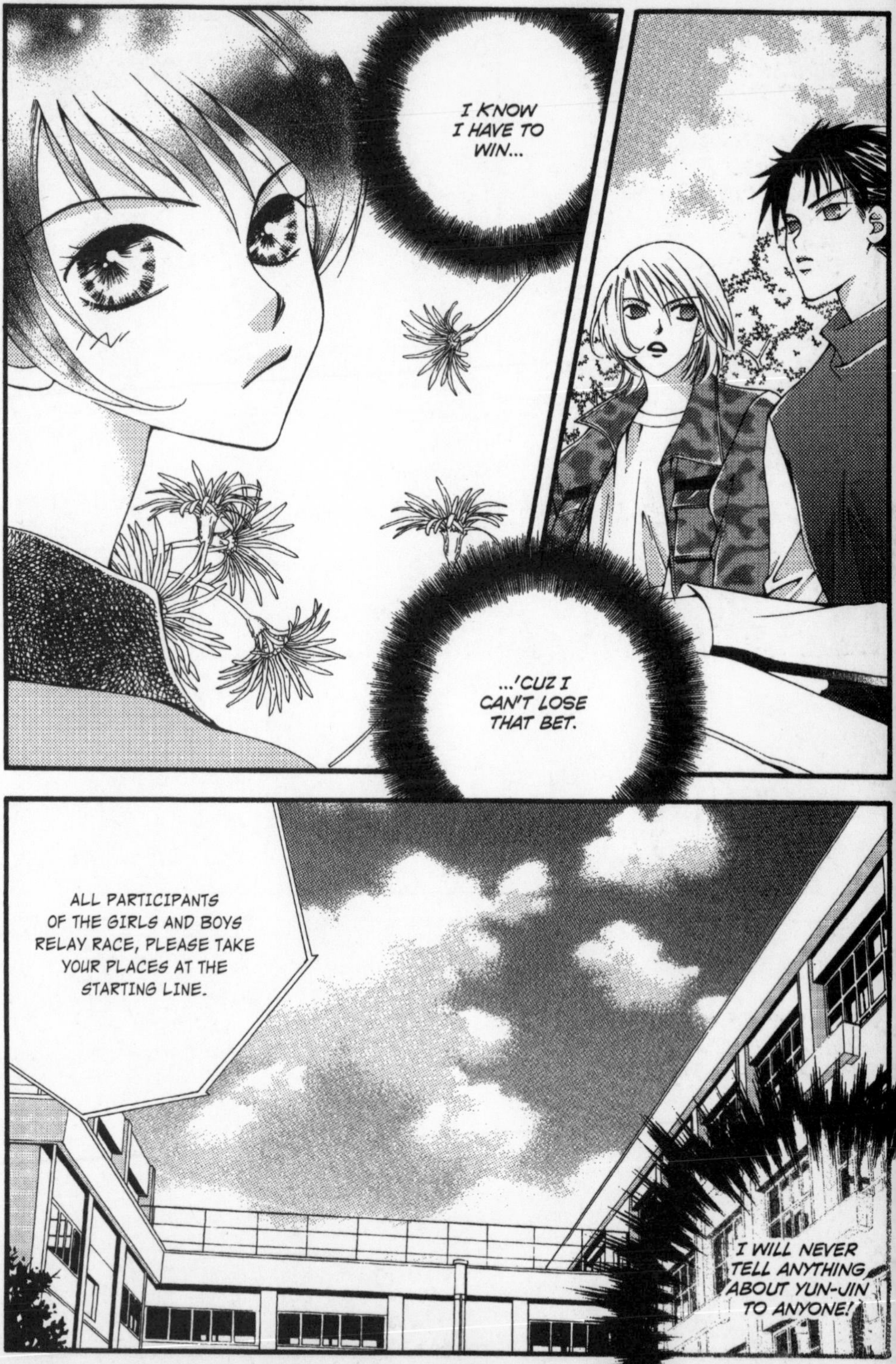
I KNOW I HAVE TO WIN...
...'CUZ I CAN'T LOSE THAT BET.
ALL PARTICIPANTS OF THE GIRLS AND BOYS RELAY RACE, PLEASE TAKE YOUR PLACES AT THE STARTING LINE.
I WILL NEVER TELL ANYTHING ABOUT YUN-JIN TO ANYONE!

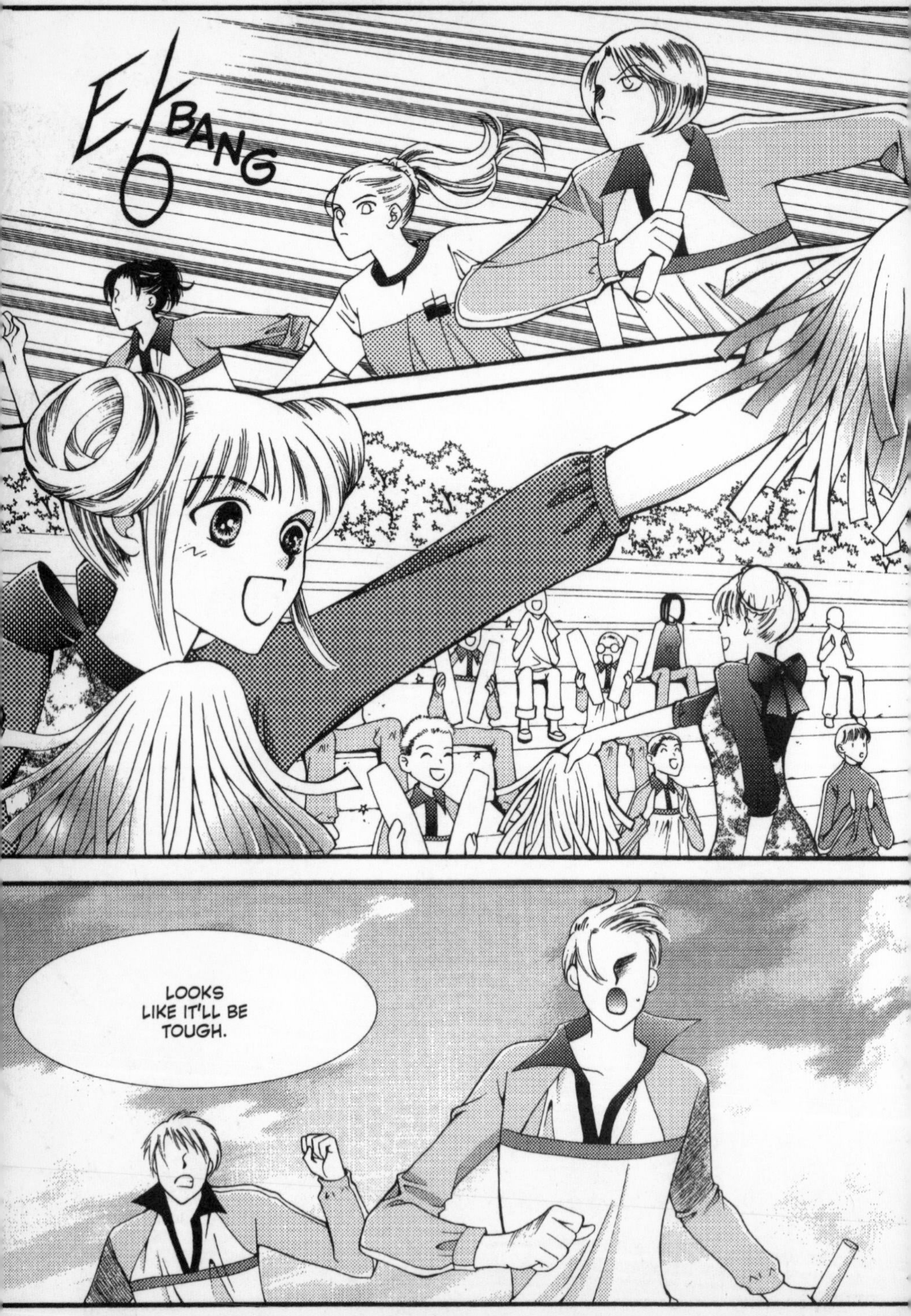
BANG
LOOKS LIKE IT'LL BE TOUGH.

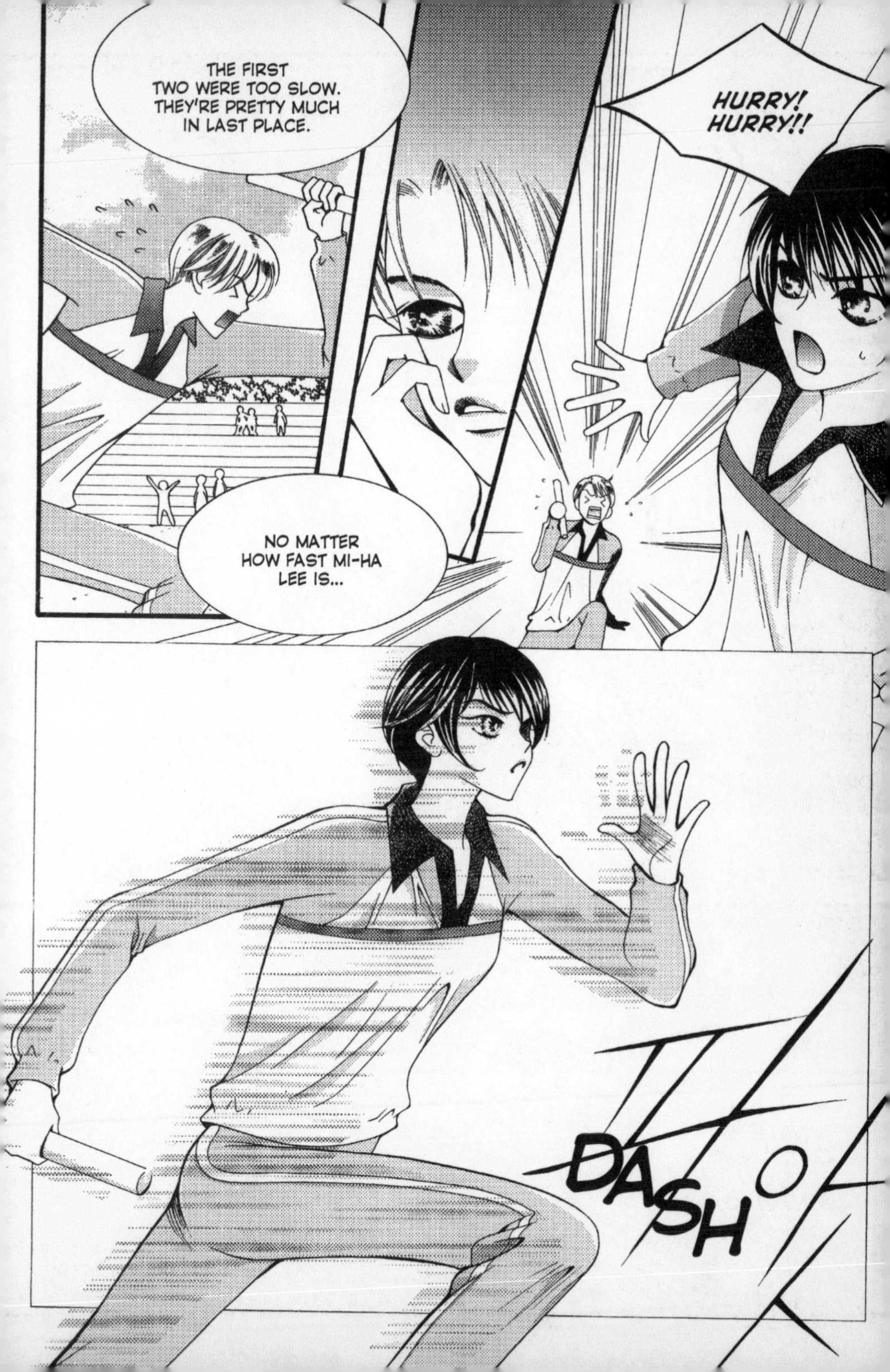

THE FIRST TWO WERE TOO SLOW. THEY'RE PRETTY MUCH IN LAST PLACE.
HURRY! HURRY!!
NO MATTER HOW FAST MI-HA LEE IS...
DASH

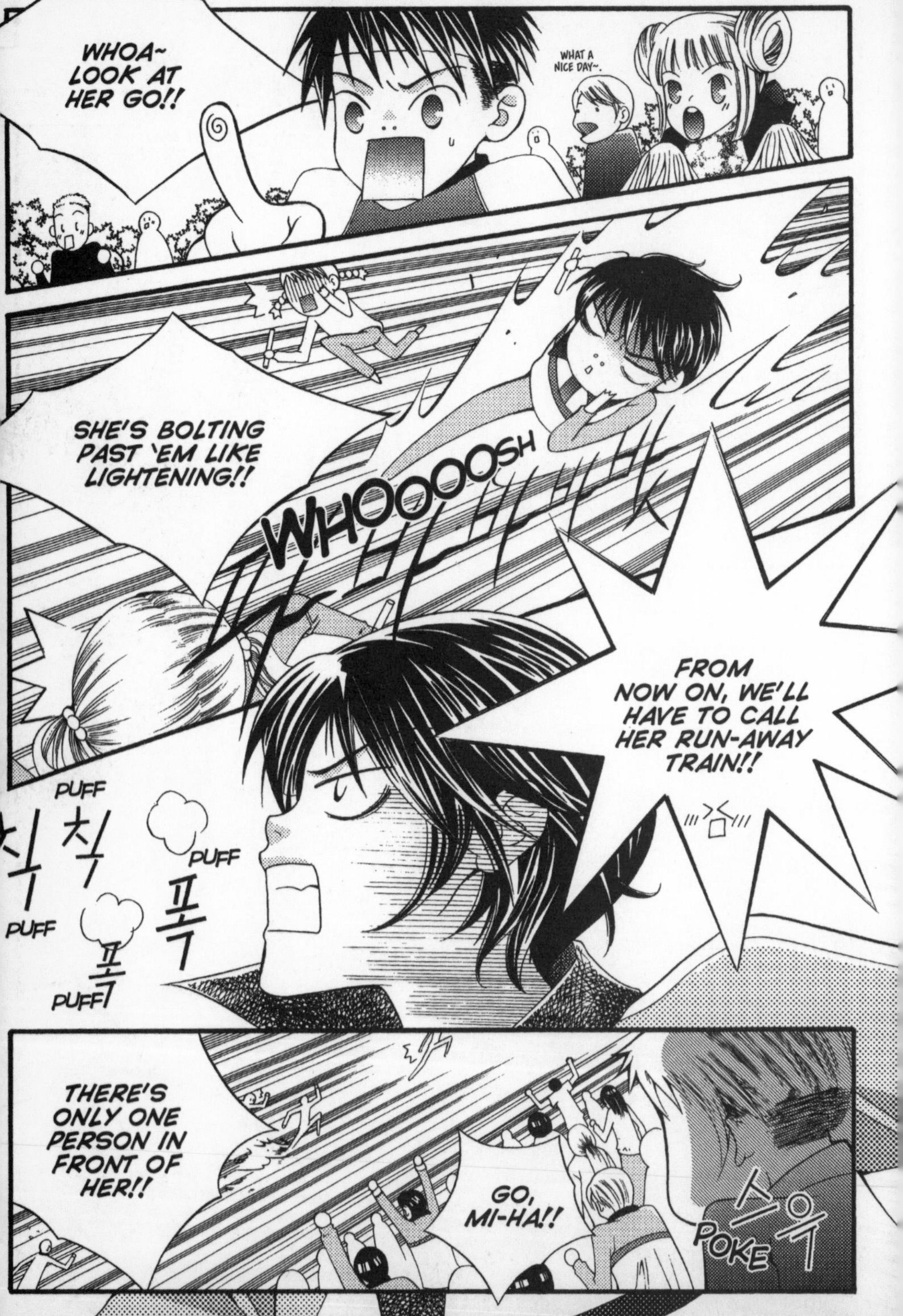
WHOA~ LOOK AT HER GO!!
WHAT A NICE DAY~.
SHE'S BOLTING PAST 'EM LIKE LIGHTENING!!
WHOOOOOSH
FROM NOW ON, WE'LL HAVE TO CALL HER RUN-AWAY TRAIN!!
PUFF
PUFF
PUFF
PUFF
THERE'S ONLY ONE PERSON IN FRONT OF HER!!
GO, MI-HA!!
POKE

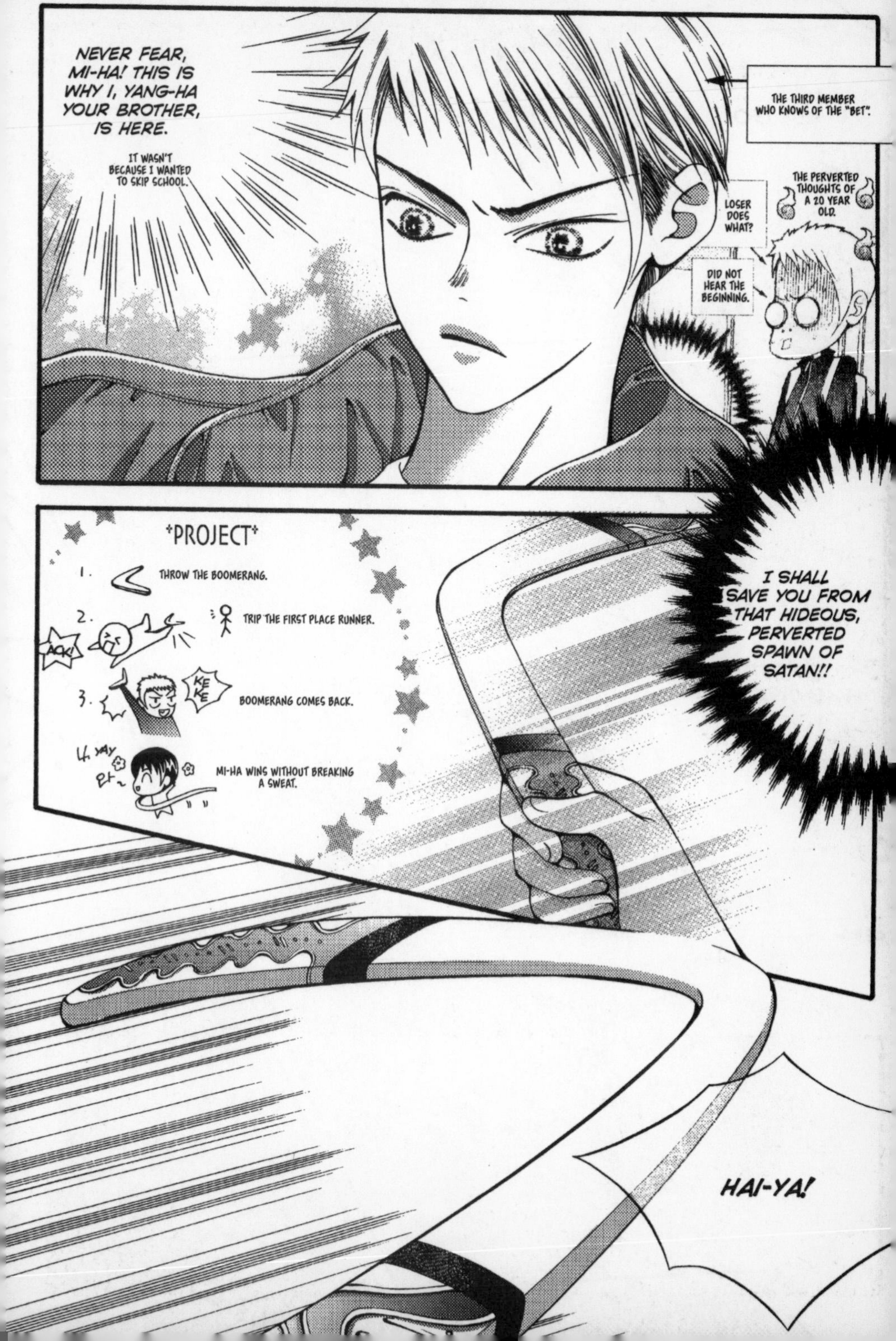
NEVER FEAR, MI-HA! THIS IS WHY I, YANG-HA YOUR BROTHER, IS HERE.
IT WASN'T BECAUSE I WANTED TO SKIP SCHOOL.
THE THIRD MEMBER WHO KNOWS OF THE "BET".
LOSER DOES WHAT?
DID NOT HEAR THE BEGINNING.
THE PERVERTED THOUGHTS OF A 20 YEAR OLD.
PROJECT
1. THROW THE BOOMERANG.
2. TRIP THE FIRST PLACE RUNNER.
ACK!
3. BOOMERANG COMES BACK.
KE KE
4. YAY
MI-HA WINS WITHOUT BREAKING A SWEAT.
I SHALL SAVE YOU FROM THAT HIDEOUS, PERVERTED SPAWN OF SATAN!!
HAI-YA!

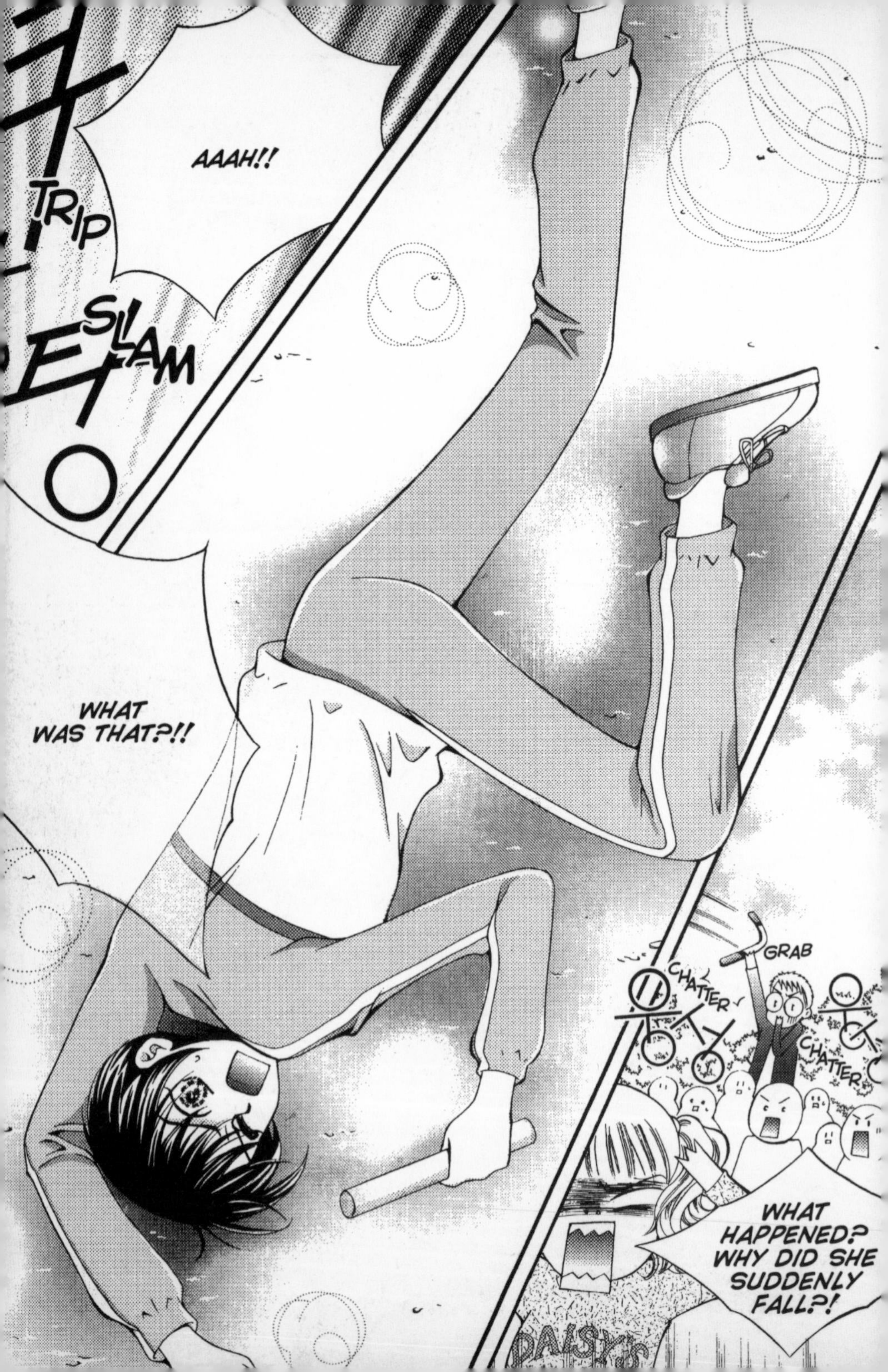
AAAH!!
TRIP
SLAM
WHAT WAS THAT?!!
GRAB
CHATTER
CHATTER
WHAT HAPPENED? WHY DID SHE SUDDENLY FALL?!

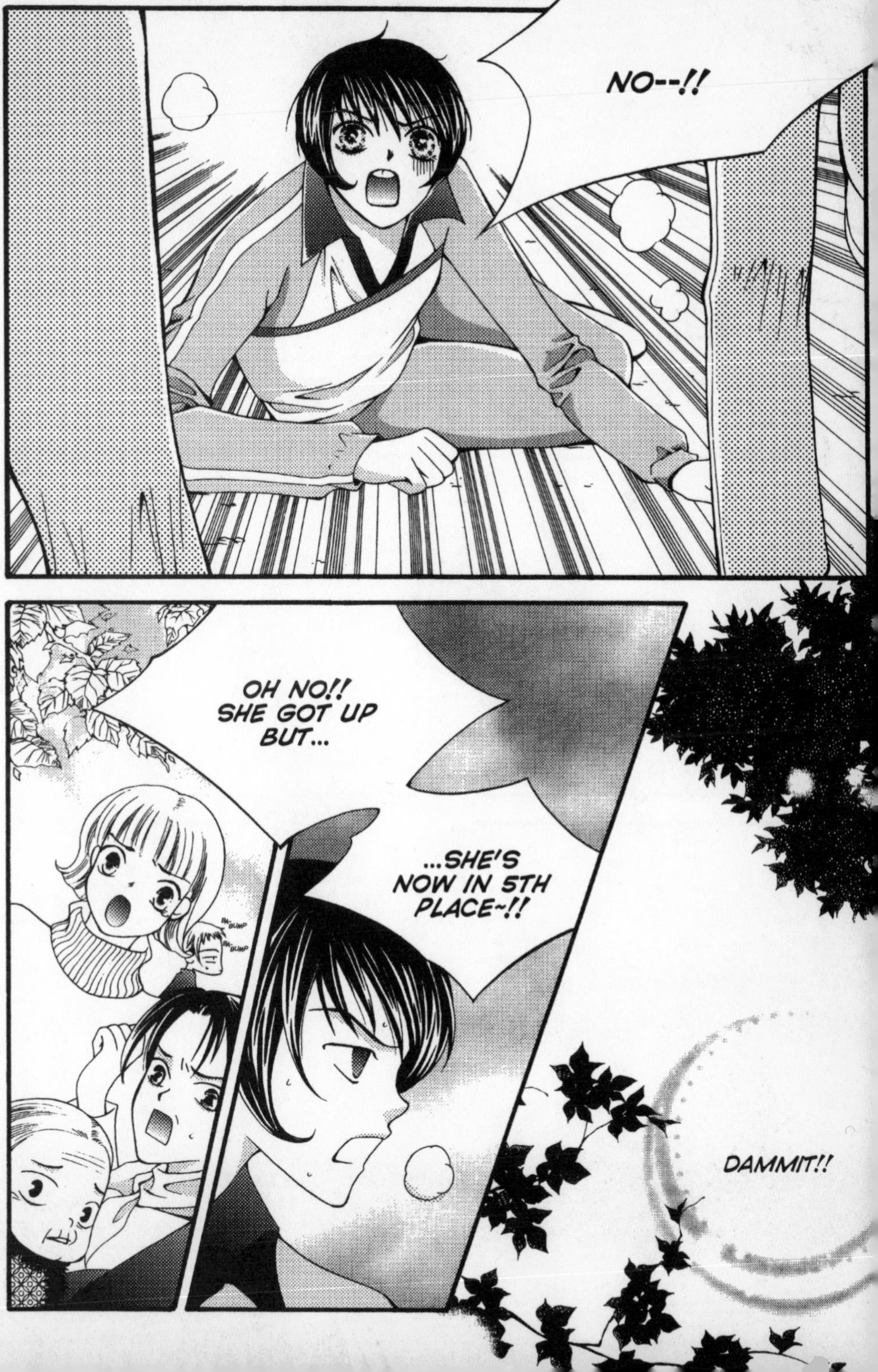
NO--!!
OH NO!! SHE GOT UP BUT...
...SHE'S NOW IN 5TH PLACE~!!
DAMMIT!!

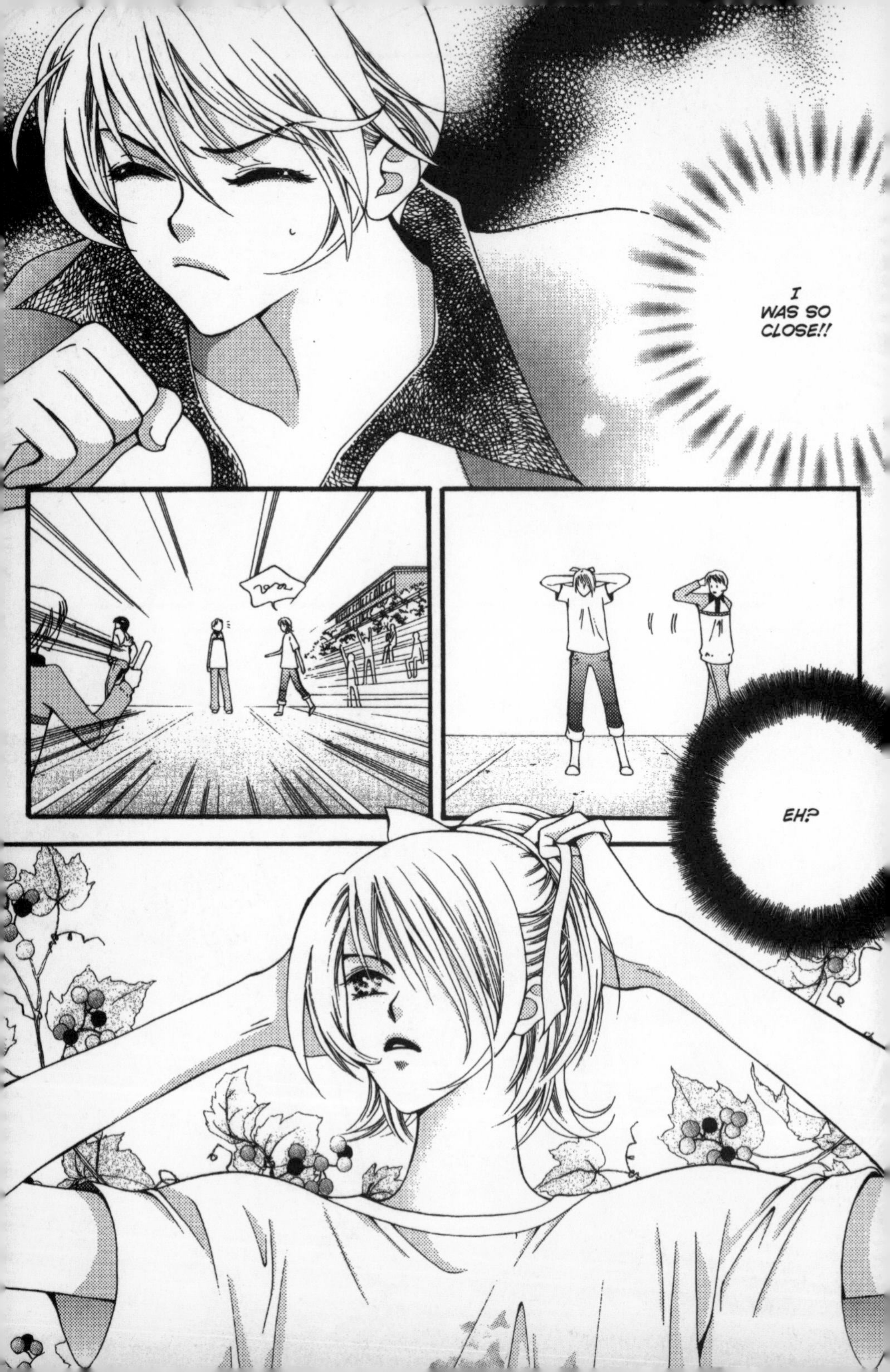
I WAS SO CLOSE!!
EH?

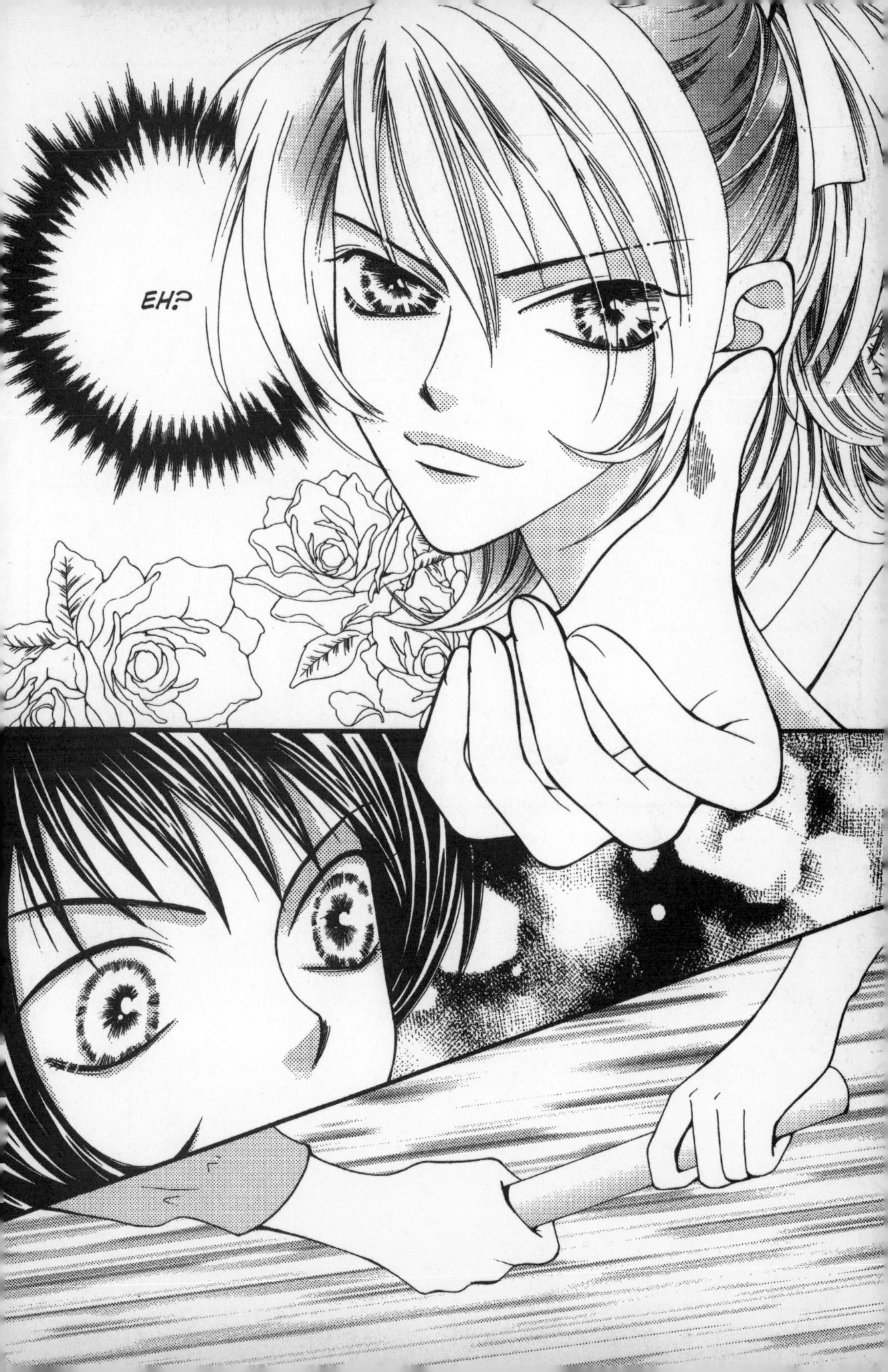
EH?

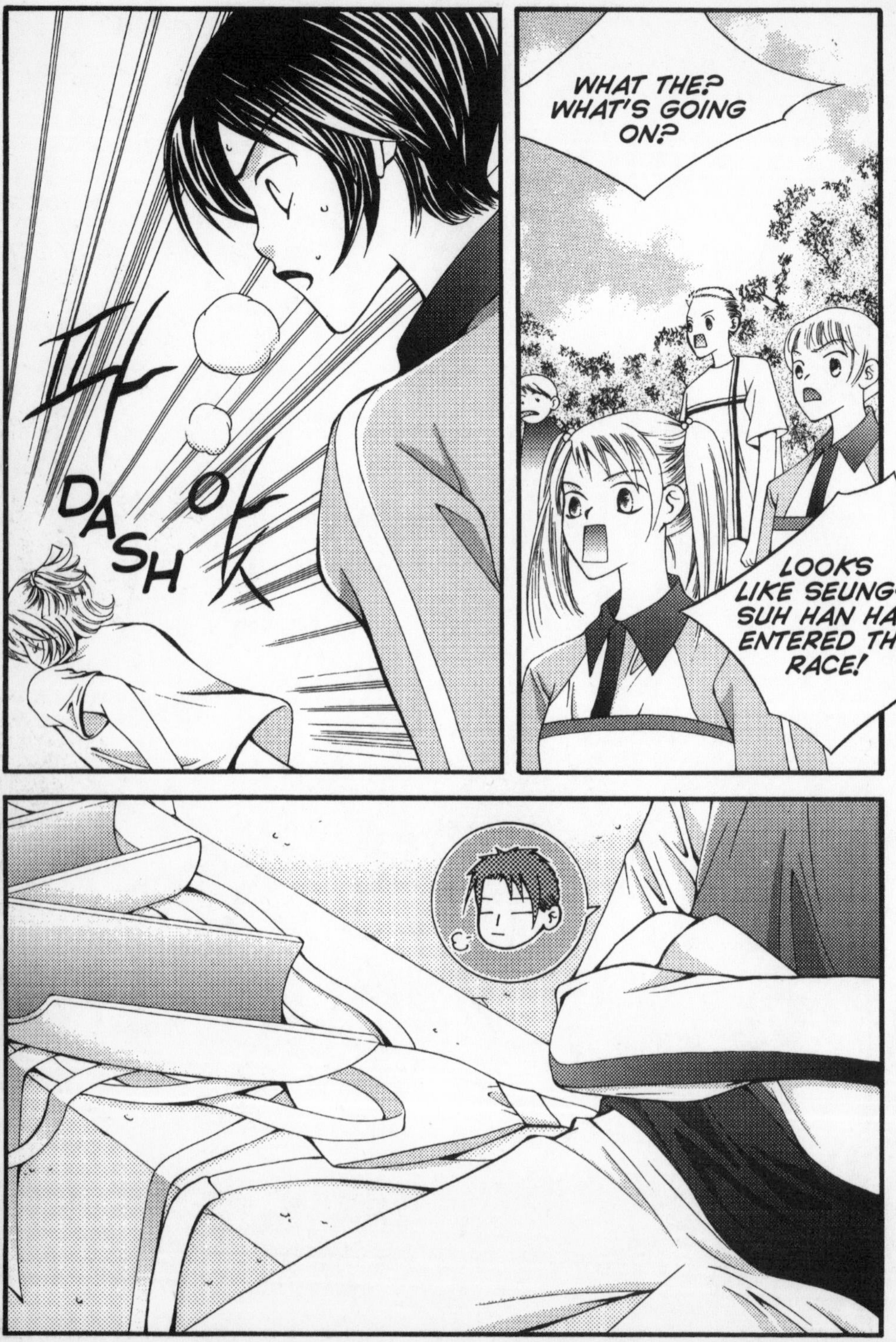
DASH
WHAT THE? WHAT'S GOING ON?
LOOKS LIKE SEUNG-SUH HAN HAS ENTERED THE RACE!

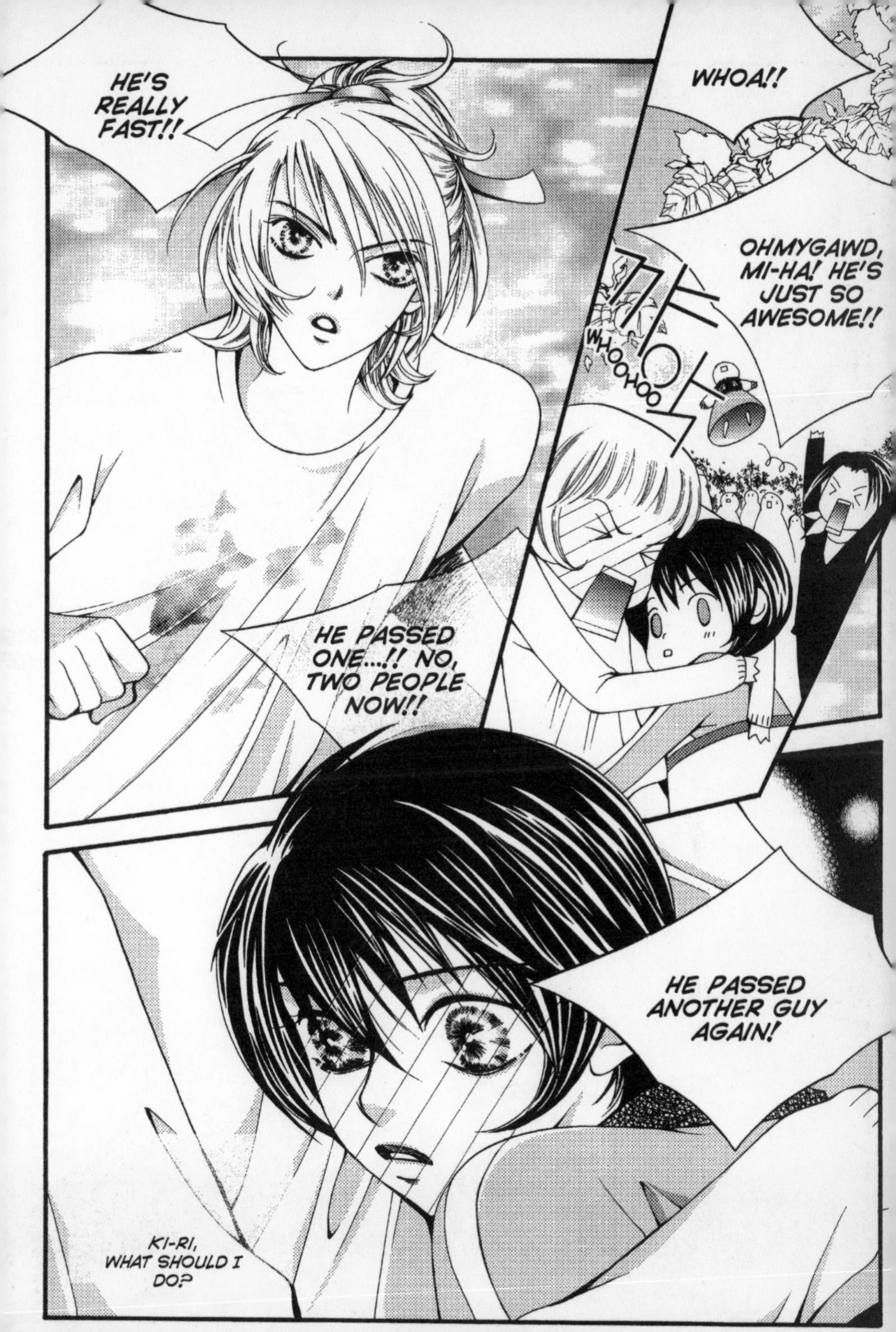
HE'S REALLY FAST!!
HE PASSED ONE...!! NO, TWO PEOPLE NOW!!
WHOA!!
OHMYGAWD, MI-HA! HE'S JUST SO AWESOME!!
WHOOHOO
HE PASSED ANOTHER GUY AGAIN!
KI-RI, WHAT SHOULD I DO?

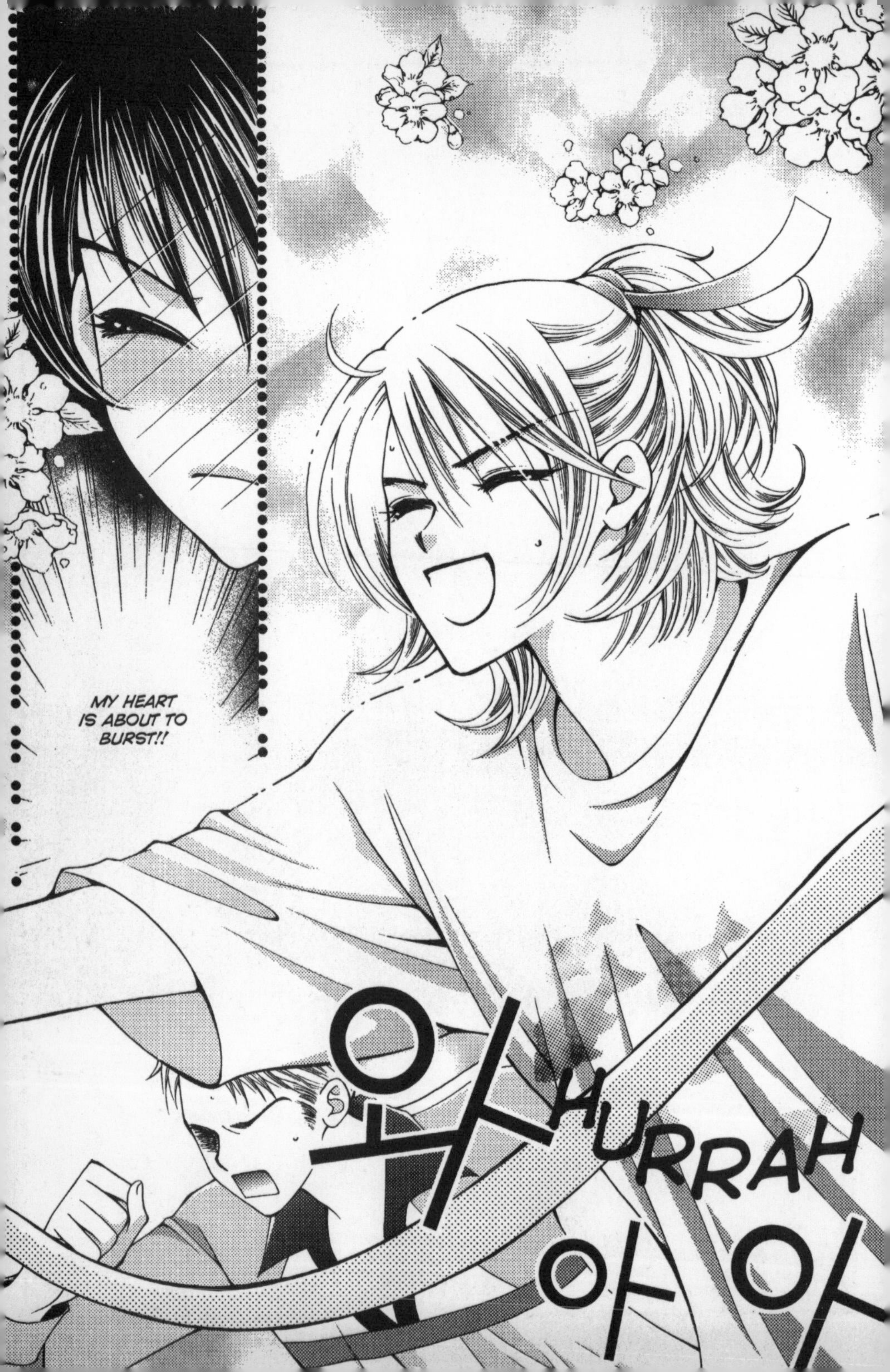
MY HEART IS ABOUT TO BURST!!
와아아
HURRAH

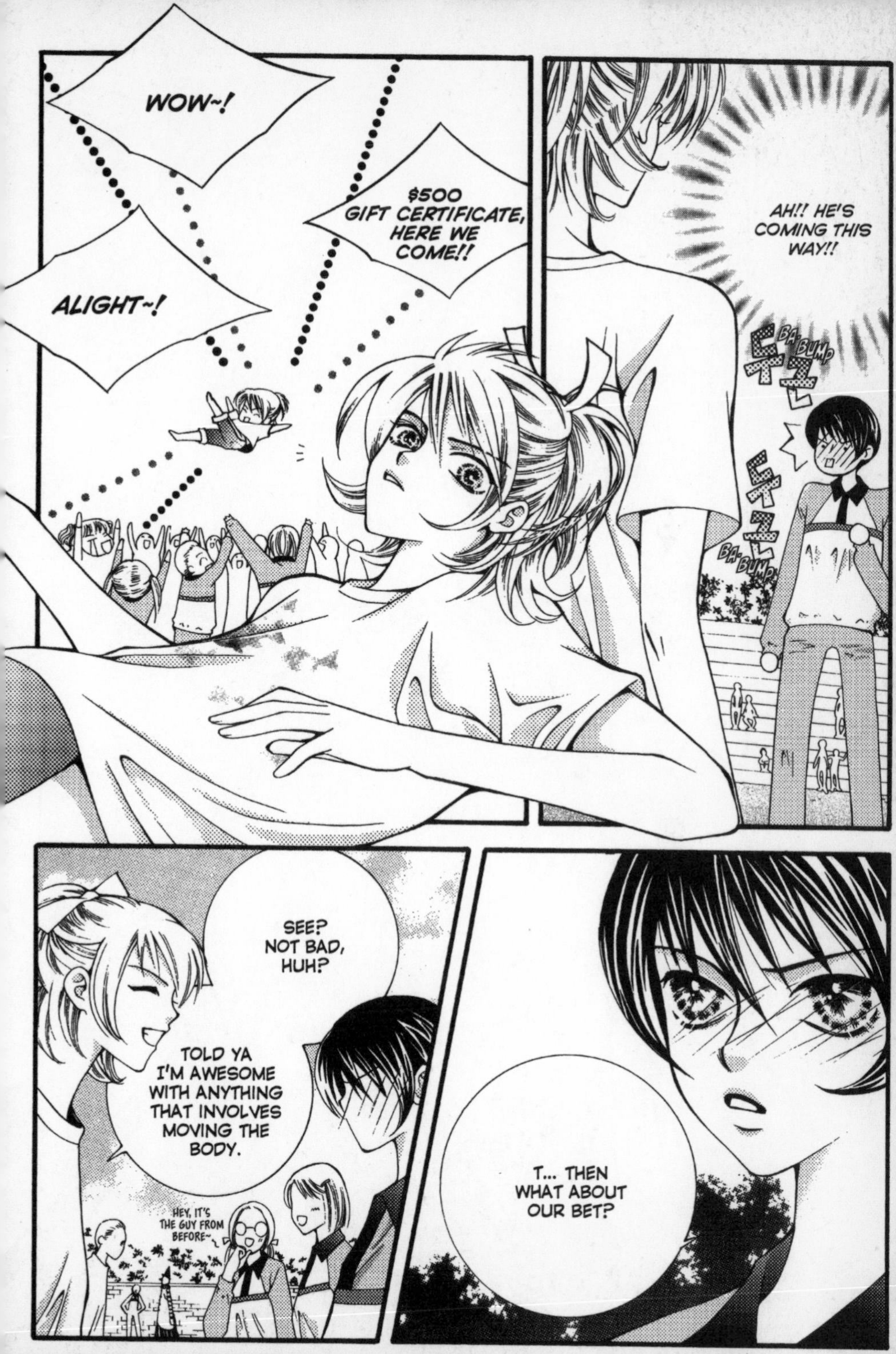
WOW~!
ALIGHT~!
$500 GIFT CERTIFICATE, HERE WE COME!!
AH!! HE'S COMING THIS WAY!!
BA-BUMP
BA-BUMP
SEE? NOT BAD, HUH?
TOLD YA I'M AWESOME WITH ANYTHING THAT INVOLVES MOVING THE BODY.
HEY, IT'S THE GUY FROM BEFORE~
T... THEN WHAT ABOUT OUR BET?

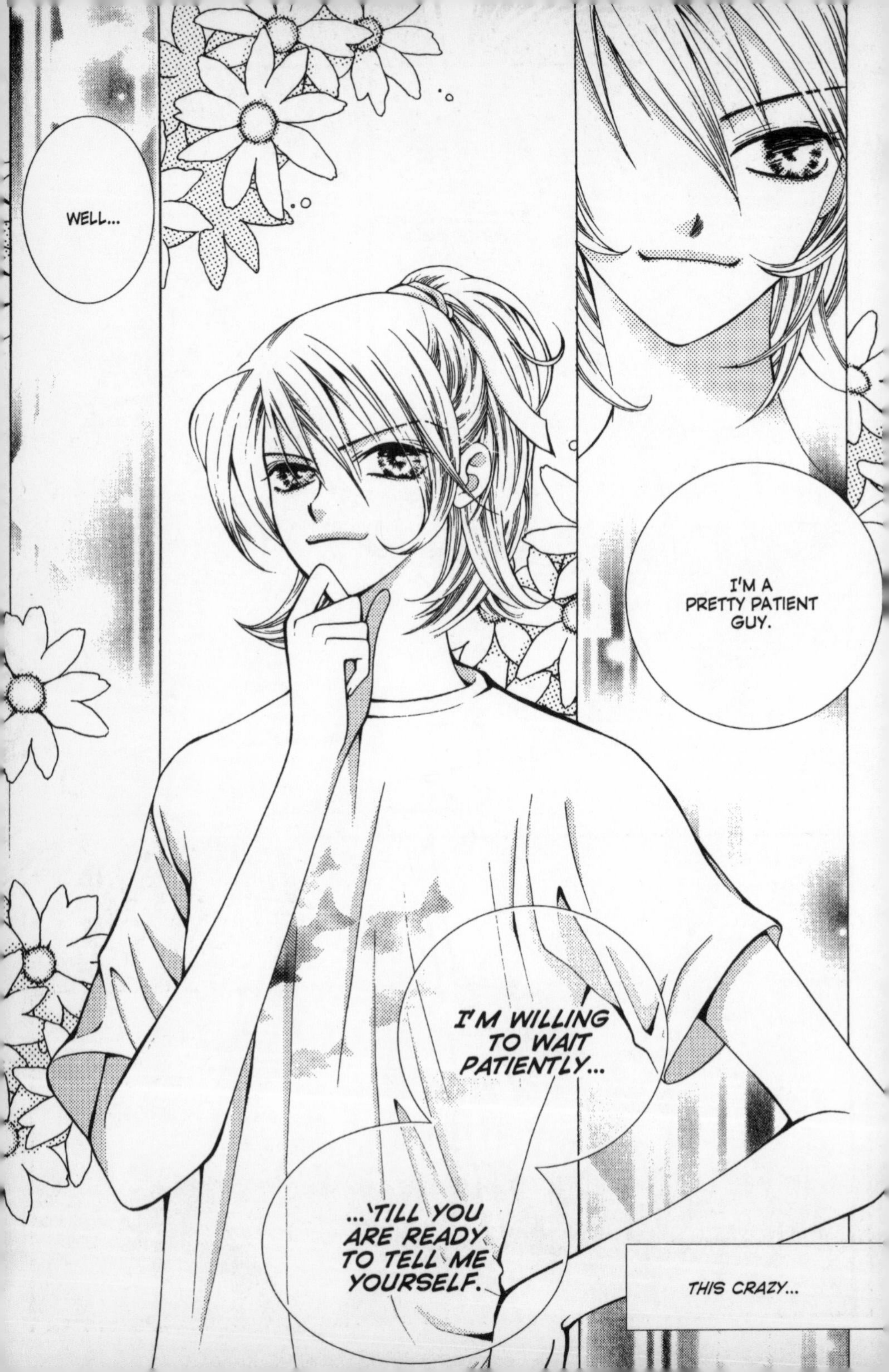
WELL...
I'M A PRETTY PATIENT GUY.
I'M WILLING TO WAIT PATIENTLY...
...'TILL YOU ARE READY TO TELL ME YOURSELF.
THIS CRAZY...

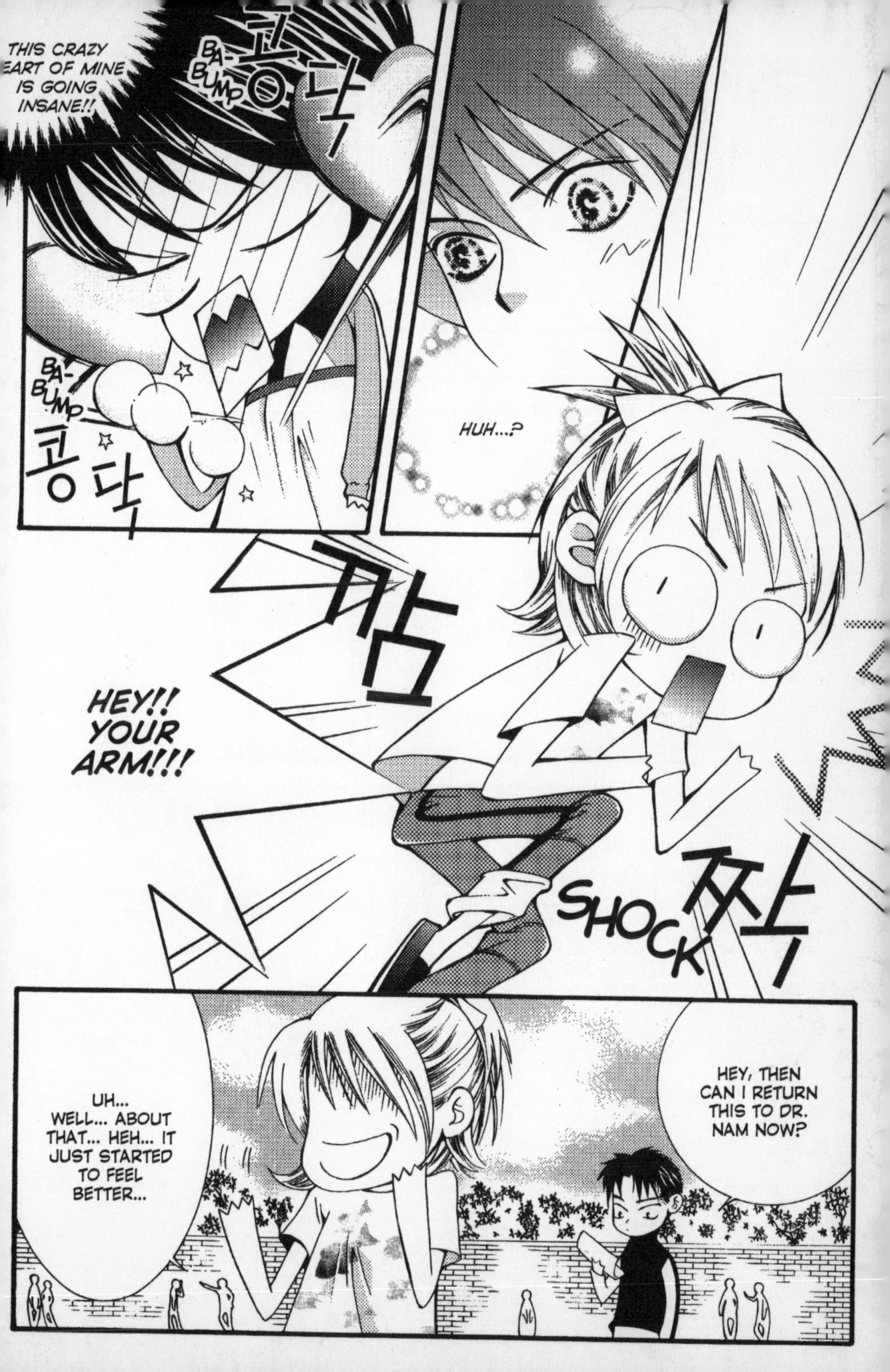
THIS CRAZY EART OF MINE IS GOING INSANE!!
BA-BUMP
콩닥
BA-BUMP
콩닥
HUH...?
깜
HEY!! YOUR ARM!!!
SHOCK
짝
UH... WELL... ABOUT THAT... HEH... IT JUST STARTED TO FEEL BETTER...
HEY, THEN CAN I RETURN THIS TO DR. NAM NOW?

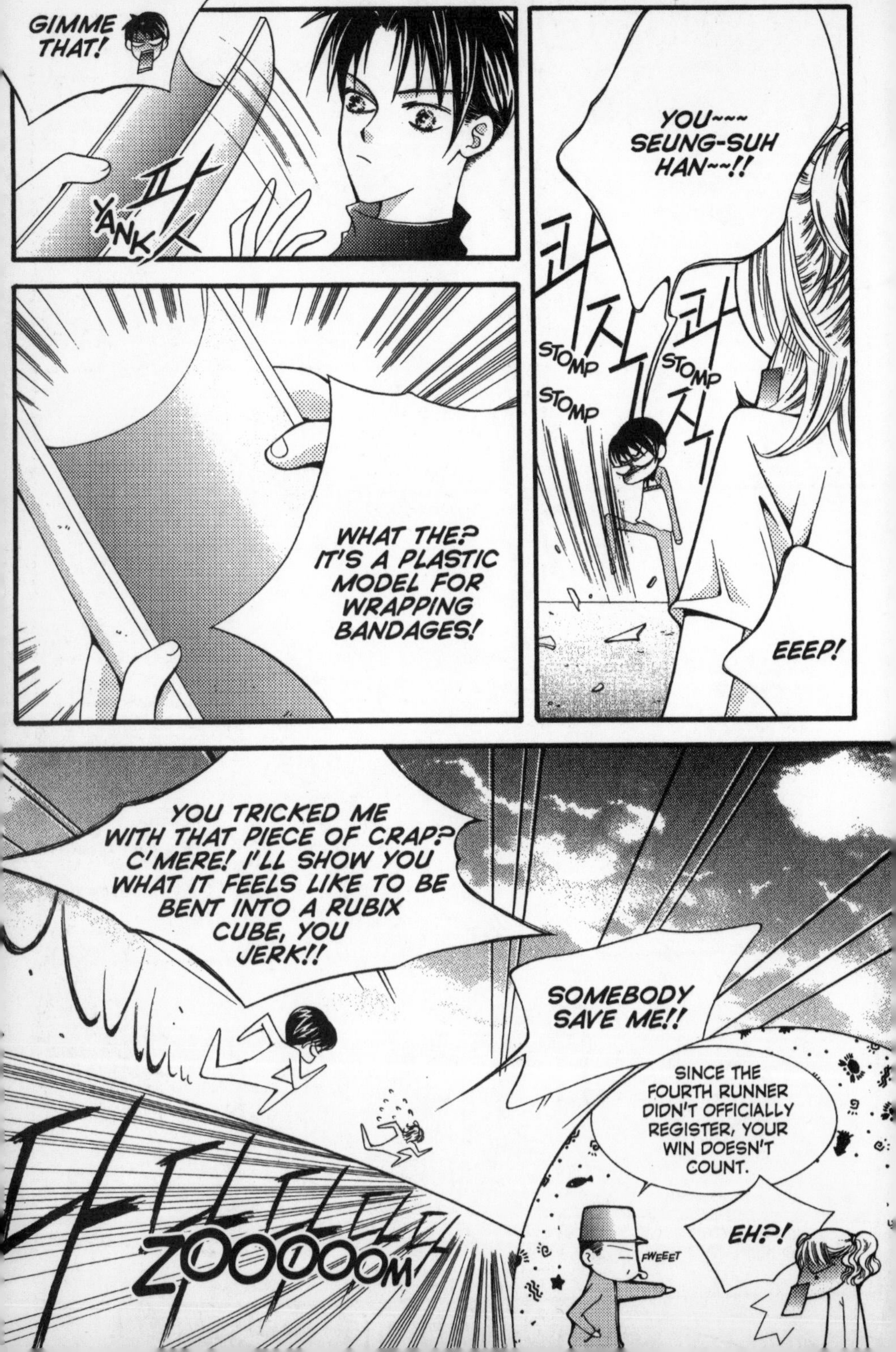
GIMME THAT!
YANK
WHAT THE? IT'S A PLASTIC MODEL FOR WRAPPING BANDAGES!
YOU~~~ SEUNG-SUH HAN~~!!
STOMP
STOMP
STOMP
EEEP!
YOU TRICKED ME WITH THAT PIECE OF CRAP? C'MERE! I'LL SHOW YOU WHAT IT FEELS LIKE TO BE BENT INTO A RUBIX CUBE, YOU JERK!!
SOMEBODY SAVE ME!!
ZOOOOOOM
SINCE THE FOURTH RUNNER DIDN'T OFFICIALLY REGISTER, YOUR WIN DOESN'T COUNT.
FWEEET
EH?!

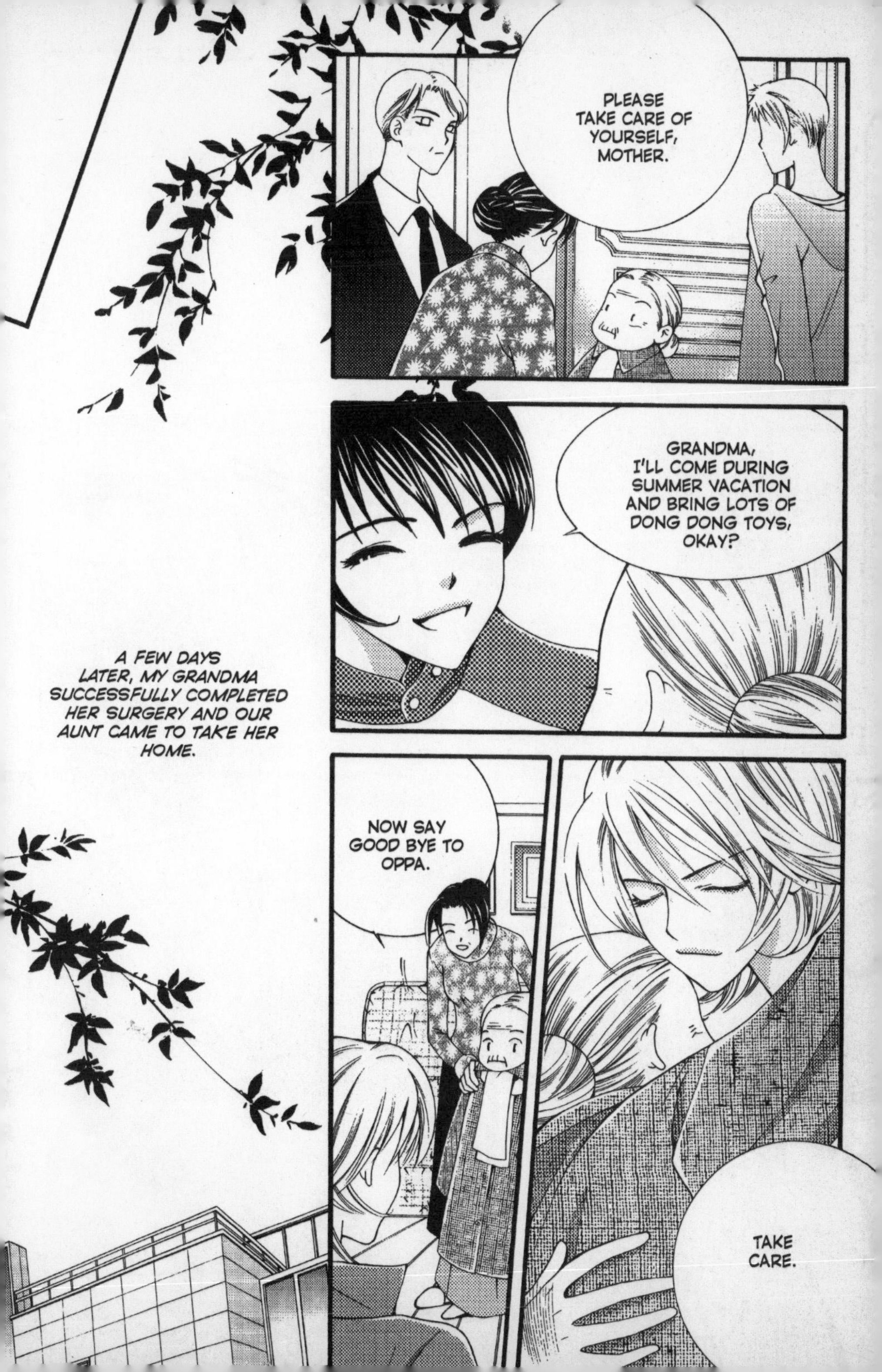
A FEW DAYS LATER, MY GRANDMA SUCCESSFULLY COMPLETED HER SURGERY AND OUR AUNT CAME TO TAKE HER HOME.
PLEASE TAKE CARE OF YOURSELF, MOTHER.
GRANDMA, I'LL COME DURING SUMMER VACATION AND BRING LOTS OF DONG DONG TOYS, OKAY?
NOW SAY GOOD BYE TO OPPA.
TAKE CARE.

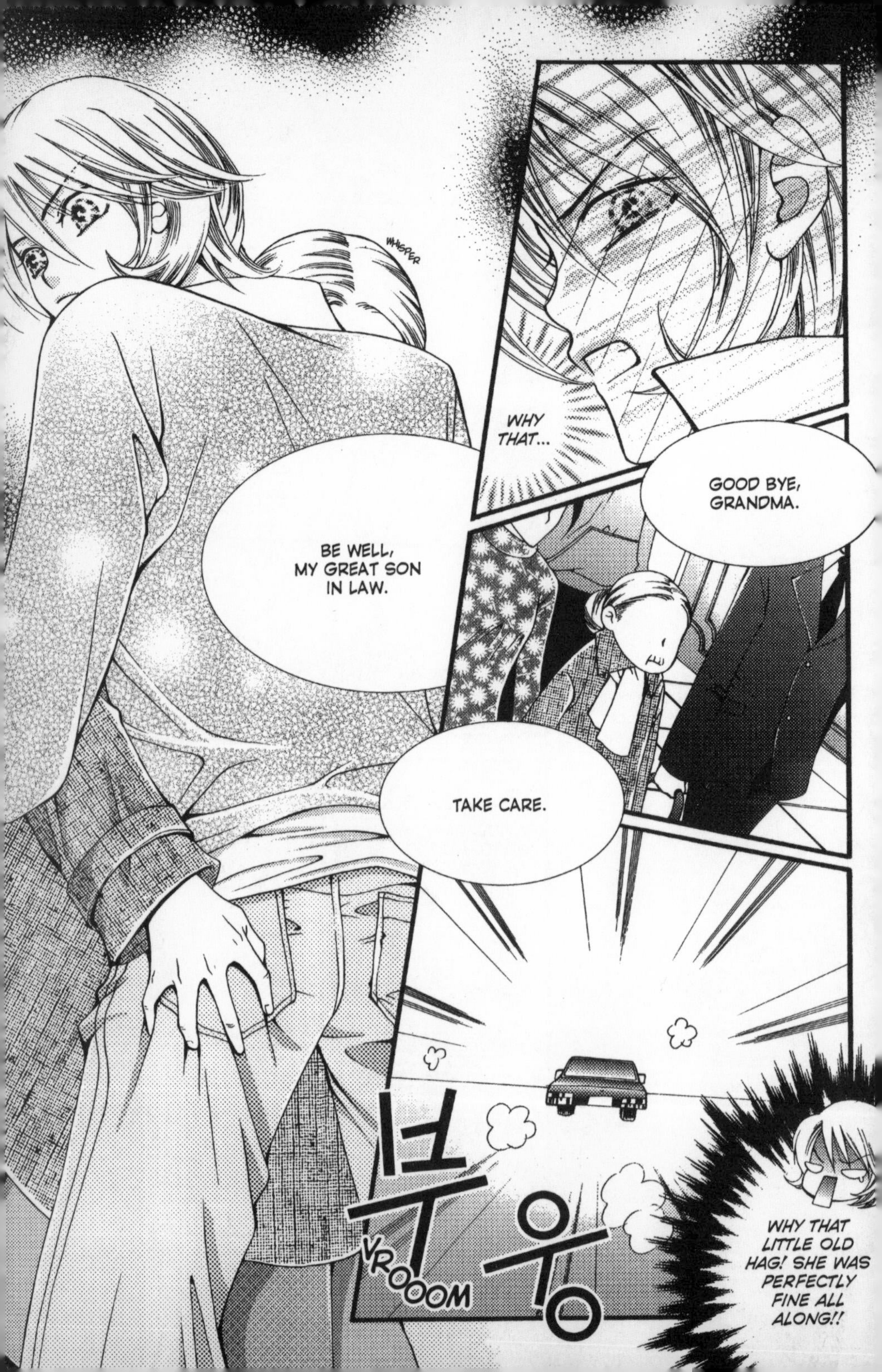
WHISPER
BE WELL, MY GREAT SON IN LAW.
TAKE CARE.
WHY THAT...
GOOD BYE, GRANDMA.
부웅
VROOOM
WHY THAT LITTLE OLD HAG! SHE WAS PERFECTLY FINE ALL ALONG!!

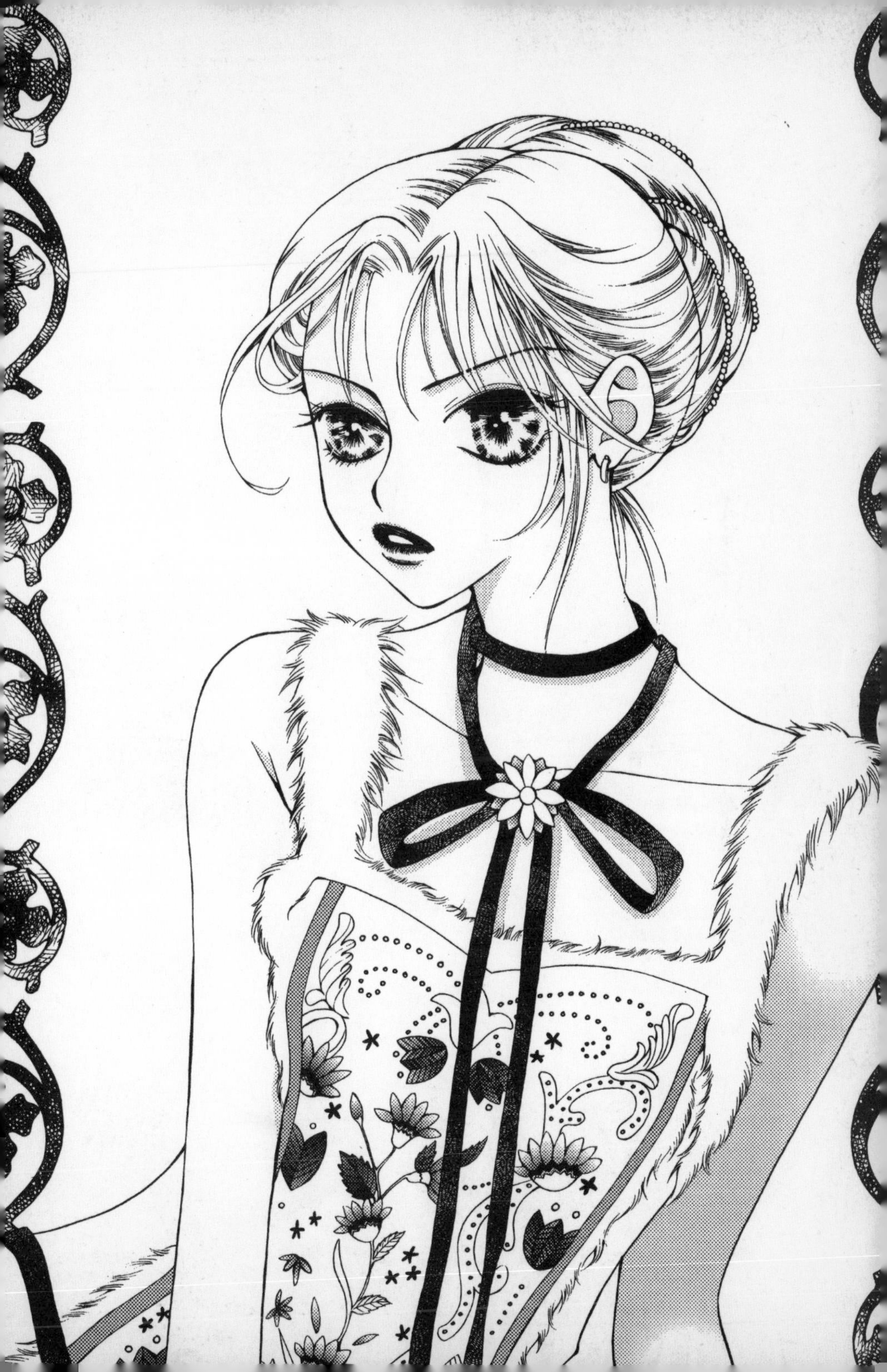

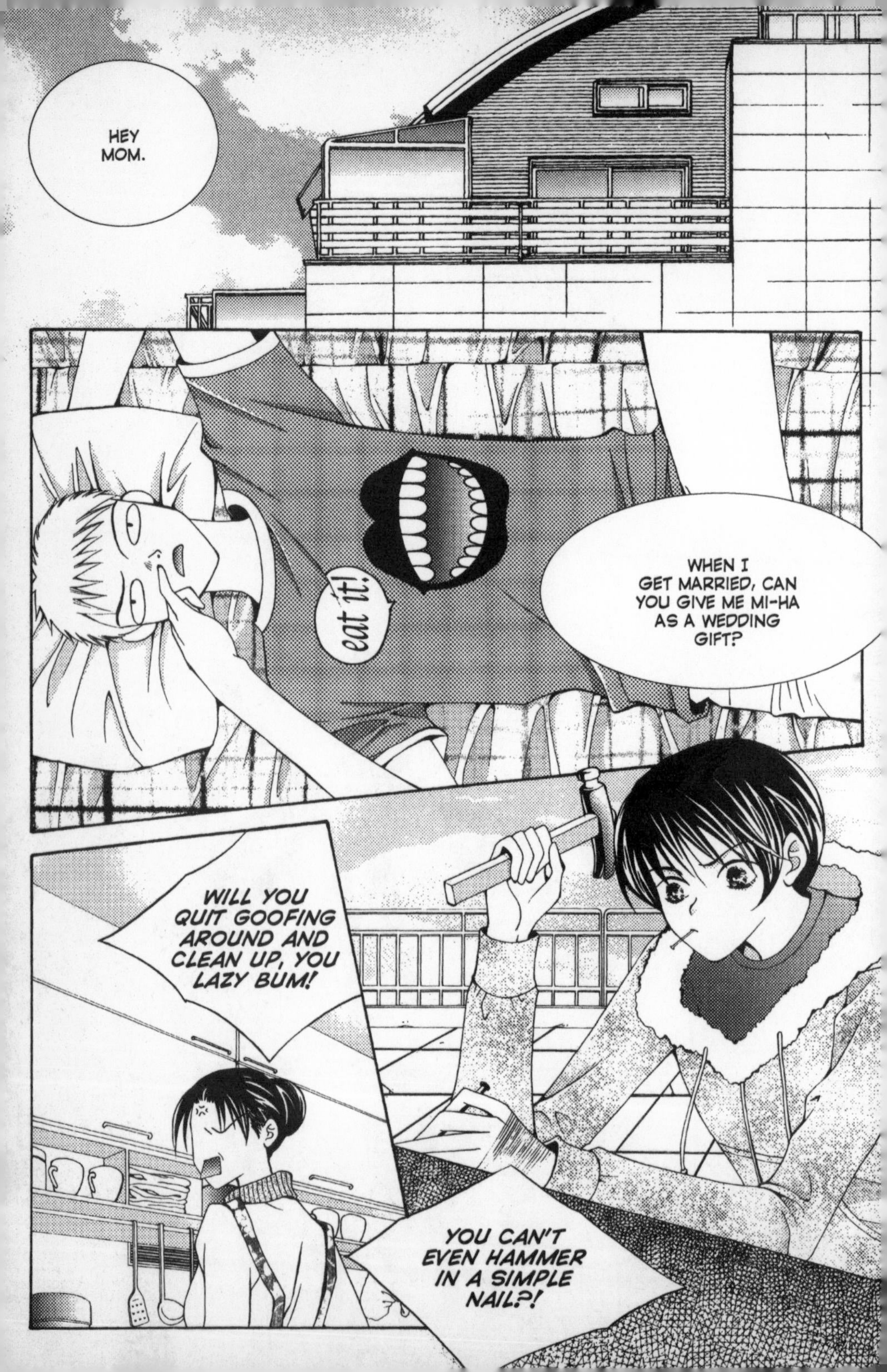
HEY MOM.
eat it!
WHEN I GET MARRIED, CAN YOU GIVE ME MI-HA AS A WEDDING GIFT?
WILL YOU QUIT GOOFING AROUND AND CLEAN UP, YOU LAZY BUM!
YOU CAN'T EVEN HAMMER IN A SIMPLE NAIL?!

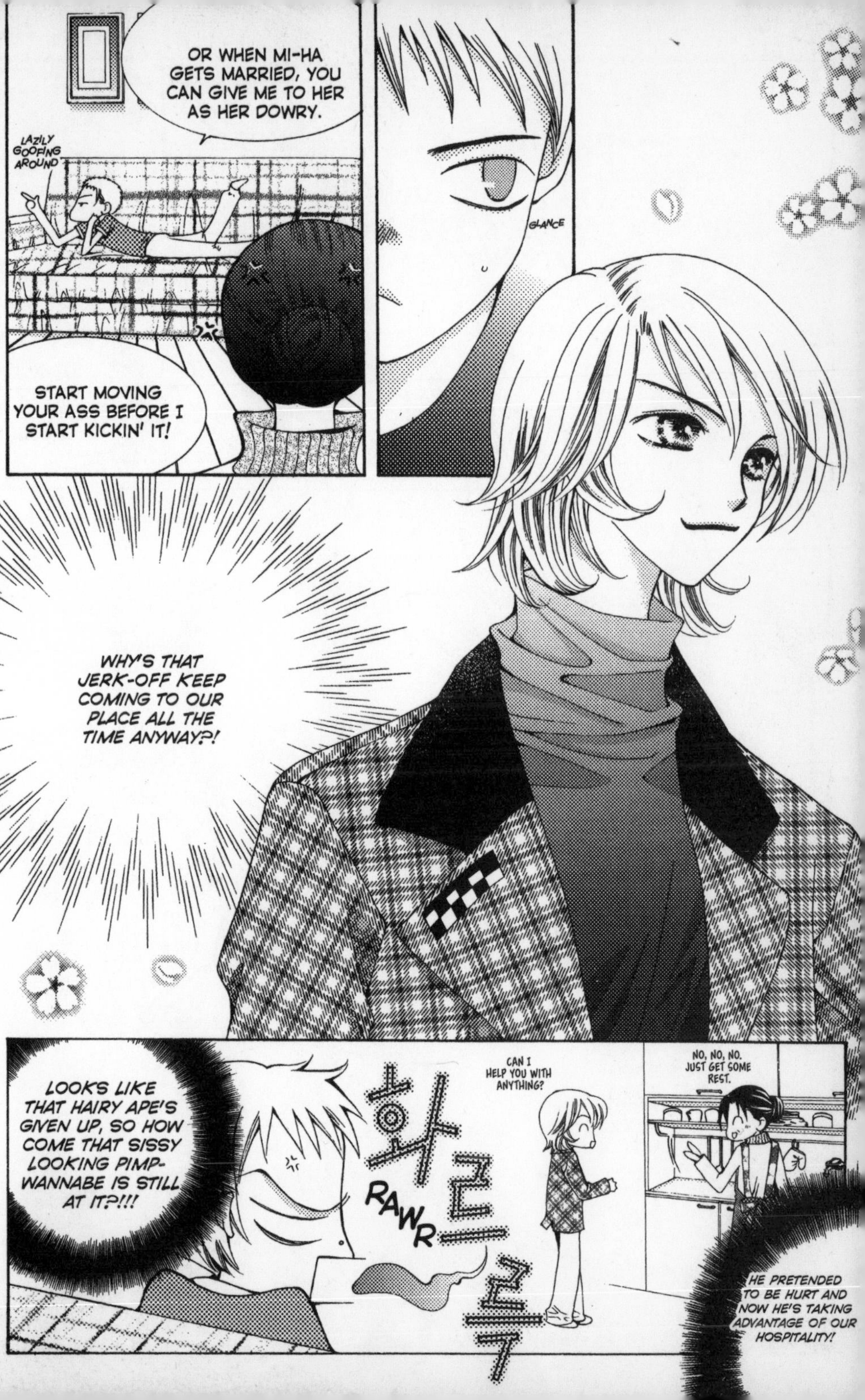
OR WHEN MI-HA GETS MARRIED, YOU CAN GIVE ME TO HER AS HER DOWRY.
LAZILY GOOFING AROUND
START MOVING YOUR ASS BEFORE I START KICKIN' IT!
GLANCE
WHY'S THAT JERK-OFF KEEP COMING TO OUR PLACE ALL THE TIME ANYWAY?!
LOOKS LIKE THAT HAIRY APE'S GIVEN UP, SO HOW COME THAT SISSY LOOKING PIMP-WANNABE IS STILL AT IT?!!!
RAWR
CAN I HELP YOU WITH ANYTHING?
NO, NO, NO. JUST GET SOME REST.
HE PRETENDED TO BE HURT AND NOW HE'S TAKING ADVANTAGE OF OUR HOSPITALITY!

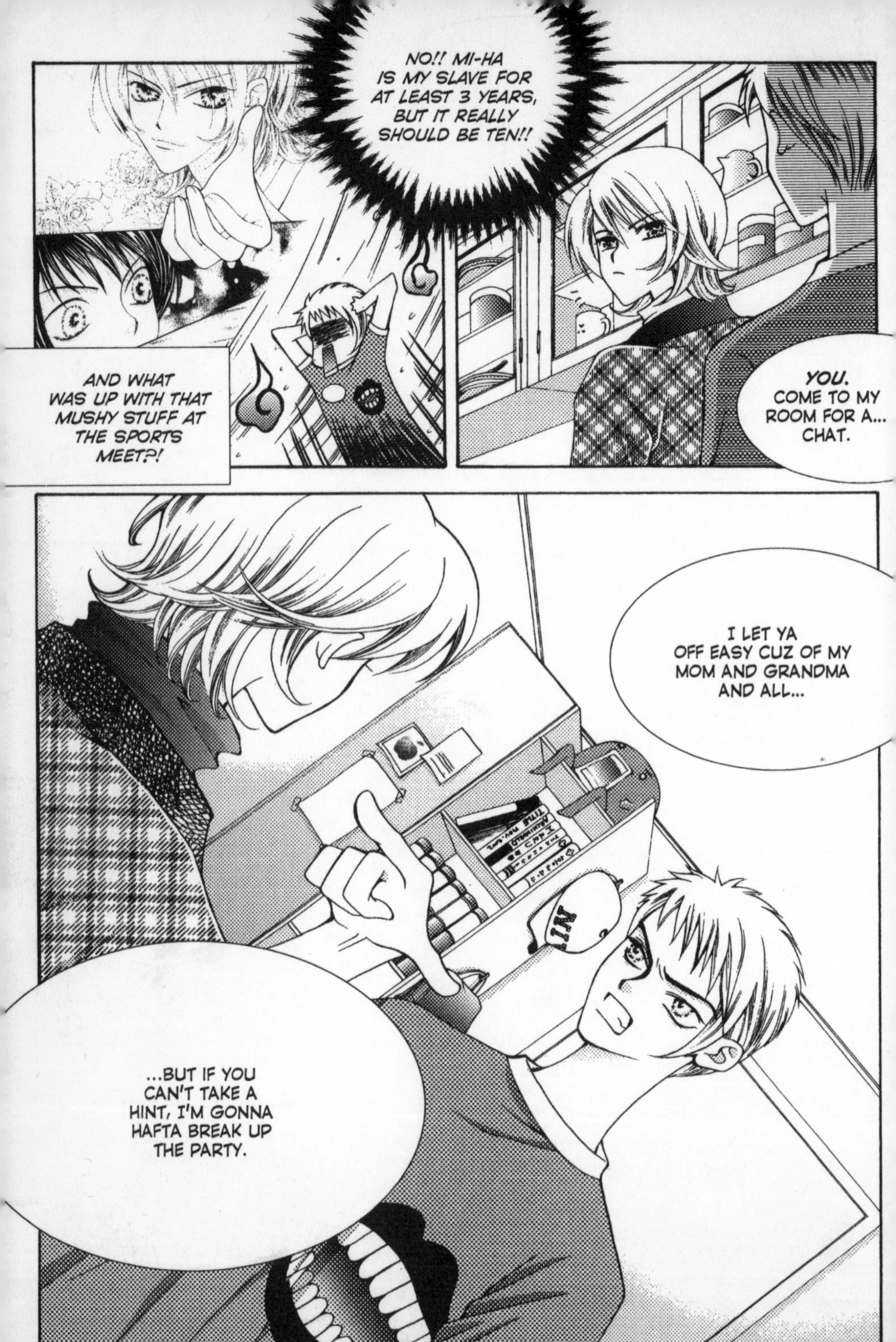
NO!! MI-HA IS MY SLAVE FOR AT LEAST 3 YEARS, BUT IT REALLY SHOULD BE TEN!!
AND WHAT WAS UP WITH THAT MUSHY STUFF AT THE SPORTS MEET?!
YOU. COME TO MY ROOM FOR A... CHAT.
I LET YA OFF EASY CUZ OF MY MOM AND GRANDMA AND ALL...
...BUT IF YOU CAN'T TAKE A HINT, I'M GONNA HAFTA BREAK UP THE PARTY.

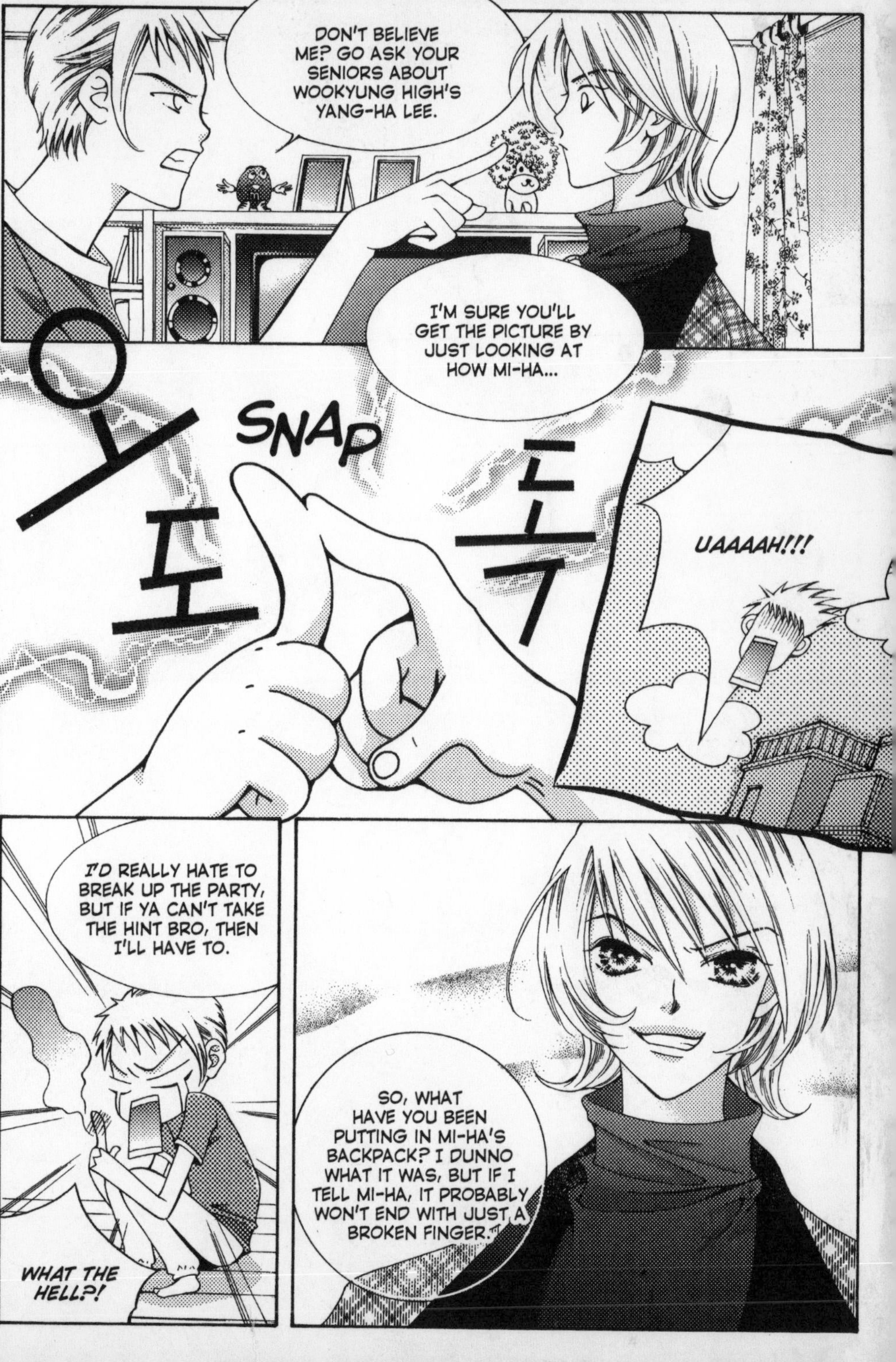
DON'T BELIEVE ME? GO ASK YOUR SENIORS ABOUT WOOKYUNG HIGH'S YANG-HA LEE.
I'M SURE YOU'LL GET THE PICTURE BY JUST LOOKING AT HOW MI-HA...
SNAP
UAAAAH!!!
I'D REALLY HATE TO BREAK UP THE PARTY, BUT IF YA CAN'T TAKE THE HINT BRO, THEN I'LL HAVE TO.
WHAT THE HELL?!
SO, WHAT HAVE YOU BEEN PUTTING IN MI-HA'S BACKPACK? I DUNNO WHAT IT WAS, BUT IF I TELL MI-HA, IT PROBABLY WON'T END WITH JUST A BROKEN FINGER.

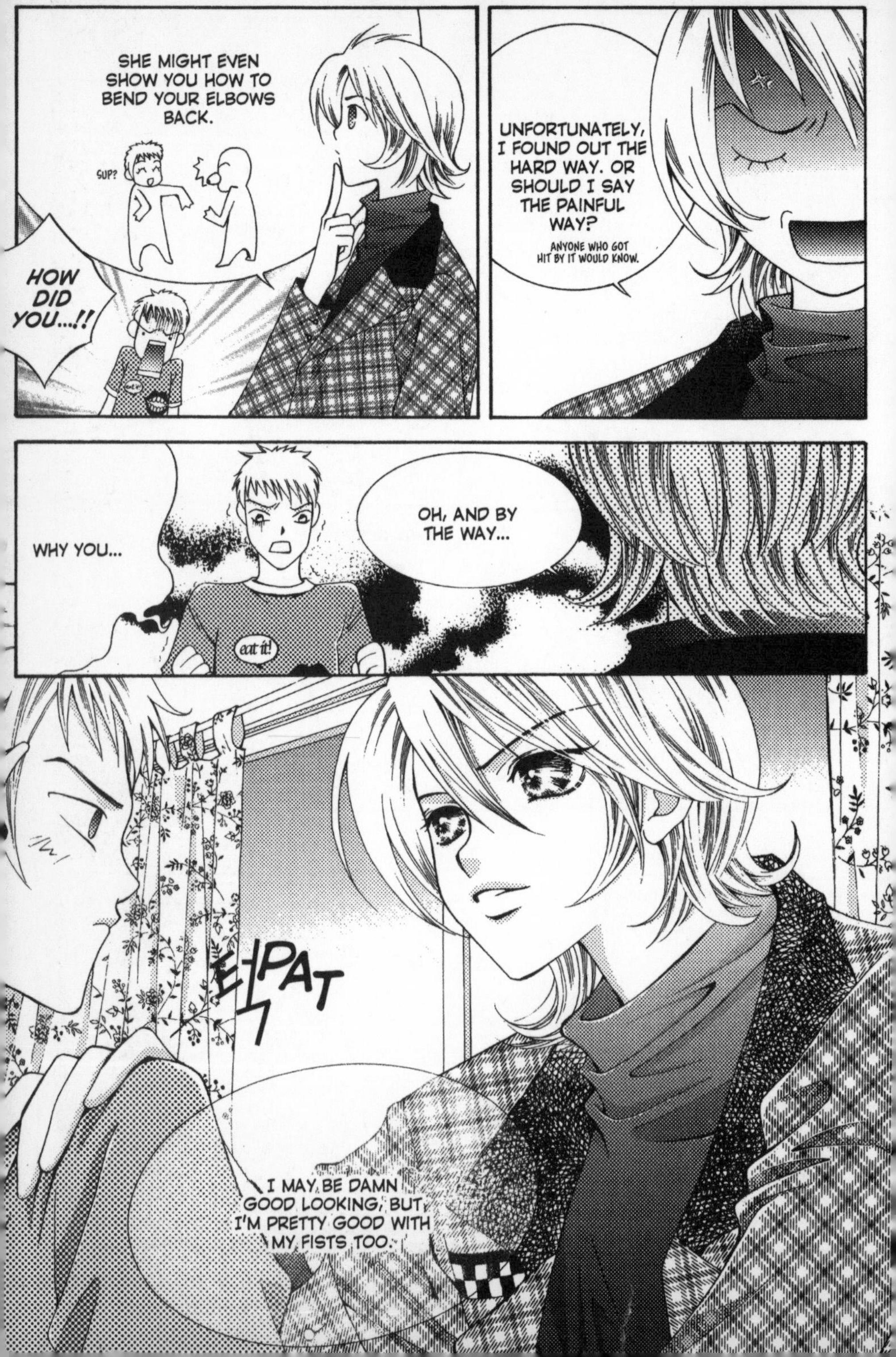
SHE MIGHT EVEN SHOW YOU HOW TO BEND YOUR ELBOWS BACK.
SUP?
HOW DID YOU...!!
UNFORTUNATELY, I FOUND OUT THE HARD WAY. OR SHOULD I SAY THE PAINFUL WAY?
ANYONE WHO GOT HIT BY IT WOULD KNOW.
WHY YOU...
eat it!
OH, AND BY THE WAY...
PAT
I MAY BE DAMN GOOD LOOKING, BUT I'M PRETTY GOOD WITH MY FISTS TOO.

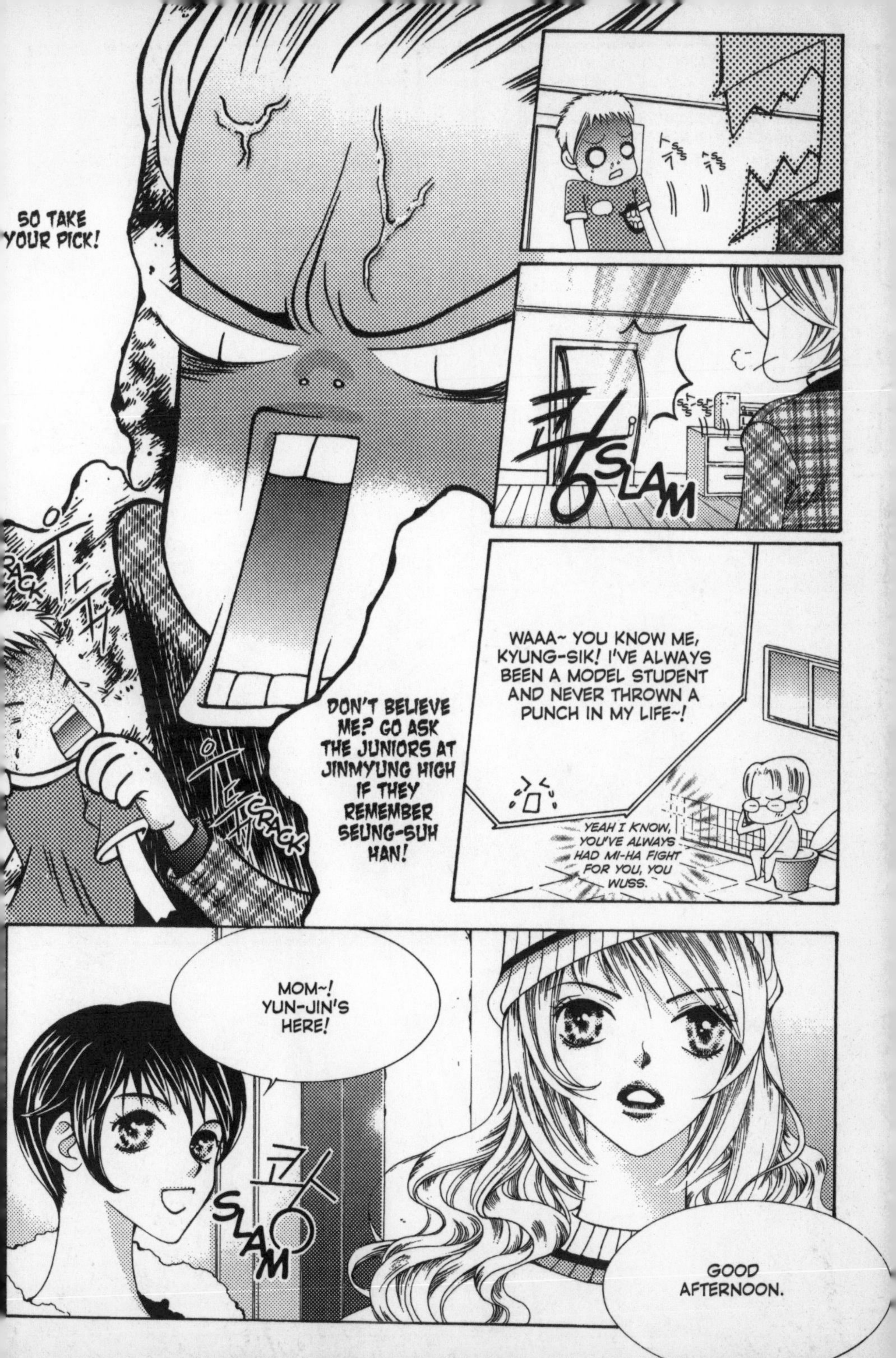
SO TAKE YOUR PICK!
CRACK
CRACK
DON'T BELIEVE ME? GO ASK THE JUNIORS AT JINMYUNG HIGH IF THEY REMEMBER SEUNG-SUH HAN!
SLAM
WAAA~ YOU KNOW ME, KYUNG-SIK! I'VE ALWAYS BEEN A MODEL STUDENT AND NEVER THROWN A PUNCH IN MY LIFE~!
YEAH I KNOW, YOU'VE ALWAYS HAD MI-HA FIGHT FOR YOU, YOU WUSS.
MOM~! YUN-JIN'S HERE!
SLAM
GOOD AFTERNOON.

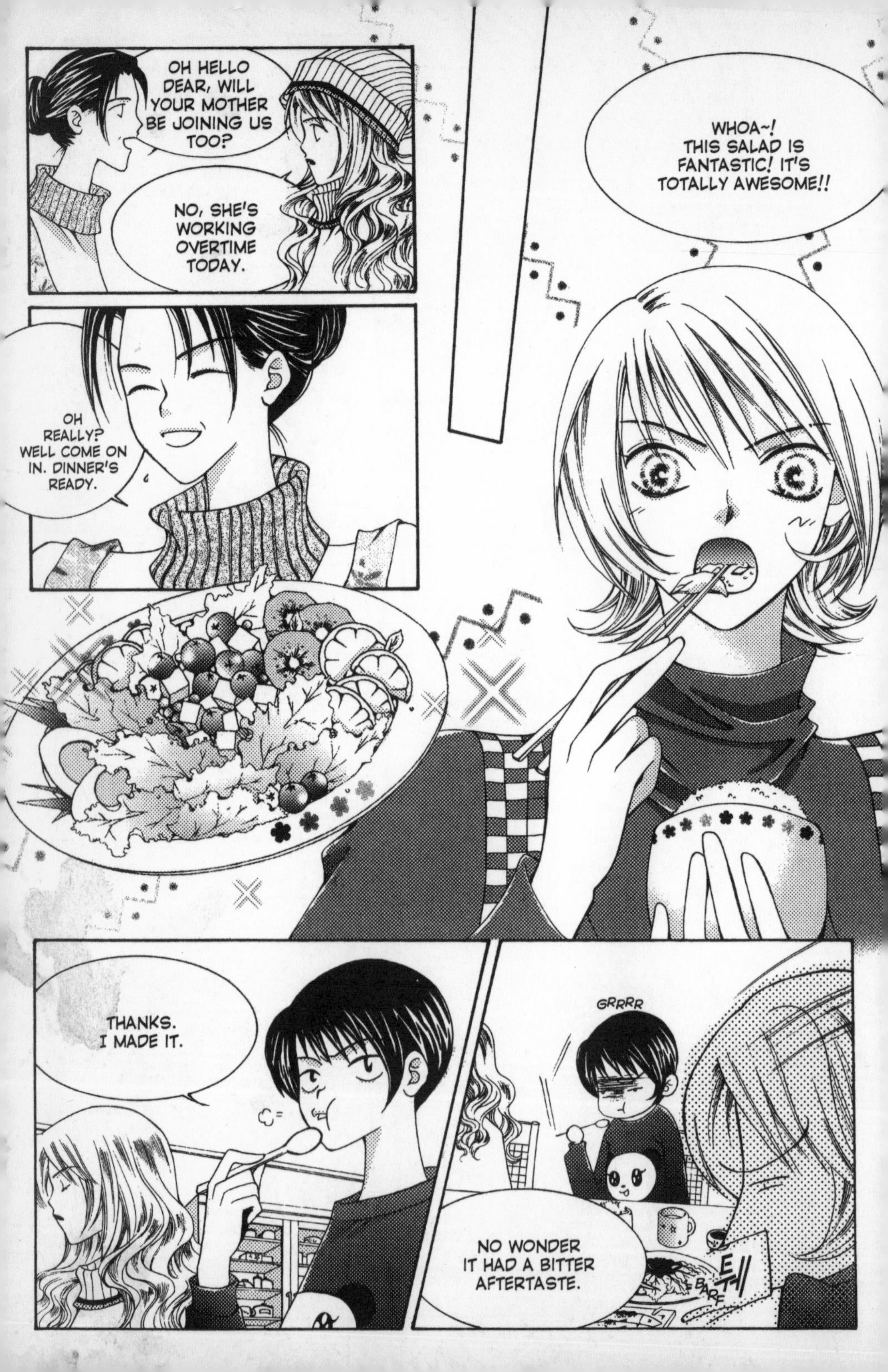
OH HELLO DEAR, WILL YOUR MOTHER BE JOINING US TOO?
NO, SHE'S WORKING OVERTIME TODAY.
OH REALLY? WELL COME ON IN. DINNER'S READY.
WHOA~! THIS SALAD IS FANTASTIC! IT'S TOTALLY AWESOME!!
THANKS. I MADE IT.
GRRRR
NO WONDER IT HAD A BITTER AFTERTASTE.
BARF

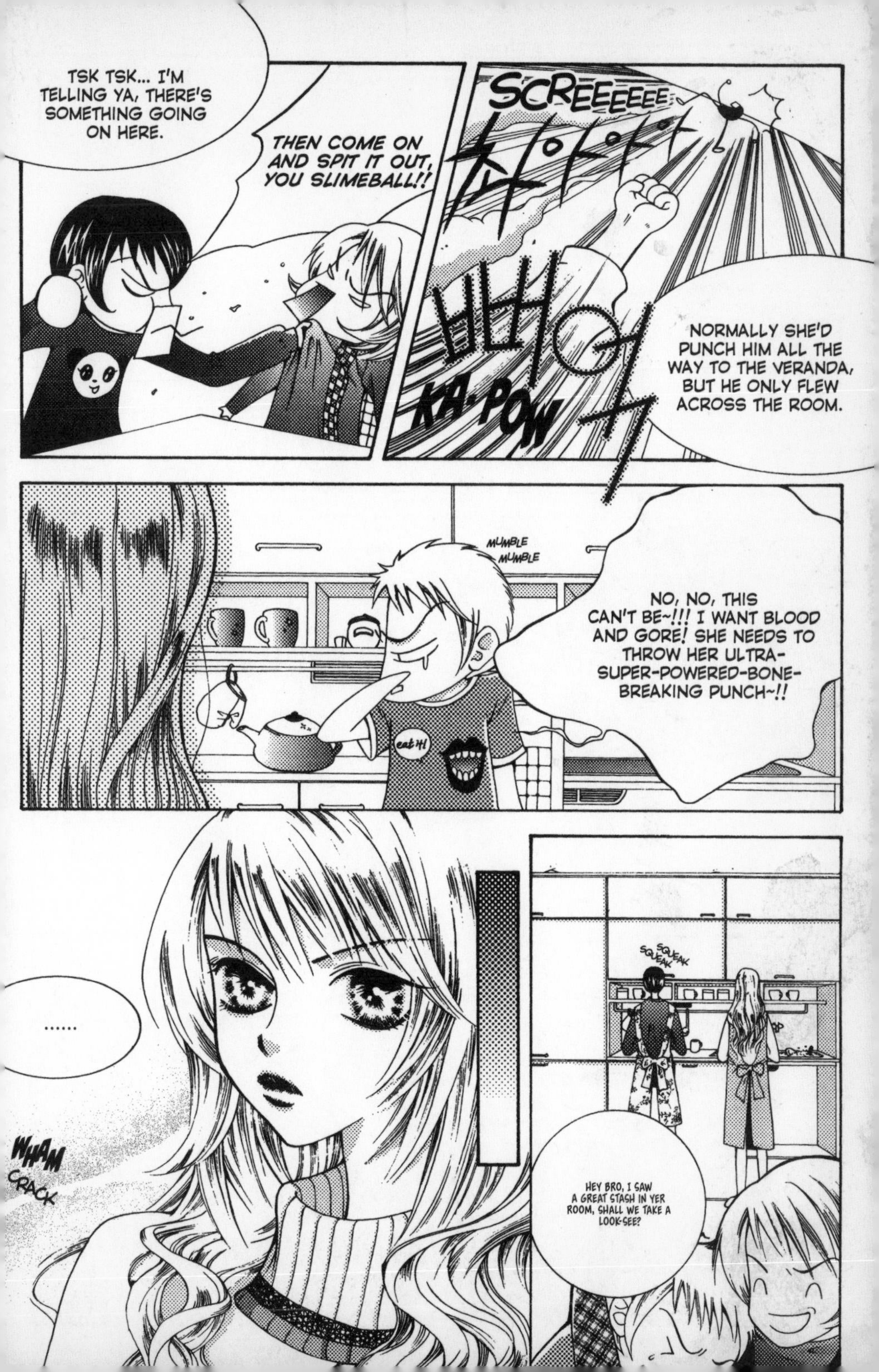
TSK TSK... I'M TELLING YA, THERE'S SOMETHING GOING ON HERE.
THEN COME ON AND SPIT IT OUT, YOU SLIMEBALL!!
SCREEEEEE
KA-POW
NORMALLY SHE'D PUNCH HIM ALL THE WAY TO THE VERANDA, BUT HE ONLY FLEW ACROSS THE ROOM.
MUMBLE MUMBLE
NO, NO, THIS CAN'T BE~!!! I WANT BLOOD AND GORE! SHE NEEDS TO THROW HER ULTRA-SUPER-POWERED-BONE-BREAKING PUNCH~!!
......
WHAM
CRACK
SQUEAK SQUEAK
HEY BRO, I SAW A GREAT STASH IN YER ROOM, SHALL WE TAKE A LOOK-SEE?

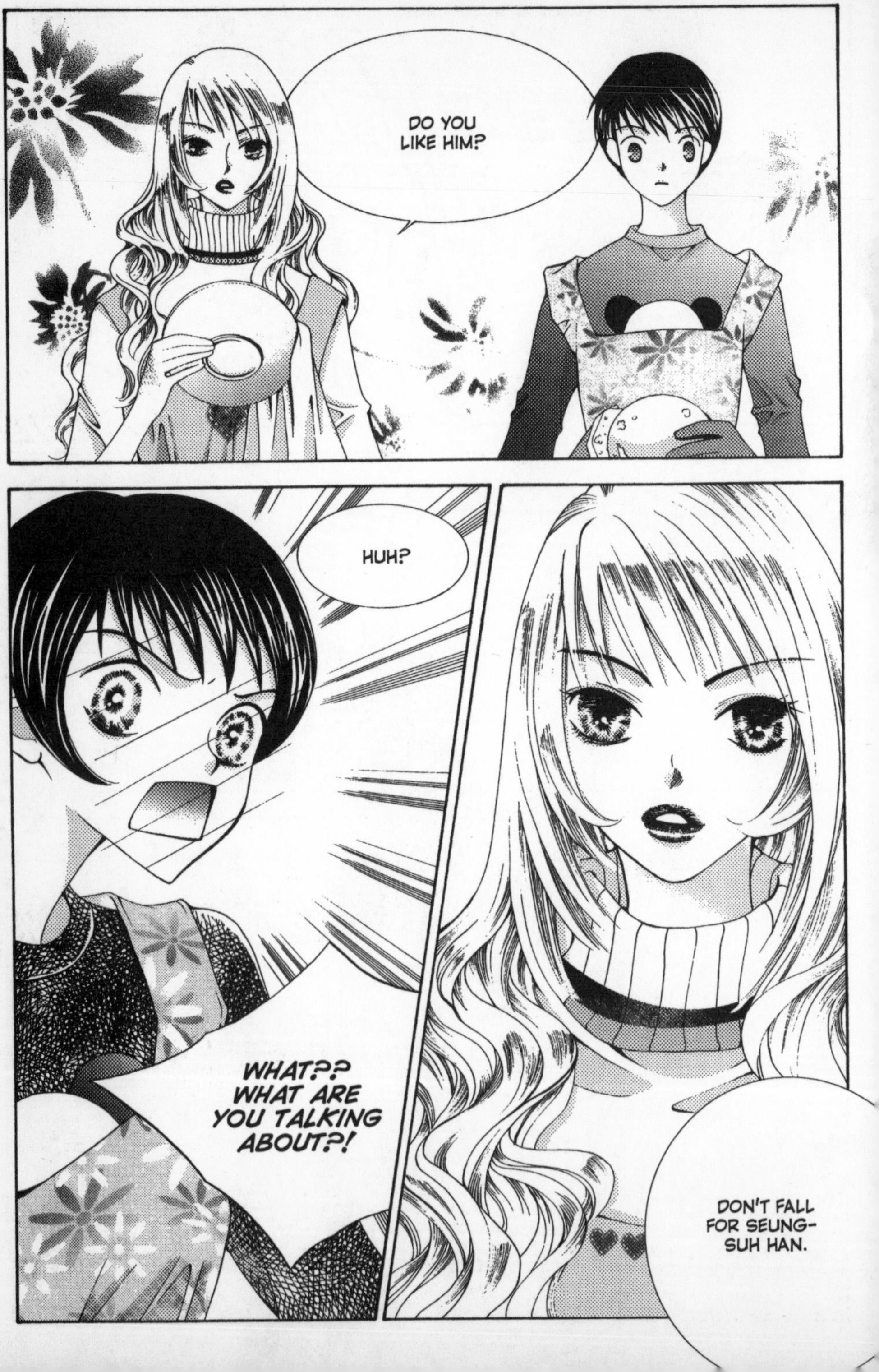
DO YOU LIKE HIM?
HUH?
WHAT?? WHAT ARE YOU TALKING ABOUT?!
DON'T FALL FOR SEUNG-SUH HAN.

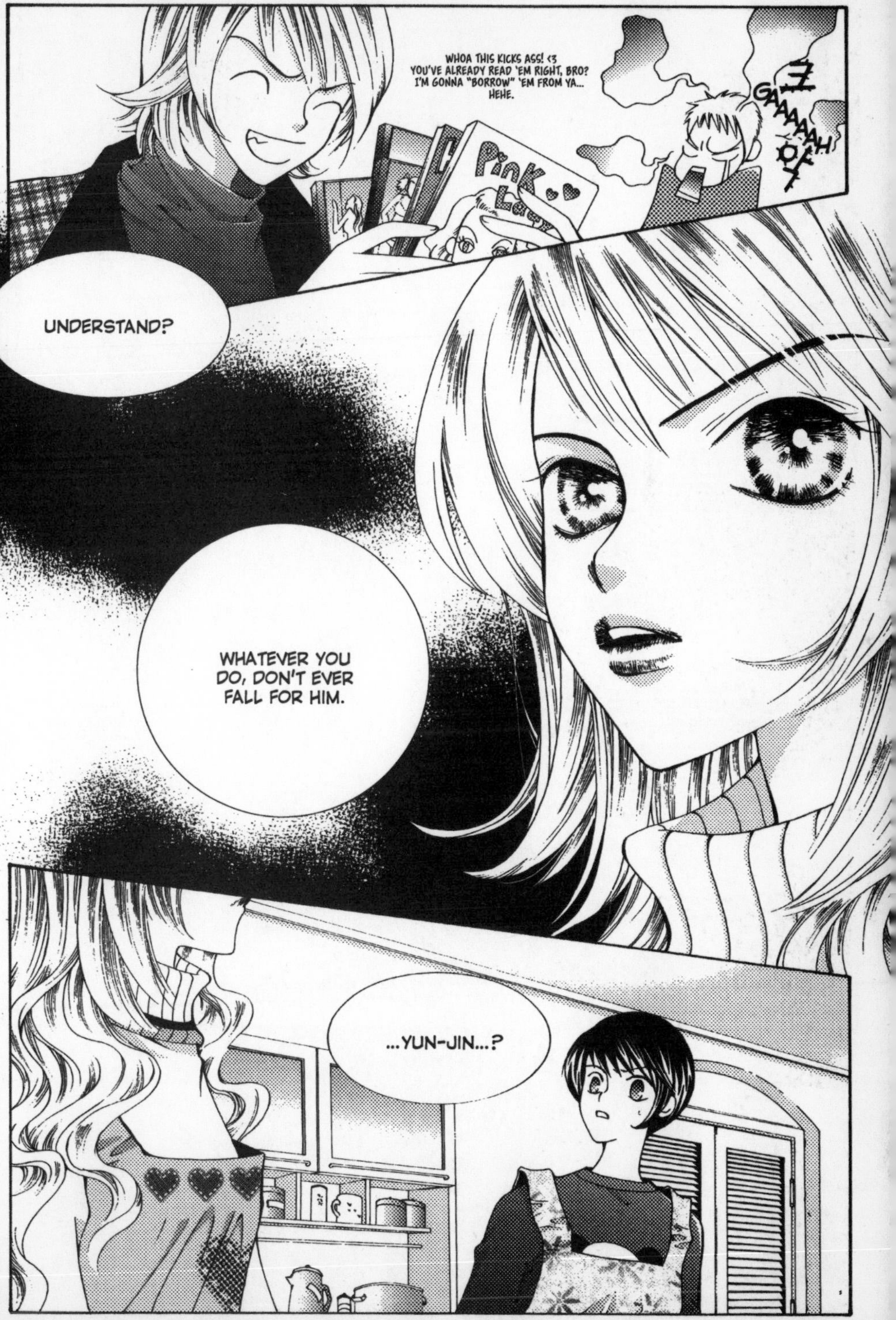
WHOA THIS KICKS ASS! <3 YOU'VE ALREADY READ 'EM RIGHT, BRO? I'M GONNA "BORROW" 'EM FROM YA... HEHE.
GAAAAAAH.
UNDERSTAND?
WHATEVER YOU DO, DON'T EVER FALL FOR HIM.
...YUN-JIN...?

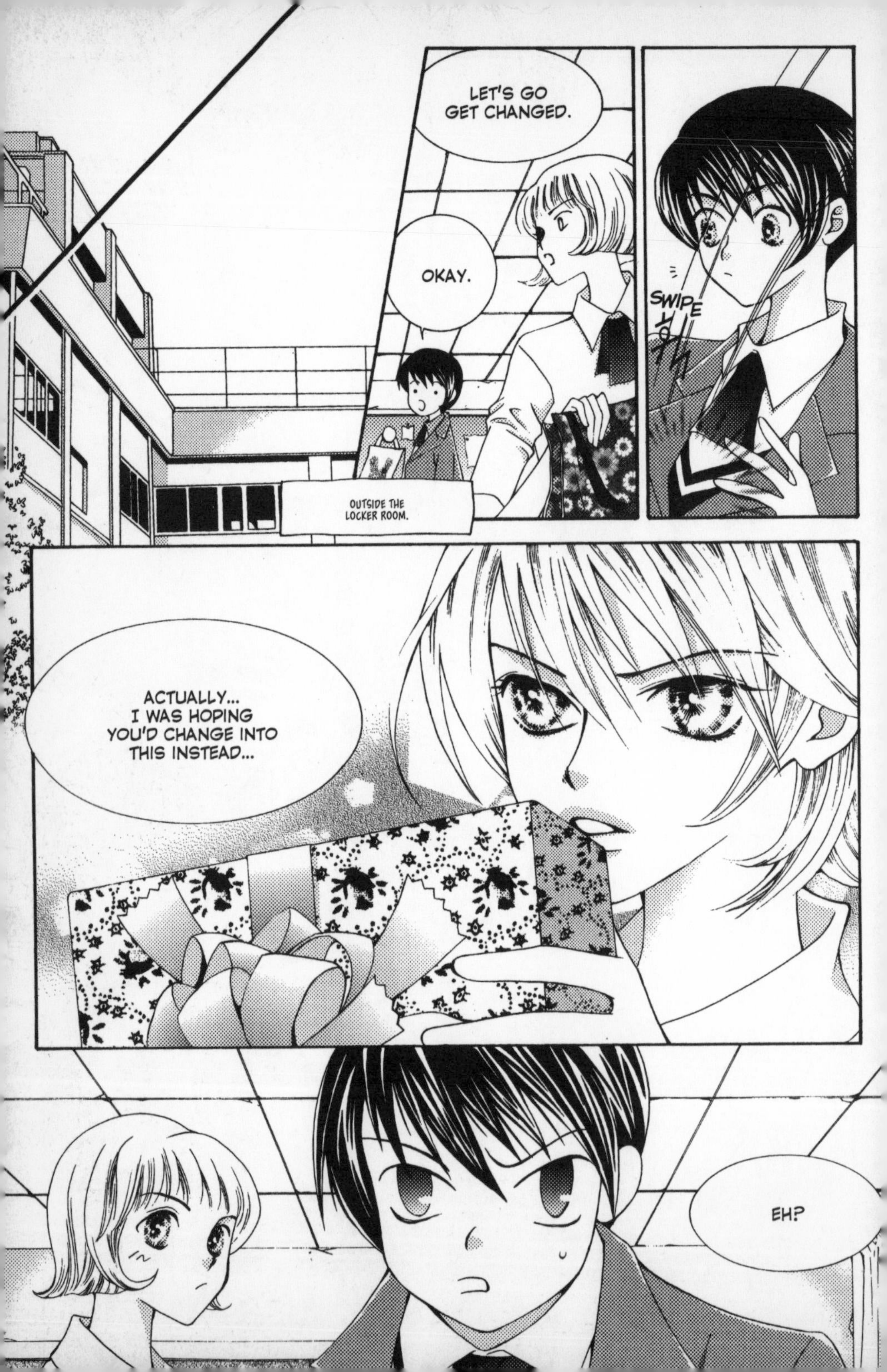
OUTSIDE THE LOCKER ROOM.
LET'S GO GET CHANGED.
OKAY.
SWIPE
ACTUALLY... I WAS HOPING YOU'D CHANGE INTO THIS INSTEAD...
EH?

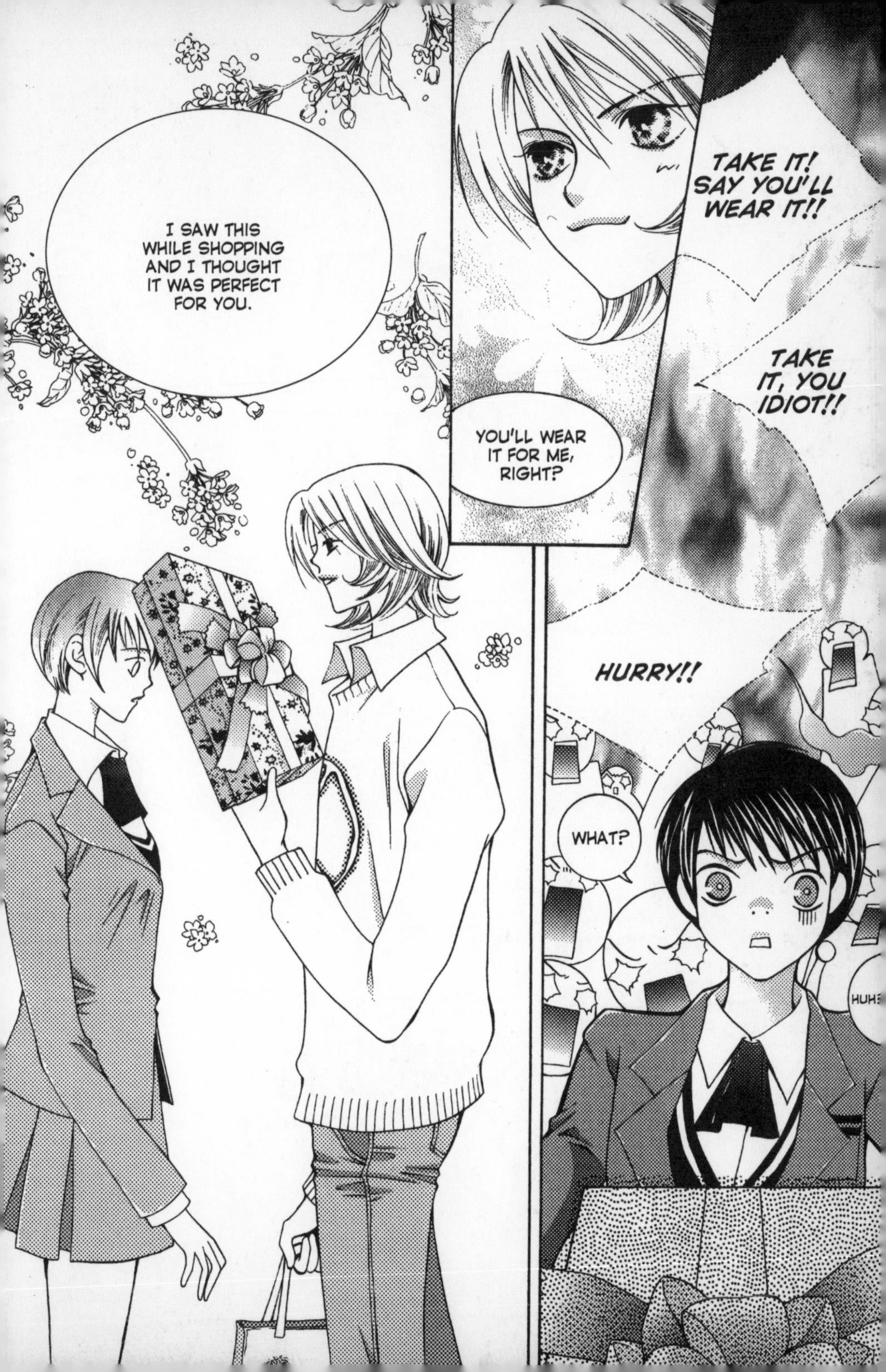
I SAW THIS WHILE SHOPPING AND I THOUGHT IT WAS PERFECT FOR YOU.
YOU'LL WEAR IT FOR ME, RIGHT?
TAKE IT! SAY YOU'LL WEAR IT!!
TAKE IT, YOU IDIOT!!
HURRY!!
WHAT?
HUH

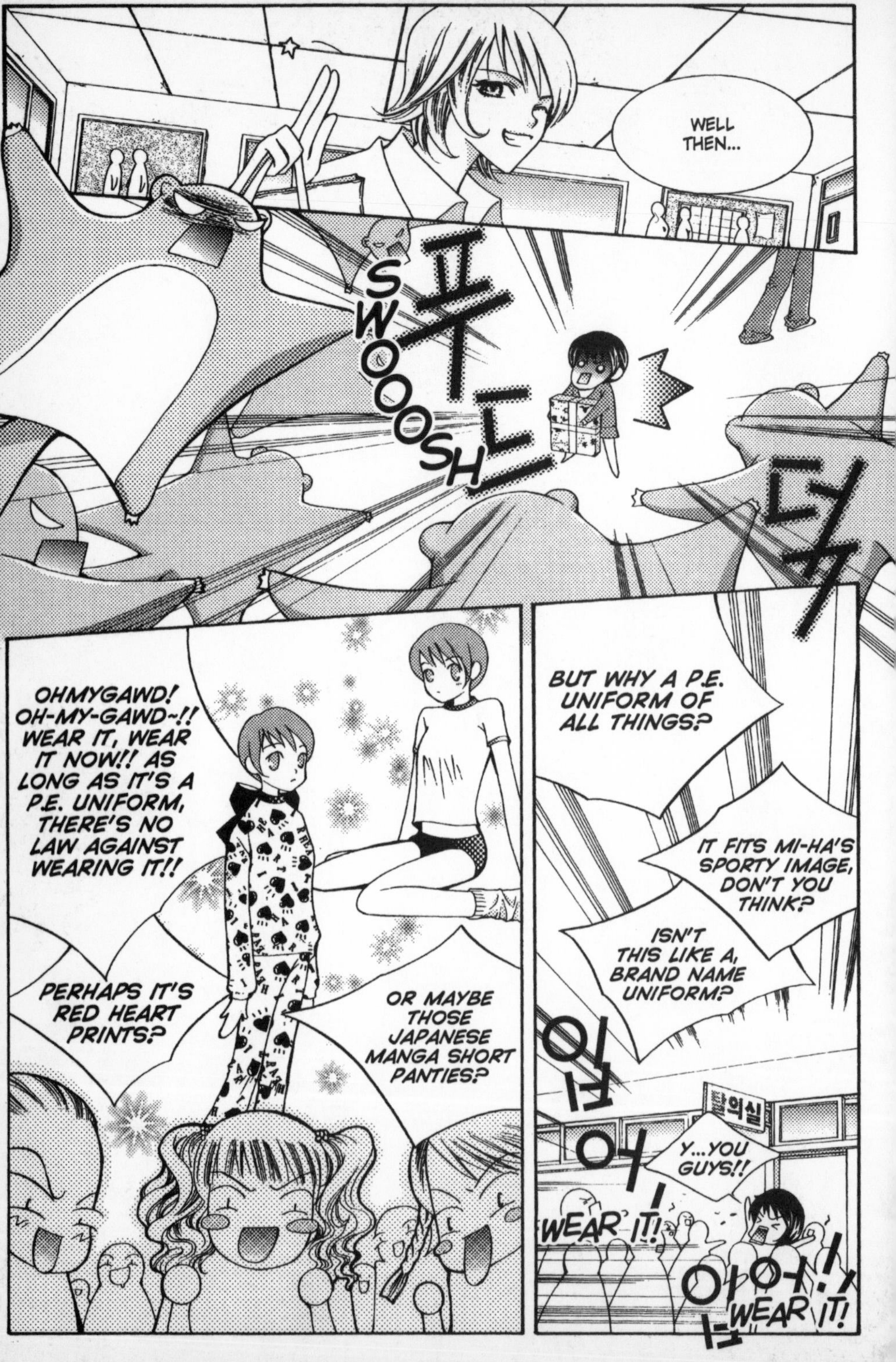
WELL THEN...
SWOOOSH
OHMYGAWD! OH-MY-GAWD~!! WEAR IT, WEAR IT NOW!! AS LONG AS IT'S A P.E. UNIFORM, THERE'S NO LAW AGAINST WEARING IT!!
PERHAPS IT'S RED HEART PRINTS?
OR MAYBE THOSE JAPANESE MANGA SHORT PANTIES?
BUT WHY A P.E. UNIFORM OF ALL THINGS?
IT FITS MI-HA'S SPORTY IMAGE, DON'T YOU THINK?
ISN'T THIS LIKE A, BRAND NAME UNIFORM?
Y...YOU GUYS!!
WEAR IT!
WEAR IT!

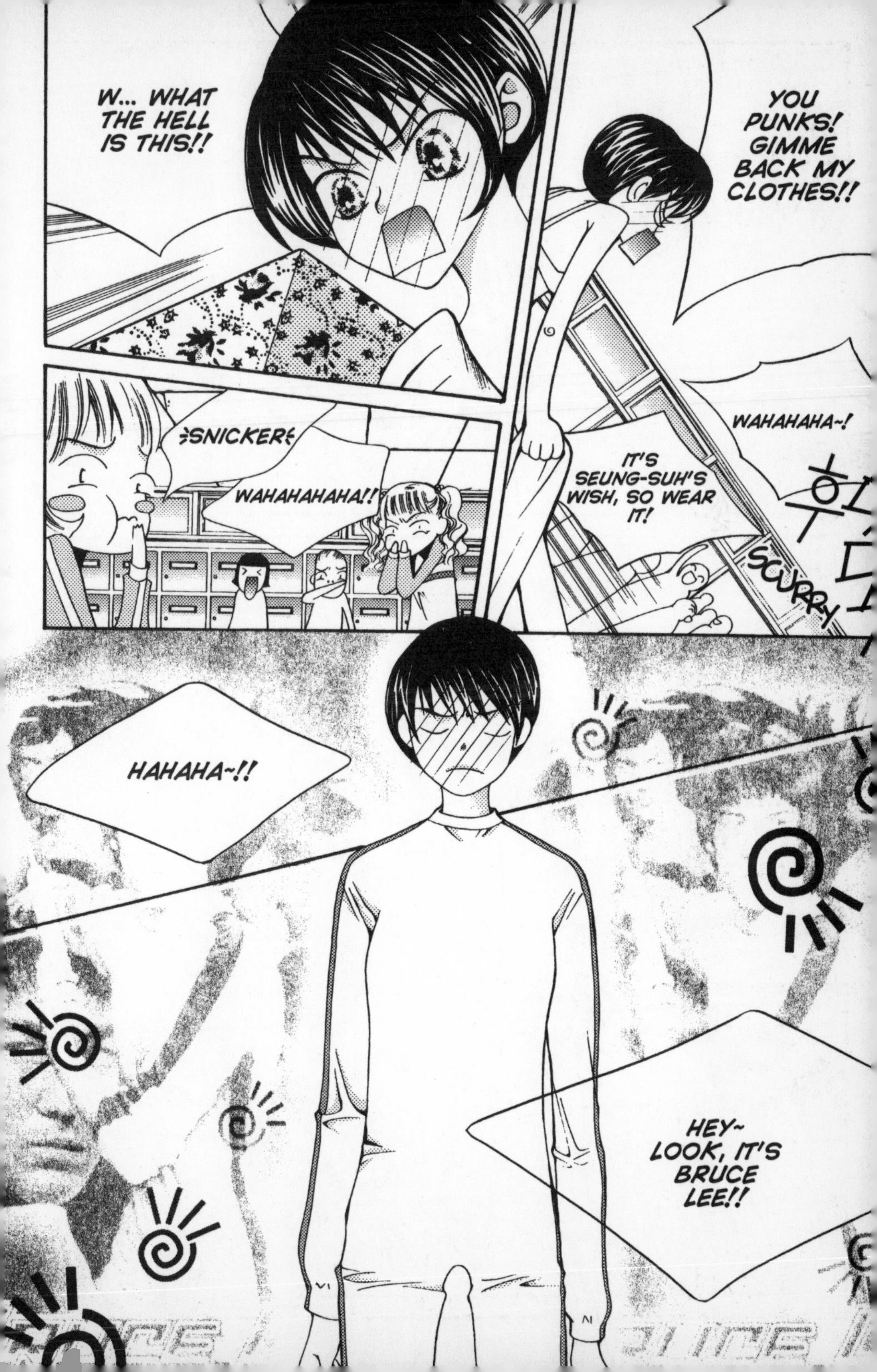
W... WHAT THE HELL IS THIS!!
YOU PUNKS! GIMME BACK MY CLOTHES!!
SNICKER
WAHAHAHAHA!!
IT'S SEUNG-SUH'S WISH, SO WEAR IT!
WAHAHAHA~!
SCURRY
HAHAHA~!!
HEY~ LOOK, IT'S BRUCE LEE!!

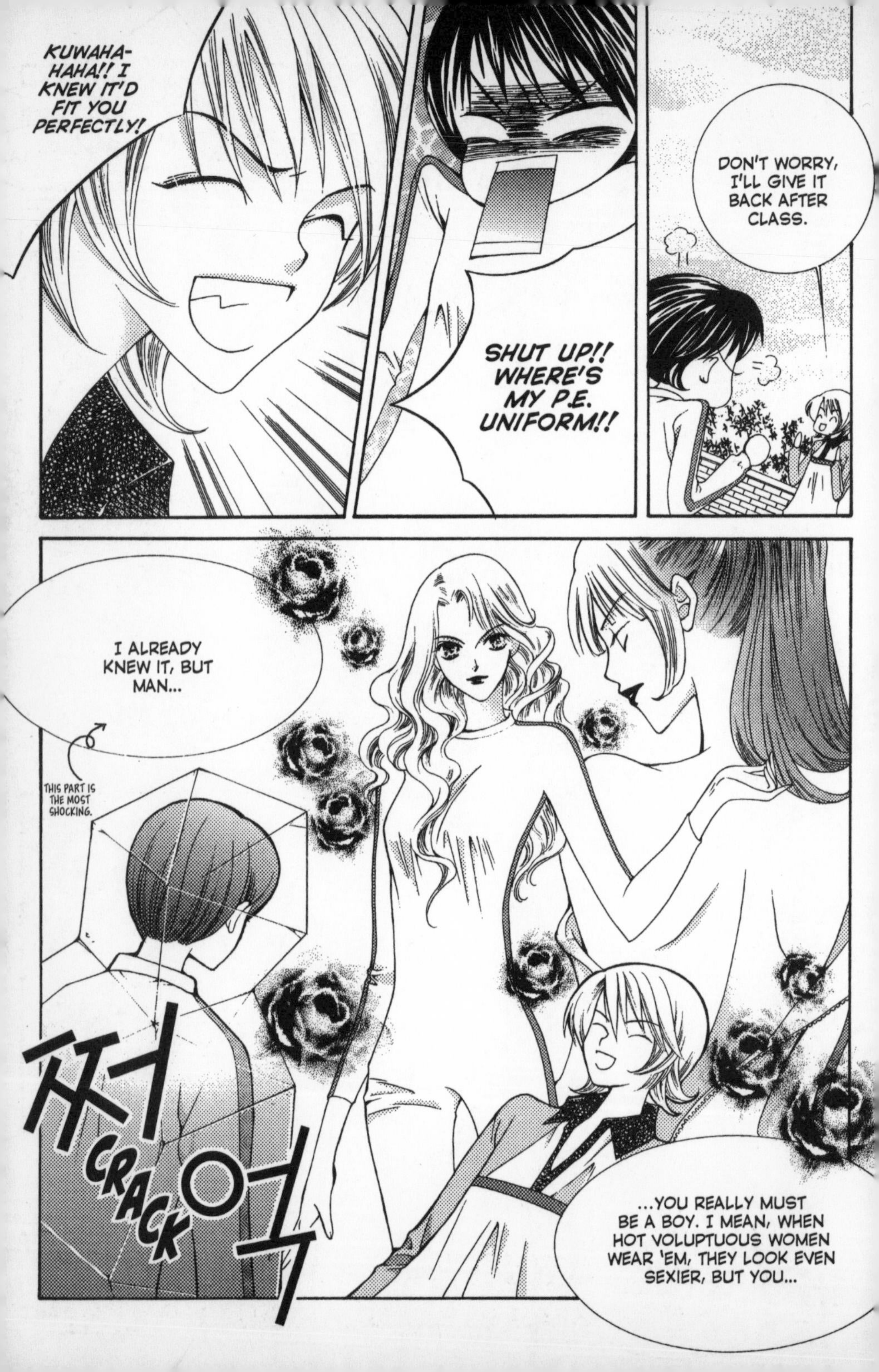
KUWAHA-HAHA!! I KNEW IT'D FIT YOU PERFECTLY!
SHUT UP!! WHERE'S MY P.E. UNIFORM!!
DON'T WORRY, I'LL GIVE IT BACK AFTER CLASS.
I ALREADY KNEW IT, BUT MAN...
THIS PART IS THE MOST SHOCKING.
CRACK
...YOU REALLY MUST BE A BOY. I MEAN, WHEN HOT VOLUPTUOUS WOMEN WEAR 'EM, THEY LOOK EVEN SEXIER, BUT YOU...

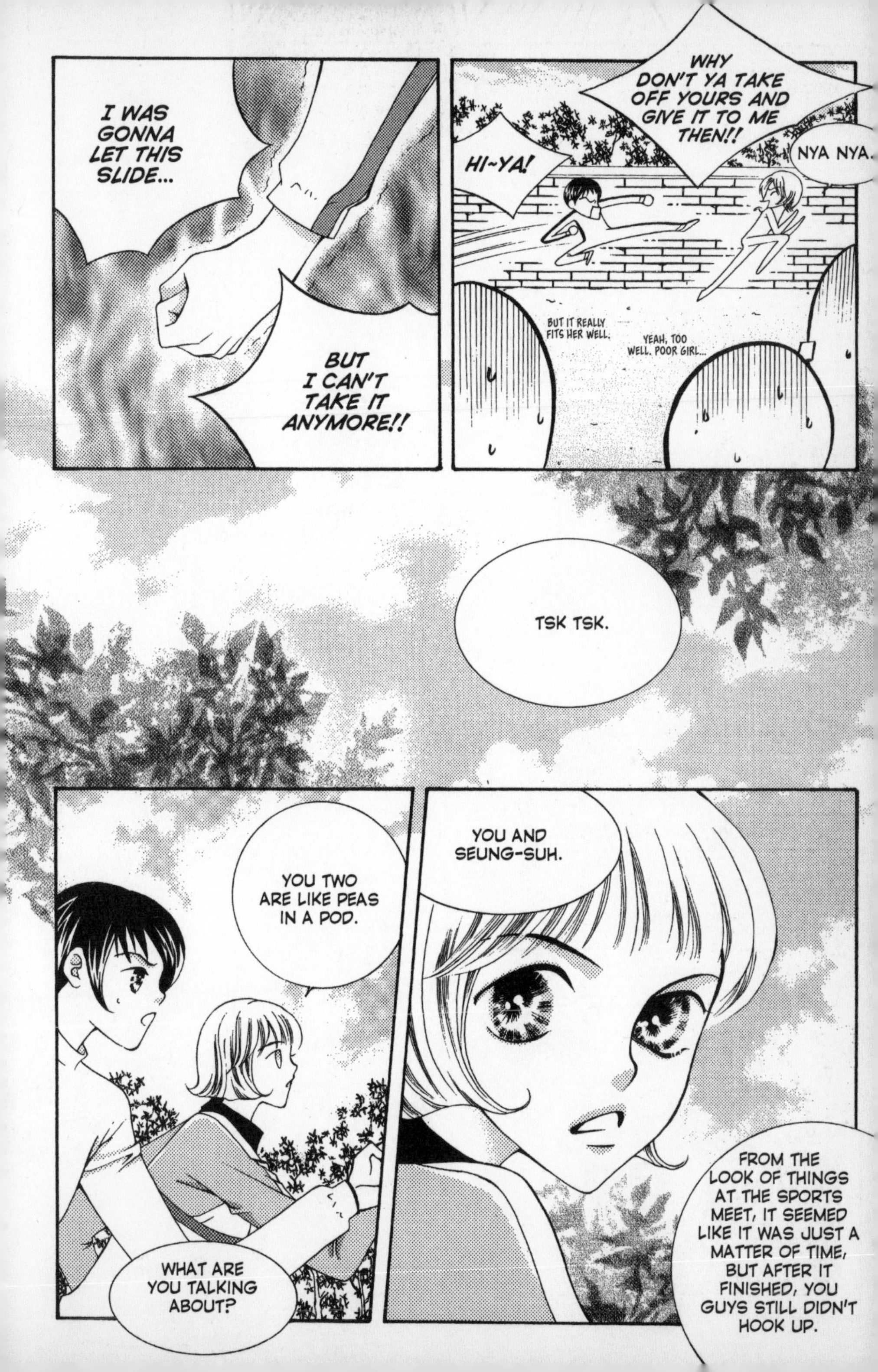
I WAS GONNA LET THIS SLIDE...
BUT I CAN'T TAKE IT ANYMORE!!
WHY DON'T YA TAKE OFF YOURS AND GIVE IT TO ME THEN!!
HI~YA!
NYA NYA.
BUT IT REALLY FITS HER WELL.
YEAH, TOO WELL. POOR GIRL...
TSK TSK.
YOU TWO ARE LIKE PEAS IN A POD.
WHAT ARE YOU TALKING ABOUT?
YOU AND SEUNG-SUH.
FROM THE LOOK OF THINGS AT THE SPORTS MEET, IT SEEMED LIKE IT WAS JUST A MATTER OF TIME, BUT AFTER IT FINISHED, YOU GUYS STILL DIDN'T HOOK UP.

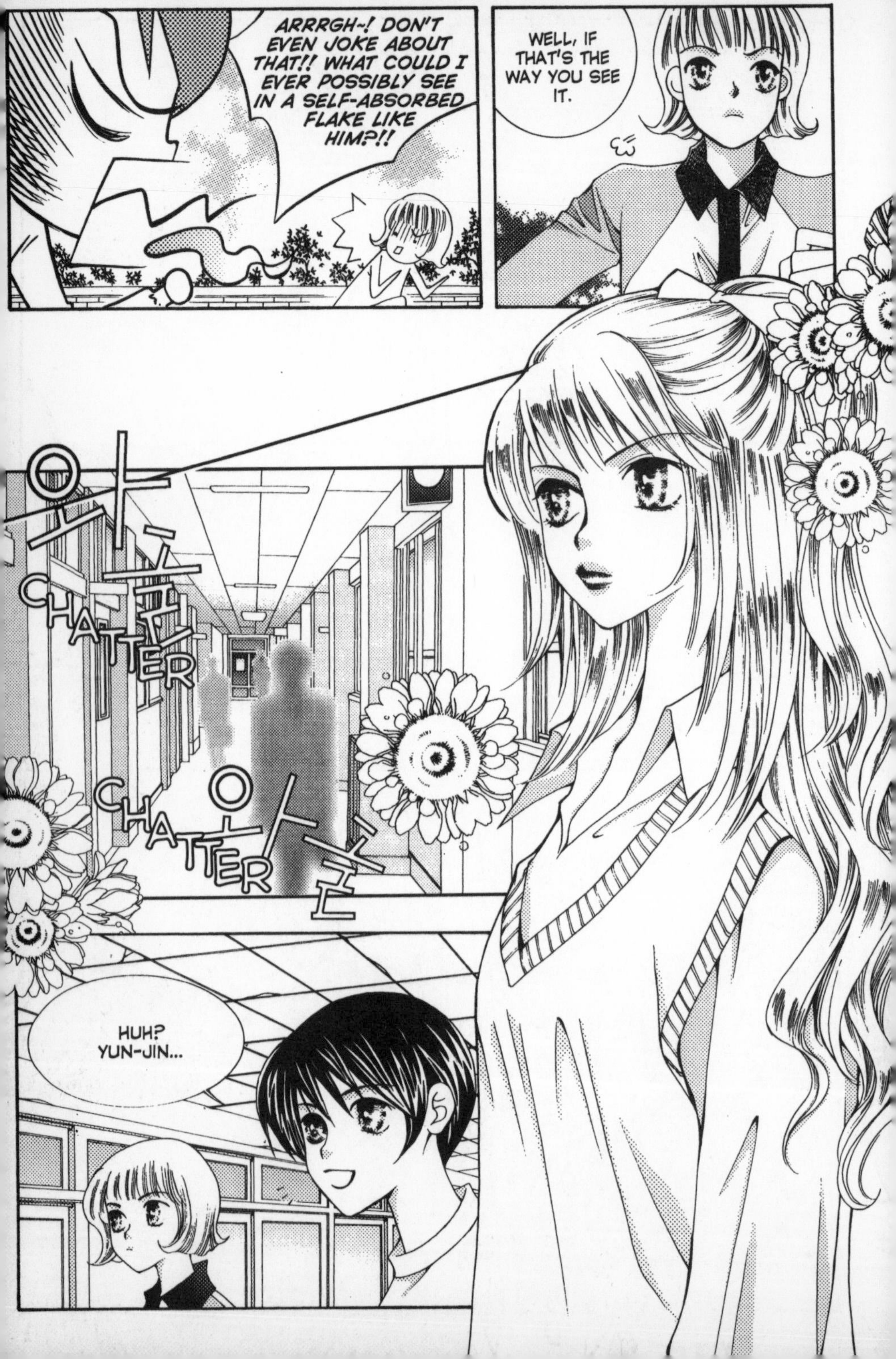
ARRRGH~! DON'T EVEN JOKE ABOUT THAT!! WHAT COULD I EVER POSSIBLY SEE IN A SELF-ABSORBED FLAKE LIKE HIM?!!
WELL, IF THAT'S THE WAY YOU SEE IT.
CHATTER
CHATTER
HUH? YUN-JIN...

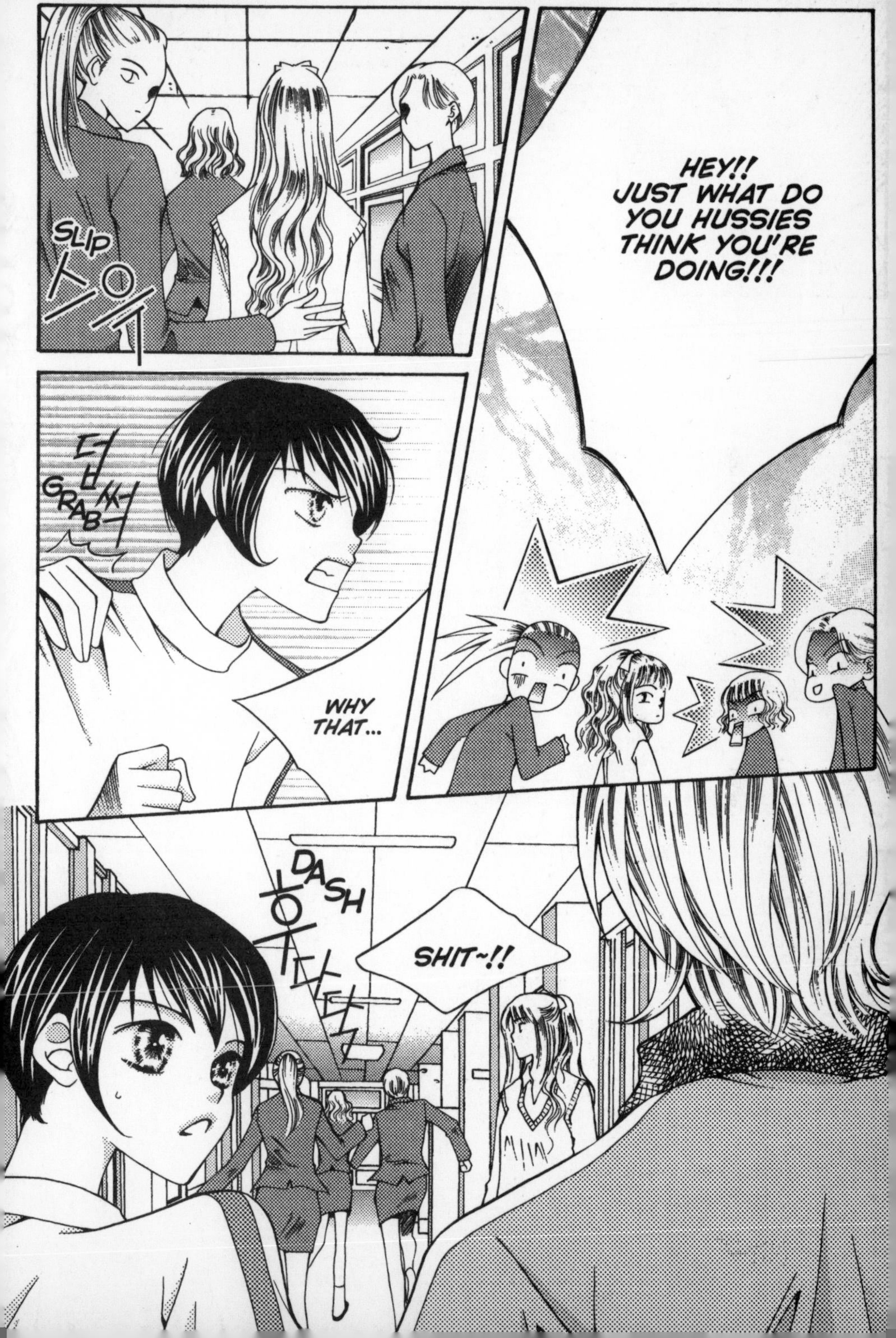
SLIP
GRAB
WHY THAT...
HEY!! JUST WHAT DO YOU HUSSIES THINK YOU'RE DOING!!!
DASH
SHIT~!!

STROLL

STRANGE, IT KINDA SEEMS LIKE SEUNG-SUH'S BEEN TAKING CARE OF YUN-JIN.

YOU'VE NOTICED THAT TOO?

YEAH, IT SEEMS LIKE LATELY, NO ON! BEEN BOTHERIN YUN-JIN BECAL OF HIM.

I CAN'T QUITE PUT MY FINGER ON IT, BUT HE SEEMS TO BE PROTECTING HER FOR SOME REASON.

탈의실

LOCKER ROOM

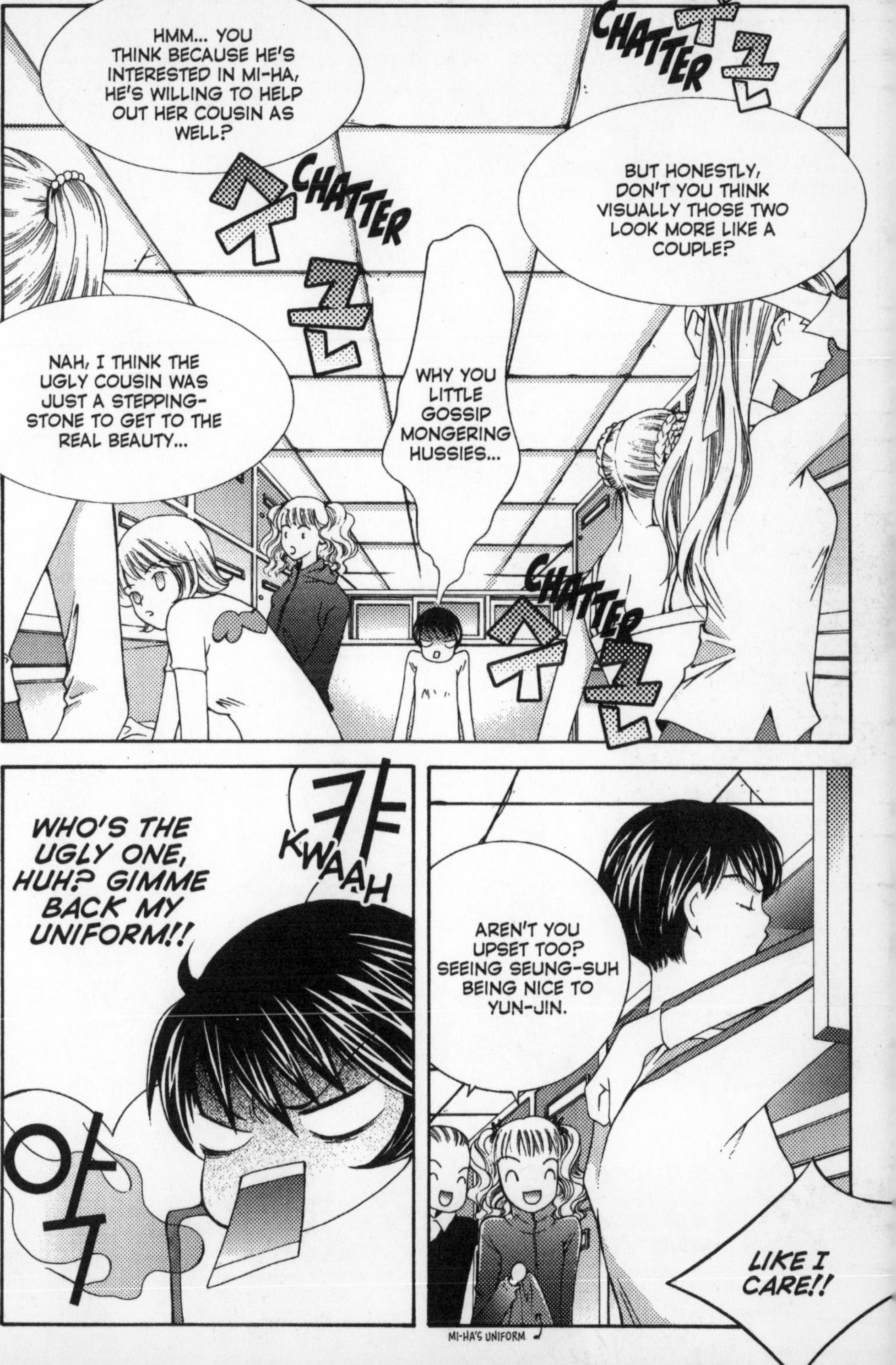
HMM... YOU THINK BECAUSE HE'S INTERESTED IN MI-HA, HE'S WILLING TO HELP OUT HER COUSIN AS WELL?
CHATTER
CHATTER
BUT HONESTLY, DON'T YOU THINK VISUALLY THOSE TWO LOOK MORE LIKE A COUPLE?
NAH, I THINK THE UGLY COUSIN WAS JUST A STEPPING-STONE TO GET TO THE REAL BEAUTY...
WHY YOU LITTLE GOSSIP MONGERING HUSSIES...
CHATTER
WHO'S THE UGLY ONE, HUH? GIMME BACK MY UNIFORM!!
캬
KWAAH
AREN'T YOU UPSET TOO? SEEING SEUNG-SUH BEING NICE TO YUN-JIN.
LIKE I CARE!!
MI-HA'S UNIFORM

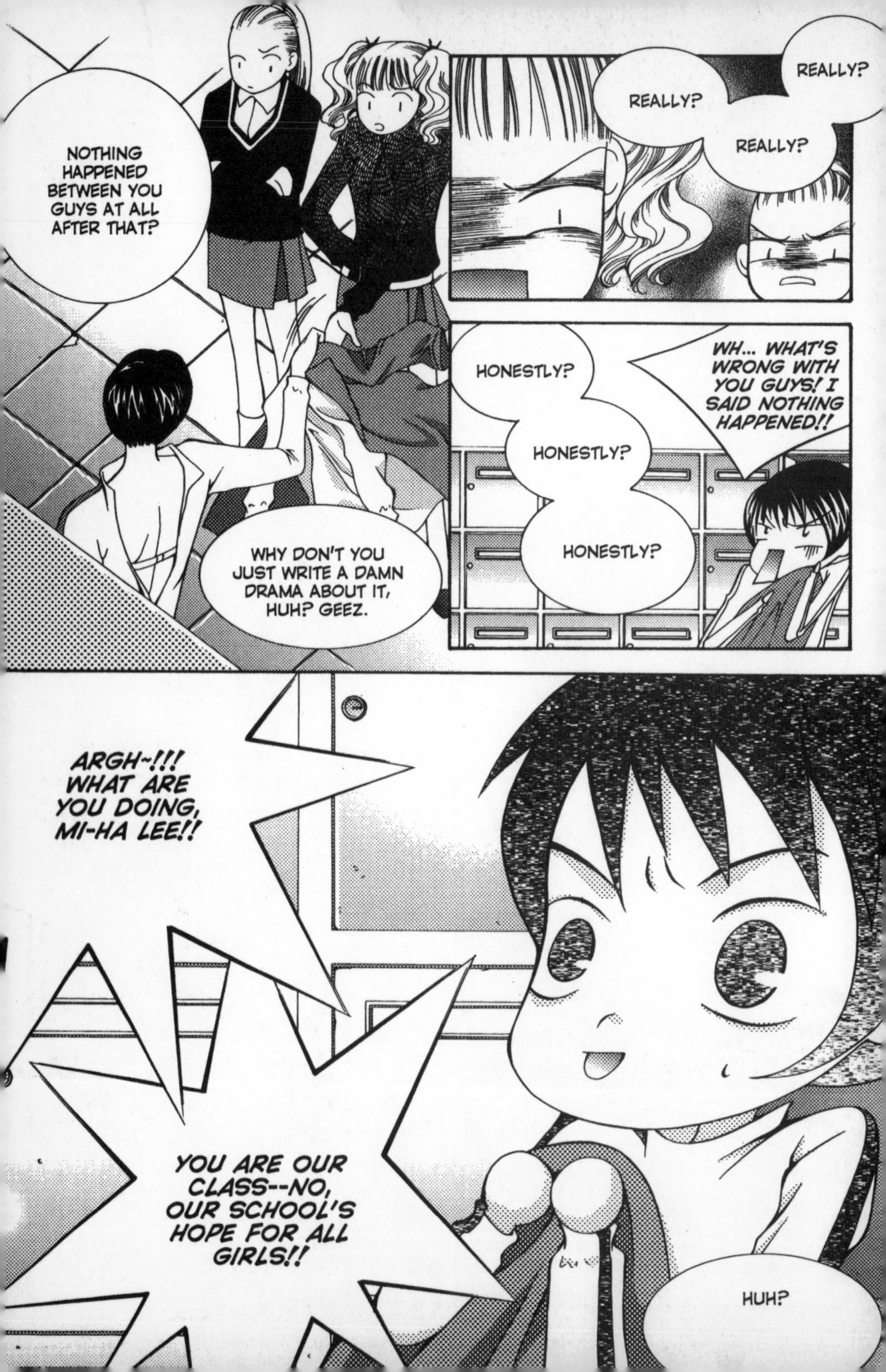
NOTHING HAPPENED BETWEEN YOU GUYS AT ALL AFTER THAT?
WHY DON'T YOU JUST WRITE A DAMN DRAMA ABOUT IT, HUH? GEEZ.
REALLY?
REALLY?
REALLY?
HONESTLY?
HONESTLY?
HONESTLY?
WH... WHAT'S WRONG WITH YOU GUYS! I SAID NOTHING HAPPENED!!
ARGH~!!! WHAT ARE YOU DOING, MI-HA LEE!!
YOU ARE OUR CLASS--NO, OUR SCHOOL'S HOPE FOR ALL GIRLS!!
HUH?

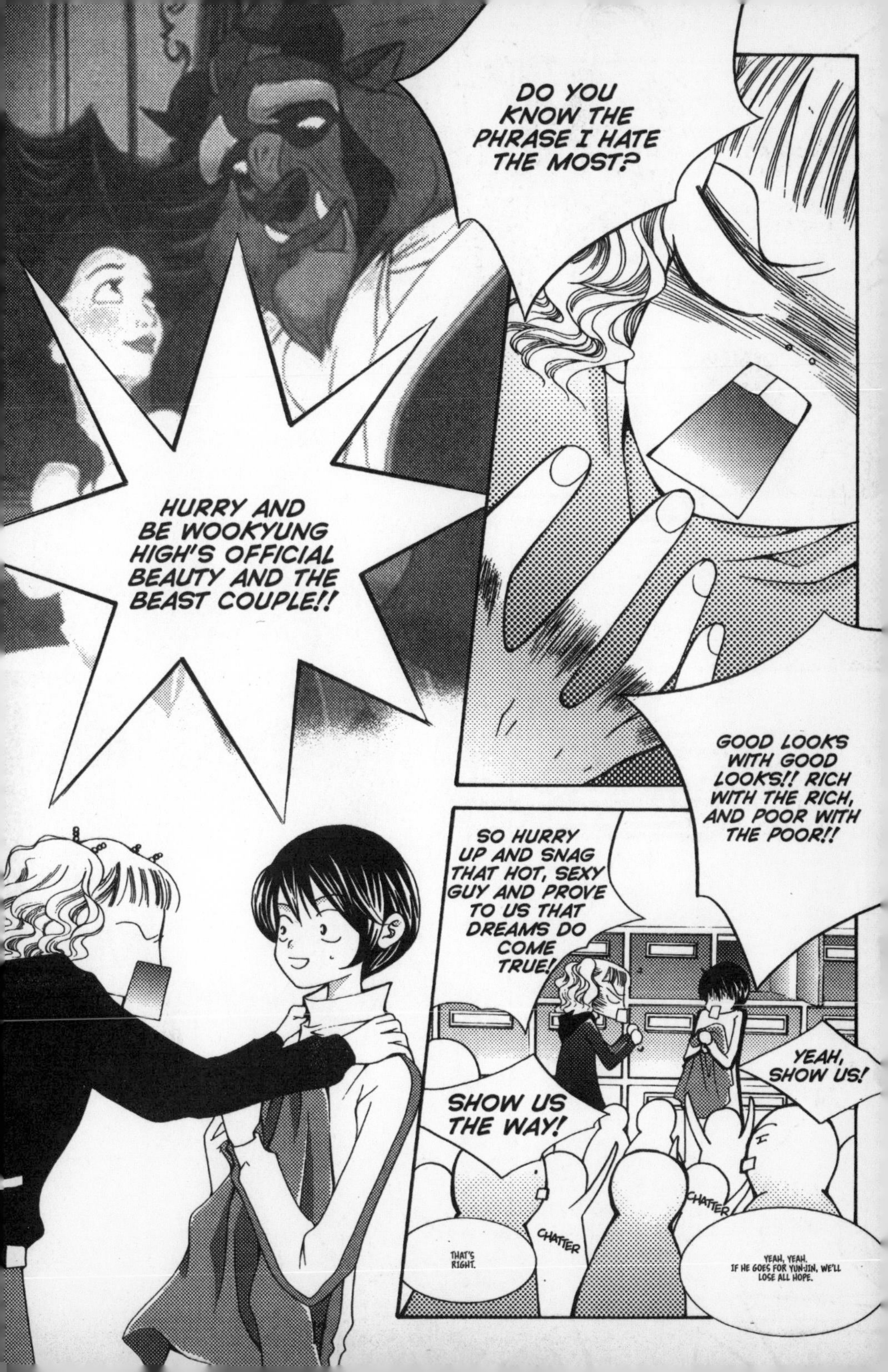
DO YOU KNOW THE PHRASE I HATE THE MOST?
HURRY AND BE WOOKYUNG HIGH'S OFFICIAL BEAUTY AND THE BEAST COUPLE!!
GOOD LOOKS WITH GOOD LOOKS!! RICH WITH THE RICH, AND POOR WITH THE POOR!!
SO HURRY UP AND SNAG THAT HOT, SEXY GUY AND PROVE TO US THAT DREAMS DO COME TRUE!
YEAH, SHOW US!
SHOW US THE WAY!
CHATTER
CHATTER
THAT'S RIGHT.
YEAH, YEAH. IF HE GOES FOR YUN-JIN, WE'LL LOSE ALL HOPE.

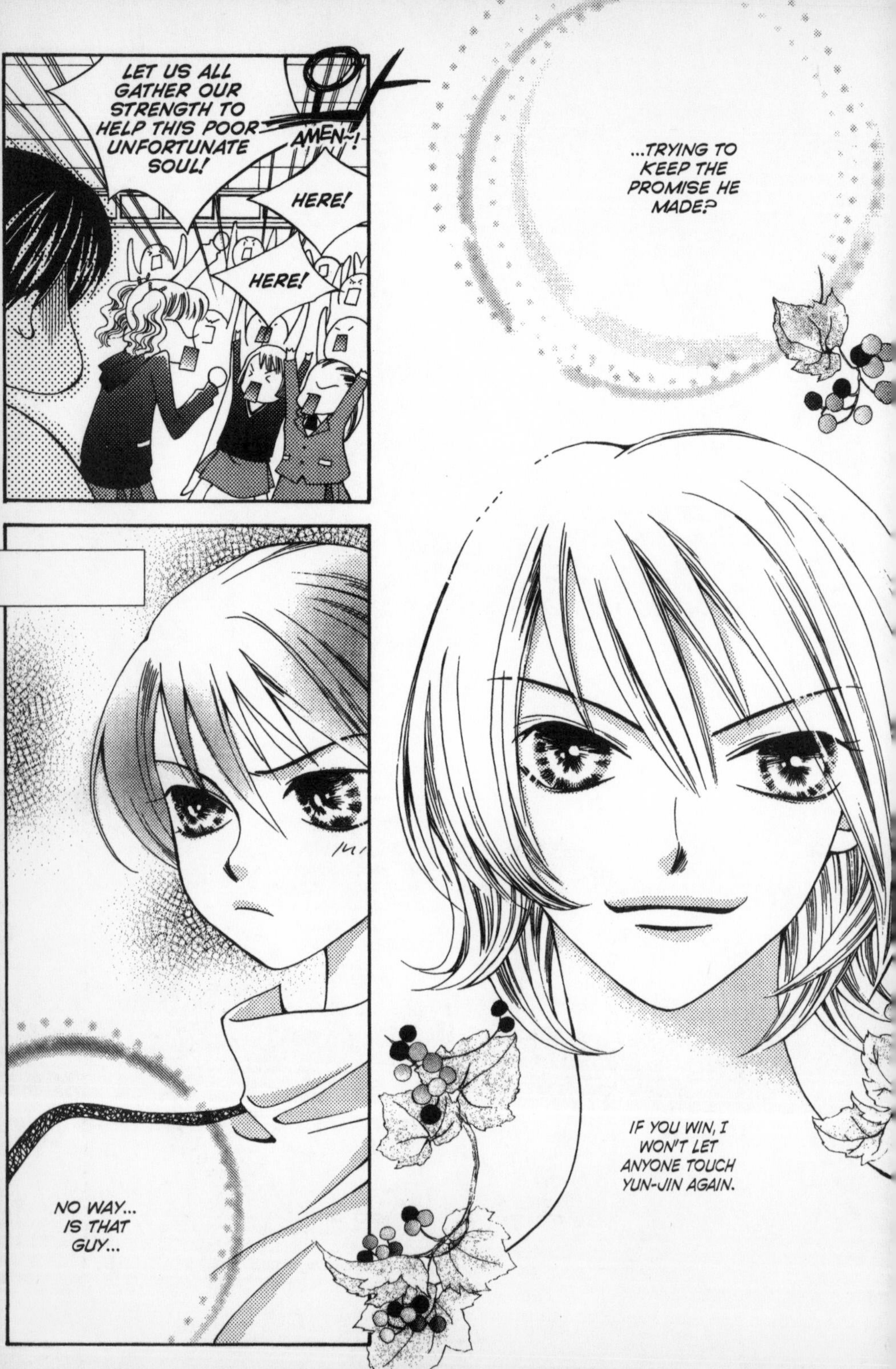
LET US ALL GATHER OUR STRENGTH TO HELP THIS POOR UNFORTUNATE SOUL!
AMEN~!
HERE!
HERE!
NO WAY... IS THAT GUY...
...TRYING TO KEEP THE PROMISE HE MADE?
IF YOU WIN, I WON'T LET ANYONE TOUCH YUN-JIN AGAIN.

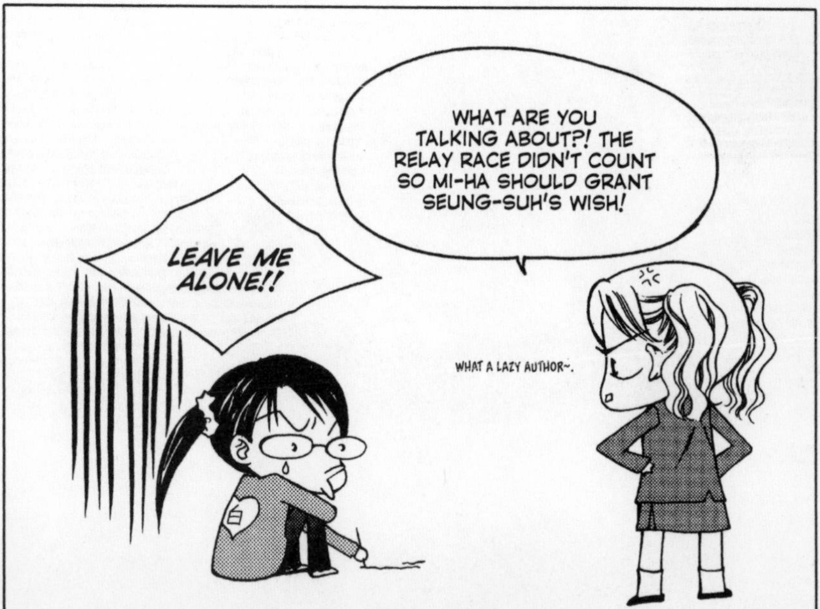
LEAVE ME ALONE!!
WHAT ARE YOU TALKING ABOUT?! THE RELAY RACE DIDN'T COUNT SO MI-HA SHOULD GRANT SEUNG-SUH'S WISH!
WHAT A LAZY AUTHOR~.

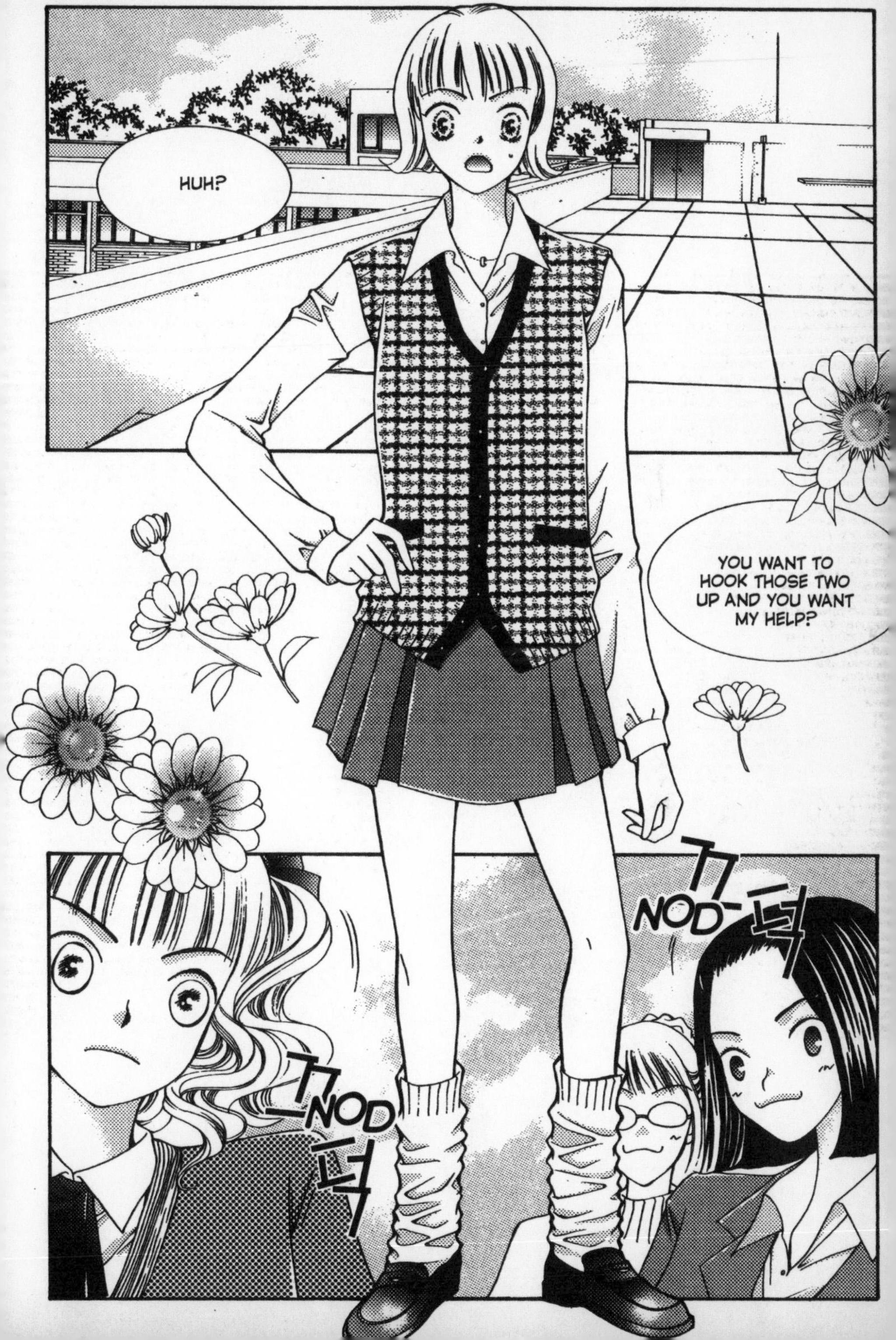
HUH?
YOU WANT TO HOOK THOSE TWO UP AND YOU WANT MY HELP?
끄 NOD 덕
끄 NOD 덕

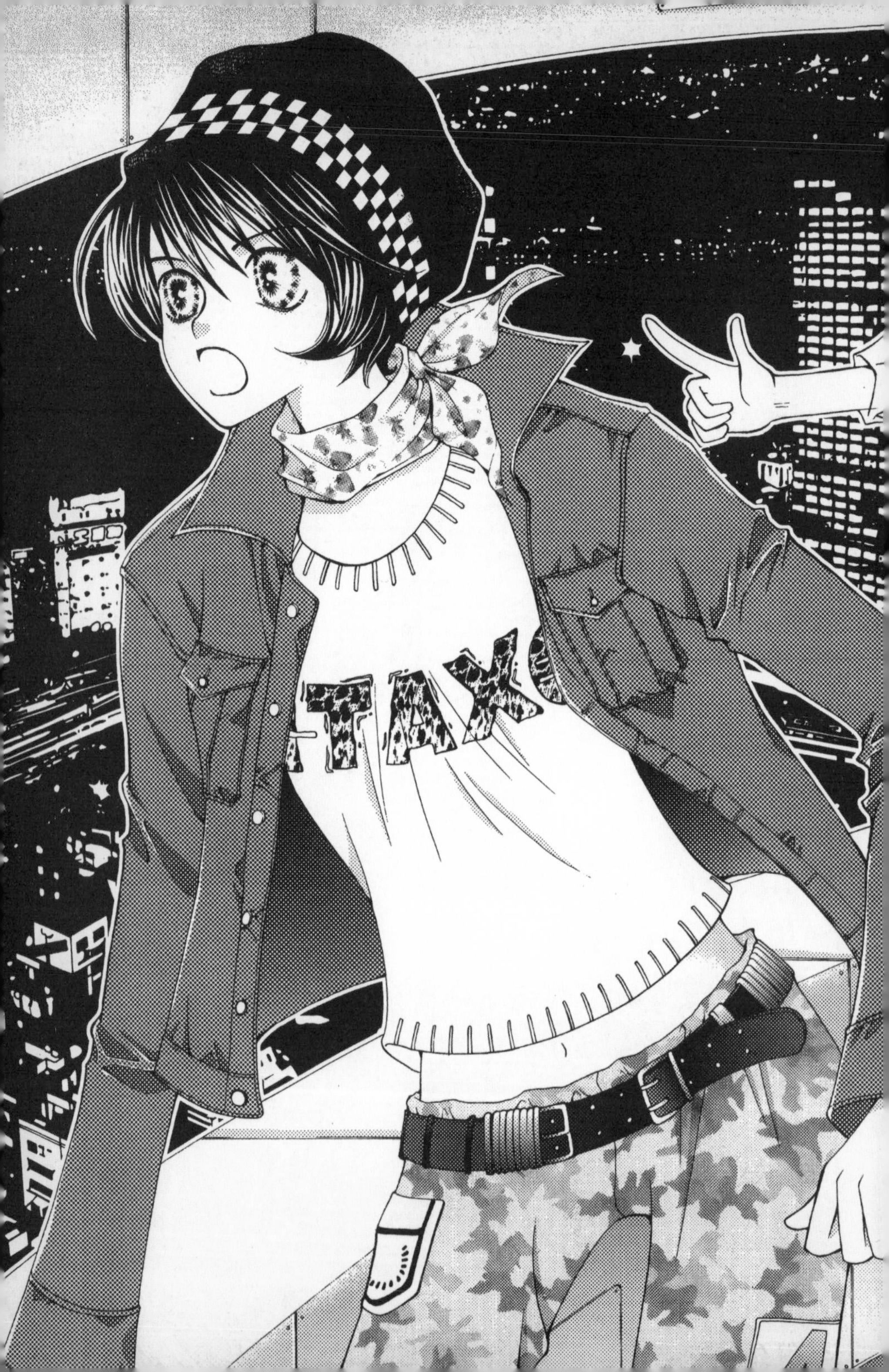

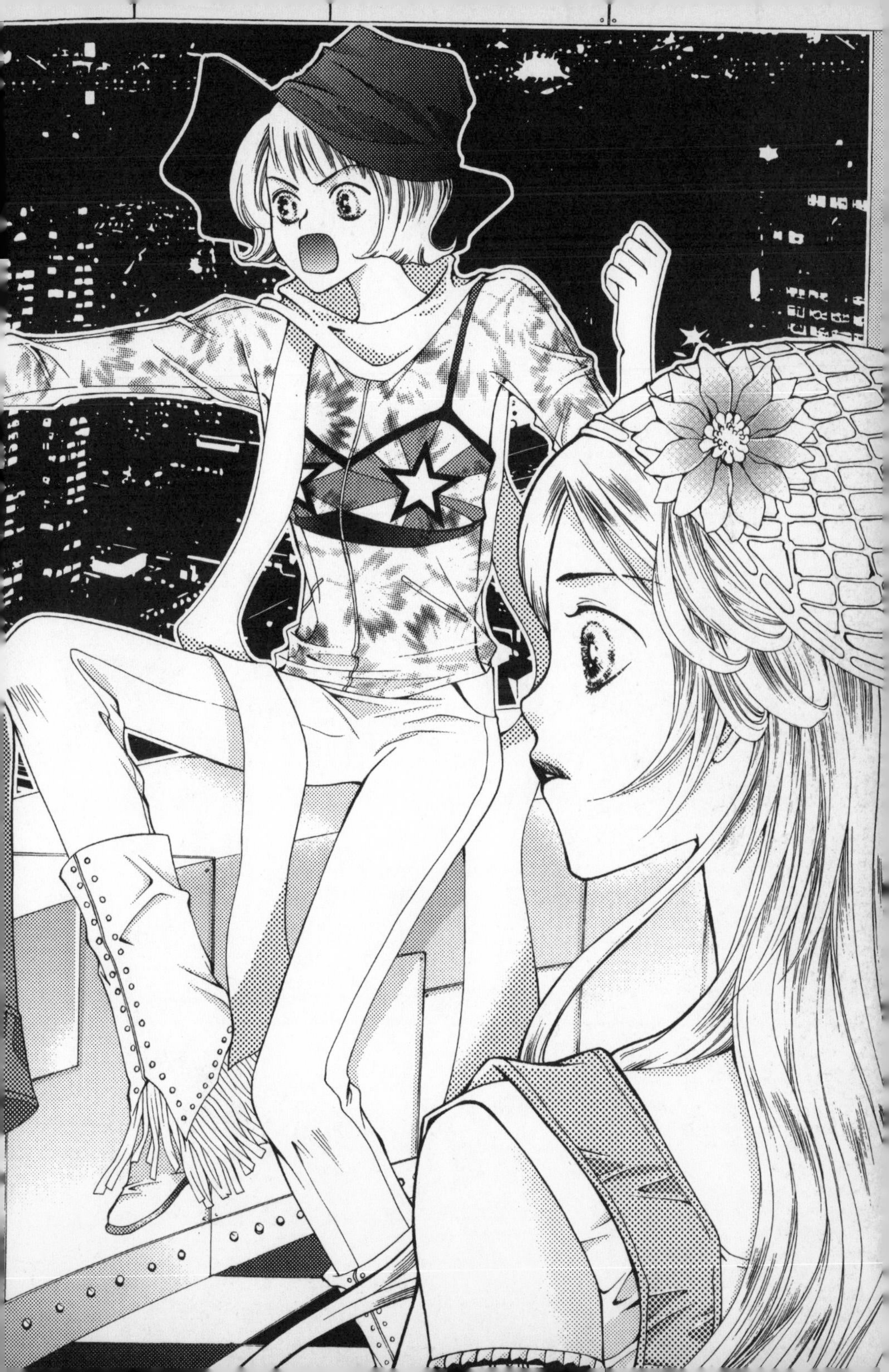

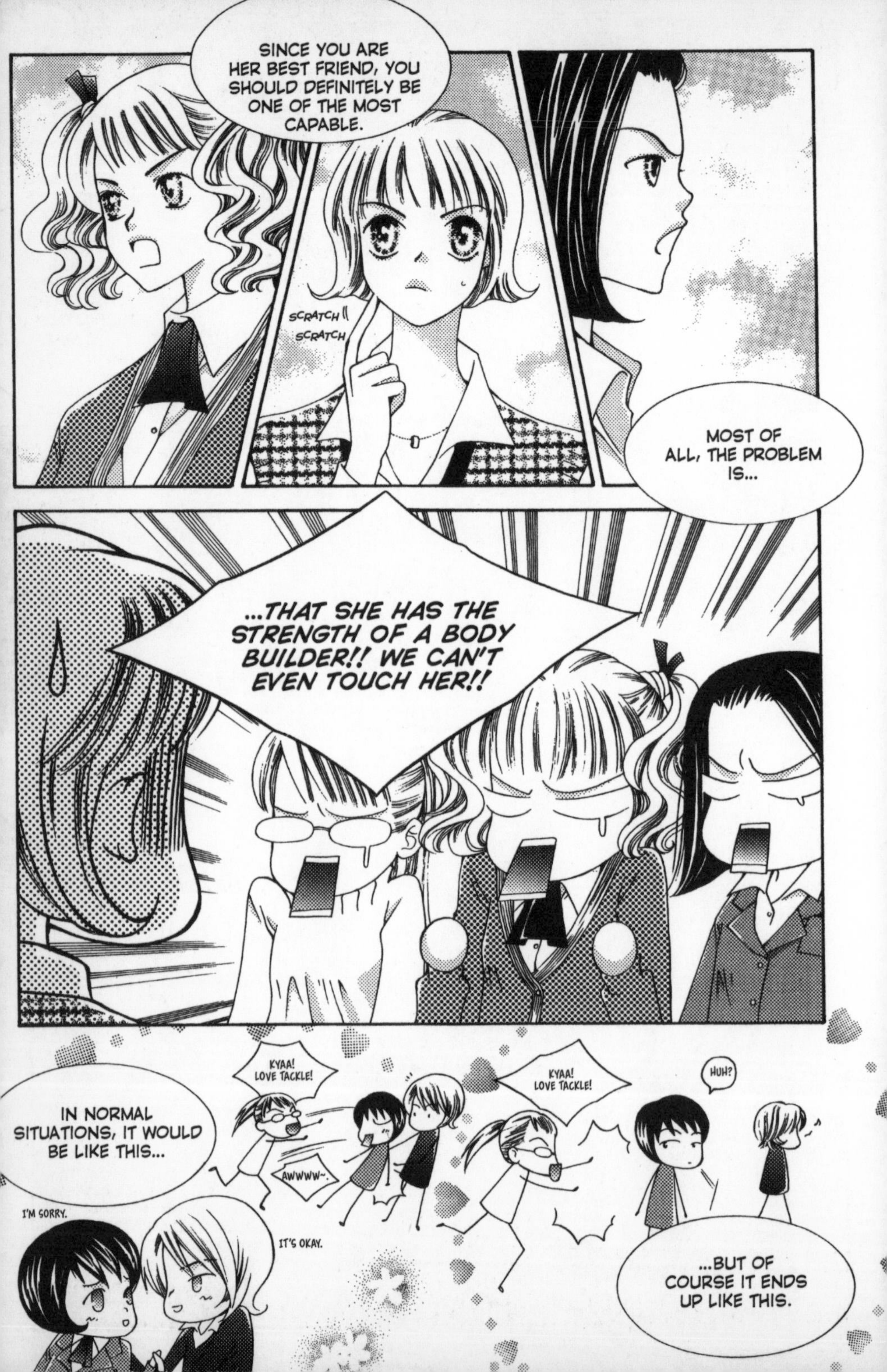
SINCE YOU ARE HER BEST FRIEND, YOU SHOULD DEFINITELY BE ONE OF THE MOST CAPABLE.
SCRATCH SCRATCH
MOST OF ALL, THE PROBLEM IS...
...THAT SHE HAS THE STRENGTH OF A BODY BUILDER!! WE CAN'T EVEN TOUCH HER!!
IN NORMAL SITUATIONS, IT WOULD BE LIKE THIS...
KYAA! LOVE TACKLE!
AWWWW~.
KYAA! LOVE TACKLE!
HUH?
I'M SORRY.
IT'S OKAY.
...BUT OF COURSE IT ENDS UP LIKE THIS.

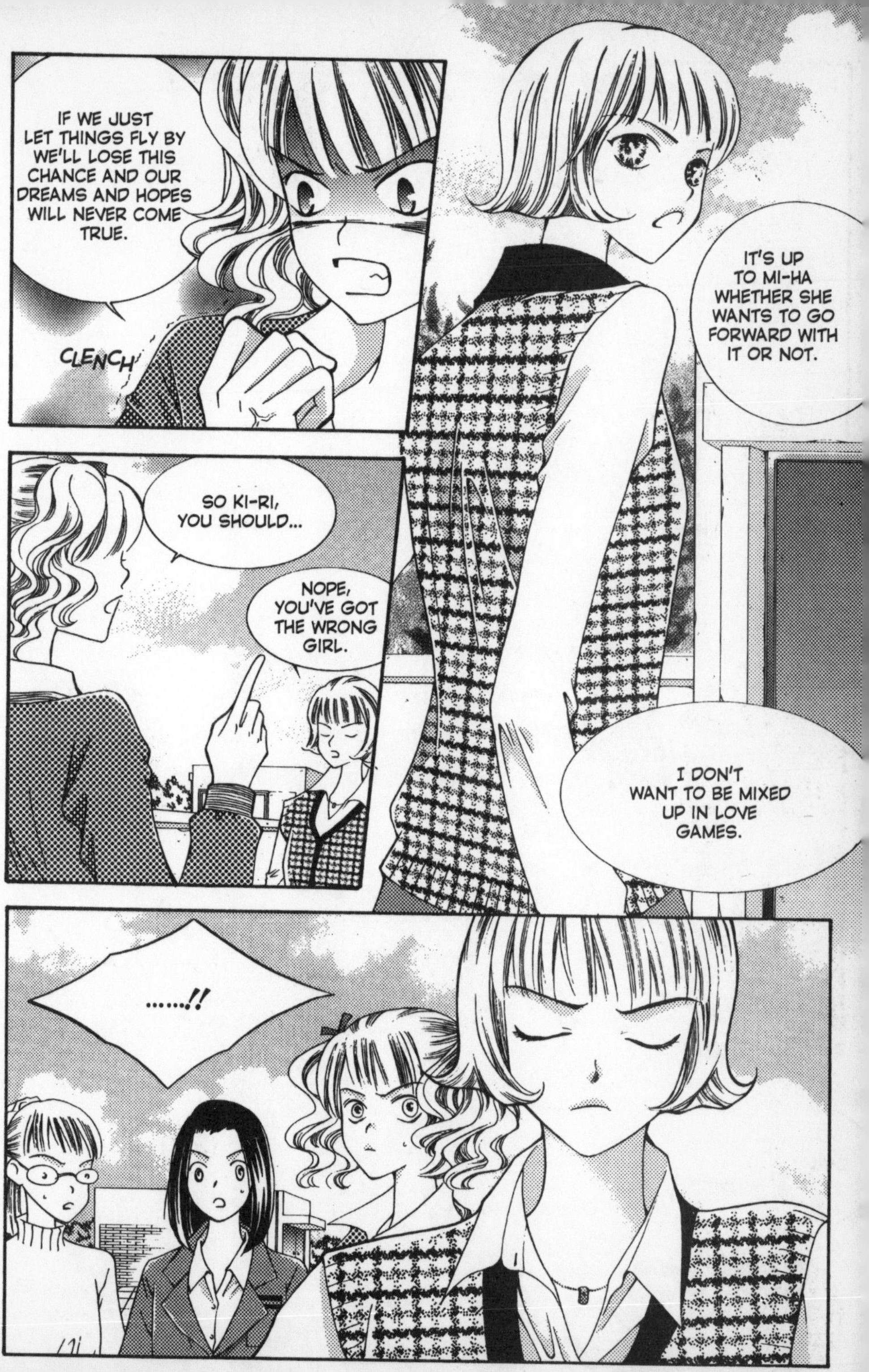
IF WE JUST LET THINGS FLY BY WE'LL LOSE THIS CHANCE AND OUR DREAMS AND HOPES WILL NEVER COME TRUE.
CLENCH
SO KI-RI, YOU SHOULD...
NOPE, YOU'VE GOT THE WRONG GIRL.
IT'S UP TO MI-HA WHETHER SHE WANTS TO GO FORWARD WITH IT OR NOT.
I DON'T WANT TO BE MIXED UP IN LOVE GAMES.
......!!

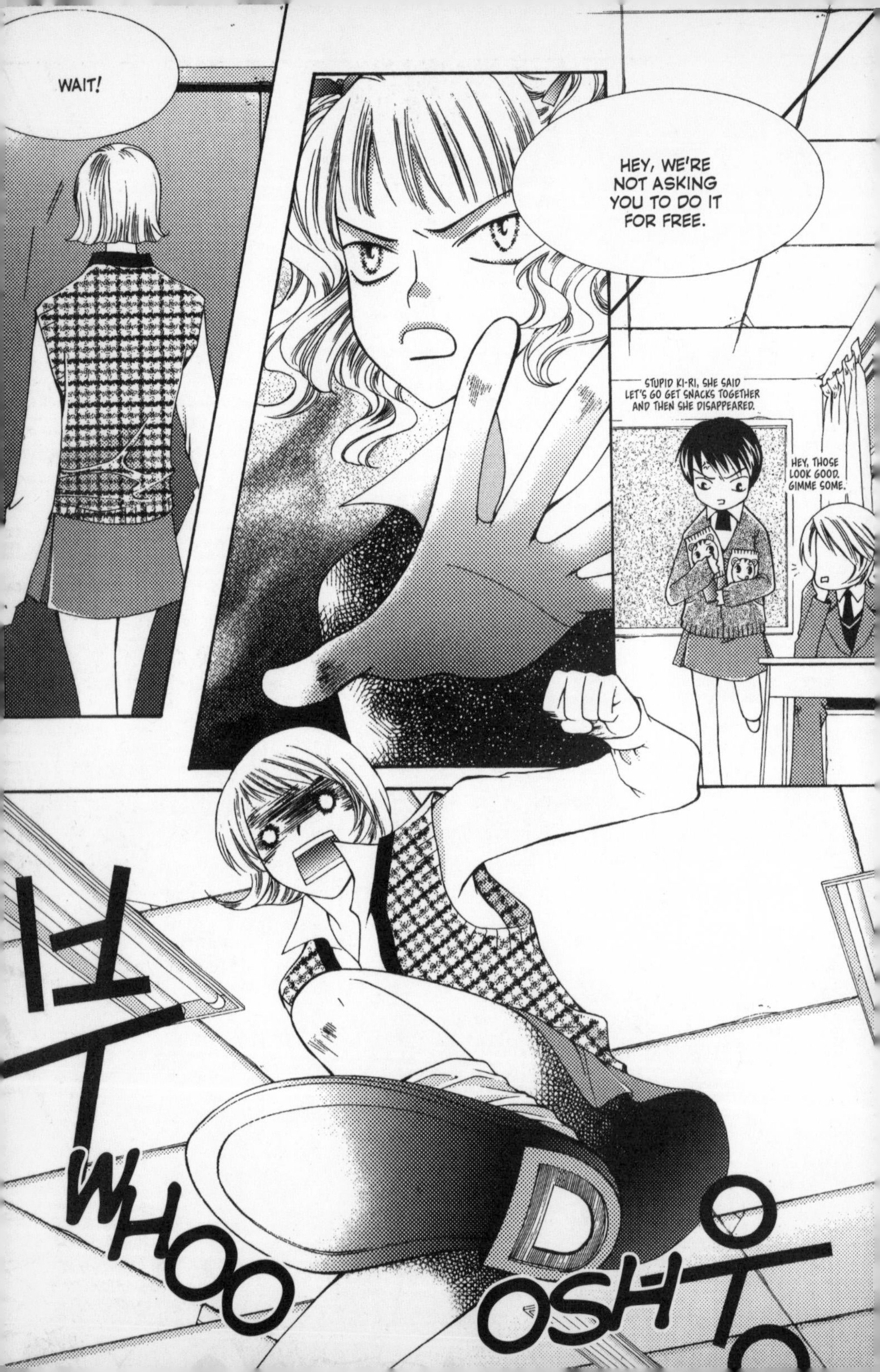
WAIT!
HEY, WE'RE NOT ASKING YOU TO DO IT FOR FREE.
STUPID KI-RI, SHE SAID LET'S GO GET SNACKS TOGETHER AND THEN SHE DISAPPEARED.
HEY, THOSE LOOK GOOD. GIMME SOME.
WHOOOSH

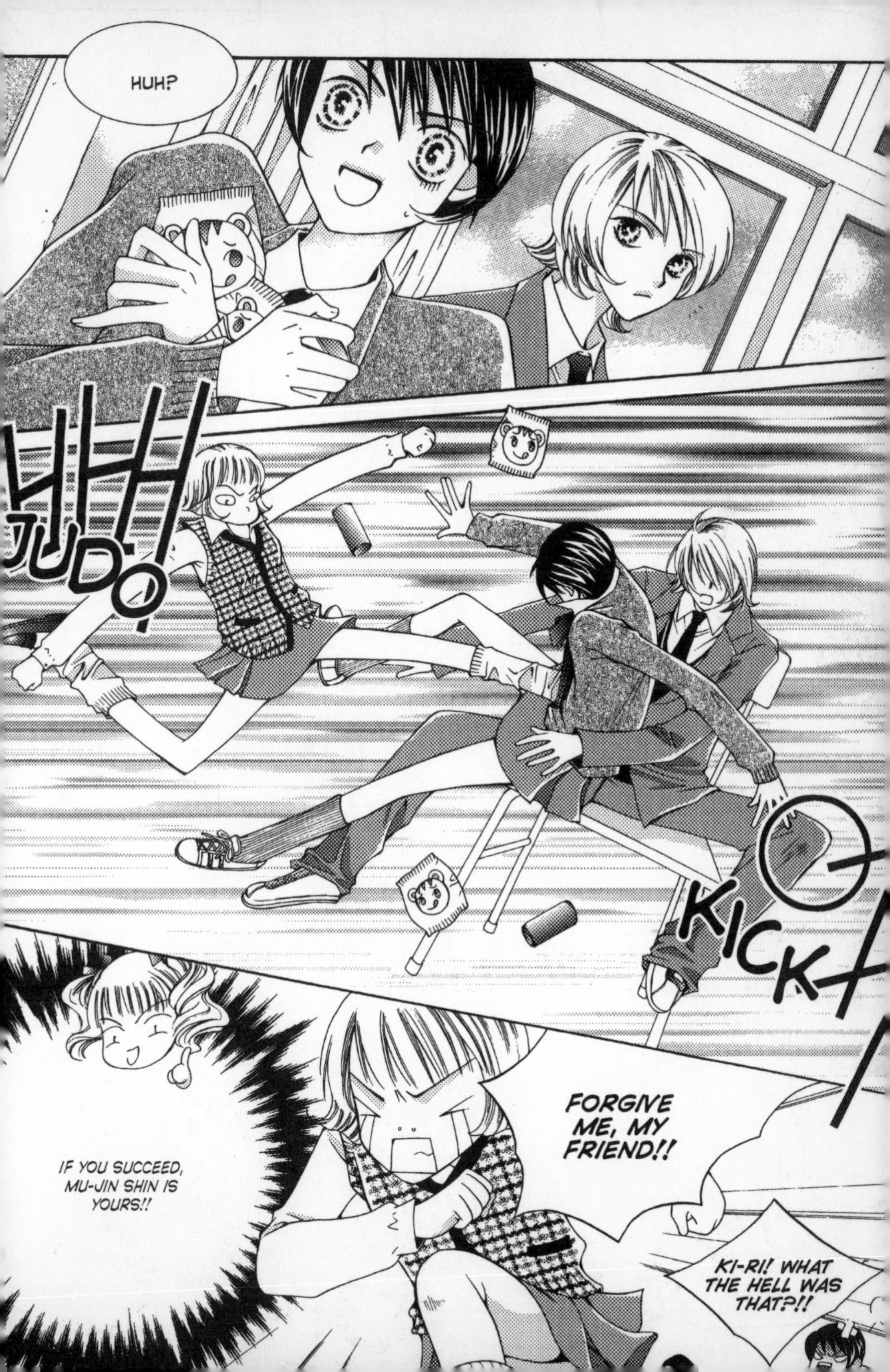
HUH?
JUDO!
KICK!
IF YOU SUCCEED, MU-JIN SHIN IS YOURS!!
FORGIVE ME, MY FRIEND!!
KI-RI! WHAT THE HELL WAS THAT?!!

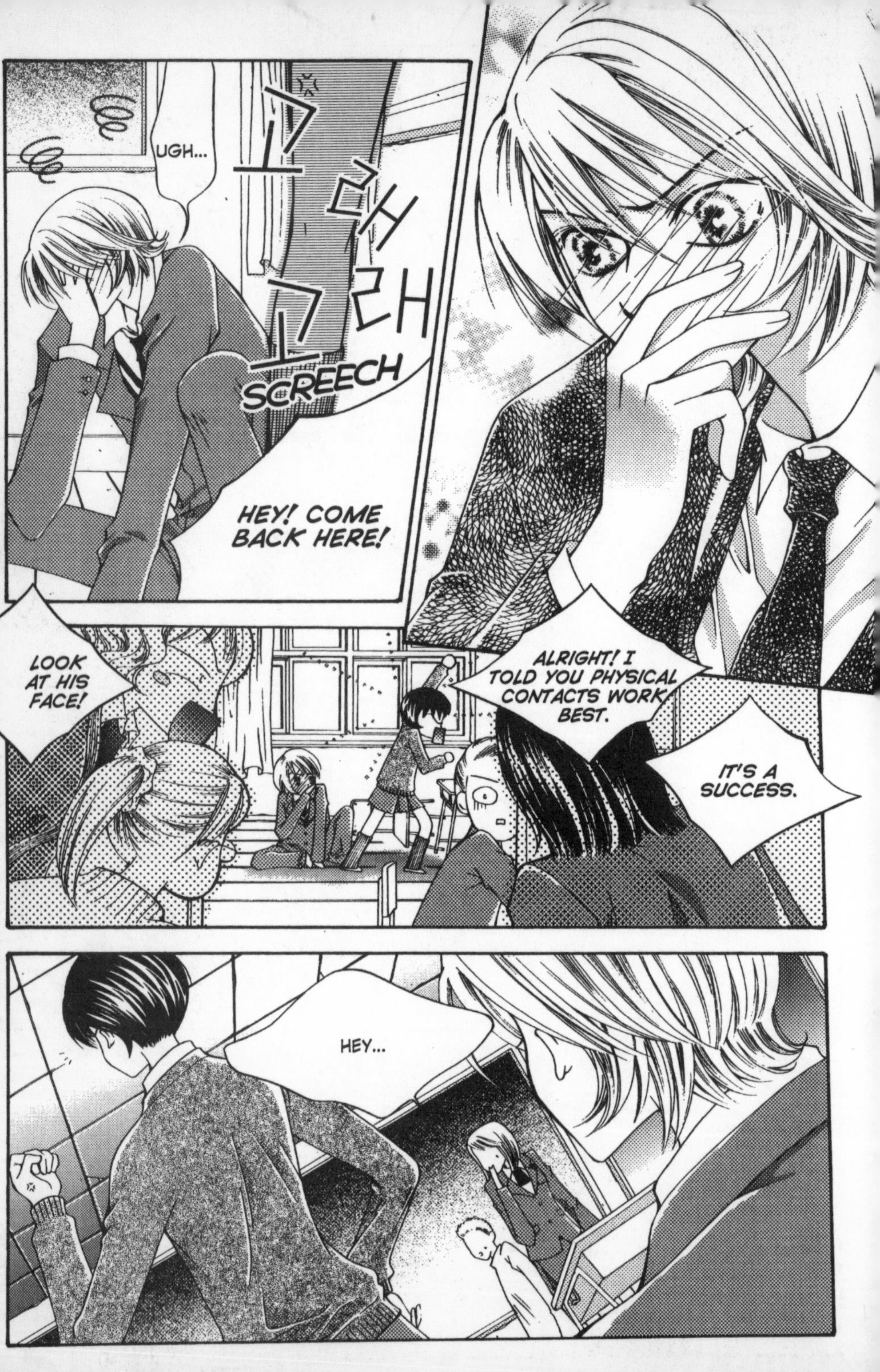
UGH...
SCREECH
HEY! COME BACK HERE!
LOOK AT HIS FACE!
ALRIGHT! I TOLD YOU PHYSICAL CONTACTS WORK BEST.
IT'S A SUCCESS.
HEY...

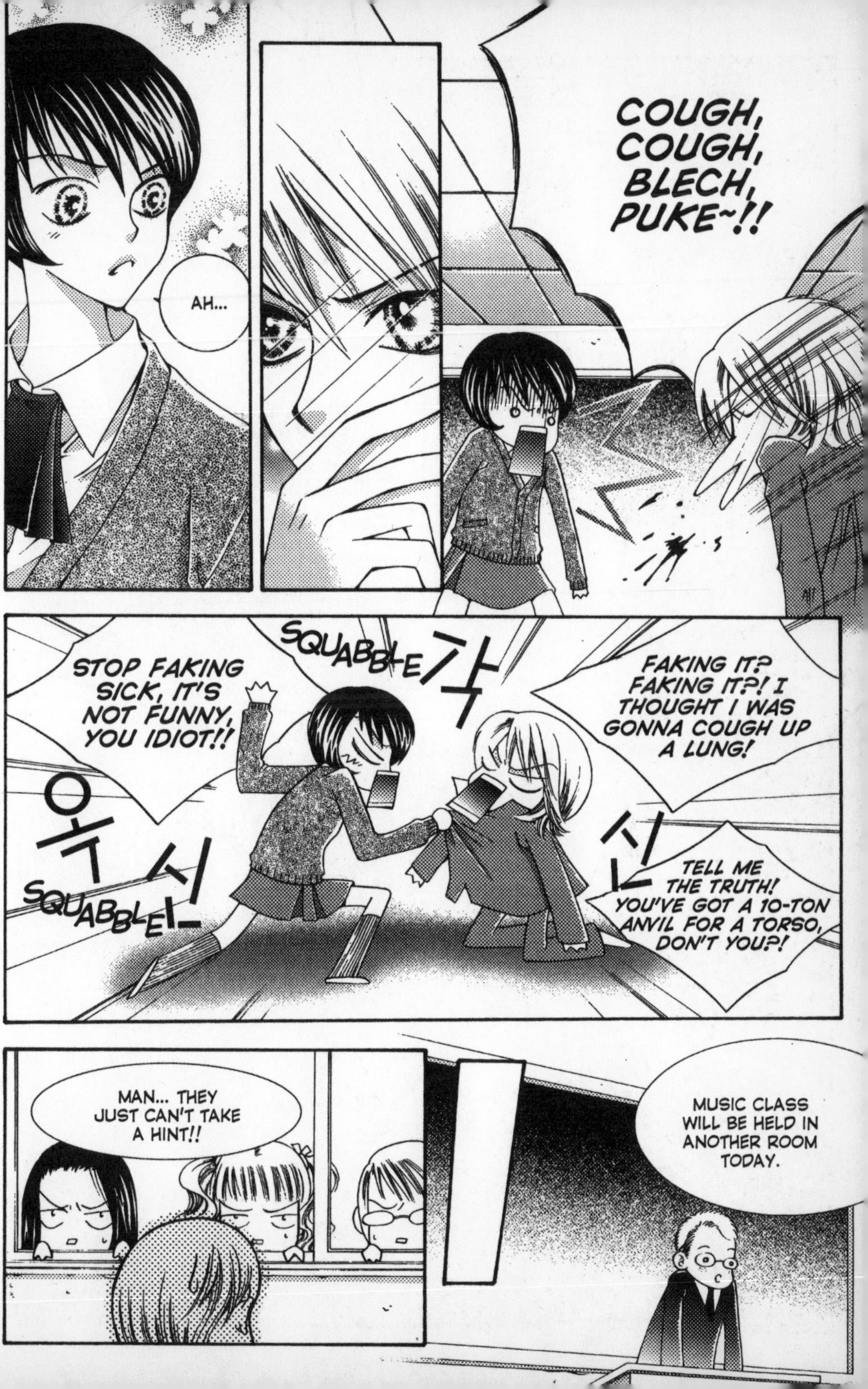
AH...
COUGH, COUGH, BLECH, PUKE~!!
SQUABBLE
STOP FAKING SICK, IT'S NOT FUNNY, YOU IDIOT!!
FAKING IT? FAKING IT?! I THOUGHT I WAS GONNA COUGH UP A LUNG!
SQUABBLE
TELL ME THE TRUTH! YOU'VE GOT A 10-TON ANVIL FOR A TORSO, DON'T YOU?!
MAN... THEY JUST CAN'T TAKE A HINT!!
MUSIC CLASS WILL BE HELD IN ANOTHER ROOM TODAY.

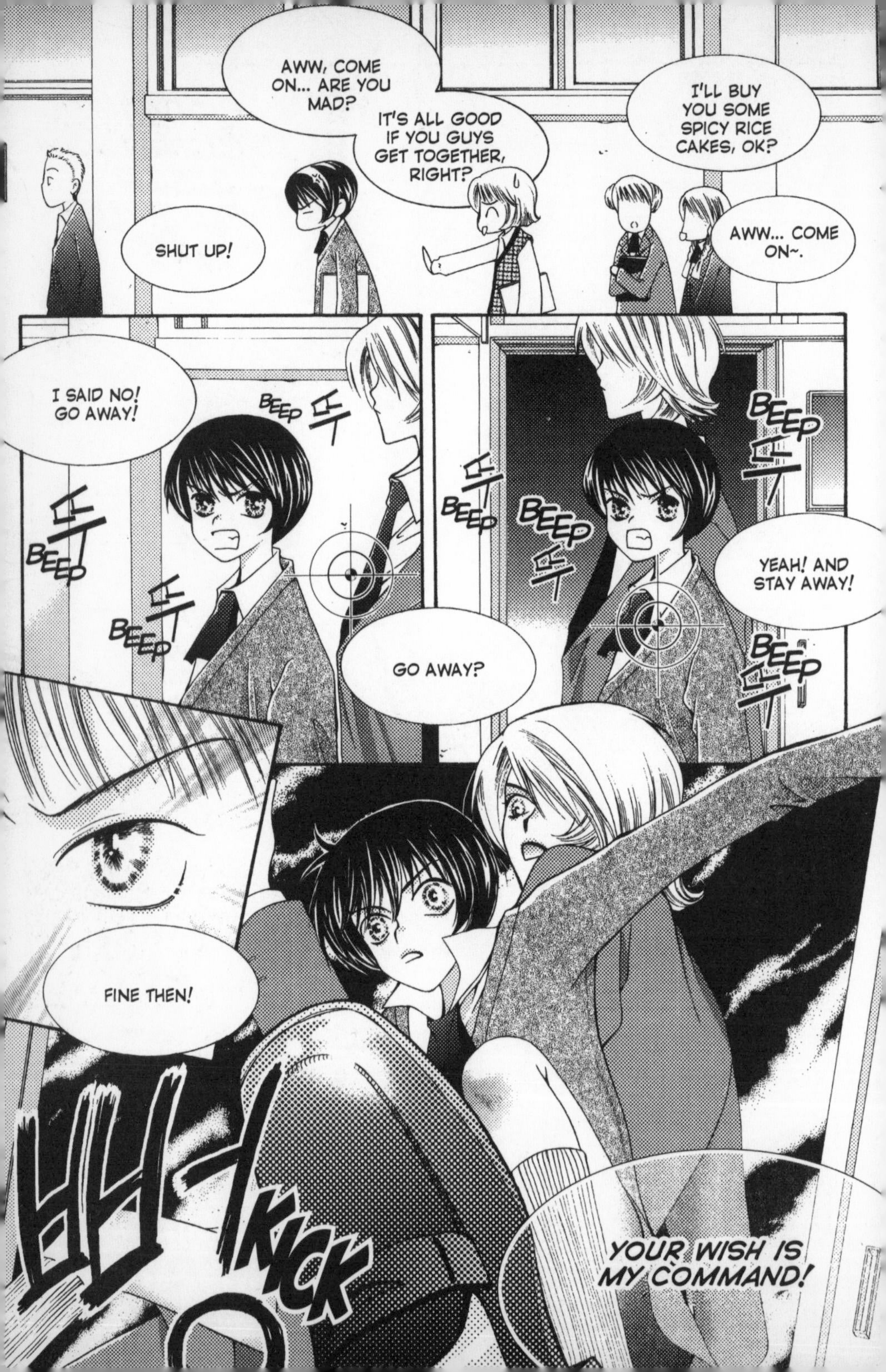
AWW, COME ON... ARE YOU MAD?
IT'S ALL GOOD IF YOU GUYS GET TOGETHER, RIGHT?
I'LL BUY YOU SOME SPICY RICE CAKES, OK?
SHUT UP!
AWW... COME ON~.
I SAID NO! GO AWAY!
BEEP
BEEP
BEEP
BEEP
BEEP
GO AWAY?
BEEP
YEAH! AND STAY AWAY!
BEEP
FINE THEN!
KICK
YOUR WISH IS MY COMMAND!

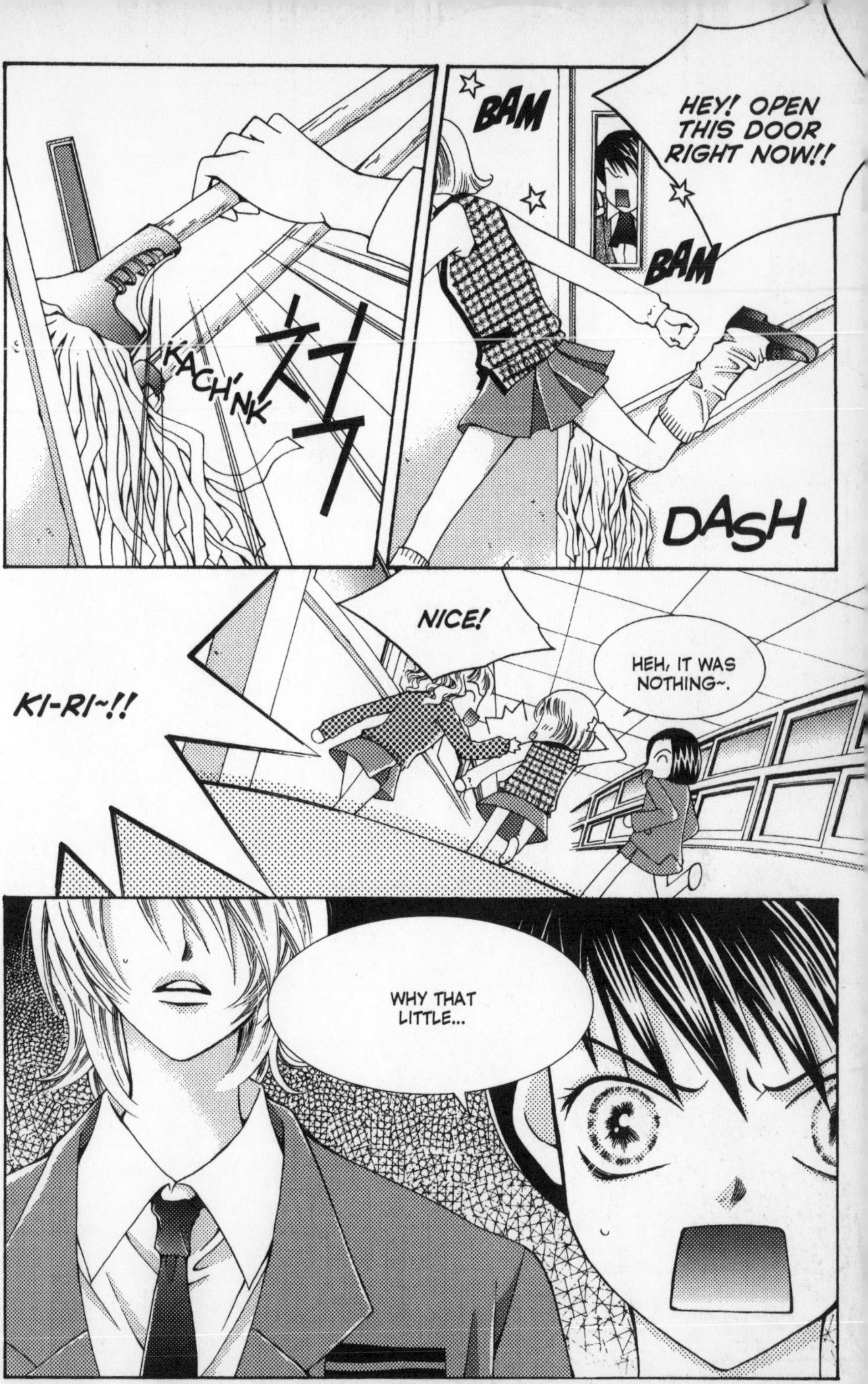
KACH'NK
BAM
HEY! OPEN THIS DOOR RIGHT NOW!!
BAM
DASH
KI-RI~!!
NICE!
HEH, IT WAS NOTHING~.
WHY THAT LITTLE...

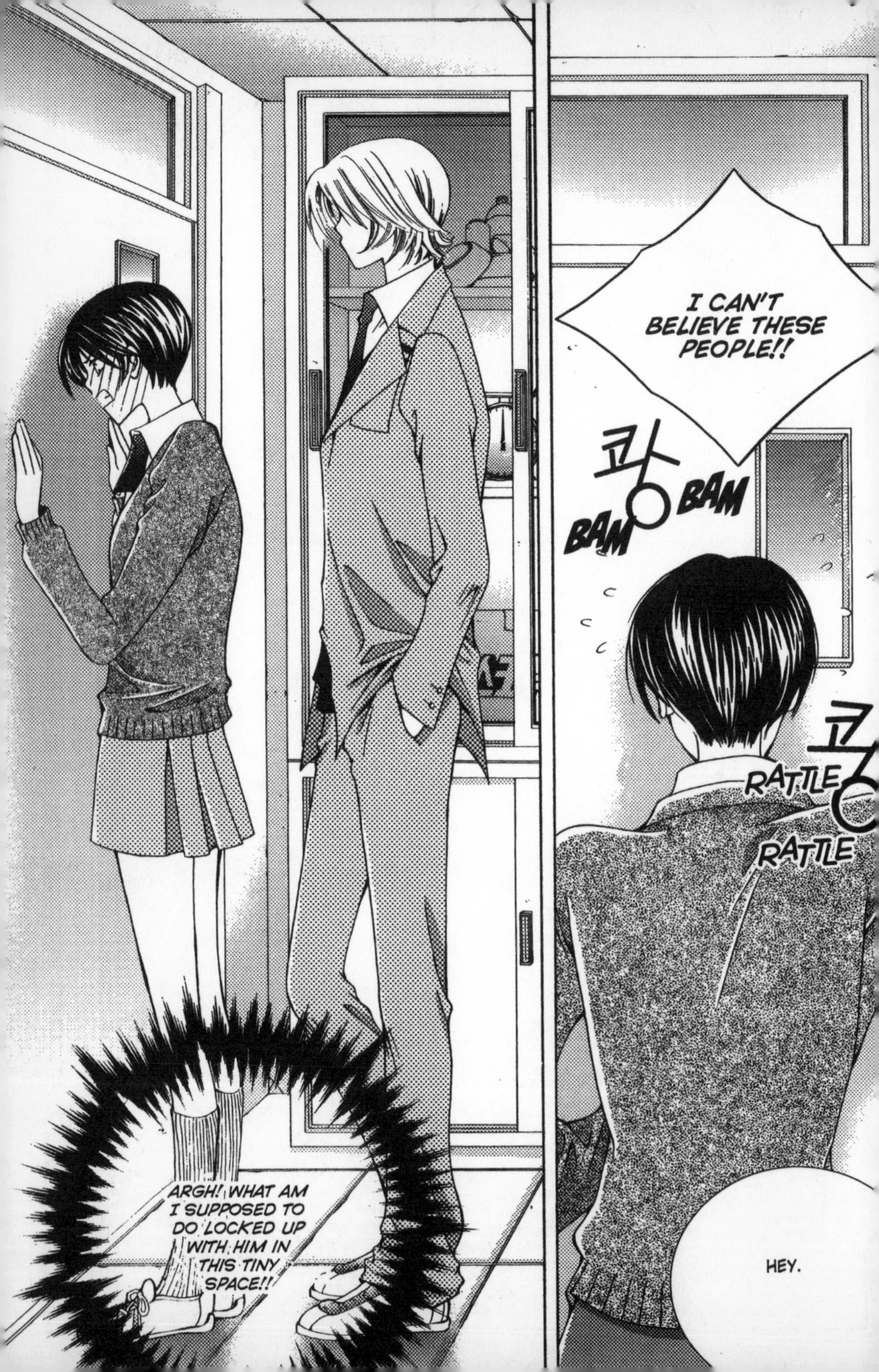
ARGH! WHAT AM I SUPPOSED TO DO LOCKED UP WITH HIM IN THIS TINY SPACE!!
I CAN'T BELIEVE THESE PEOPLE!!
쾅
BAM BAM
RATTLE RATTLE
HEY.

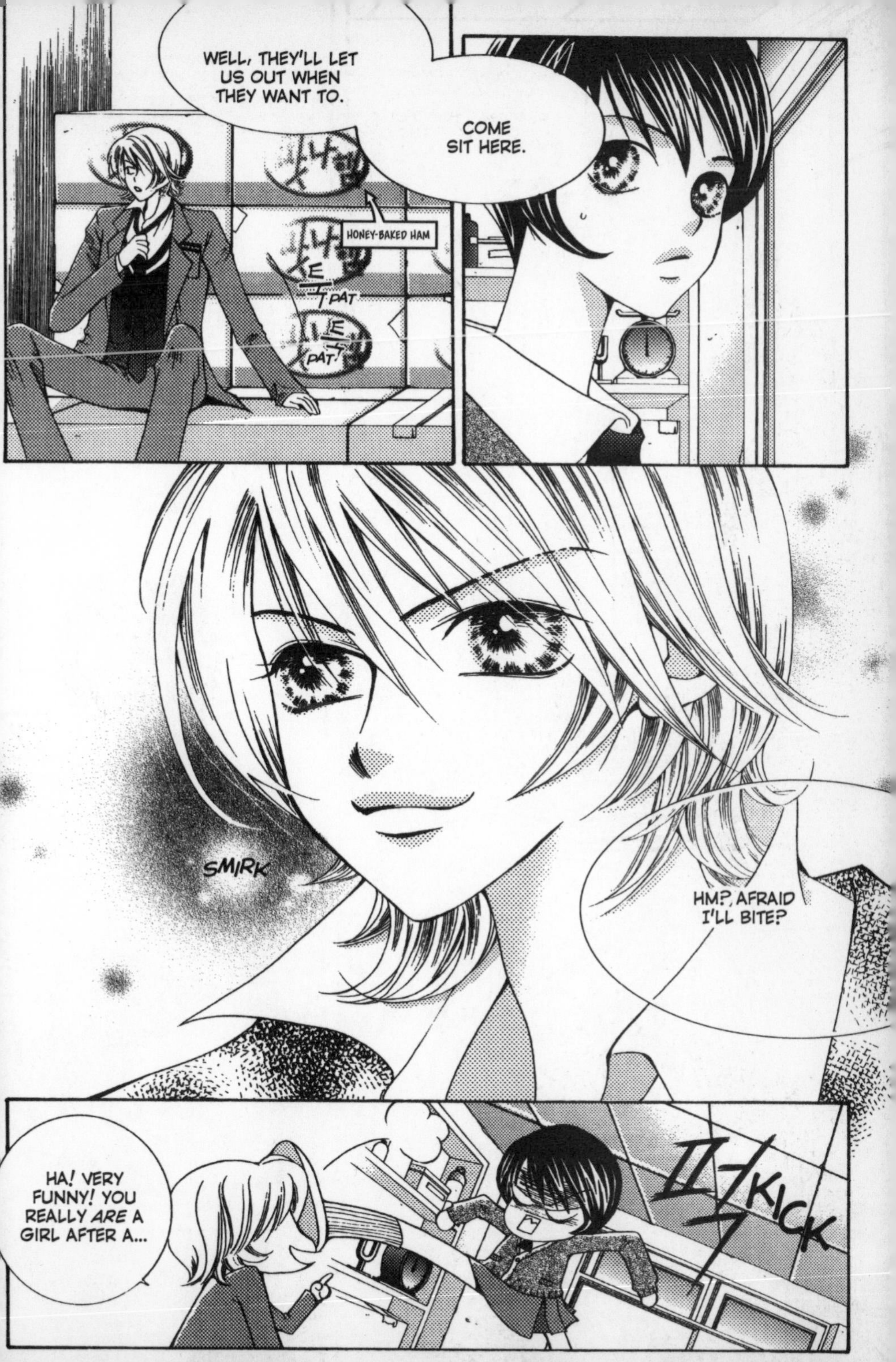
WELL, THEY'LL LET US OUT WHEN THEY WANT TO.
COME SIT HERE.
HONEY-BAKED HAM
PAT
PAT
SMIRK
HM?, AFRAID I'LL BITE?
HA! VERY FUNNY! YOU REALLY ARE A GIRL AFTER A...
KICK

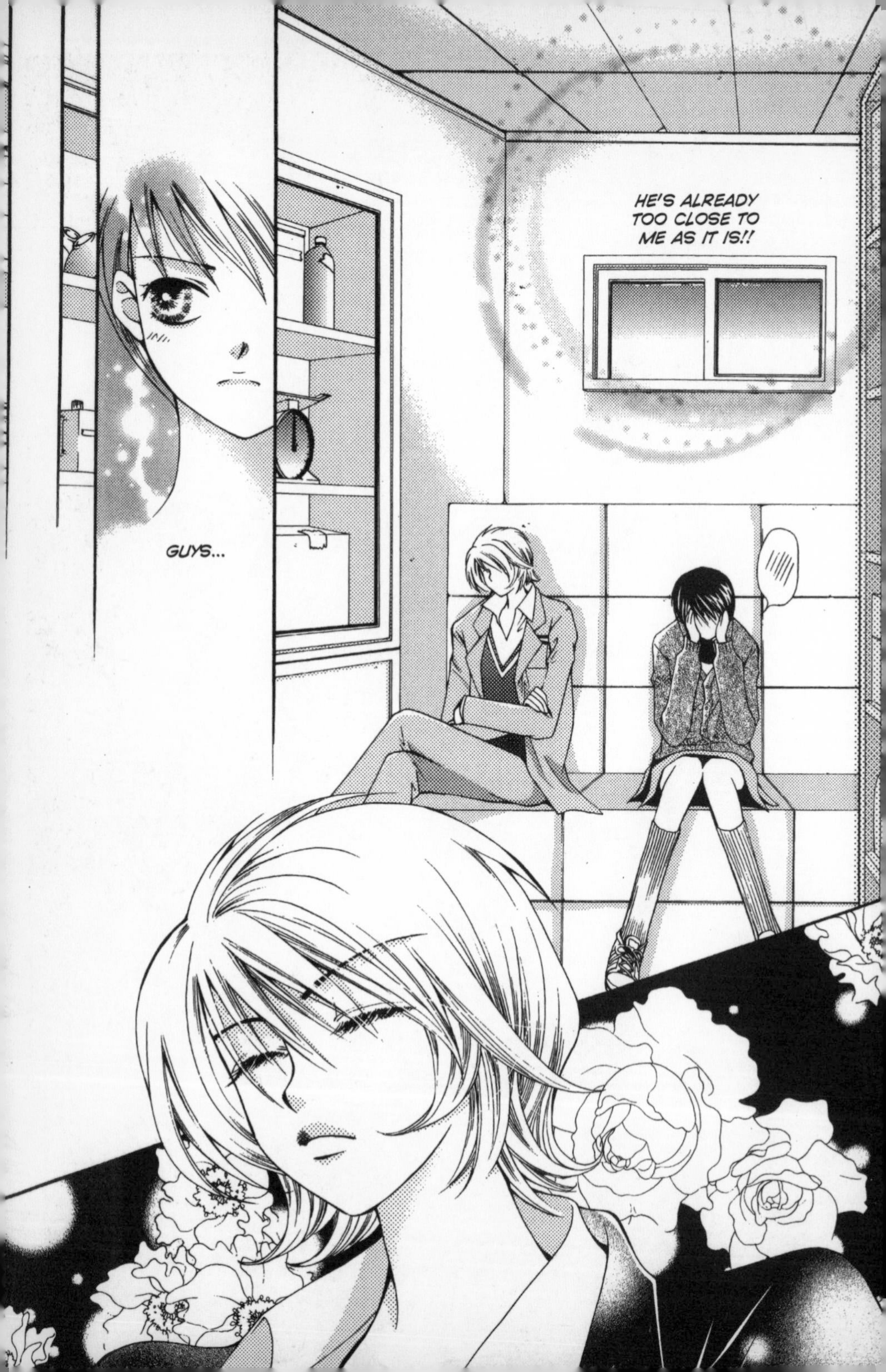
GUYS...
HE'S ALREADY TOO CLOSE TO ME AS IT IS!!

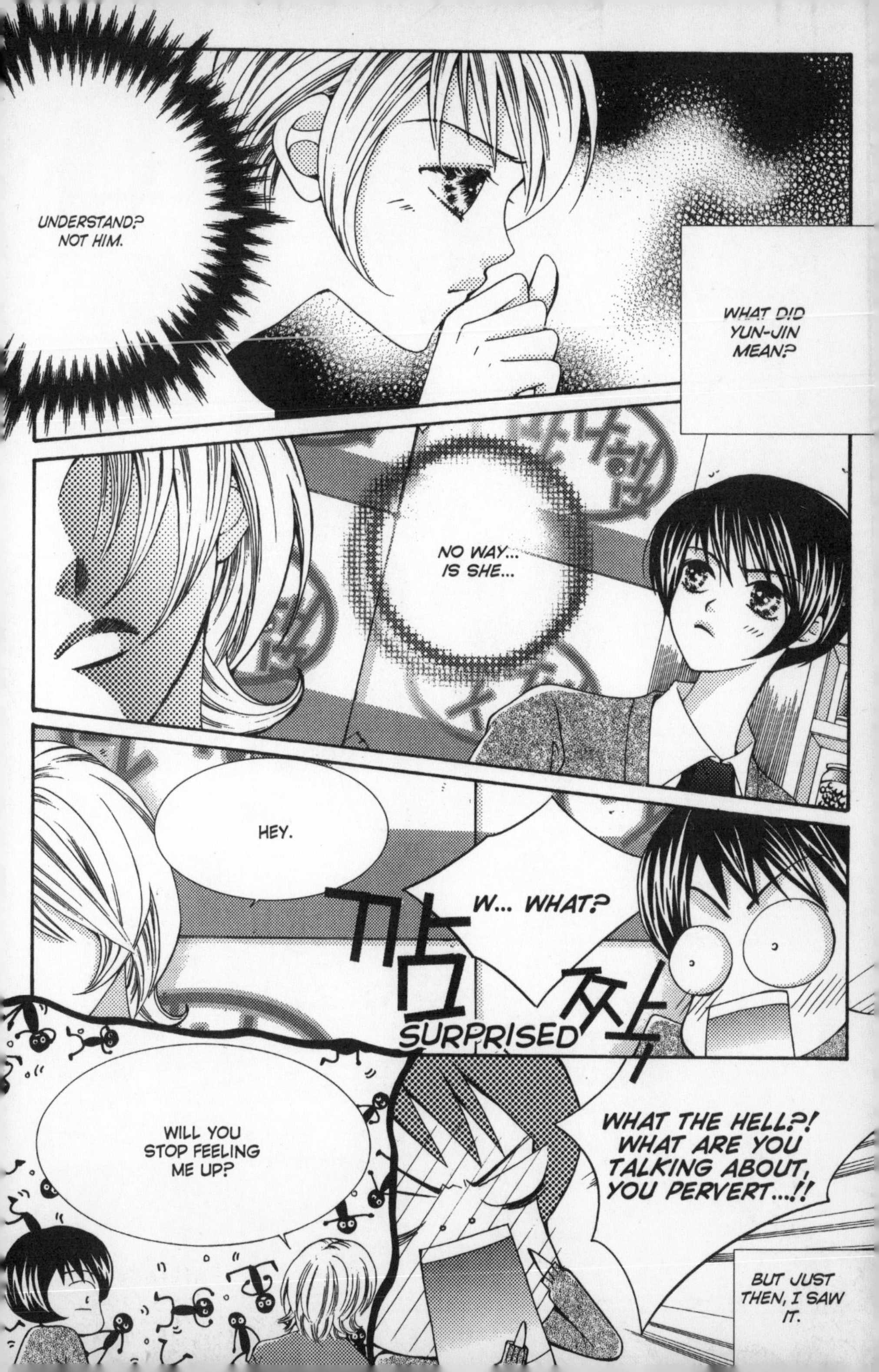
UNDERSTAND? NOT HIM.
WHAT DID YUN-JIN MEAN?
NO WAY... IS SHE...
HEY.
W... WHAT?
SURPRISED
WILL YOU STOP FEELING ME UP?
WHAT THE HELL?! WHAT ARE YOU TALKING ABOUT, YOU PERVERT...!!
BUT JUST THEN, I SAW IT.

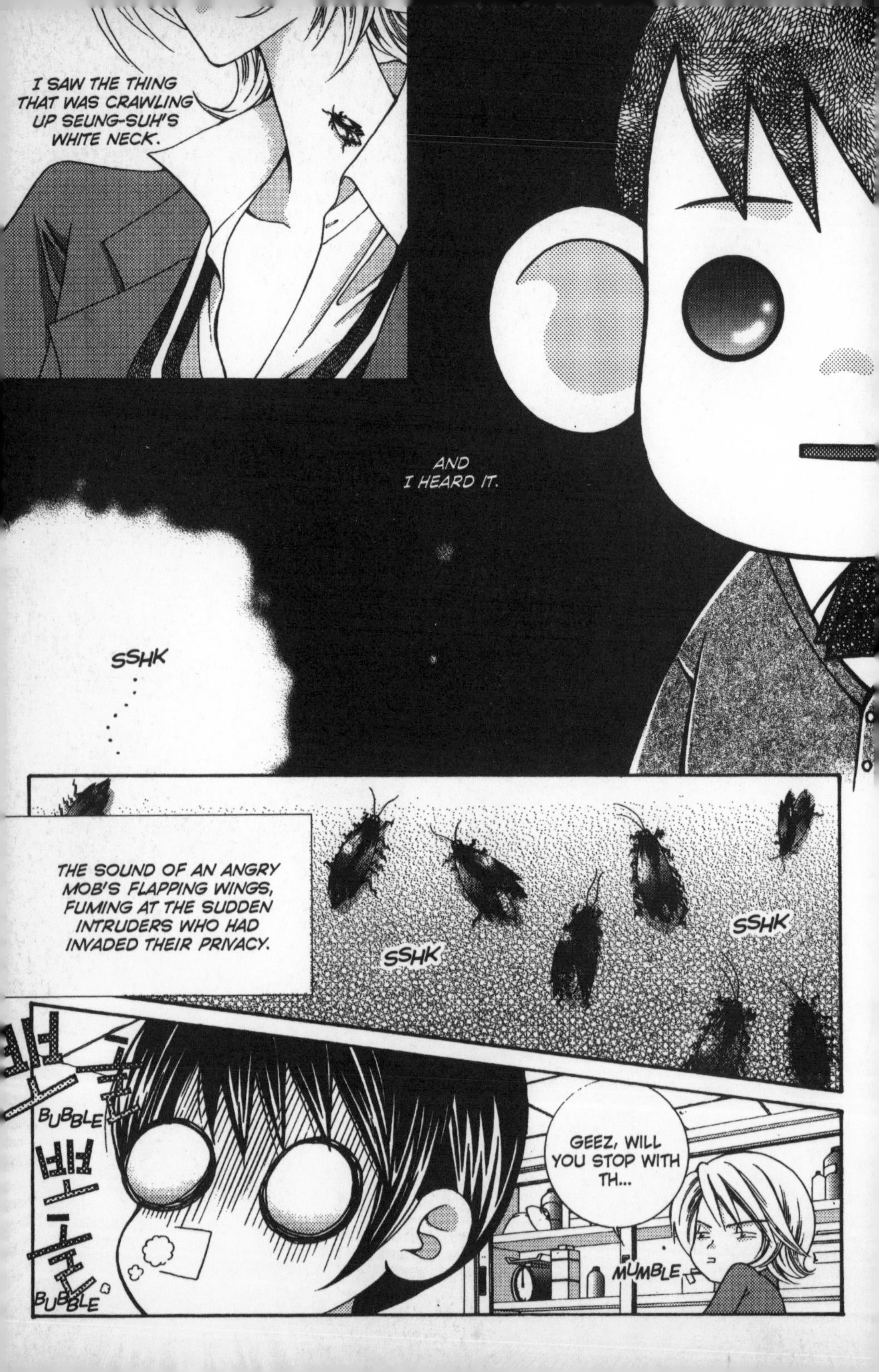
I SAW THE THING THAT WAS CRAWLING UP SEUNG-SUH'S WHITE NECK.
AND I HEARD IT.
SSHK
THE SOUND OF AN ANGRY MOB'S FLAPPING WINGS, FUMING AT THE SUDDEN INTRUDERS WHO HAD INVADED THEIR PRIVACY.
SSHK
SSHK
BUBBLE
BUBBLE
GEEZ, WILL YOU STOP WITH TH...
MUMBLE

SSHK
SSHK
SSHK
SSHK
I'M SURE WE BOTH PRAYED IN HARMONY.
PLEASE DEAR GOD, DON'T LET THEM FLY!!
MORE THAN WORDS ♪

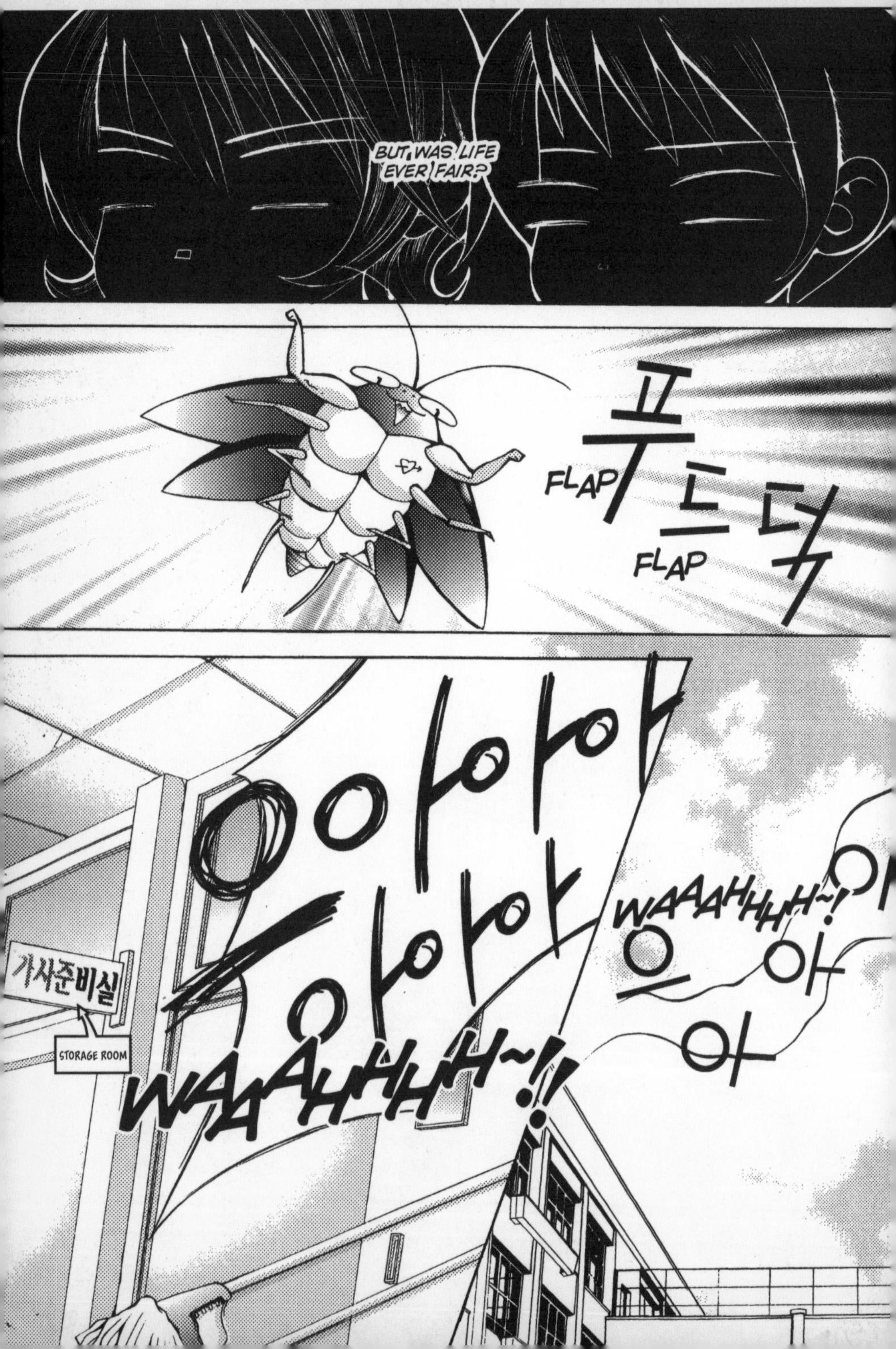
BUT, WAS LIFE EVER FAIR?
FLAP
푸드덕
FLAP
가사준비실
STORAGE ROOM
WAAAHHHH~!!
WAAAHHHH~!

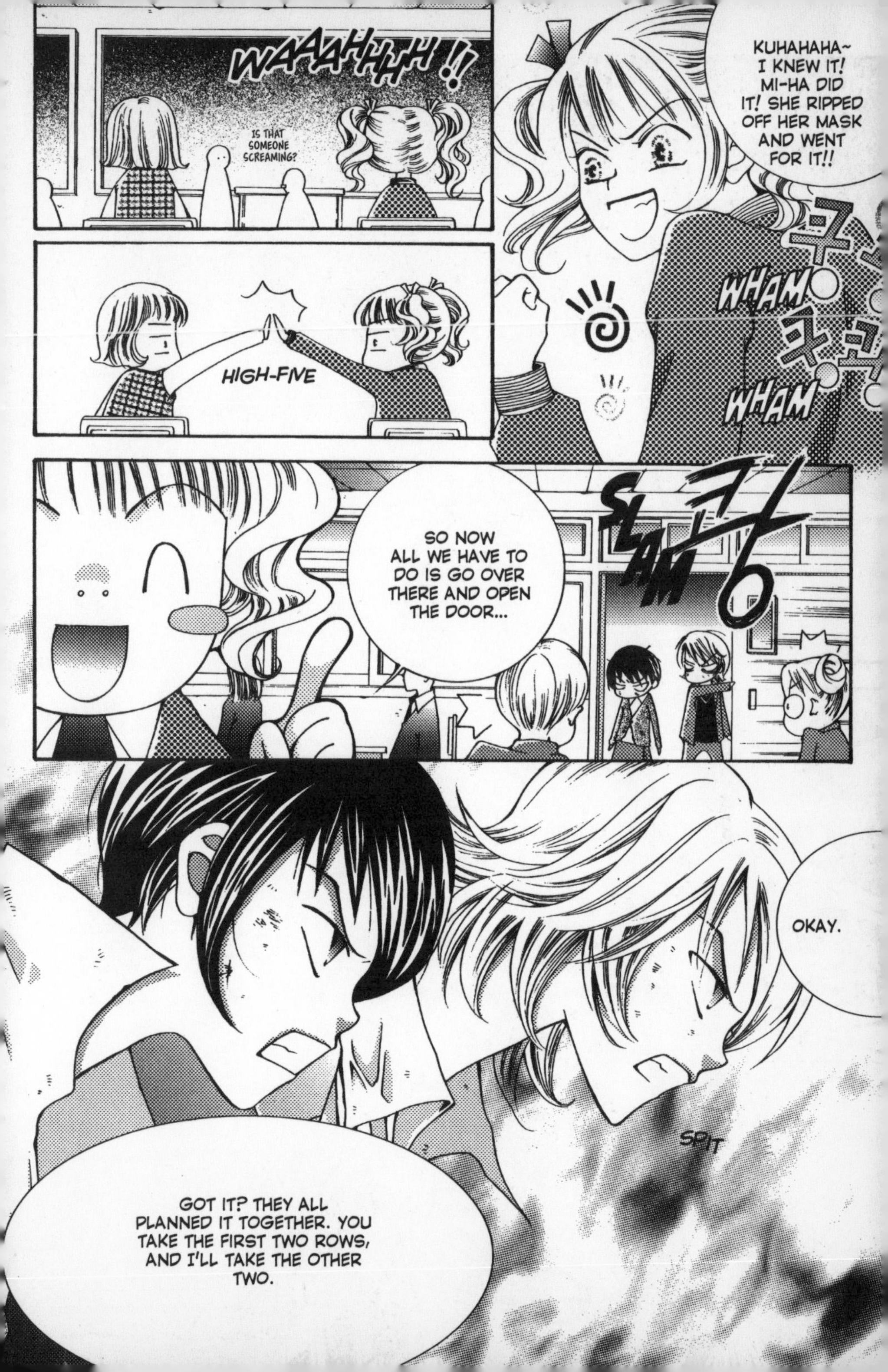
WAAAHHHH!!
IS THAT SOMEONE SCREAMING?
HIGH-FIVE
KUHAHAHA~ I KNEW IT! MI-HA DID IT! SHE RIPPED OFF HER MASK AND WENT FOR IT!!
WHAM
WHAM
SO NOW ALL WE HAVE TO DO IS GO OVER THERE AND OPEN THE DOOR...
SLAM
OKAY.
GOT IT? THEY ALL PLANNED IT TOGETHER. YOU TAKE THE FIRST TWO ROWS, AND I'LL TAKE THE OTHER TWO.
SPIT

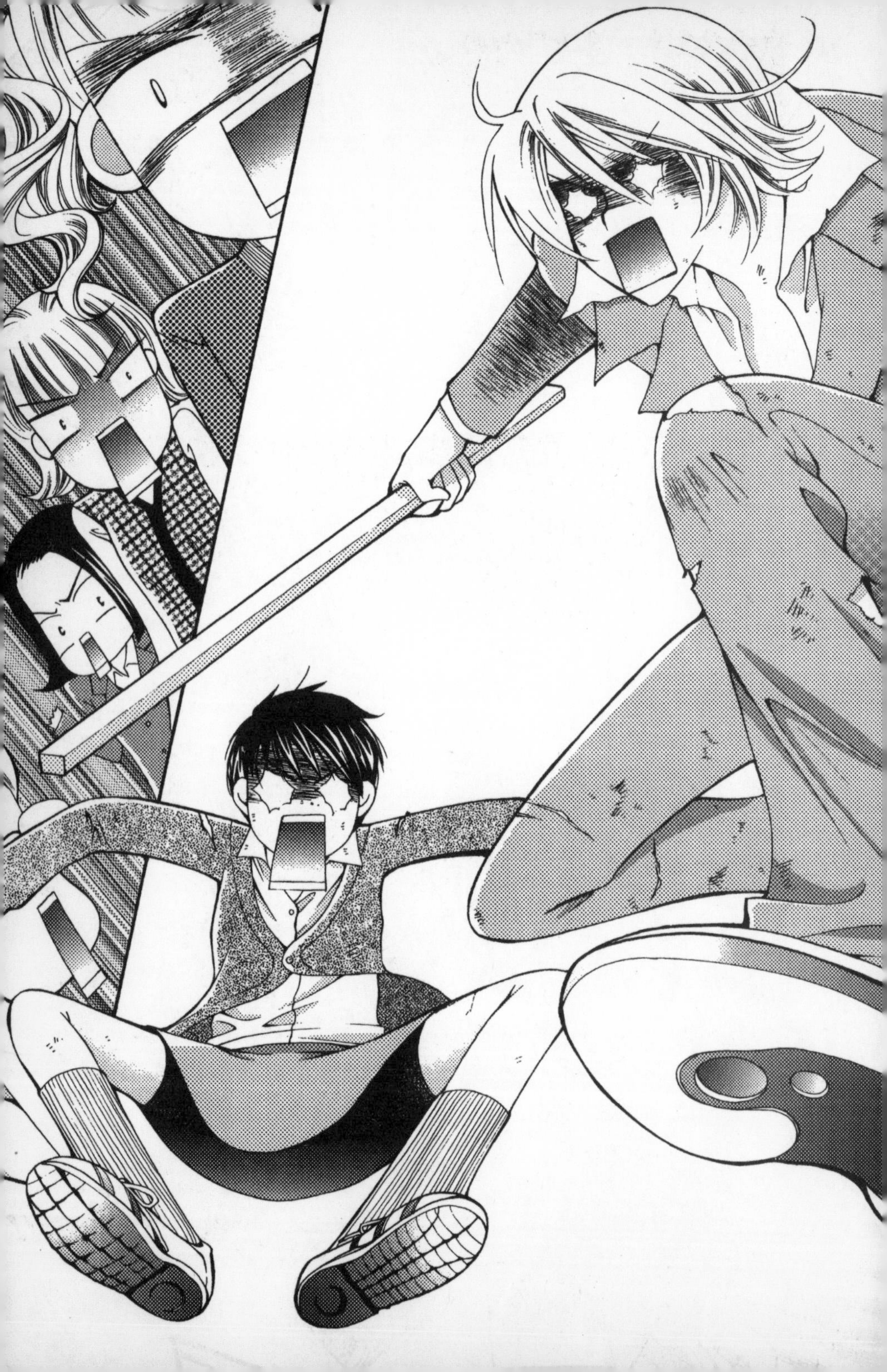

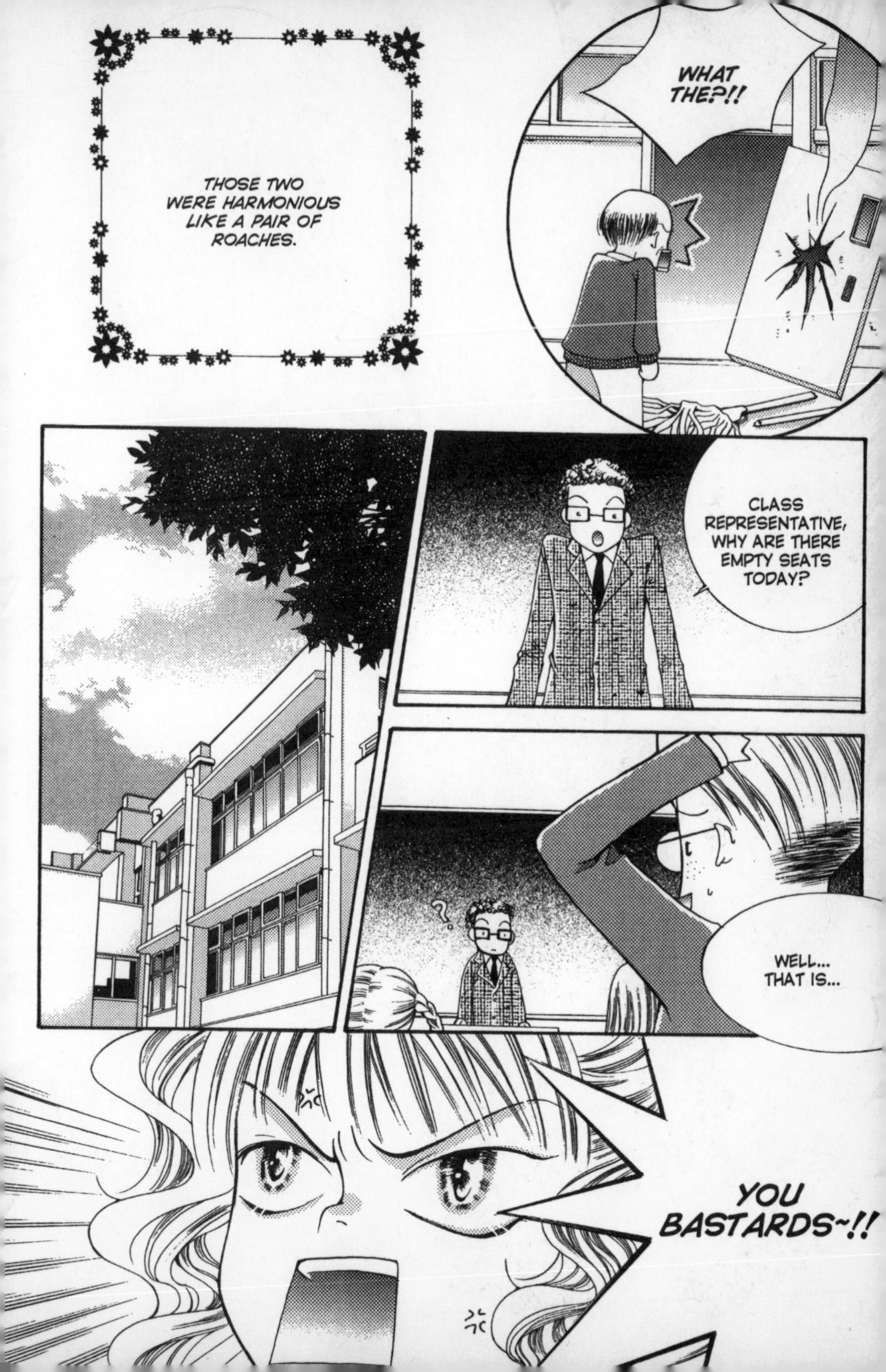
THOSE TWO WERE HARMONIOUS LIKE A PAIR OF ROACHES.
WHAT THE?!!
CLASS REPRESENTATIVE, WHY ARE THERE EMPTY SEATS TODAY?
WELL... THAT IS...
YOU BASTARDS~!!

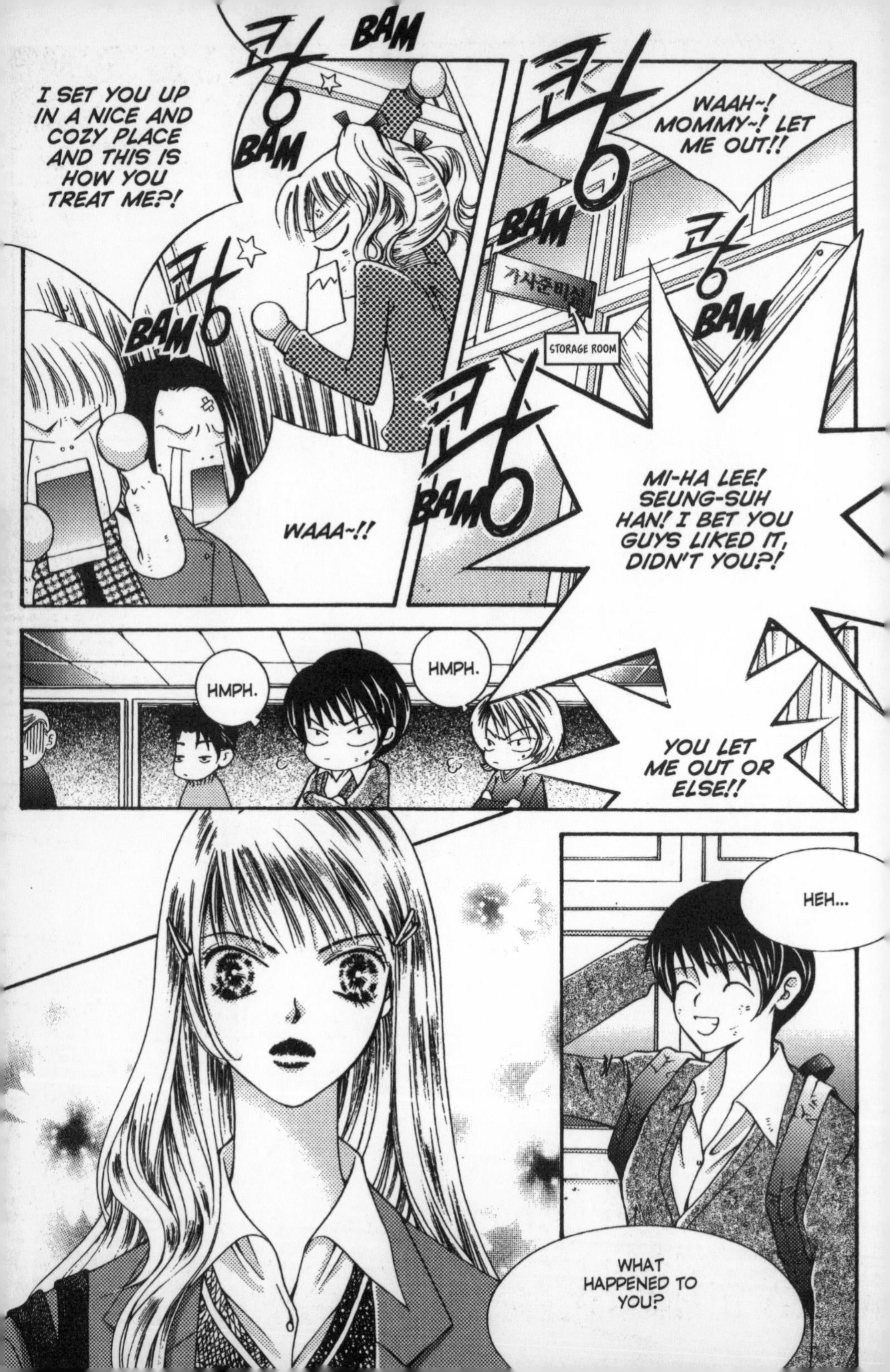

쾅
BAM
I SET YOU UP IN A NICE AND COZY PLACE AND THIS IS HOW YOU TREAT ME?!
쾅
BAM
쾅
BAM
쾅
BAM
WAAA~!!
쾅
BAM
WAAH~! MOMMY~! LET ME OUT!!
STORAGE ROOM
쾅
BAM
MI-HA LEE! SEUNG-SUH HAN! I BET YOU GUYS LIKED IT, DIDN'T YOU?!
YOU LET ME OUT OR ELSE!!
HMPH.
HMPH.
HEH...
WHAT HAPPENED TO YOU?

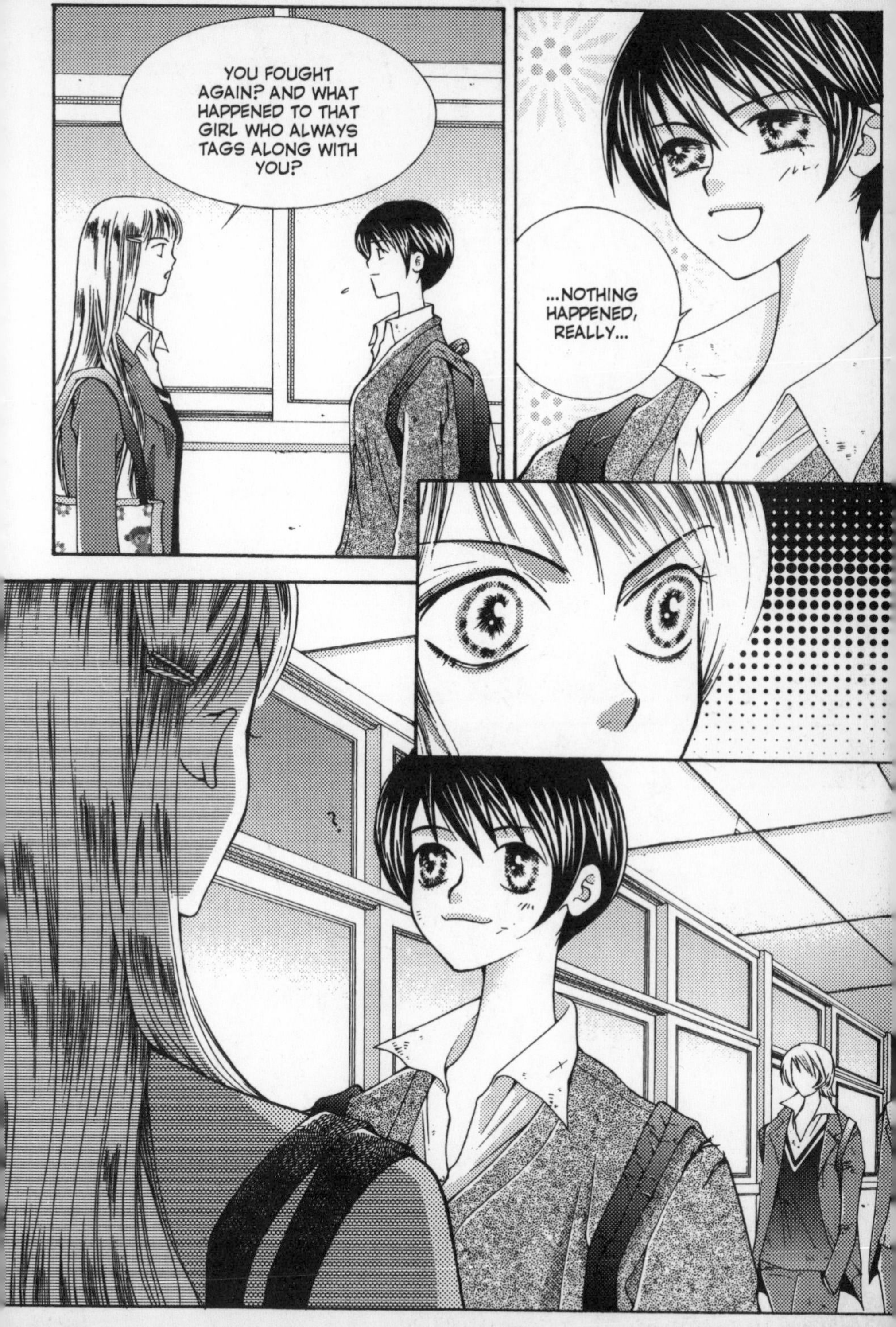
YOU FOUGHT AGAIN? AND WHAT HAPPENED TO THAT GIRL WHO ALWAYS TAGS ALONG WITH YOU?
...NOTHING HAPPENED, REALLY...

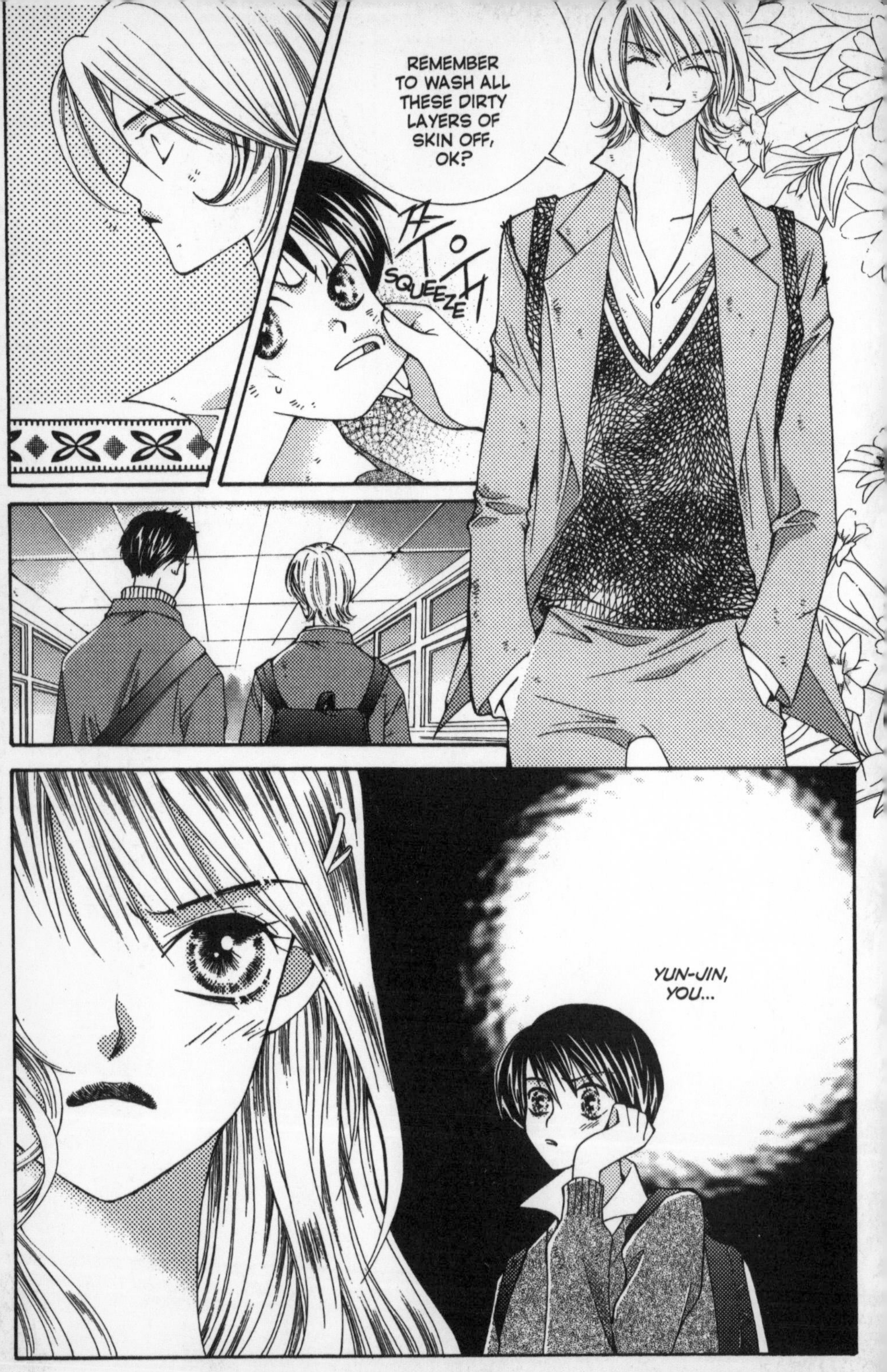
REMEMBER TO WASH ALL THESE DIRTY LAYERS OF SKIN OFF, OK?
SQUEEZE
YUN-JIN, YOU...

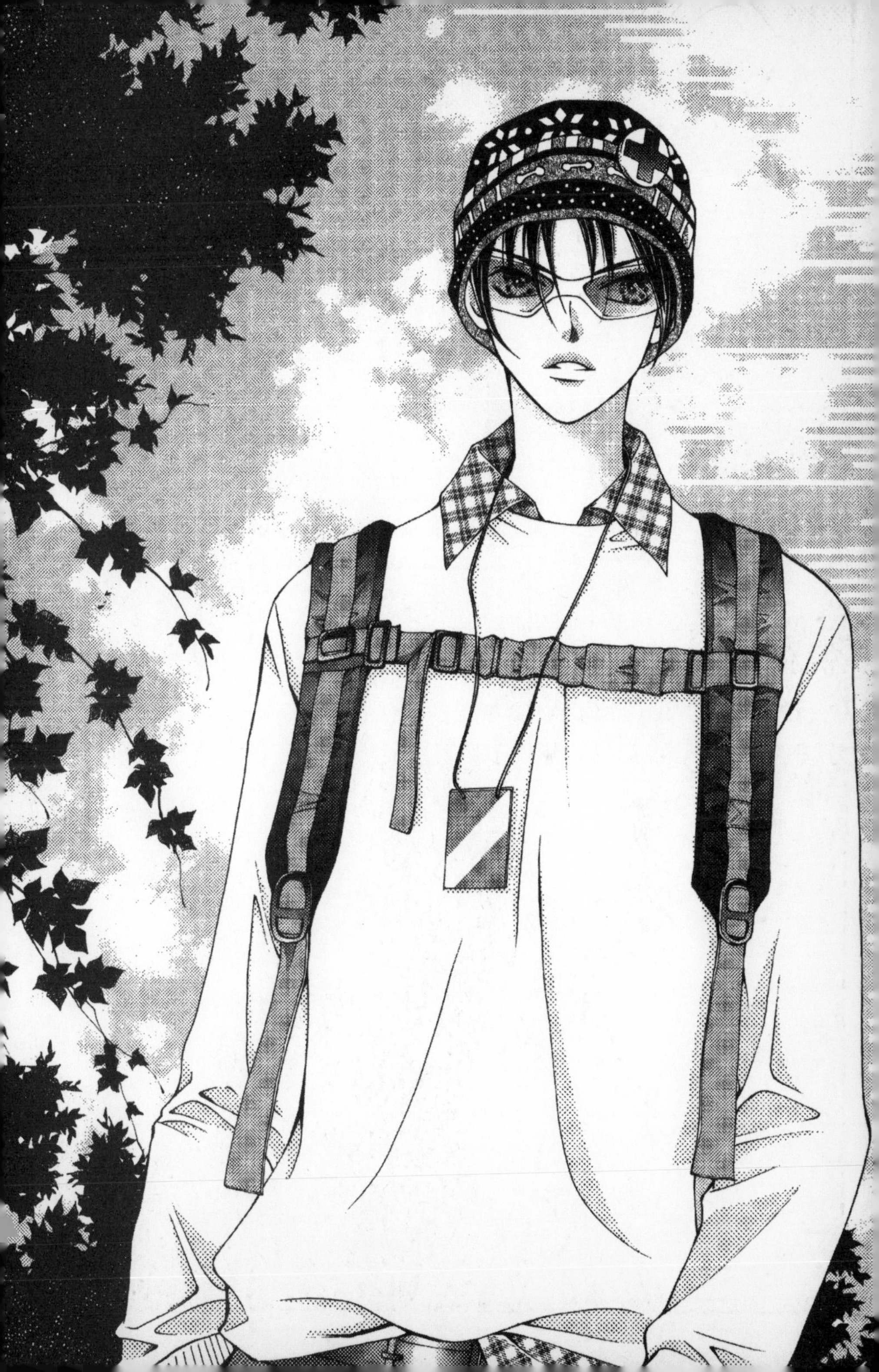

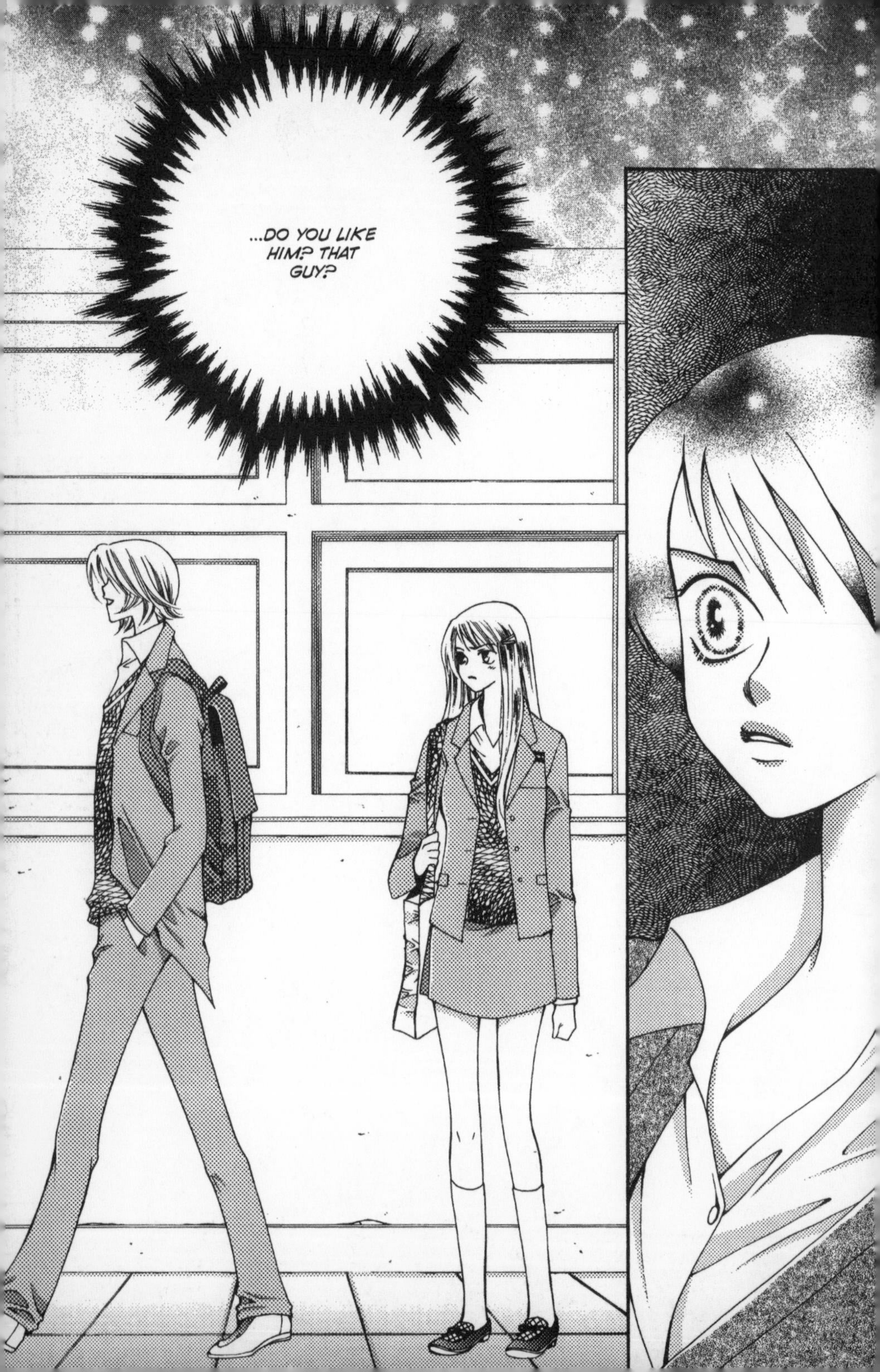
...DO YOU LIKE HIM? THAT GUY?

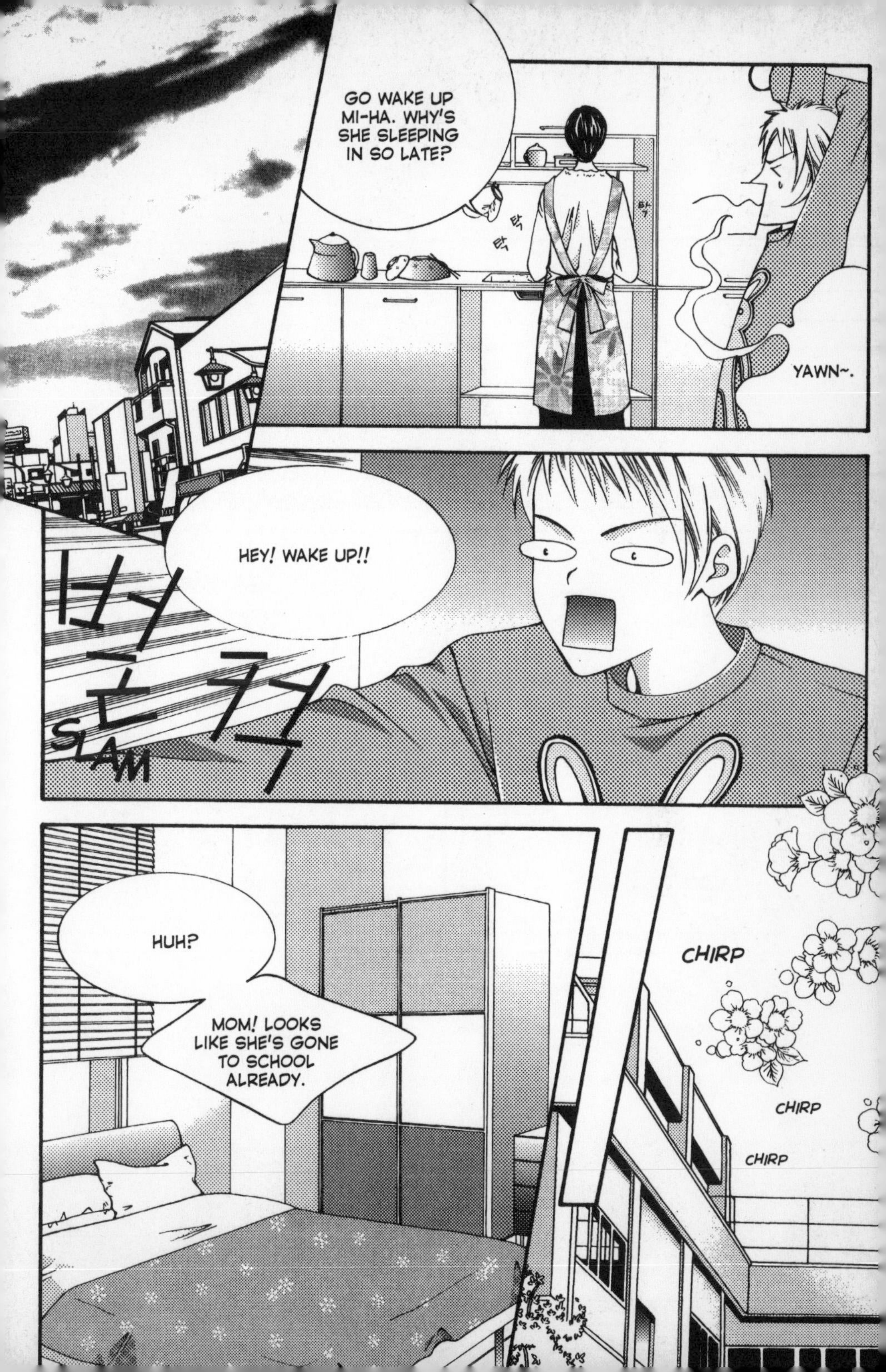
GO WAKE UP MI-HA. WHY'S SHE SLEEPING IN SO LATE?
YAWN~.
SLAM
HEY! WAKE UP!!
HUH?
MOM! LOOKS LIKE SHE'S GONE TO SCHOOL ALREADY.
CHIRP
CHIRP
CHIRP

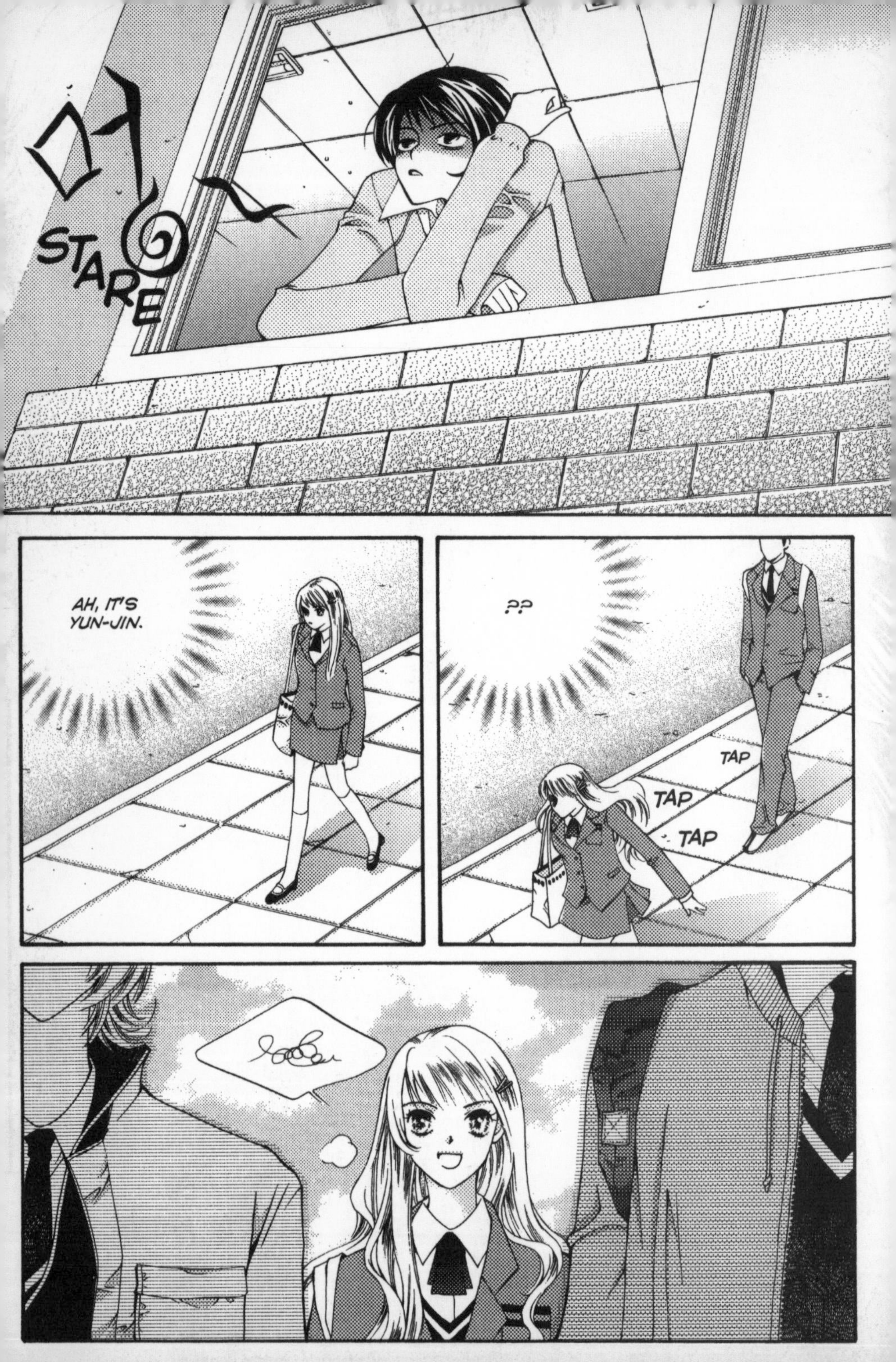
STARE
AH, IT'S YUN-JIN.
??
TAP
TAP
TAP

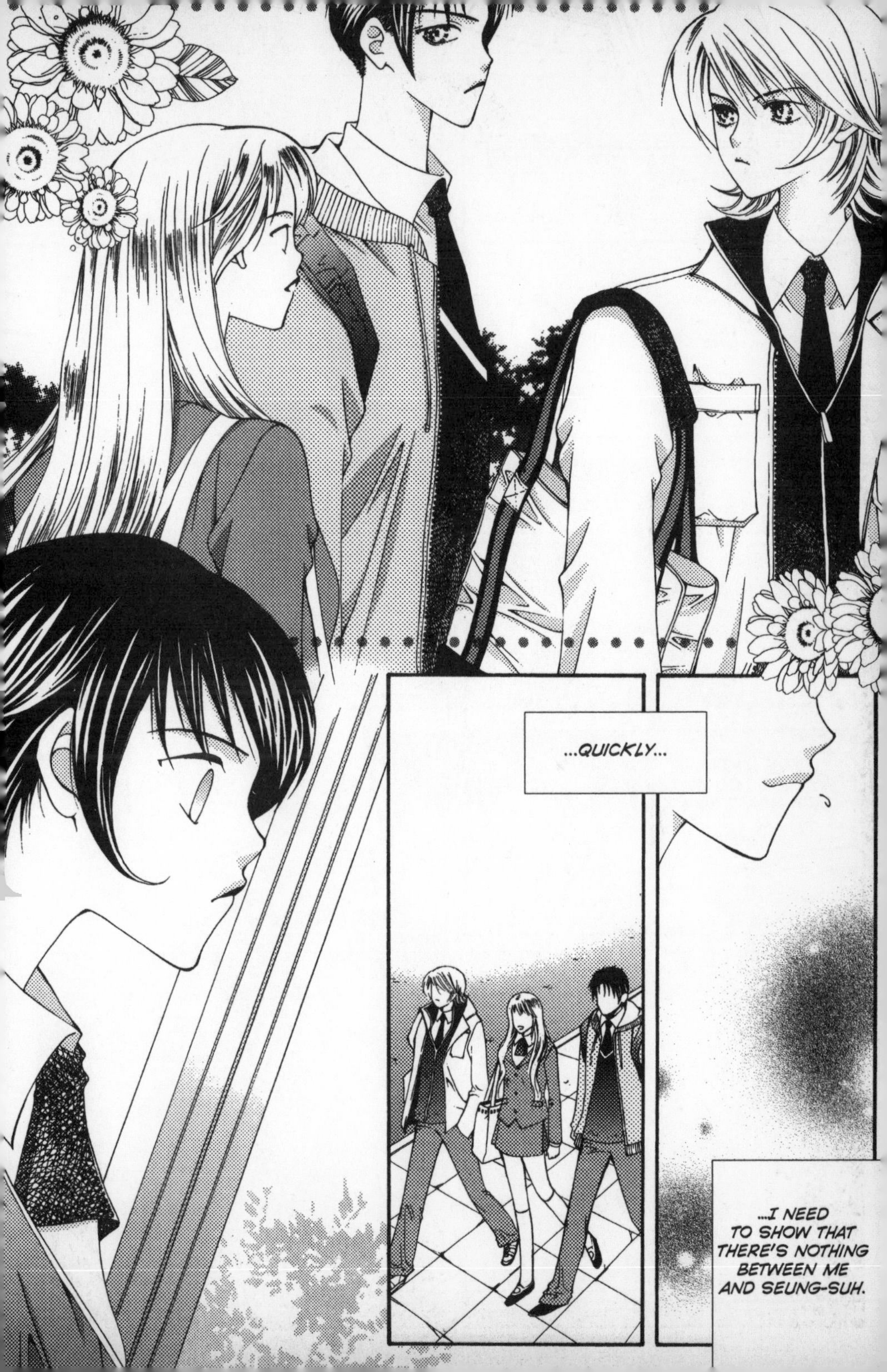
...QUICKLY...
...I NEED TO SHOW THAT THERE'S NOTHING BETWEEN ME AND SEUNG-SUH.

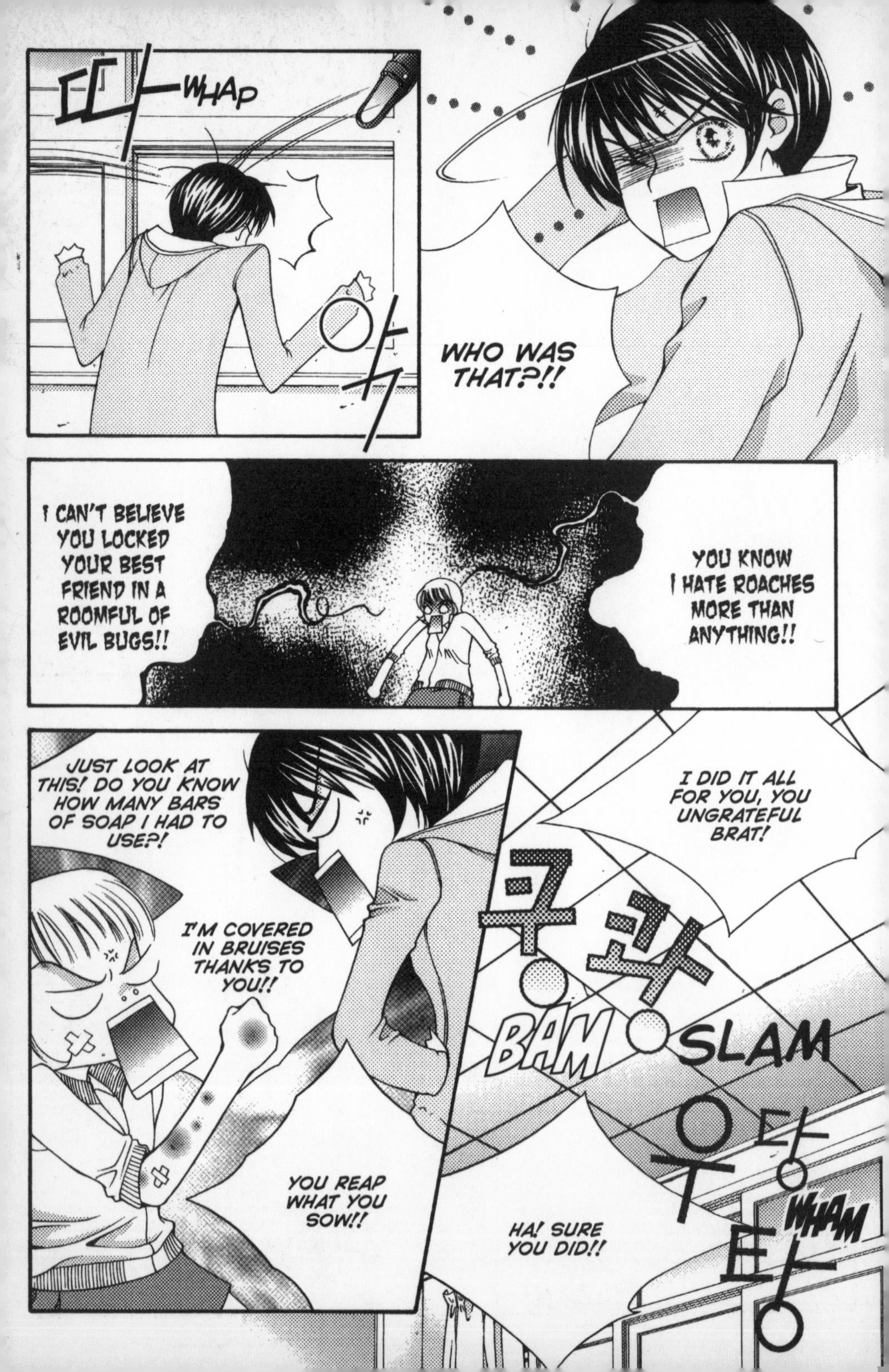
WHAP
WHO WAS THAT?!!
I CAN'T BELIEVE YOU LOCKED YOUR BEST FRIEND IN A ROOMFUL OF EVIL BUGS!!
YOU KNOW I HATE ROACHES MORE THAN ANYTHING!!
JUST LOOK AT THIS! DO YOU KNOW HOW MANY BARS OF SOAP I HAD TO USE?!
I'M COVERED IN BRUISES THANKS TO YOU!!
I DID IT ALL FOR YOU, YOU UNGRATEFUL BRAT!
BAM
SLAM
YOU REAP WHAT YOU SOW!!
HA! SURE YOU DID!!
WHAM

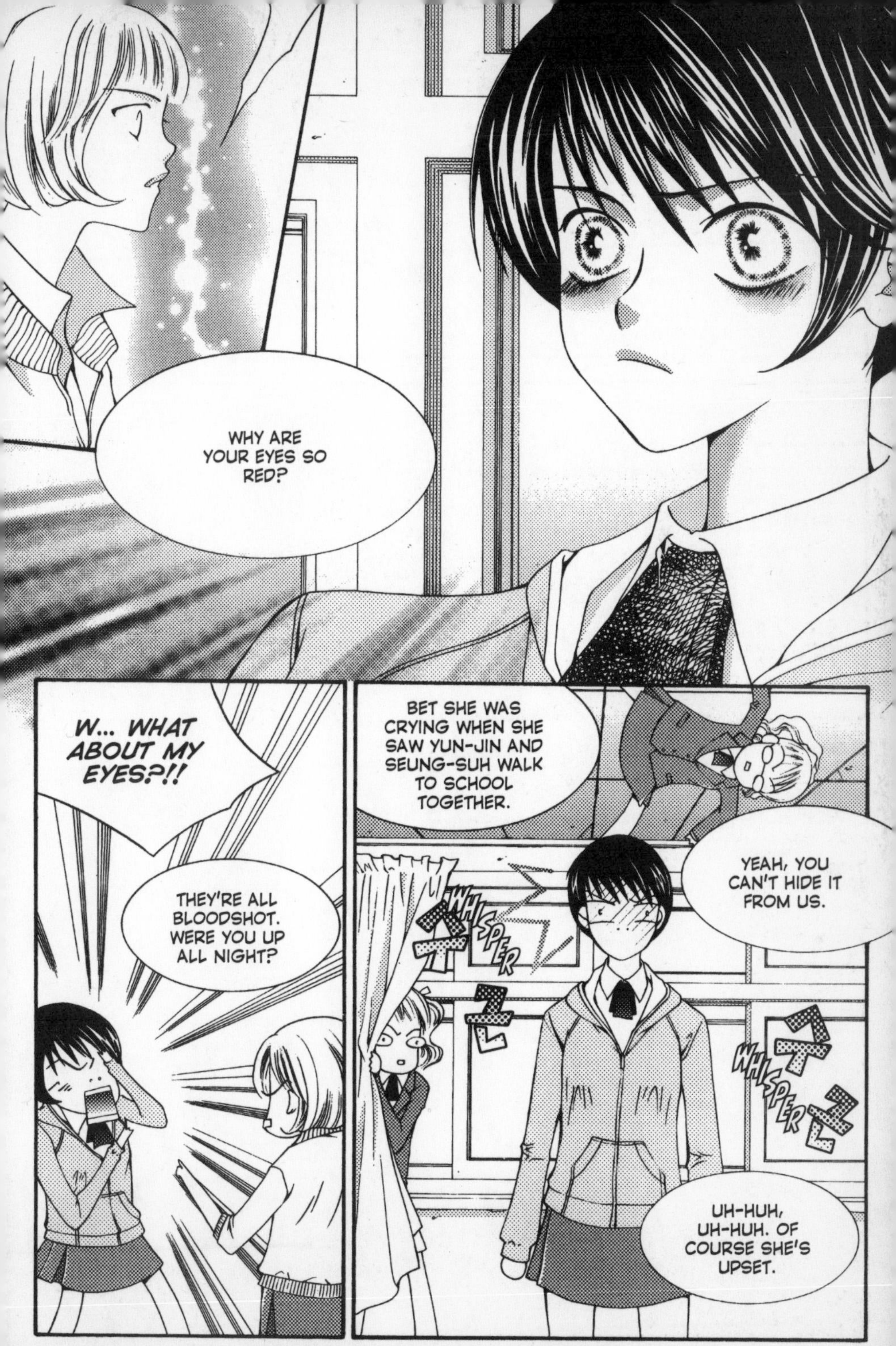
WHY ARE YOUR EYES SO RED?
W... WHAT ABOUT MY EYES?!!
THEY'RE ALL BLOODSHOT. WERE YOU UP ALL NIGHT?
BET SHE WAS CRYING WHEN SHE SAW YUN-JIN AND SEUNG-SUH WALK TO SCHOOL TOGETHER.
WHISPER
YEAH, YOU CAN'T HIDE IT FROM US.
WHISPER
UH-HUH, UH-HUH. OF COURSE SHE'S UPSET.

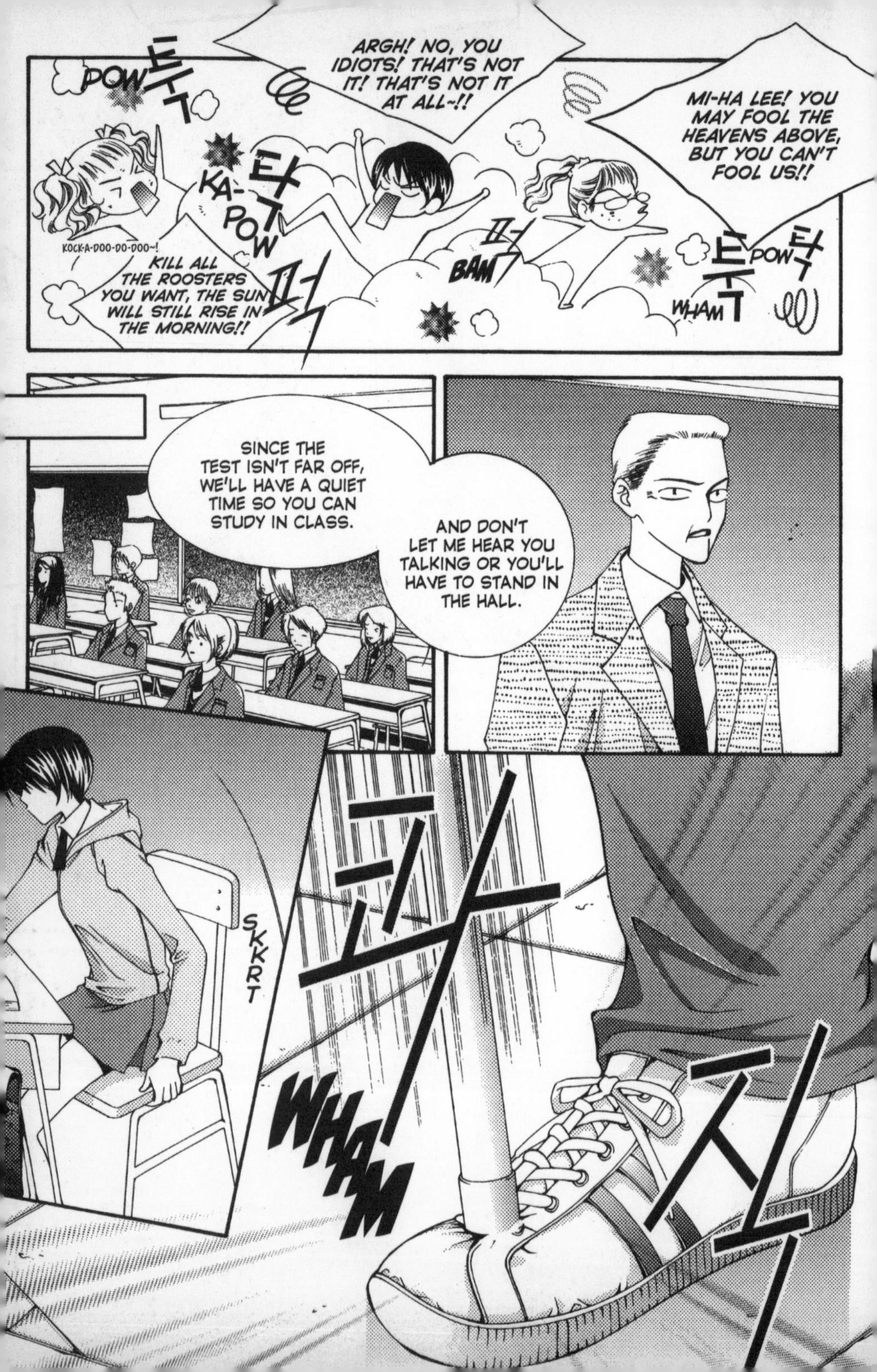
POW
ARGH! NO, YOU IDIOTS! THAT'S NOT IT! THAT'S NOT IT AT ALL~!!
MI-HA LEE! YOU MAY FOOL THE HEAVENS ABOVE, BUT YOU CAN'T FOOL US!!
KA-POW
KOCK-A-DOO-DO-DOO~!
KILL ALL THE ROOSTERS YOU WANT, THE SUN WILL STILL RISE IN THE MORNING!!
BAM
POW
WHAM
SINCE THE TEST ISN'T FAR OFF, WE'LL HAVE A QUIET TIME SO YOU CAN STUDY IN CLASS.
AND DON'T LET ME HEAR YOU TALKING OR YOU'LL HAVE TO STAND IN THE HALL.
SKKRT
WHAM

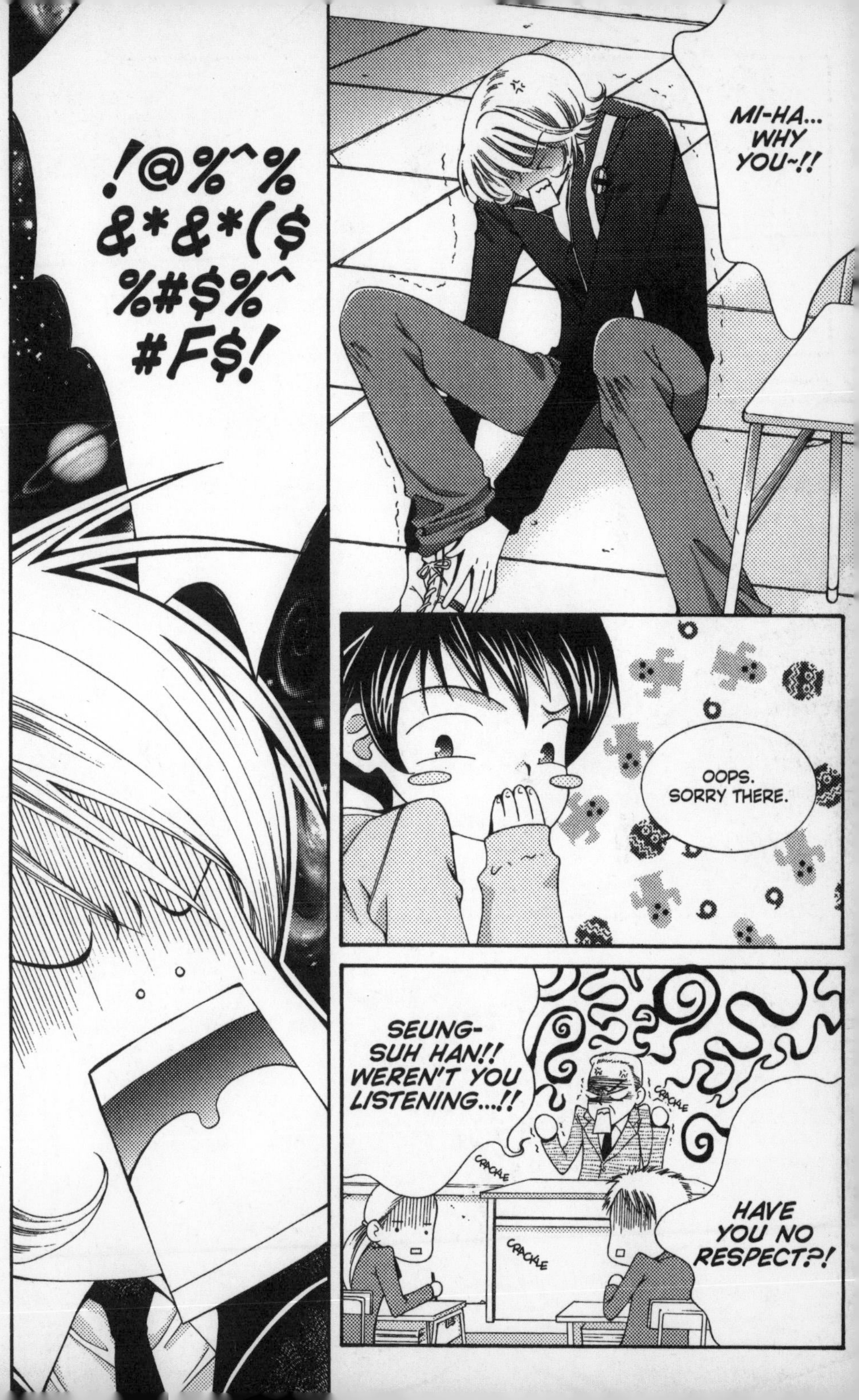
!@%^%
&*&*($
%#$%^
#F$!
MI-HA... WHY YOU~!!
OOPS. SORRY THERE.
SEUNG-SUH HAN!! WEREN'T YOU LISTENING...!!
CRACKLE
CRACKLE
CRACKLE
HAVE YOU NO RESPECT?!

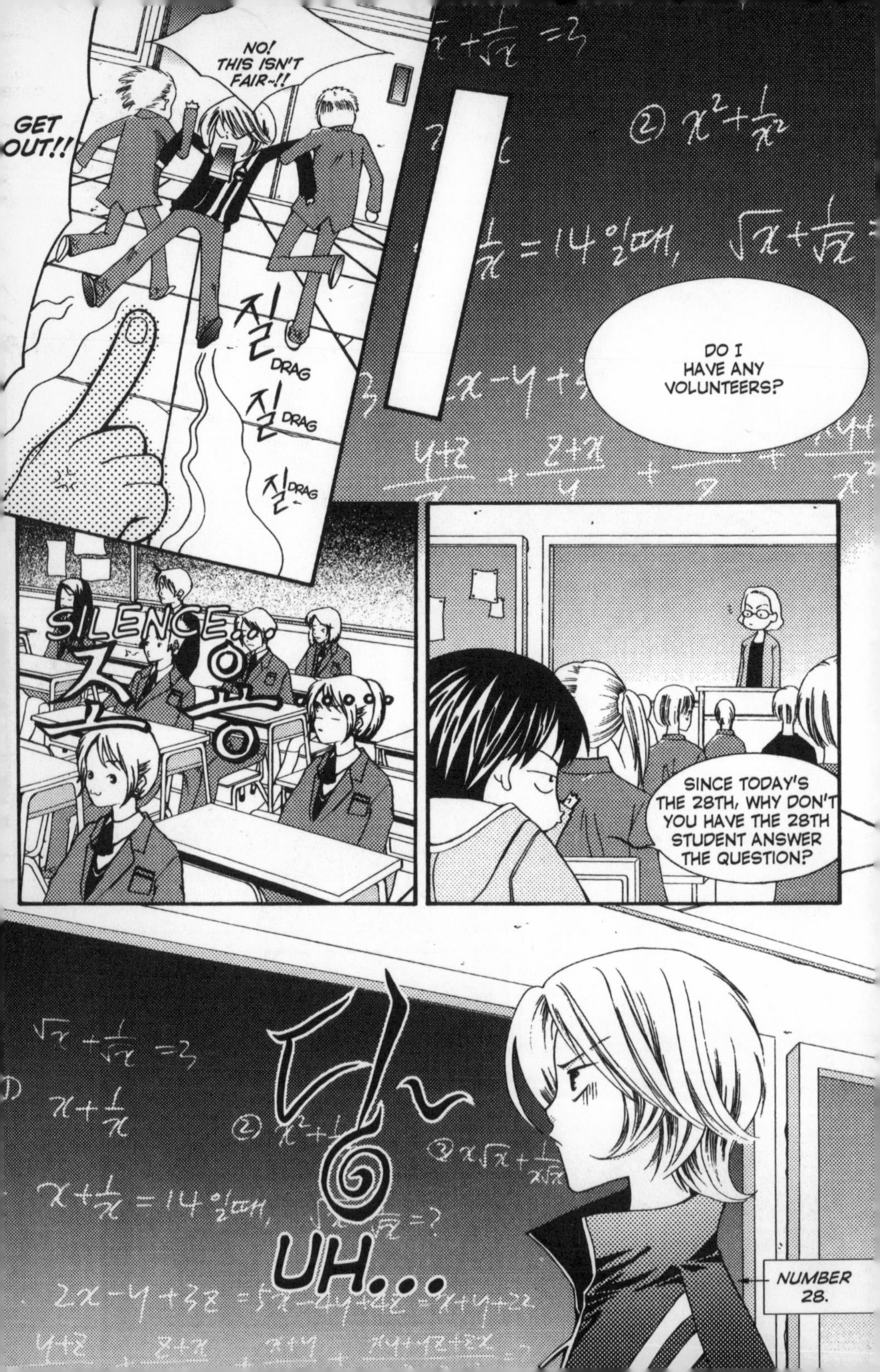
GET OUT!!
NO! THIS ISN'T FAIR~!!
질 DRAG
질 DRAG
질 DRAG~
DO I HAVE ANY VOLUNTEERS?
SILENCE...
조용
SINCE TODAY'S THE 28TH, WHY DON'T YOU HAVE THE 28TH STUDENT ANSWER THE QUESTION?
UH...
NUMBER 28.

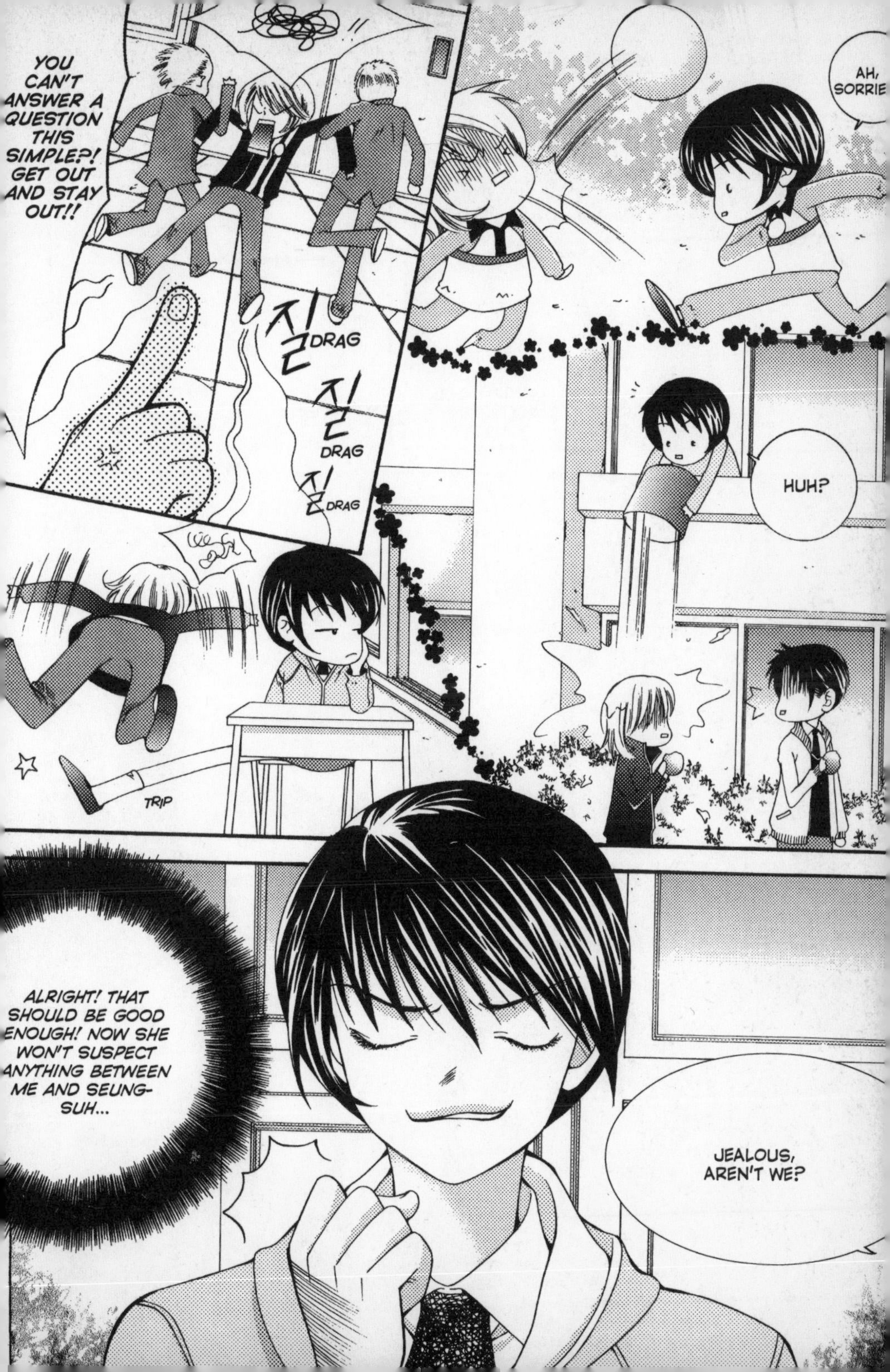
YOU CAN'T ANSWER A QUESTION THIS SIMPLE?! GET OUT AND STAY OUT!!
질 DRAG
질 DRAG
질 DRAG
AH, SORRIE
TRIP
HUH?
ALRIGHT! THAT SHOULD BE GOOD ENOUGH! NOW SHE WON'T SUSPECT ANYTHING BETWEEN ME AND SEUNG-SUH...
JEALOUS, AREN'T WE?

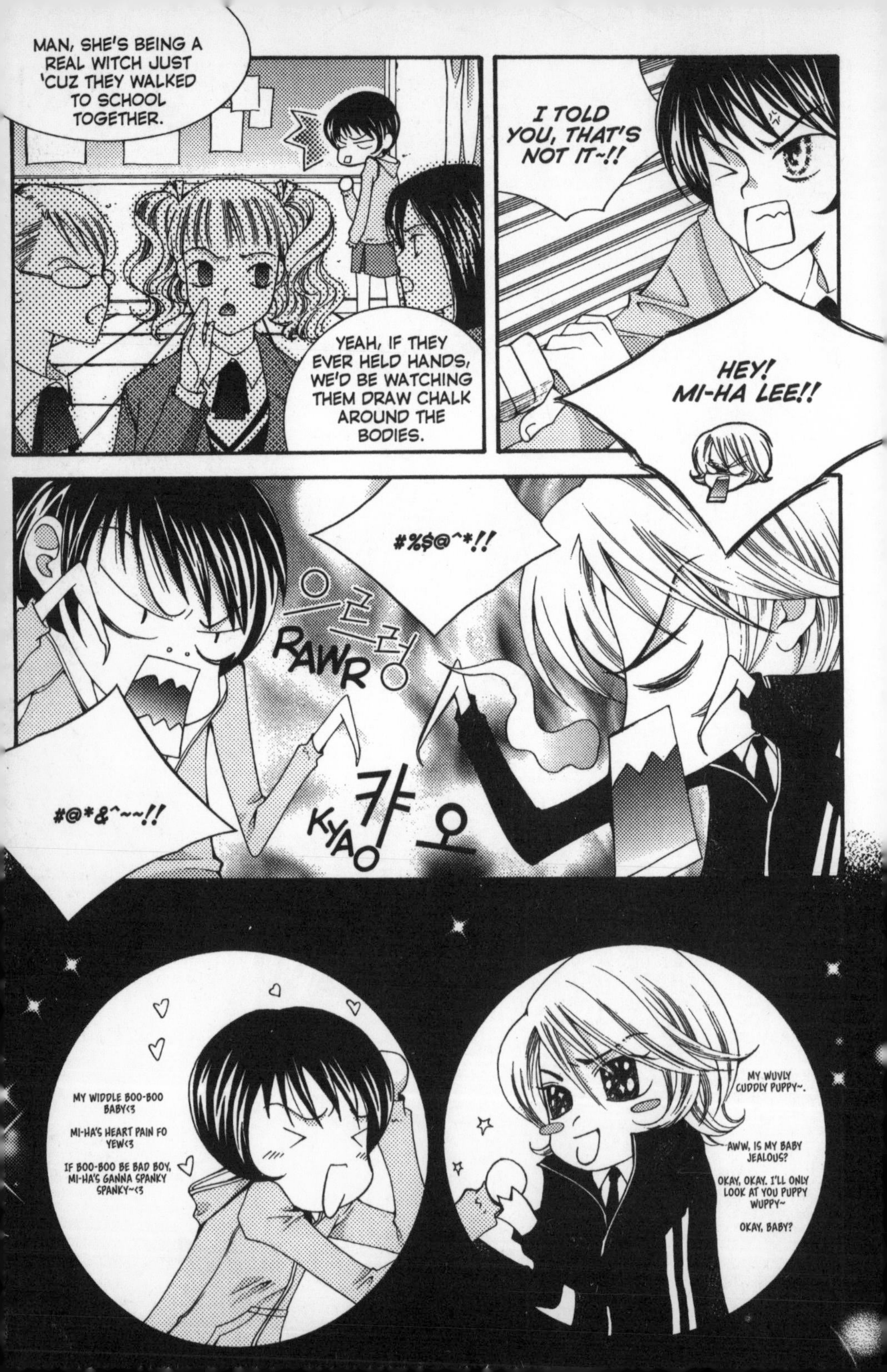
MAN, SHE'S BEING A REAL WITCH JUST 'CUZ THEY WALKED TO SCHOOL TOGETHER.
YEAH, IF THEY EVER HELD HANDS, WE'D BE WATCHING THEM DRAW CHALK AROUND THE BODIES.
I TOLD YOU, THAT'S NOT IT~!!
HEY! MI-HA LEE!!
#%$@^*!!
으르렁
RAWR
#@*&^~~!!
캬오
KYAO
MY WIDDLE BOO-BOO BABY<3
MI-HA'S HEART PAIN FO YEW<3
IF BOO-BOO BE BAD BOY, MI-HA'S GANNA SPANKY SPANKY~<3
MY WUVLY CUDDLY PUPPY~.
AWW, IS MY BABY JEALOUS?
OKAY, OKAY. I'LL ONLY LOOK AT YOU PUPPY WUPPY~
OKAY, BABY?

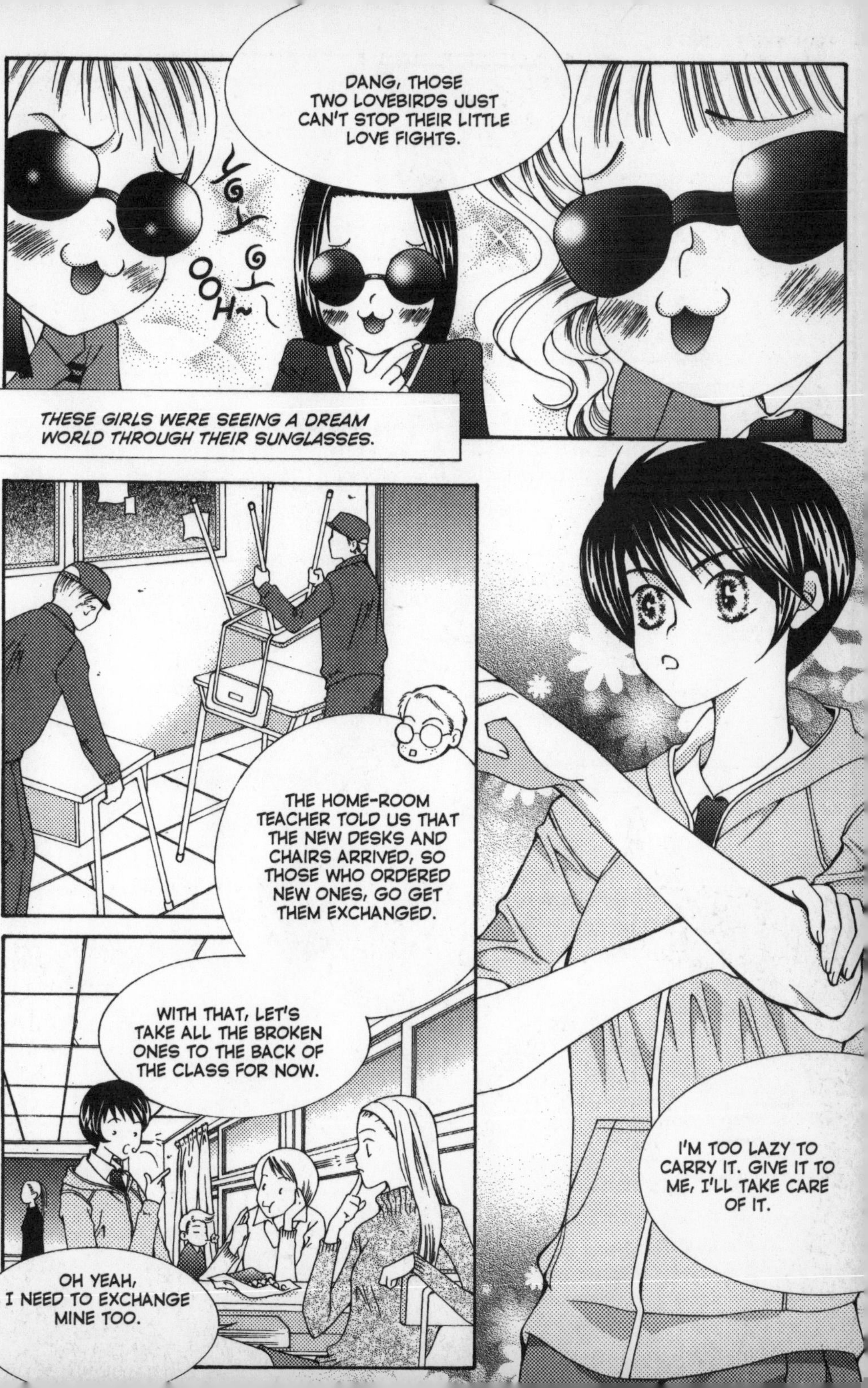
DANG, THOSE TWO LOVEBIRDS JUST CAN'T STOP THEIR LITTLE LOVE FIGHTS.
OOH~
THESE GIRLS WERE SEEING A DREAM WORLD THROUGH THEIR SUNGLASSES.
THE HOME-ROOM TEACHER TOLD US THAT THE NEW DESKS AND CHAIRS ARRIVED, SO THOSE WHO ORDERED NEW ONES, GO GET THEM EXCHANGED.
WITH THAT, LET'S TAKE ALL THE BROKEN ONES TO THE BACK OF THE CLASS FOR NOW.
OH YEAH, I NEED TO EXCHANGE MINE TOO.
I'M TOO LAZY TO CARRY IT. GIVE IT TO ME, I'LL TAKE CARE OF IT.

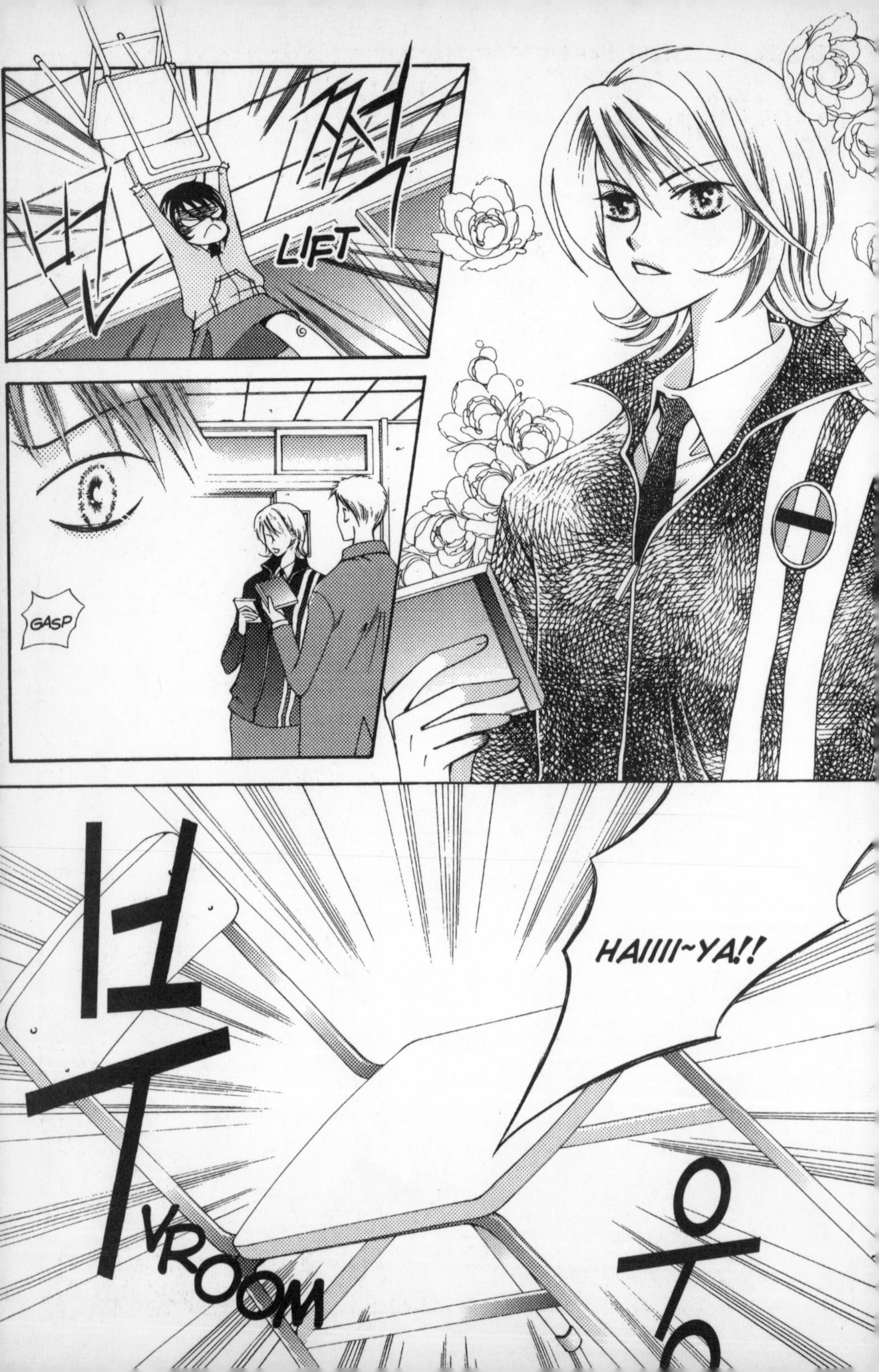
LIFT
GASP
HAIIII~YA!!
VROOM

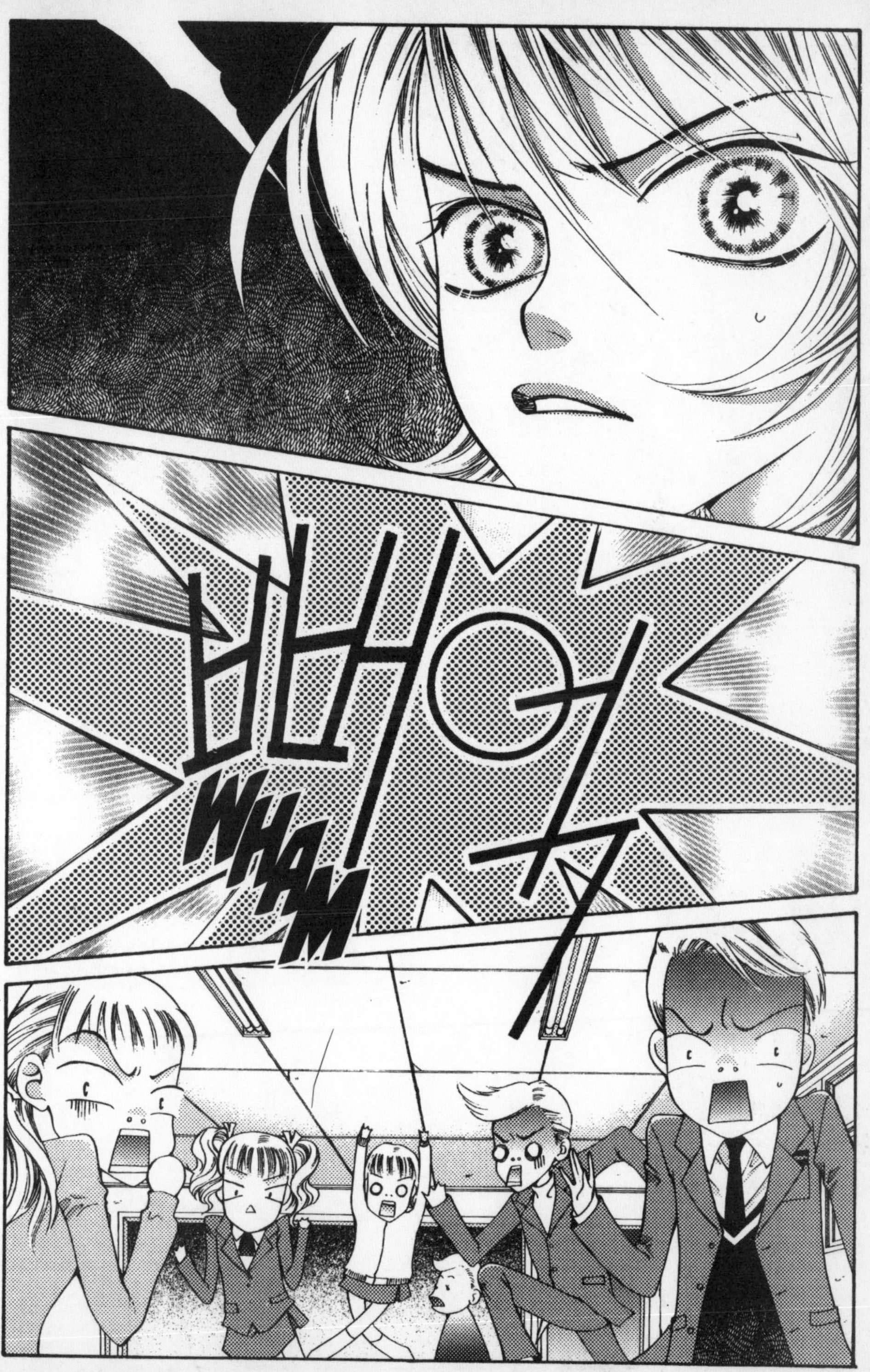
WHAM

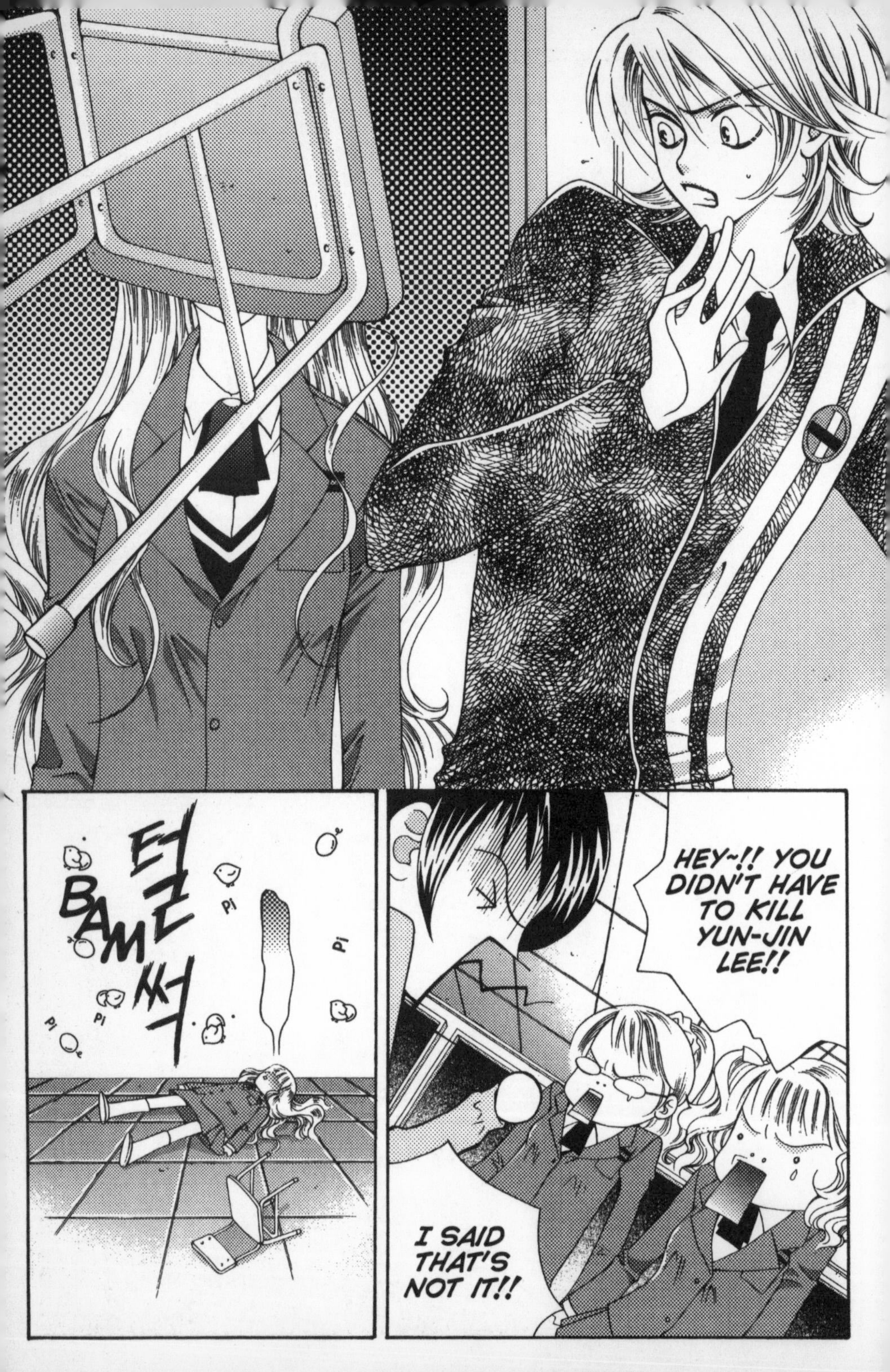
털썩
BAM
Pi
HEY~!! YOU DIDN'T HAVE TO KILL YUN-JIN LEE!!
I SAID THAT'S NOT IT!!

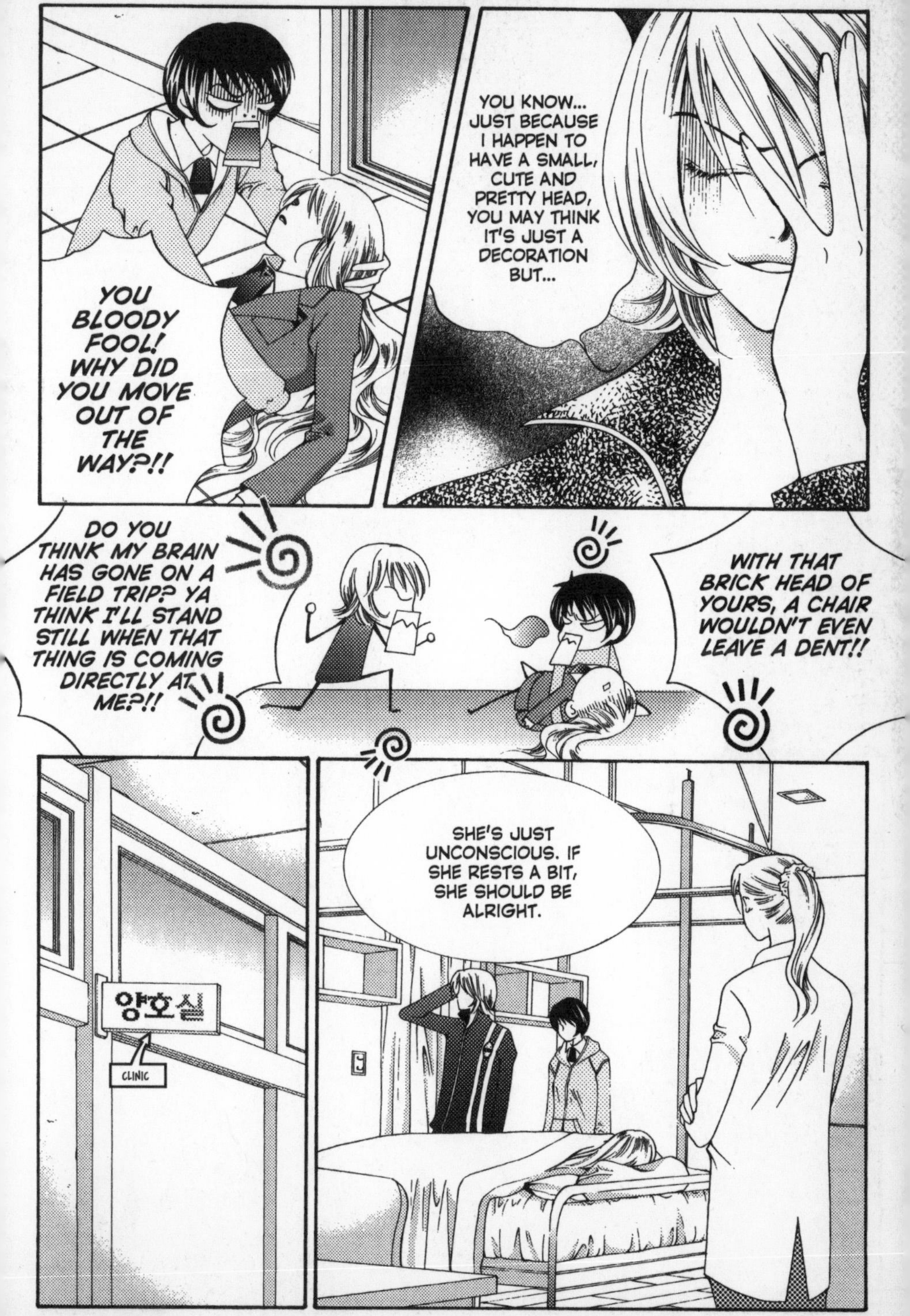

YOU BLOODY FOOL! WHY DID YOU MOVE OUT OF THE WAY?!!
YOU KNOW... JUST BECAUSE I HAPPEN TO HAVE A SMALL, CUTE AND PRETTY HEAD, YOU MAY THINK IT'S JUST A DECORATION BUT...
DO YOU THINK MY BRAIN HAS GONE ON A FIELD TRIP? YA THINK I'LL STAND STILL WHEN THAT THING IS COMING DIRECTLY AT ME?!!
WITH THAT BRICK HEAD OF YOURS, A CHAIR WOULDN'T EVEN LEAVE A DENT!!
양호실
CLINIC
SHE'S JUST UNCONSCIOUS. IF SHE RESTS A BIT, SHE SHOULD BE ALRIGHT.

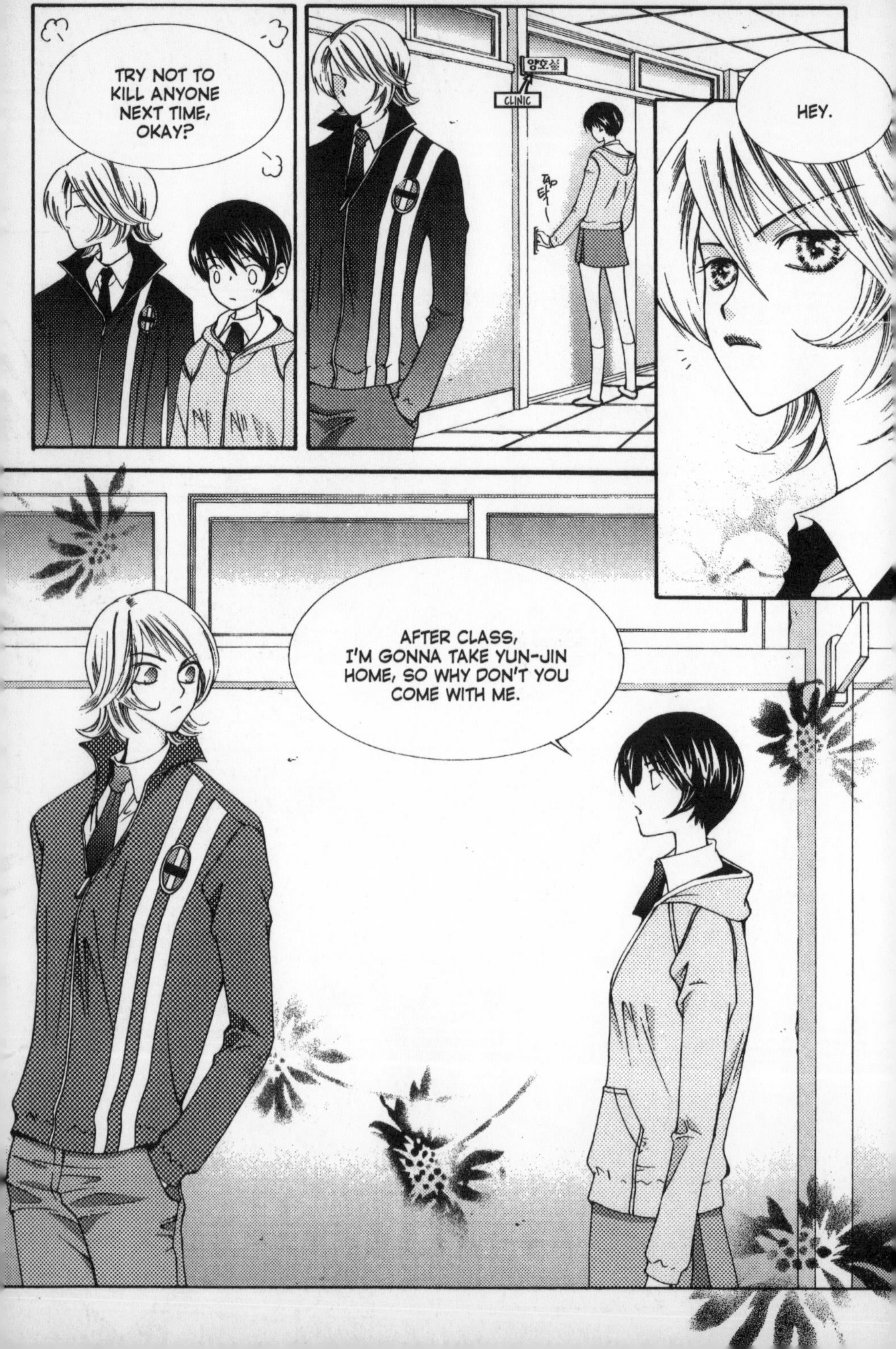
TRY NOT TO KILL ANYONE NEXT TIME, OKAY?
양호실
CLINIC
TAP
탁
HEY.
AFTER CLASS, I'M GONNA TAKE YUN-JIN HOME, SO WHY DON'T YOU COME WITH ME.

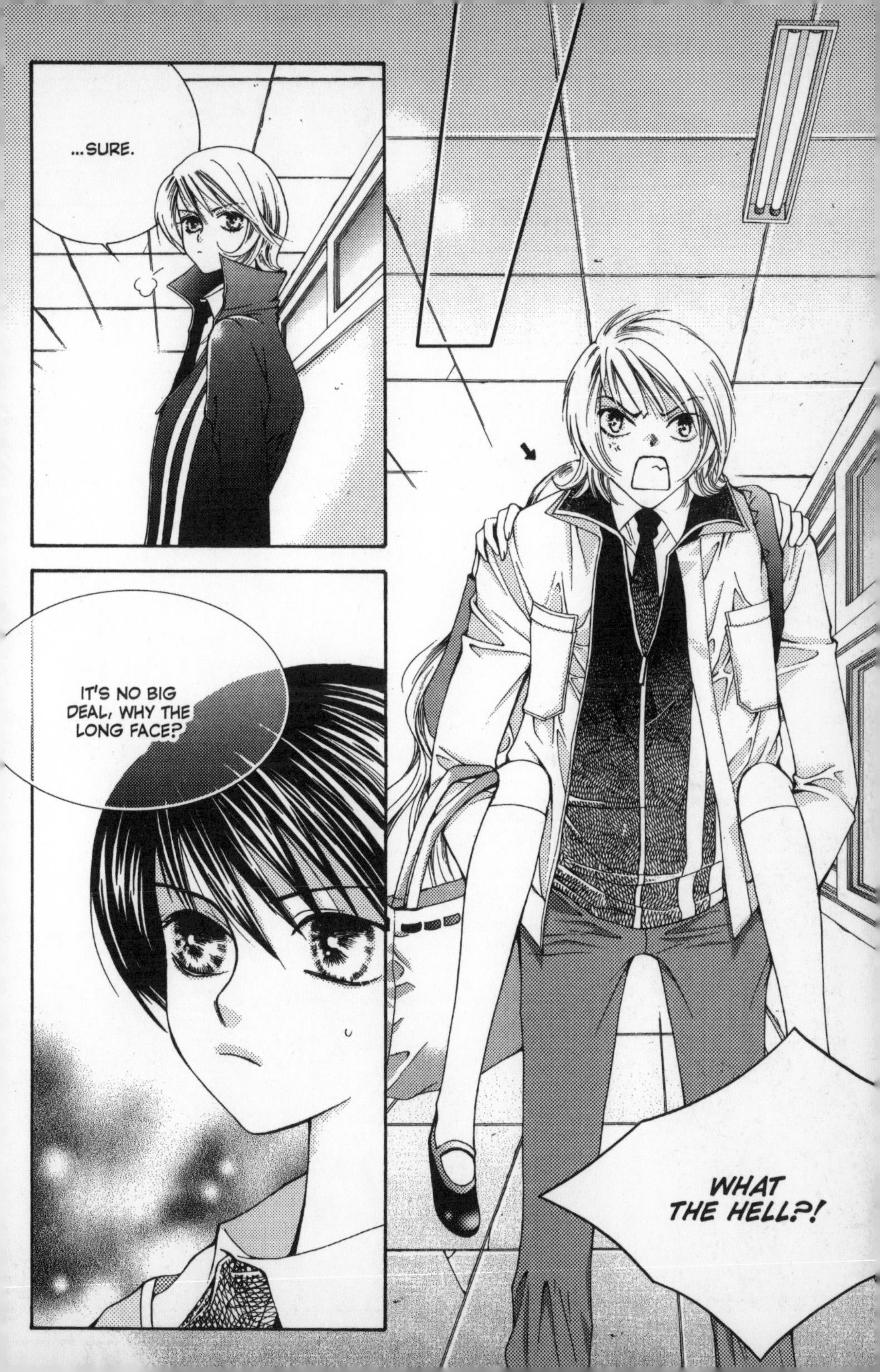
...SURE.
IT'S NO BIG DEAL, WHY THE LONG FACE?
WHAT THE HELL?!

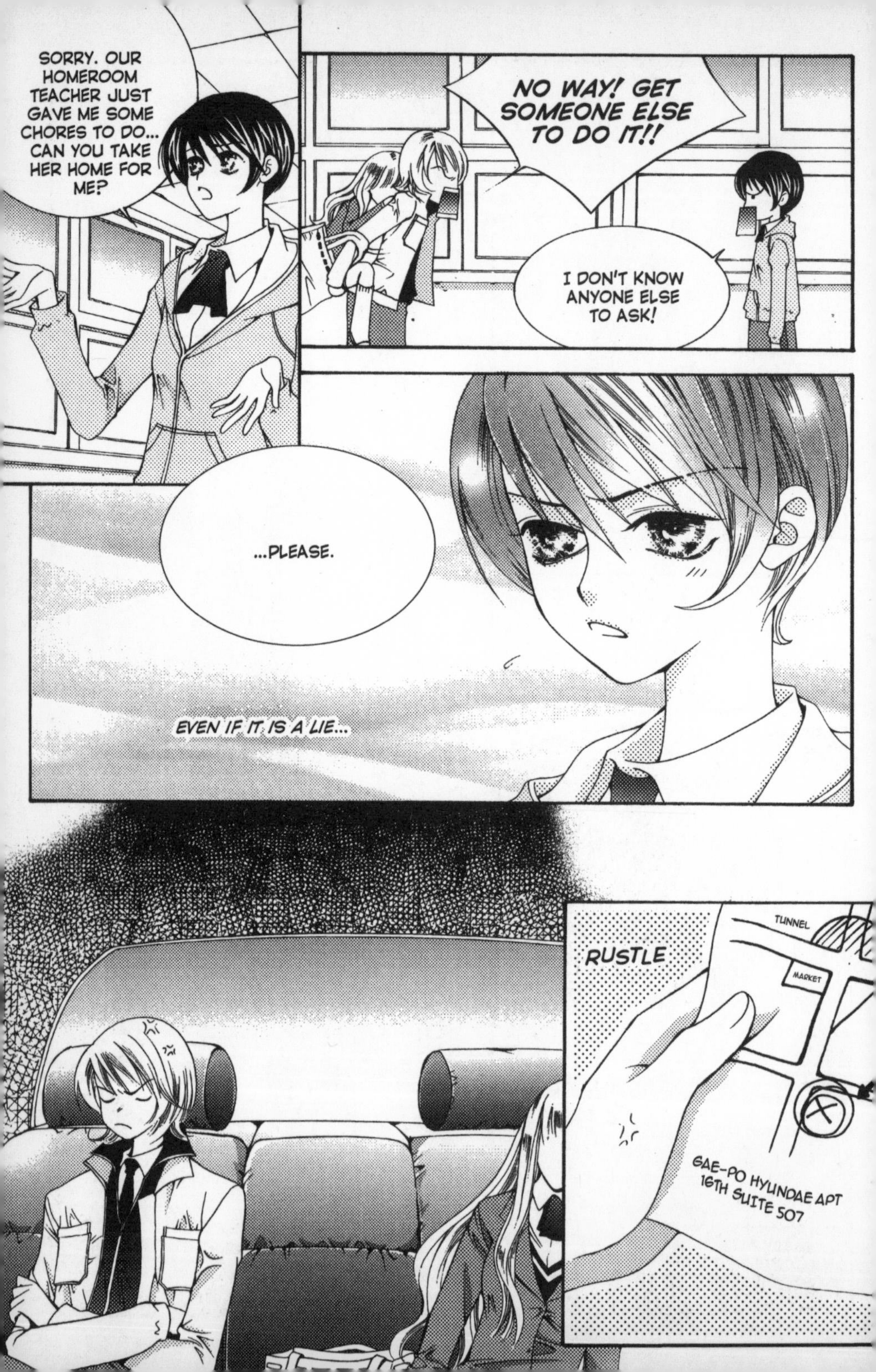
SORRY. OUR HOMEROOM TEACHER JUST GAVE ME SOME CHORES TO DO... CAN YOU TAKE HER HOME FOR ME?
NO WAY! GET SOMEONE ELSE TO DO IT!!
I DON'T KNOW ANYONE ELSE TO ASK!
...PLEASE.
EVEN IF IT IS A LIE...
RUSTLE
TUNNEL
MARKET
GAE-PO HYUNDAE APT 16TH SUITE 507

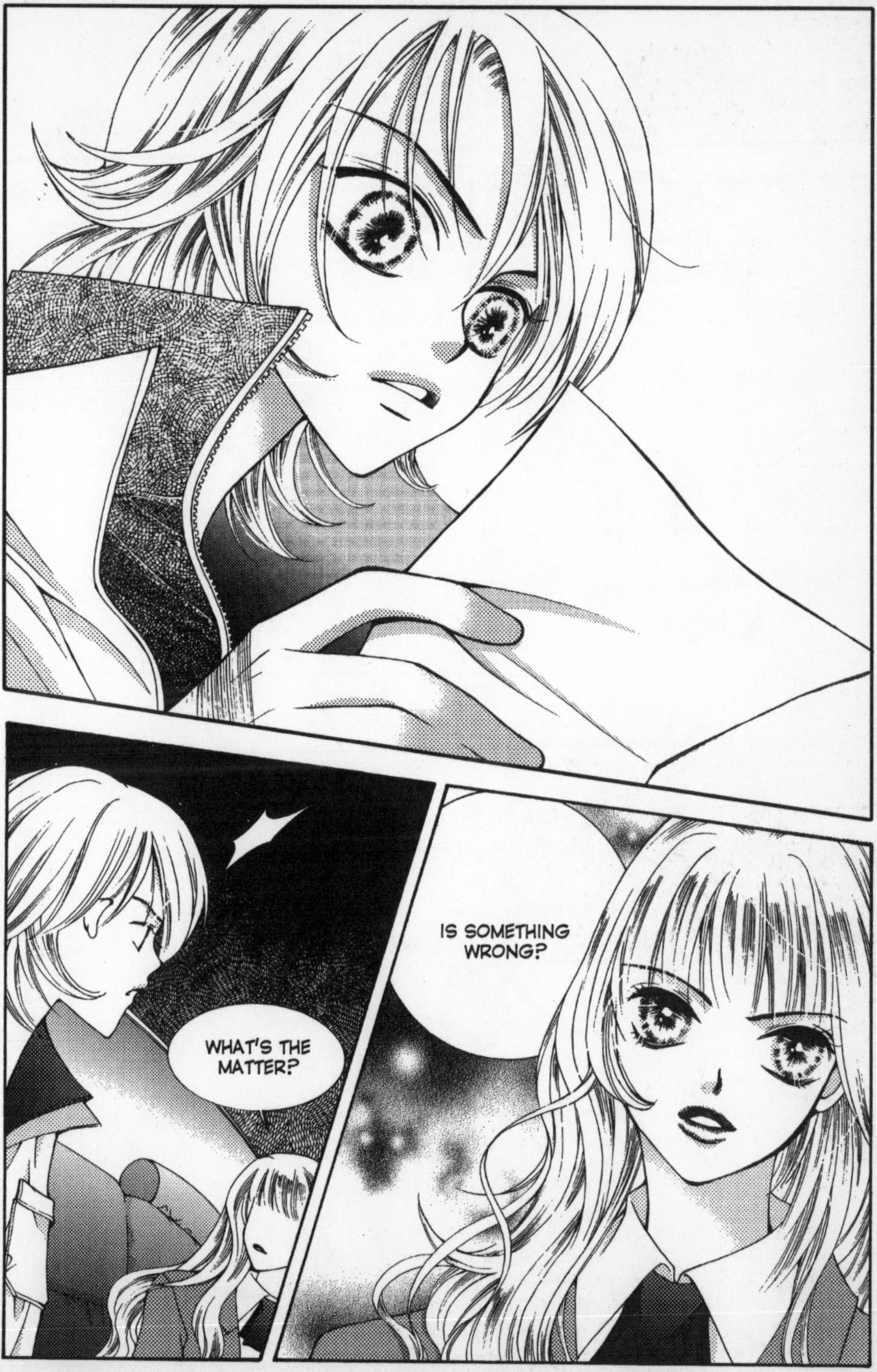
WHAT'S THE MATTER?
IS SOMETHING WRONG?

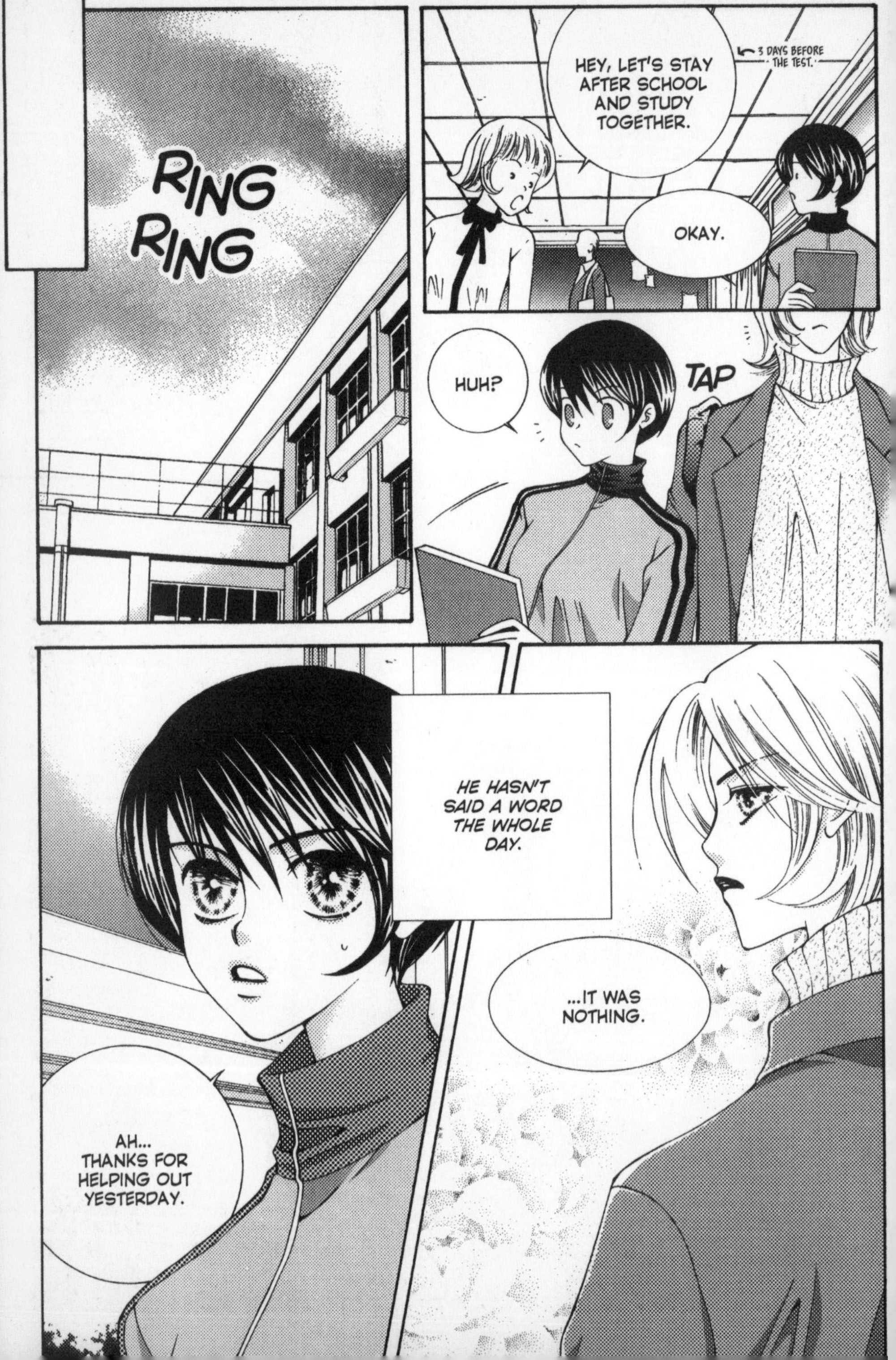
RING RING
3 DAYS BEFORE THE TEST.
HEY, LET'S STAY AFTER SCHOOL AND STUDY TOGETHER.
OKAY.
HUH?
TAP
HE HASN'T SAID A WORD THE WHOLE DAY.
AH... THANKS FOR HELPING OUT YESTERDAY.
...IT WAS NOTHING.

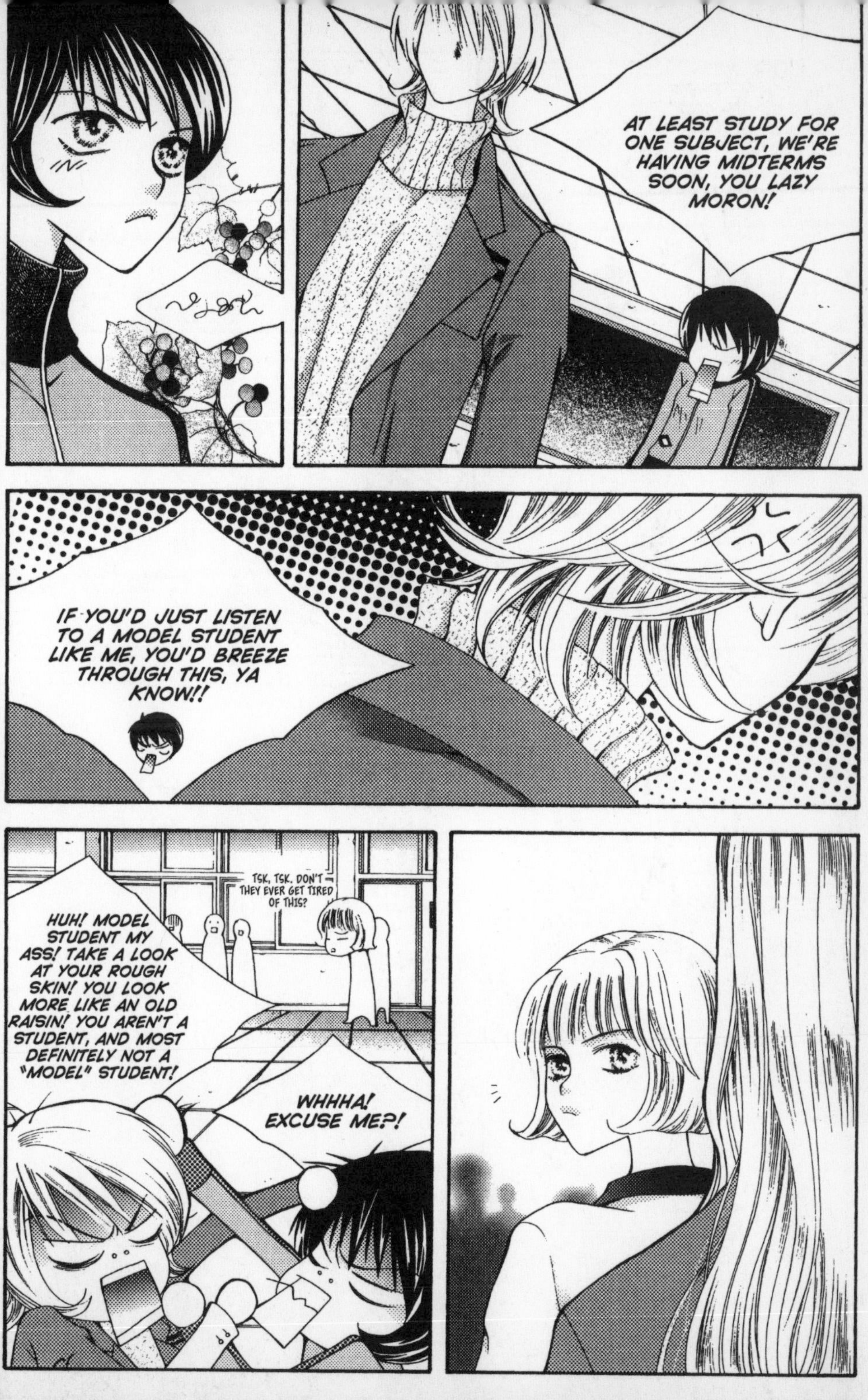
AT LEAST STUDY FOR ONE SUBJECT, WE'RE HAVING MIDTERMS SOON, YOU LAZY MORON!
IF YOU'D JUST LISTEN TO A MODEL STUDENT LIKE ME, YOU'D BREEZE THROUGH THIS, YA KNOW!!
HUH! MODEL STUDENT MY ASS! TAKE A LOOK AT YOUR ROUGH SKIN! YOU LOOK MORE LIKE AN OLD RAISIN! YOU AREN'T A STUDENT, AND MOST DEFINITELY NOT A "MODEL" STUDENT!
TSK, TSK. DON'T THEY EVER GET TIRED OF THIS?
WHHHA! EXCUSE ME?!

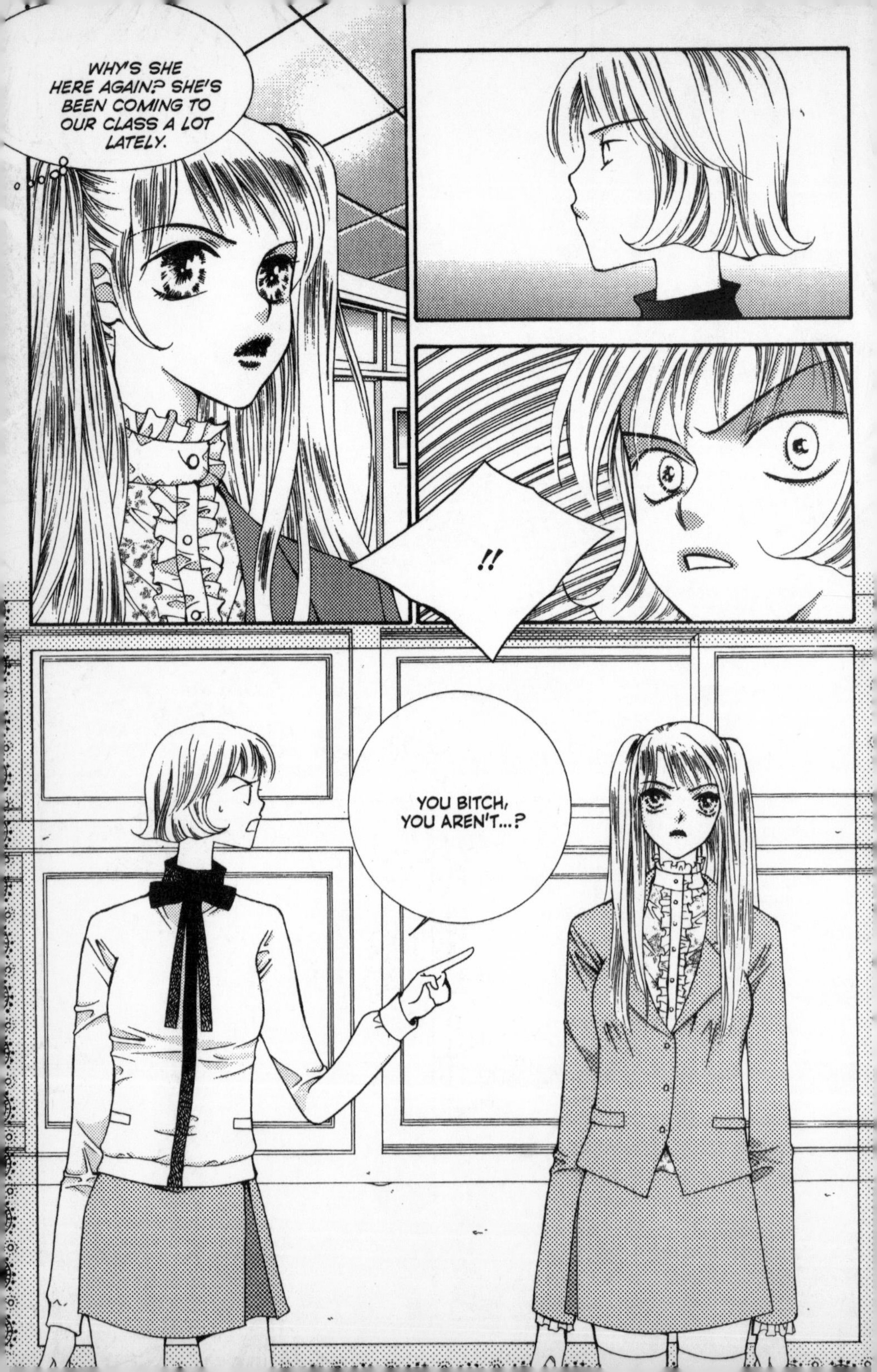
WHY'S SHE HERE AGAIN? SHE'S BEEN COMING TO OUR CLASS A LOT LATELY.
!!
YOU BITCH, YOU AREN'T...?

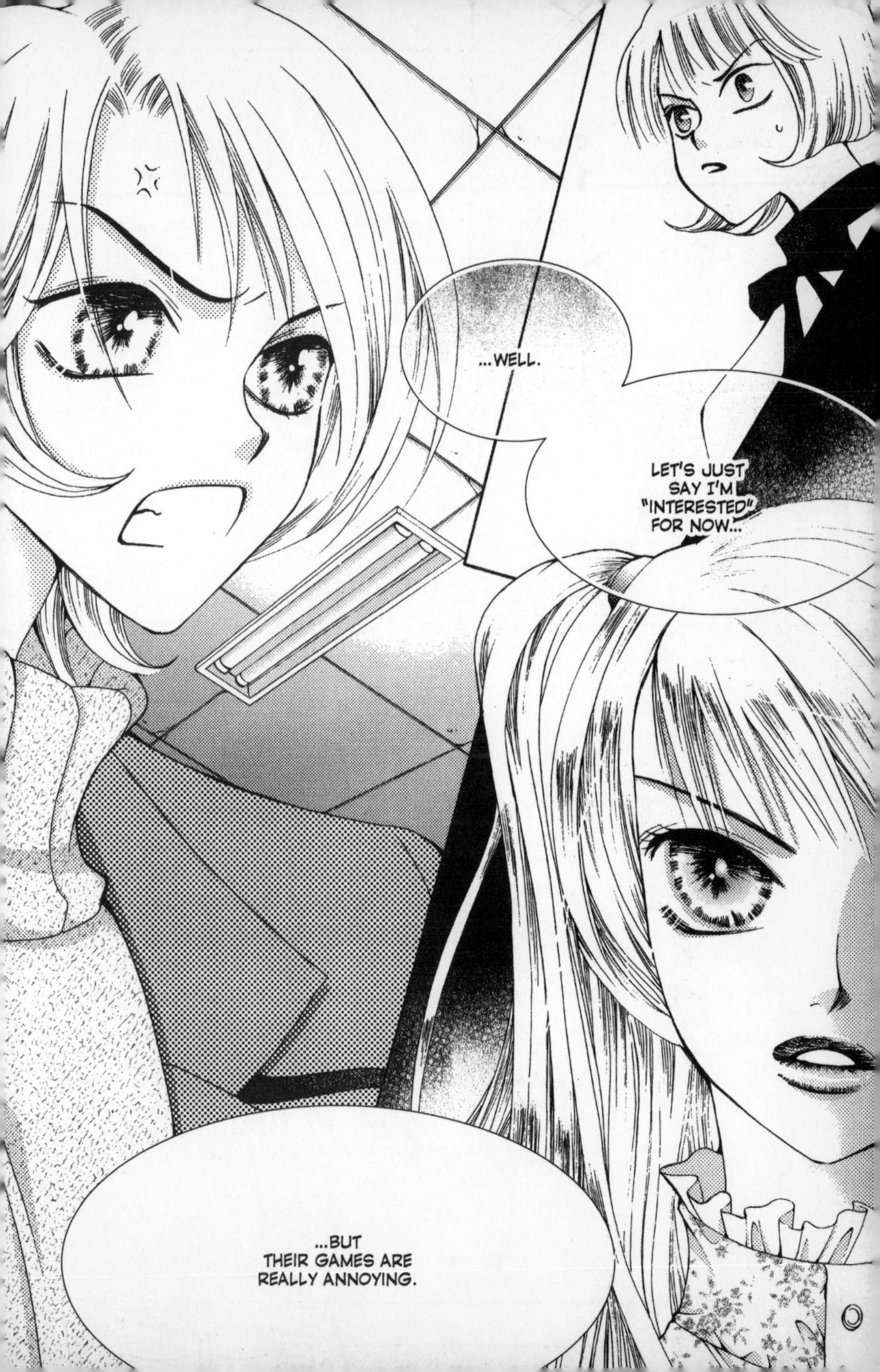
...WELL.
LET'S JUST SAY I'M "INTERESTED" FOR NOW...
...BUT THEIR GAMES ARE REALLY ANNOYING.

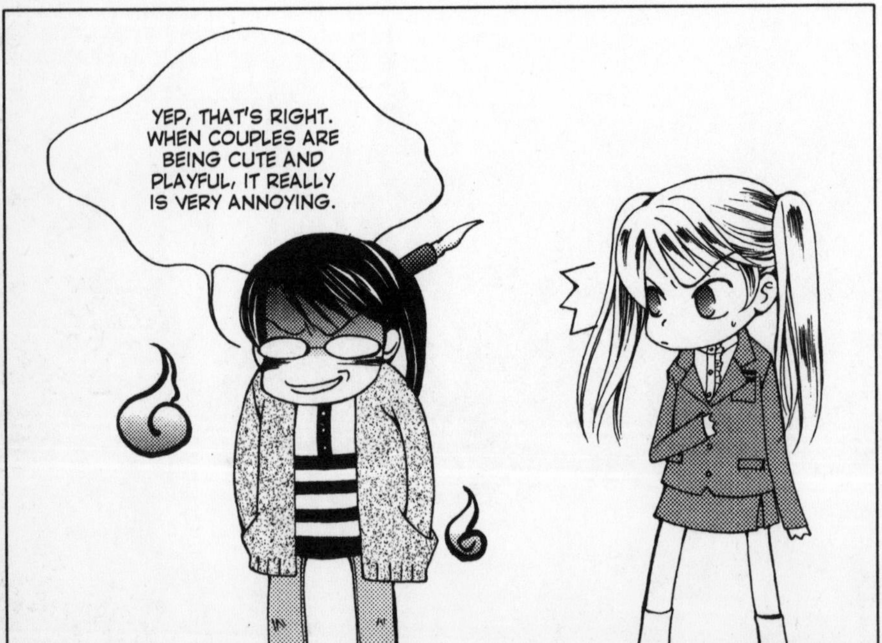
YEP, THAT'S RIGHT. WHEN COUPLES ARE BEING CUTE AND PLAYFUL, IT REALLY IS VERY ANNOYING.

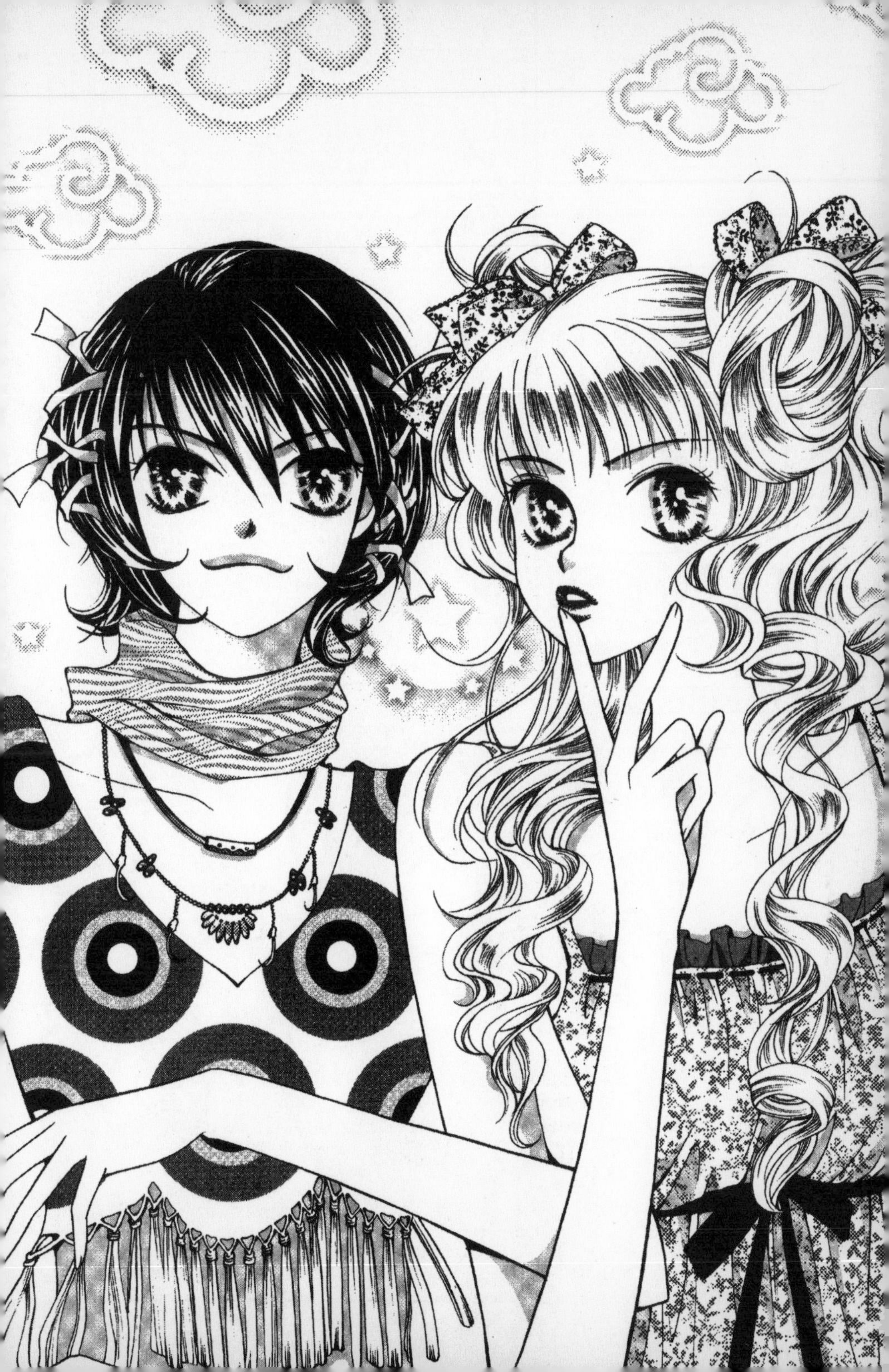

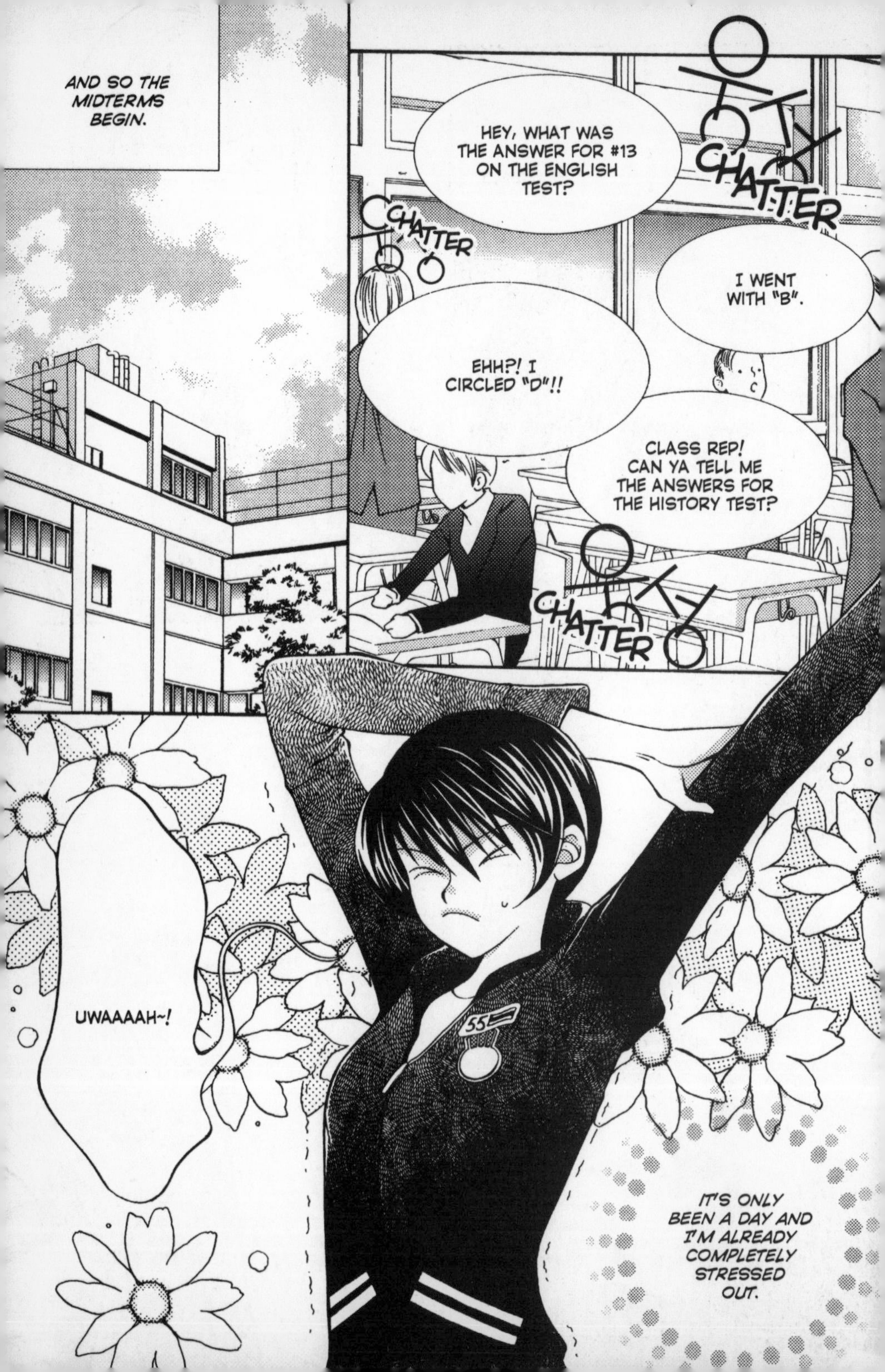
AND SO THE MIDTERMS BEGIN.
HEY, WHAT WAS THE ANSWER FOR #13 ON THE ENGLISH TEST?
CHATTER
CHATTER
I WENT WITH "B".
EHH?! I CIRCLED "D"!!
CLASS REP! CAN YA TELL ME THE ANSWERS FOR THE HISTORY TEST?
CHATTER
UWAAAAH~!
IT'S ONLY BEEN A DAY AND I'M ALREADY COMPLETELY STRESSED OUT.

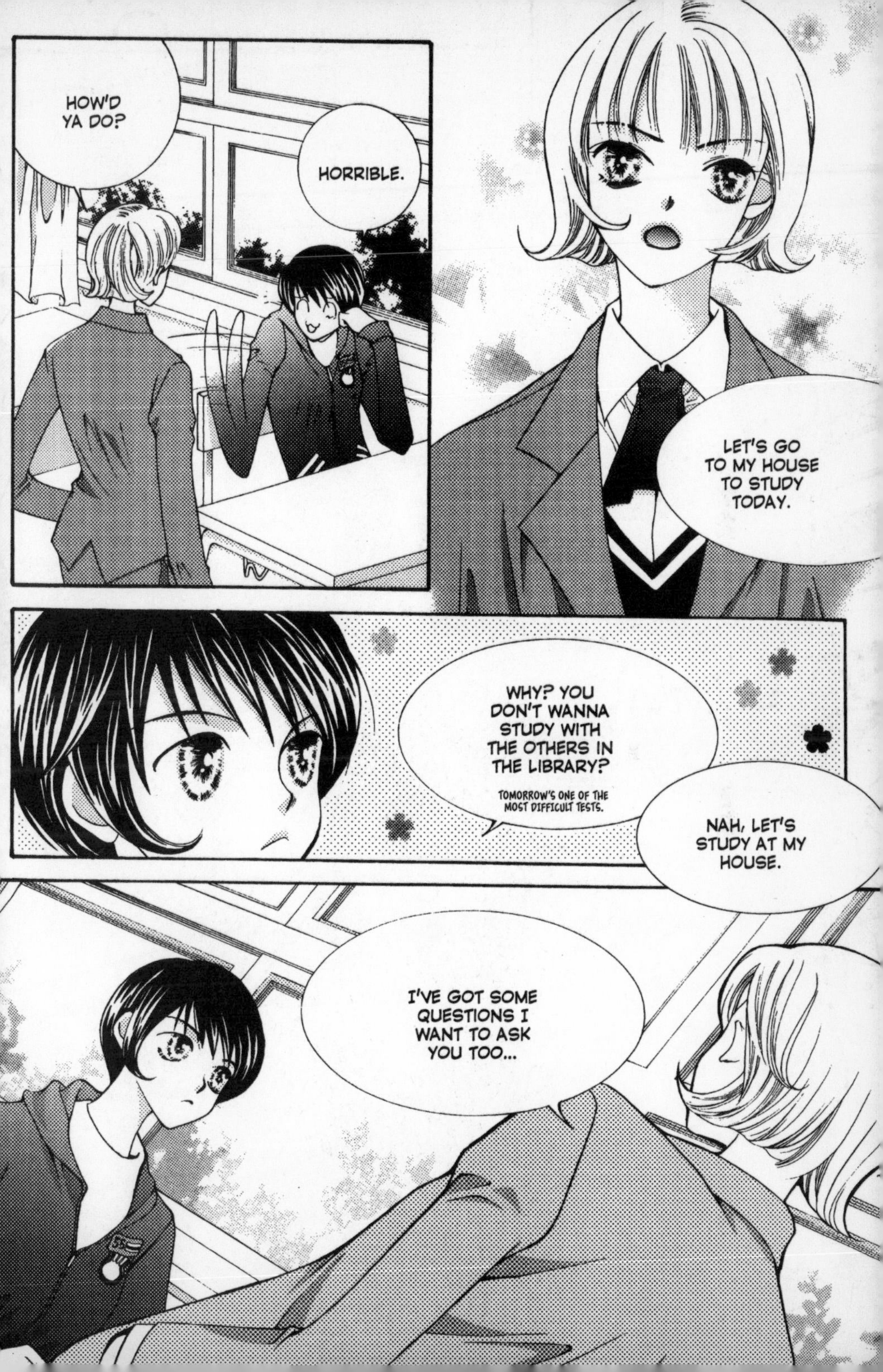
HOW'D YA DO?
HORRIBLE.
LET'S GO TO MY HOUSE TO STUDY TODAY.
WHY? YOU DON'T WANNA STUDY WITH THE OTHERS IN THE LIBRARY?
TOMORROW'S ONE OF THE MOST DIFFICULT TESTS.
NAH, LET'S STUDY AT MY HOUSE.
I'VE GOT SOME QUESTIONS I WANT TO ASK YOU TOO...

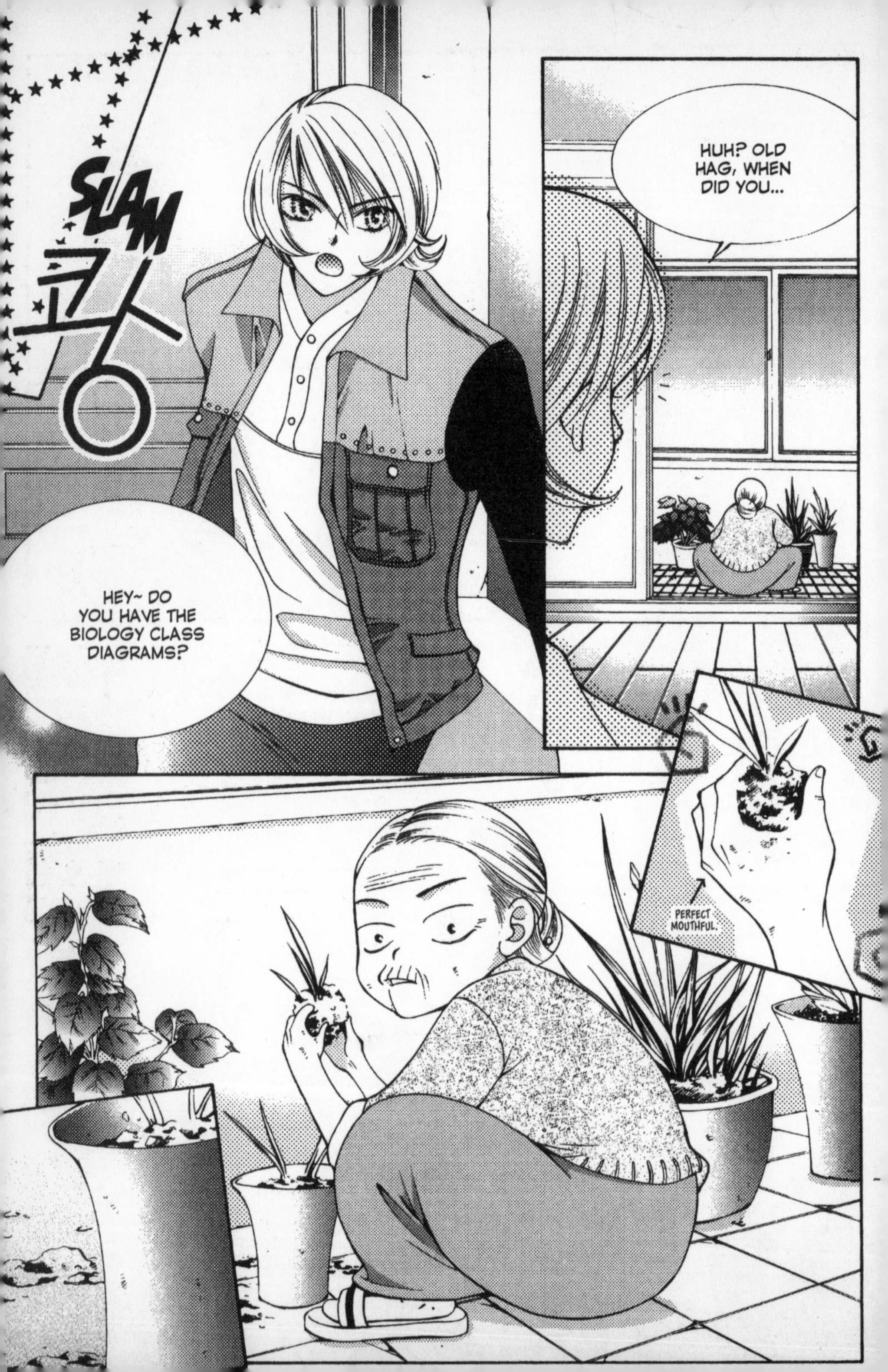
SLAM
쾅
HEY~ DO YOU HAVE THE BIOLOGY CLASS DIAGRAMS?
HUH? OLD HAG, WHEN DID YOU...
PERFECT MOUTHFUL.

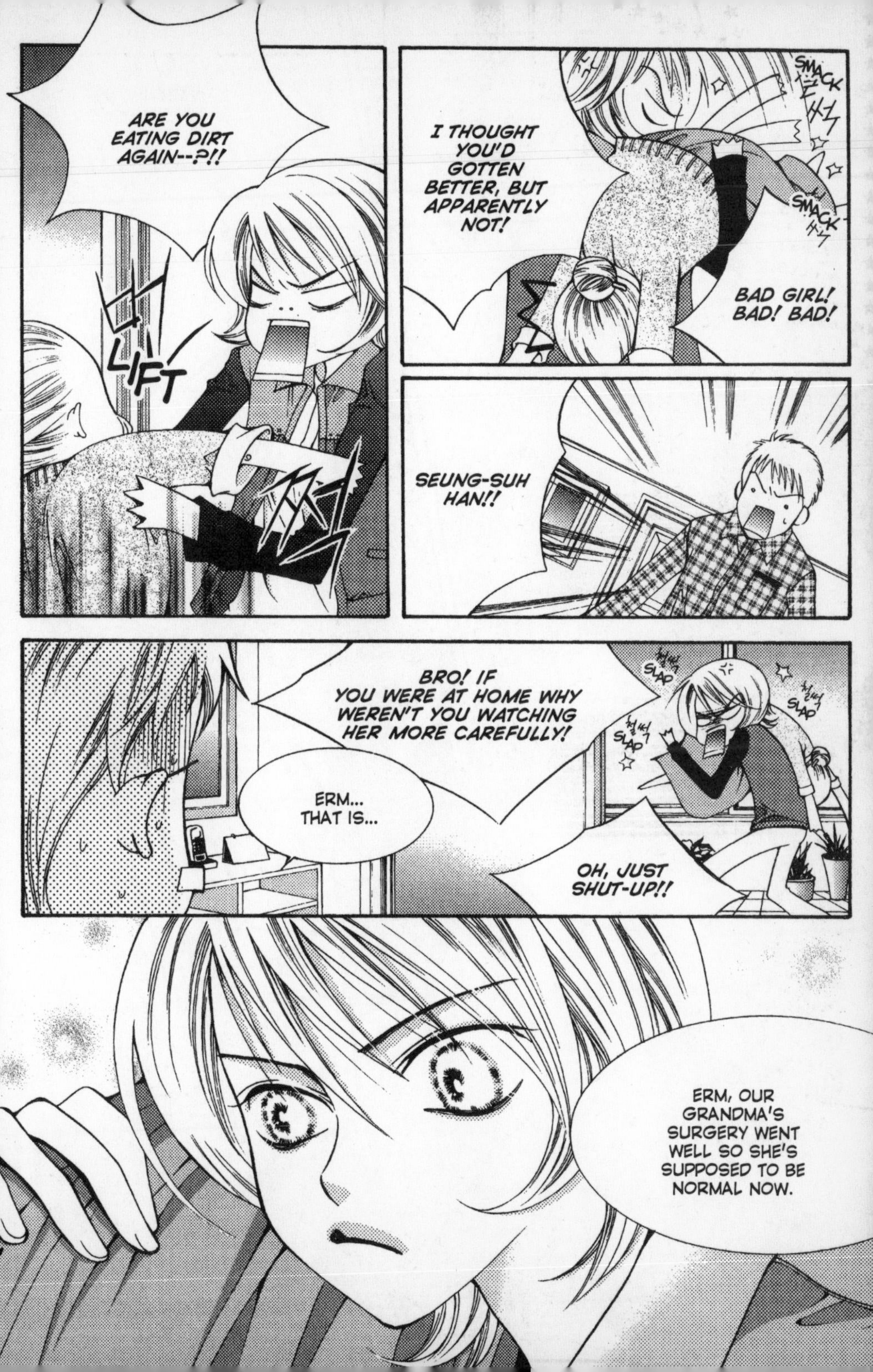
ARE YOU EATING DIRT AGAIN--?!!
LIFT
I THOUGHT YOU'D GOTTEN BETTER, BUT APPARENTLY NOT!
SMACK
SMACK
BAD GIRL! BAD! BAD!
SEUNG-SUH HAN!!
BRO! IF YOU WERE AT HOME WHY WEREN'T YOU WATCHING HER MORE CAREFULLY!
SLAP
SLAP
SLAP
ERM... THAT IS...
OH, JUST SHUT-UP!!
ERM, OUR GRANDMA'S SURGERY WENT WELL SO SHE'S SUPPOSED TO BE NORMAL NOW.

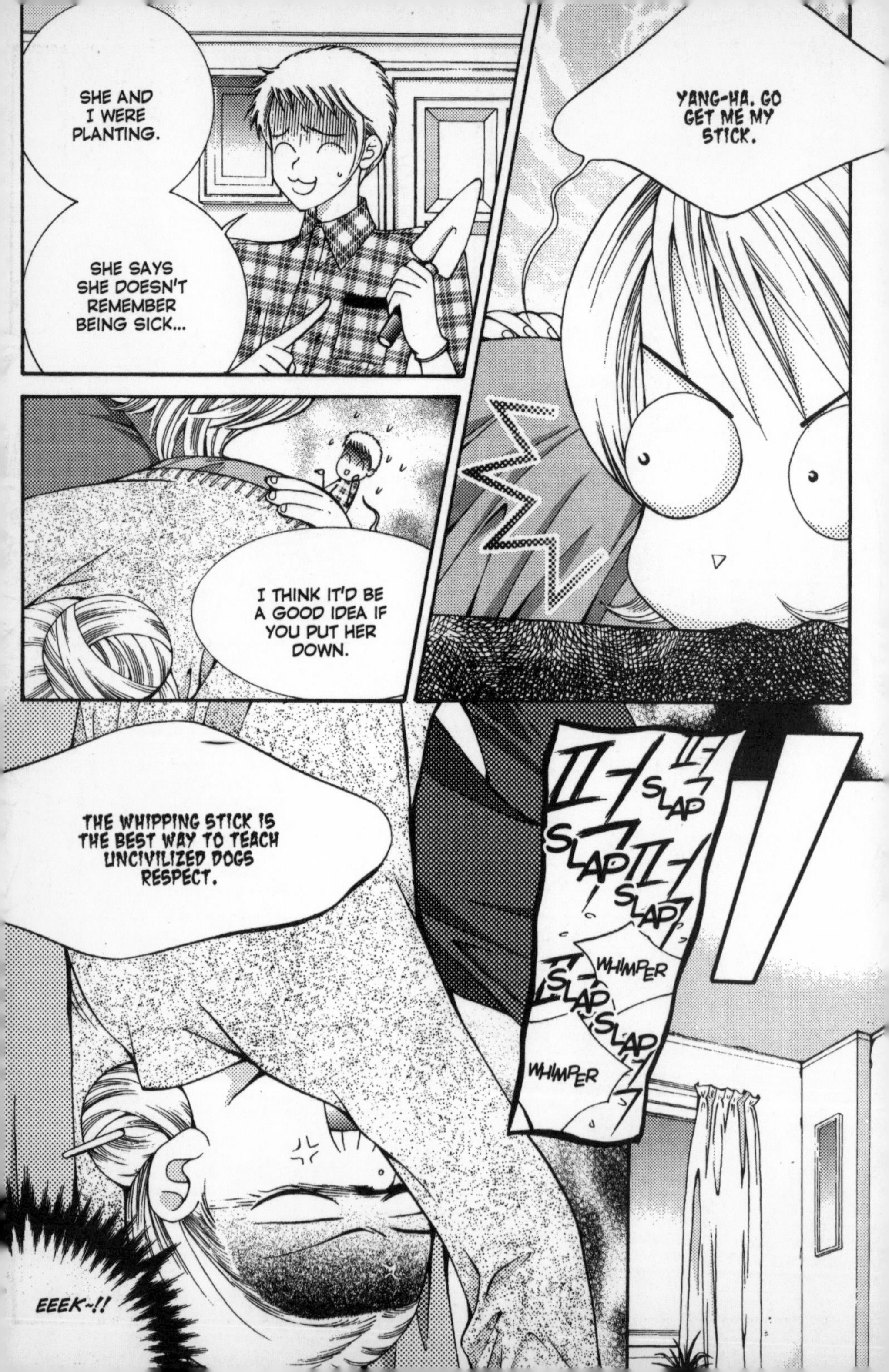

SHE AND I WERE PLANTING.
SHE SAYS SHE DOESN'T REMEMBER BEING SICK...
I THINK IT'D BE A GOOD IDEA IF YOU PUT HER DOWN.
YANG-HA. GO GET ME MY STICK.
THE WHIPPING STICK IS THE BEST WAY TO TEACH UNCIVILIZED DOGS RESPECT.
SLAP
SLAP
SLAP
WHIMPER
SLAP
SLAP
WHIMPER
EEEK~!!

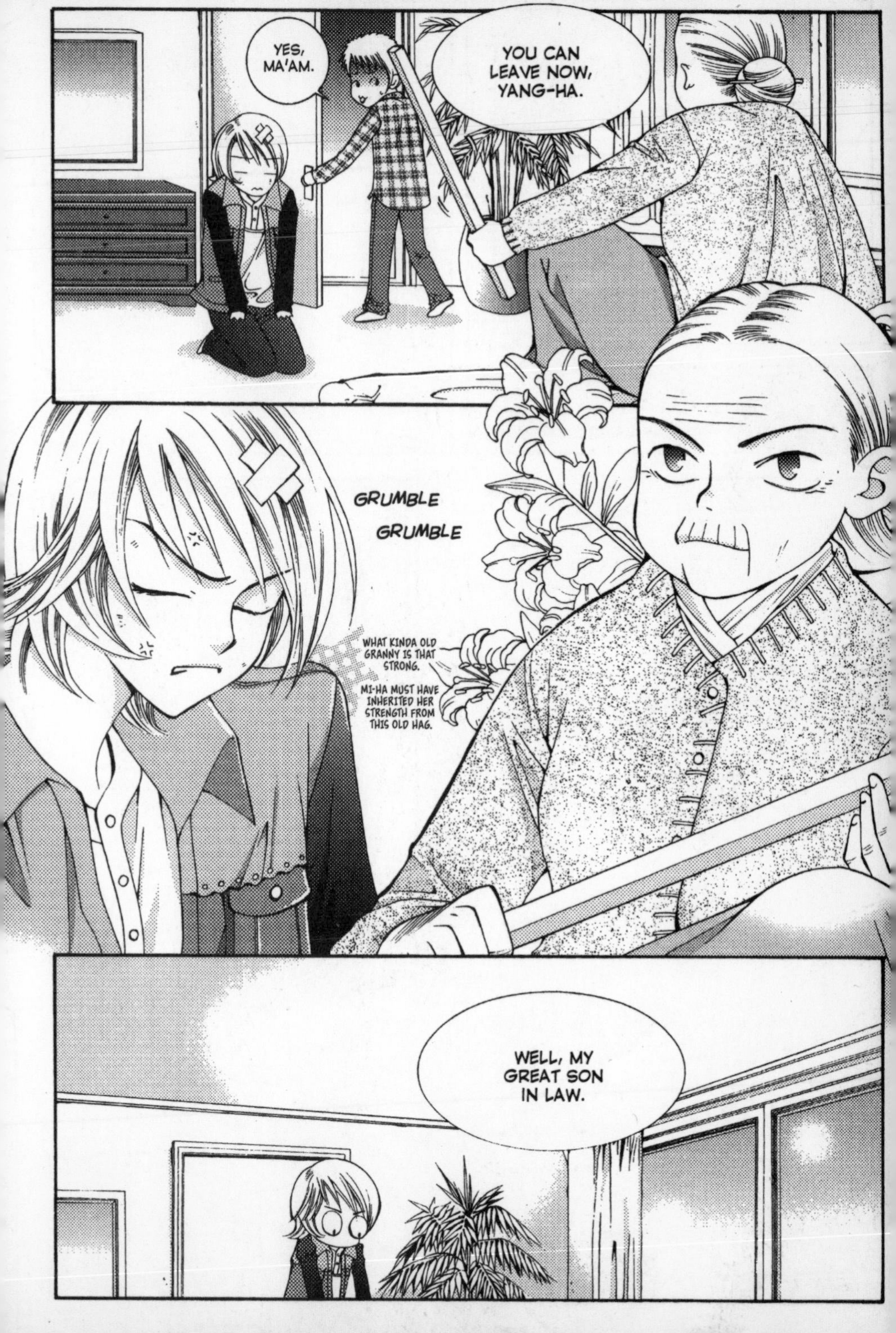
YES, MA'AM.
YOU CAN LEAVE NOW, YANG-HA.
GRUMBLE
GRUMBLE
WHAT KINDA OLD GRANNY IS THAT STRONG.
MI-HA MUST HAVE INHERITED HER STRENGTH FROM THIS OLD HAG.
WELL, MY GREAT SON IN LAW.

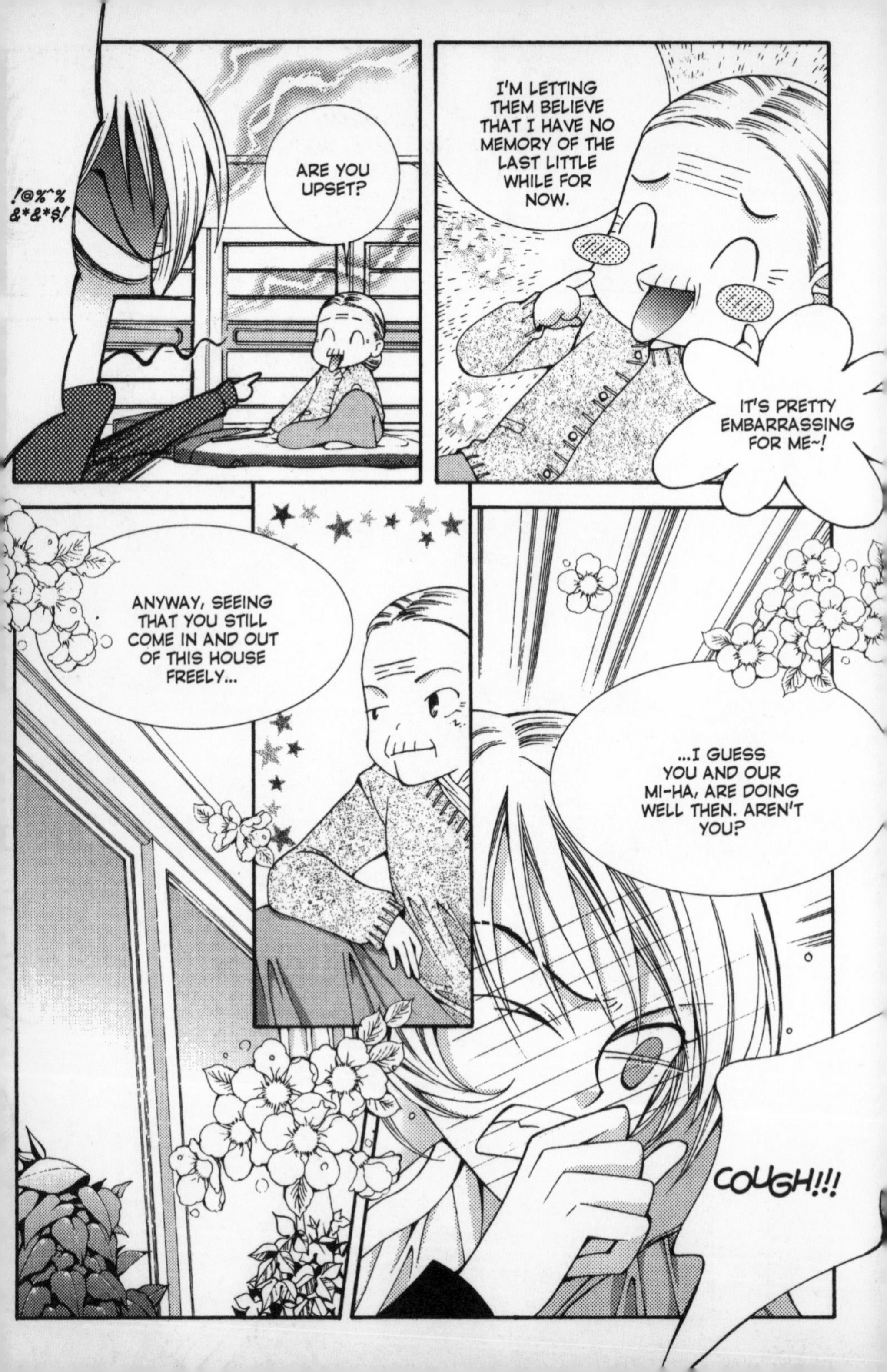
!@%^%
&*&*$!
ARE YOU UPSET?
I'M LETTING THEM BELIEVE THAT I HAVE NO MEMORY OF THE LAST LITTLE WHILE FOR NOW.
IT'S PRETTY EMBARRASSING FOR ME~!
ANYWAY, SEEING THAT YOU STILL COME IN AND OUT OF THIS HOUSE FREELY...
...I GUESS YOU AND OUR MI-HA, ARE DOING WELL THEN. AREN'T YOU?
COUGH!!!

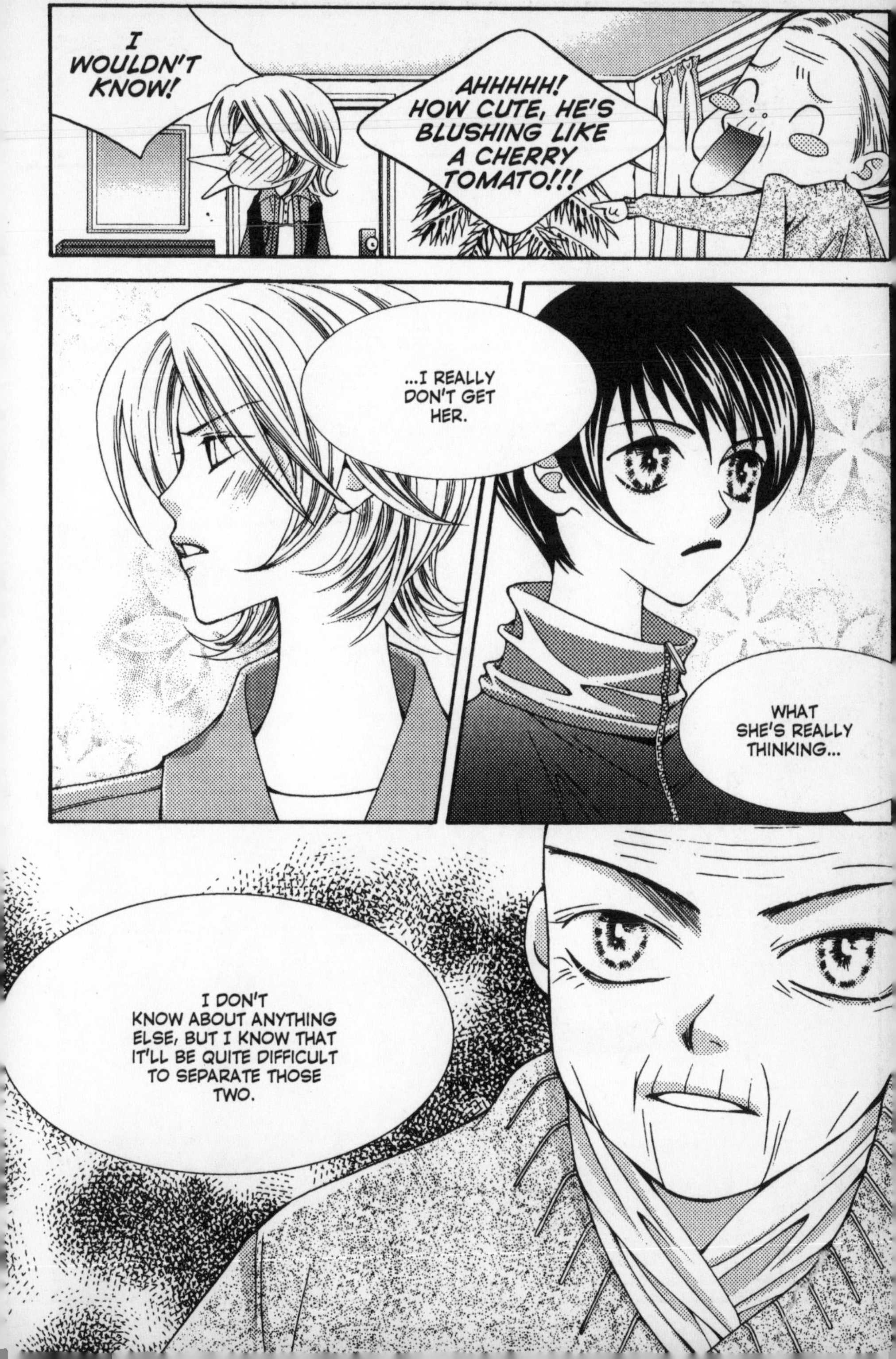
I WOULDN'T KNOW!
AHHHHH! HOW CUTE, HE'S BLUSHING LIKE A CHERRY TOMATO!!!
...I REALLY DON'T GET HER.
WHAT SHE'S REALLY THINKING...
I DON'T KNOW ABOUT ANYTHING ELSE, BUT I KNOW THAT IT'LL BE QUITE DIFFICULT TO SEPARATE THOSE TWO.

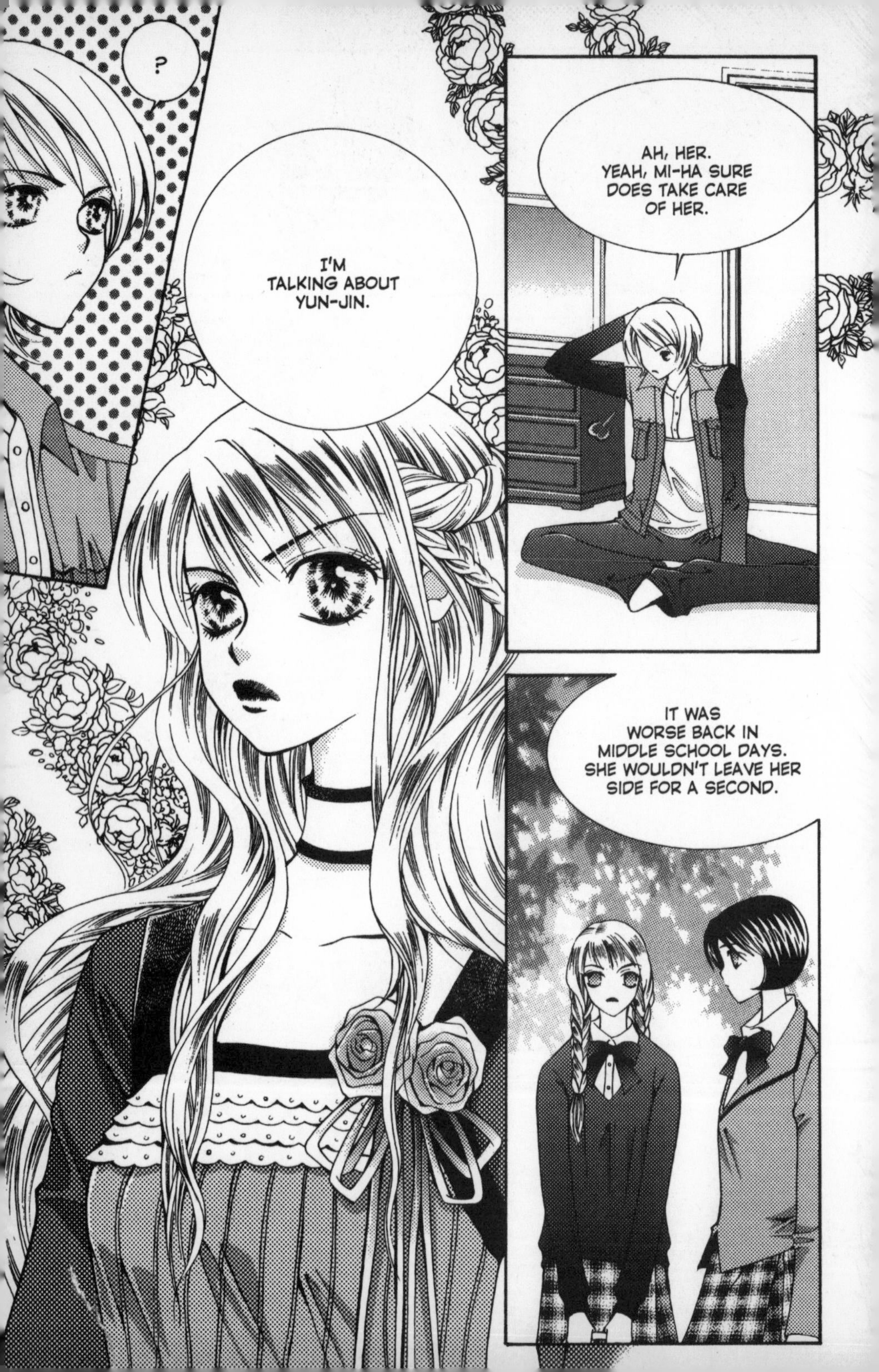
?
I'M TALKING ABOUT YUN-JIN.
AH, HER. YEAH, MI-HA SURE DOES TAKE CARE OF HER.
IT WAS WORSE BACK IN MIDDLE SCHOOL DAYS. SHE WOULDN'T LEAVE HER SIDE FOR A SECOND.

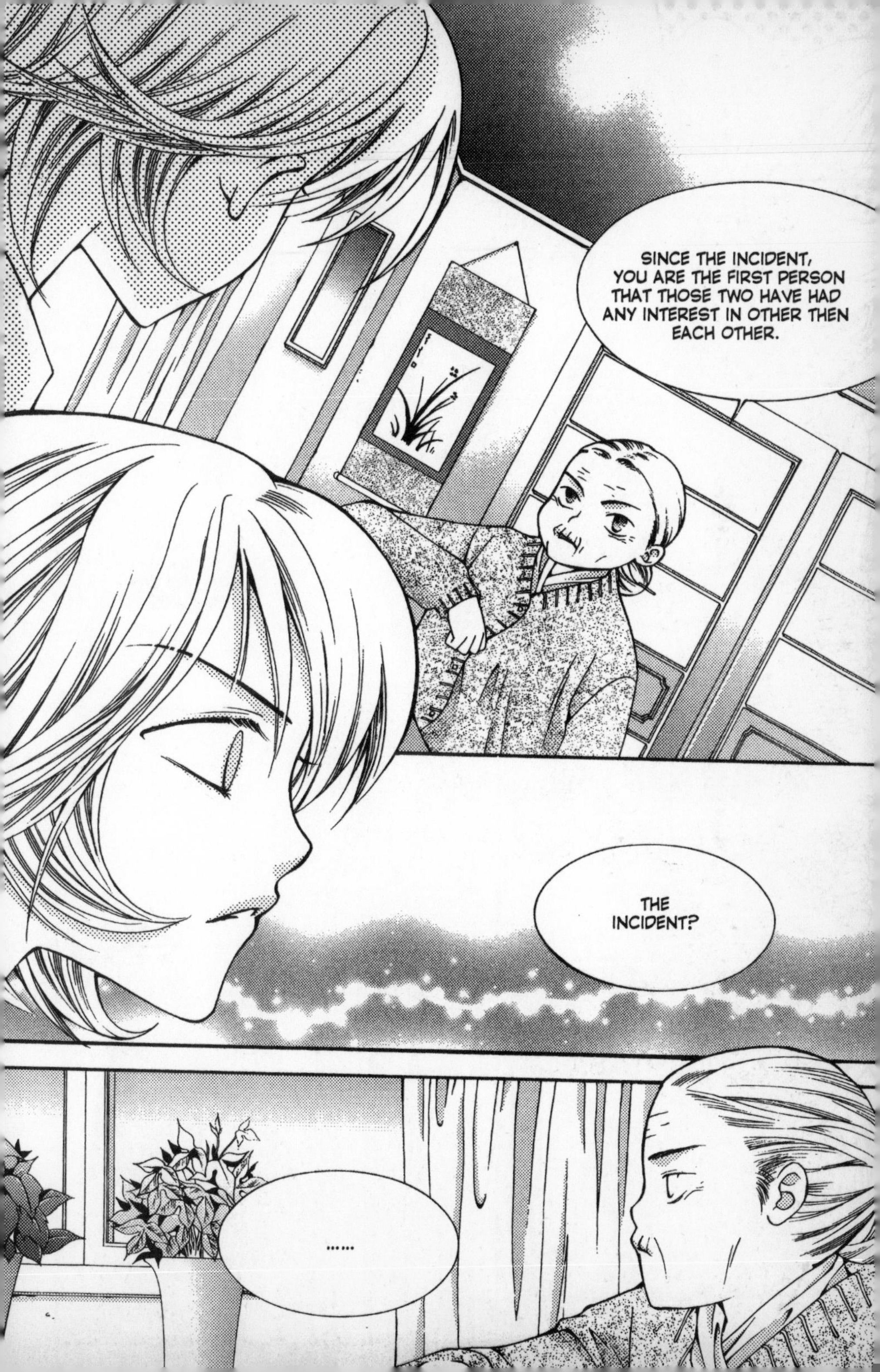
SINCE THE INCIDENT, YOU ARE THE FIRST PERSON THAT THOSE TWO HAVE HAD ANY INTEREST IN OTHER THEN EACH OTHER.
THE INCIDENT?
......

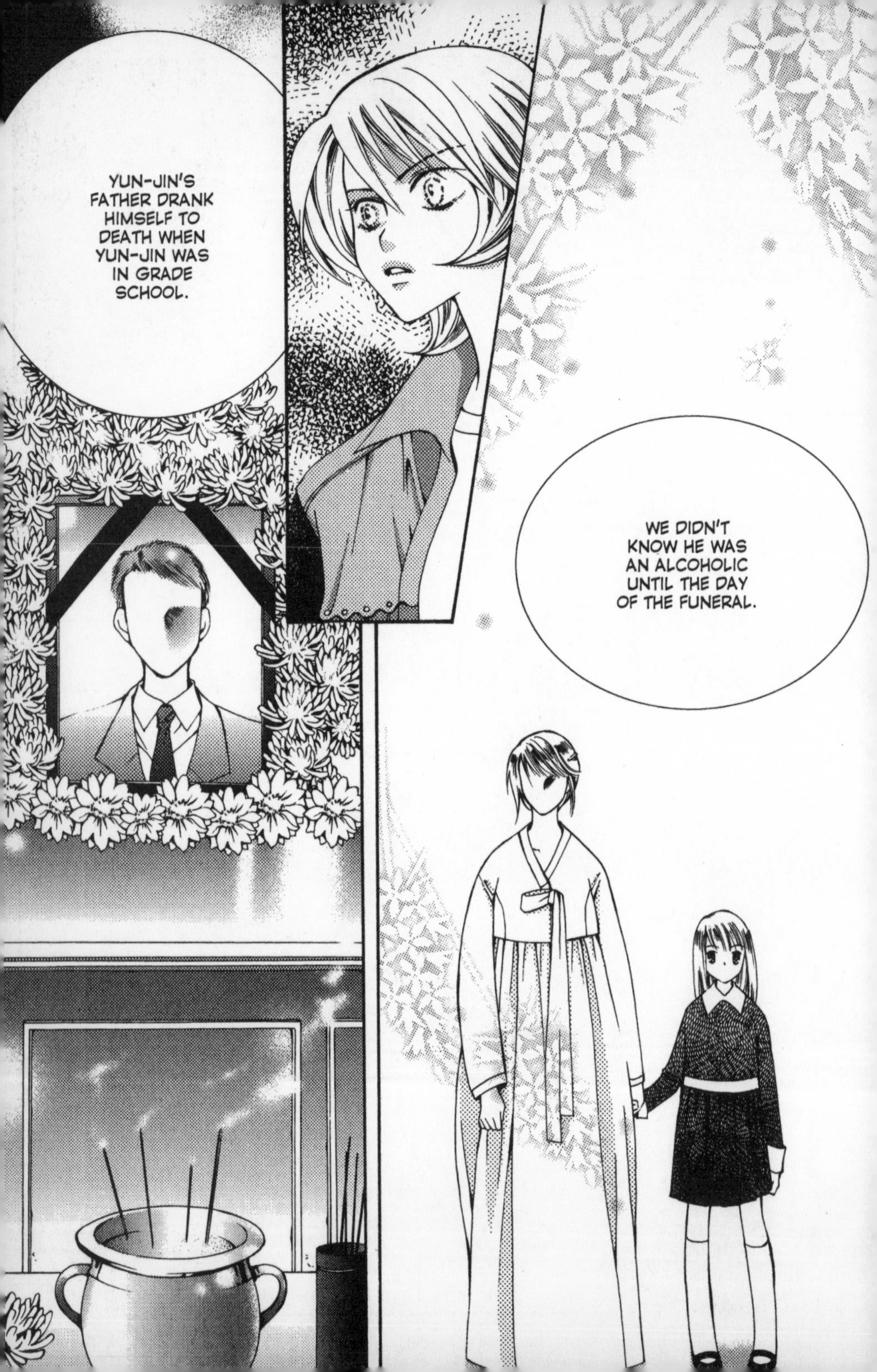
YUN-JIN'S FATHER DRANK HIMSELF TO DEATH WHEN YUN-JIN WAS IN GRADE SCHOOL.
WE DIDN'T KNOW HE WAS AN ALCOHOLIC UNTIL THE DAY OF THE FUNERAL.

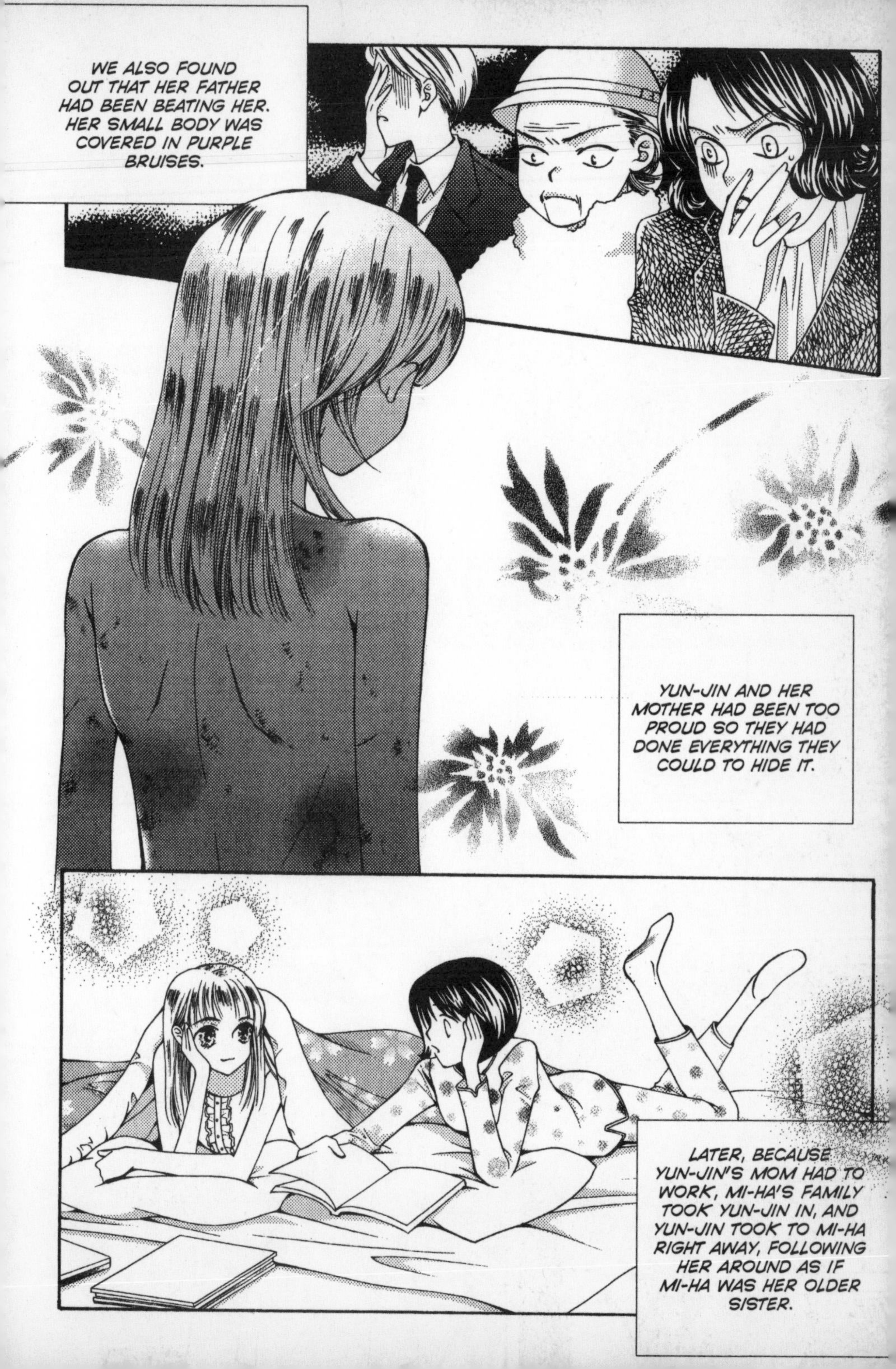
WE ALSO FOUND OUT THAT HER FATHER HAD BEEN BEATING HER. HER SMALL BODY WAS COVERED IN PURPLE BRUISES.
YUN-JIN AND HER MOTHER HAD BEEN TOO PROUD SO THEY HAD DONE EVERYTHING THEY COULD TO HIDE IT.
LATER, BECAUSE YUN-JIN'S MOM HAD TO WORK, MI-HA'S FAMILY TOOK YUN-JIN IN, AND YUN-JIN TOOK TO MI-HA RIGHT AWAY, FOLLOWING HER AROUND AS IF MI-HA WAS HER OLDER SISTER.

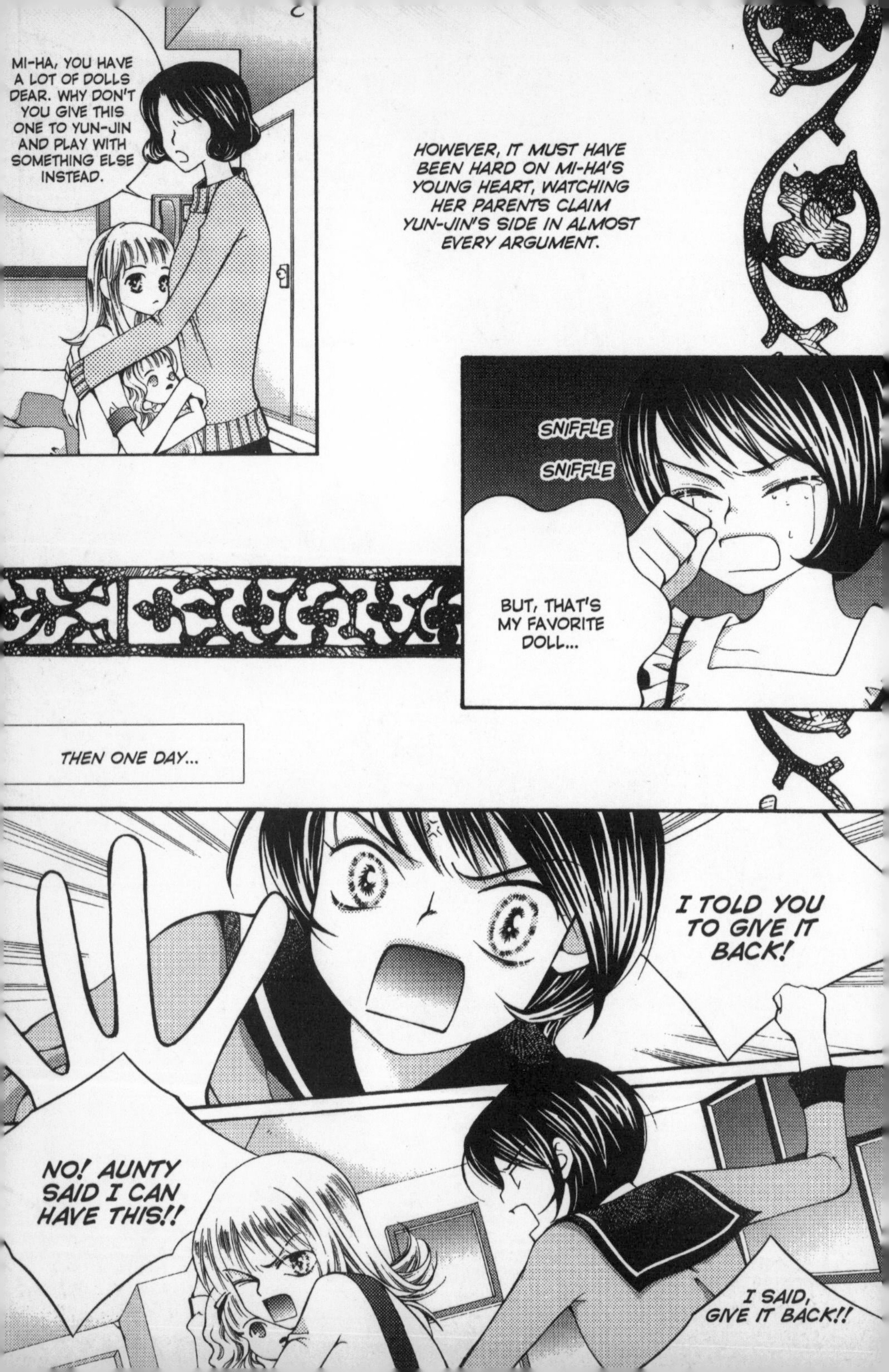
MI-HA, YOU HAVE A LOT OF DOLLS DEAR. WHY DON'T YOU GIVE THIS ONE TO YUN-JIN AND PLAY WITH SOMETHING ELSE INSTEAD.
HOWEVER, IT MUST HAVE BEEN HARD ON MI-HA'S YOUNG HEART, WATCHING HER PARENTS CLAIM YUN-JIN'S SIDE IN ALMOST EVERY ARGUMENT.
SNIFFLE
SNIFFLE
BUT, THAT'S MY FAVORITE DOLL...
THEN ONE DAY...
I TOLD YOU TO GIVE IT BACK!
NO! AUNTY SAID I CAN HAVE THIS!!
I SAID, GIVE IT BACK!!

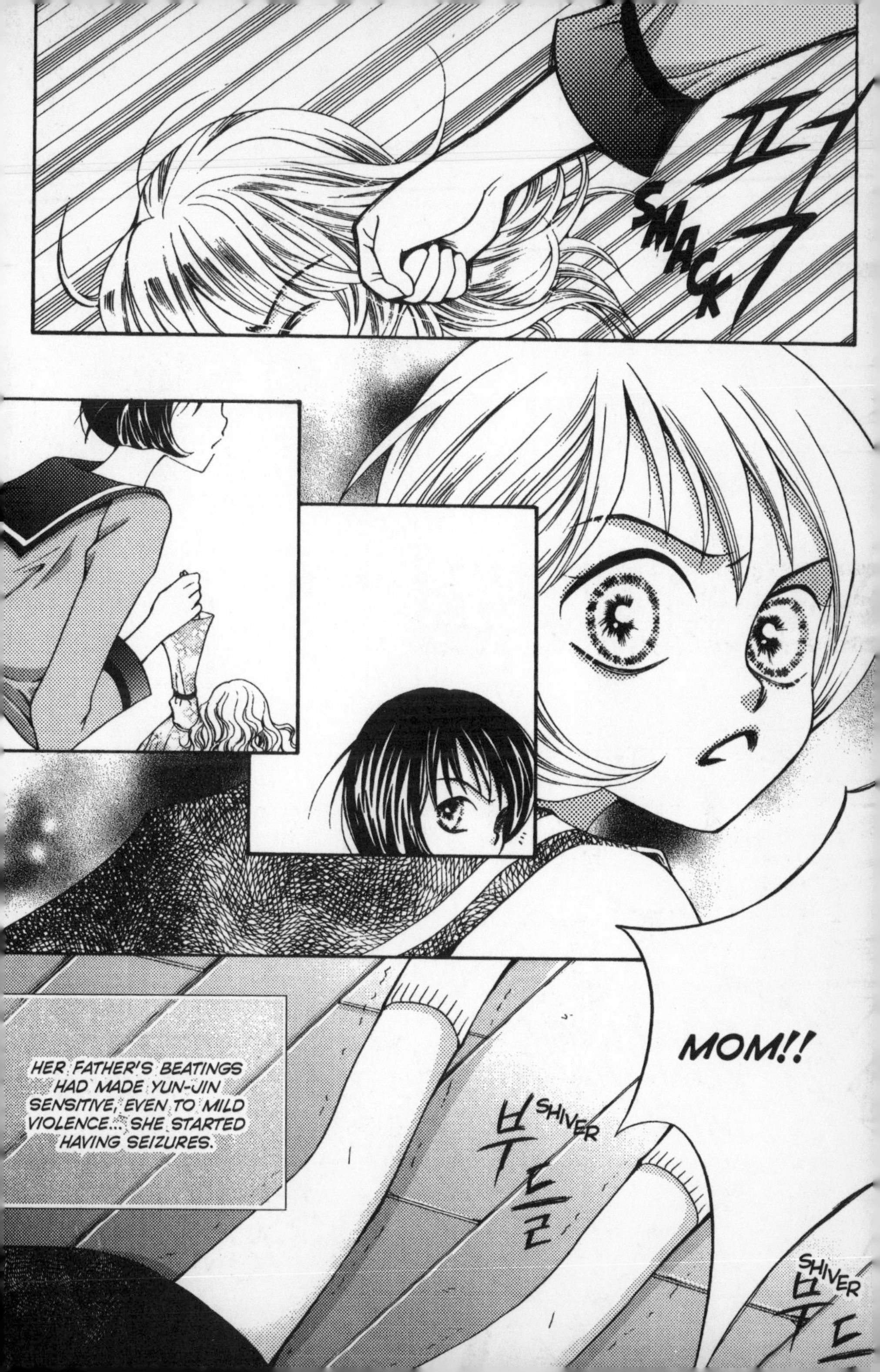
SHACK
HER FATHER'S BEATINGS HAD MADE YUN-JIN SENSITIVE, EVEN TO MILD VIOLENCE... SHE STARTED HAVING SEIZURES.
MOM!!
SHIVER
부들
SHIVER

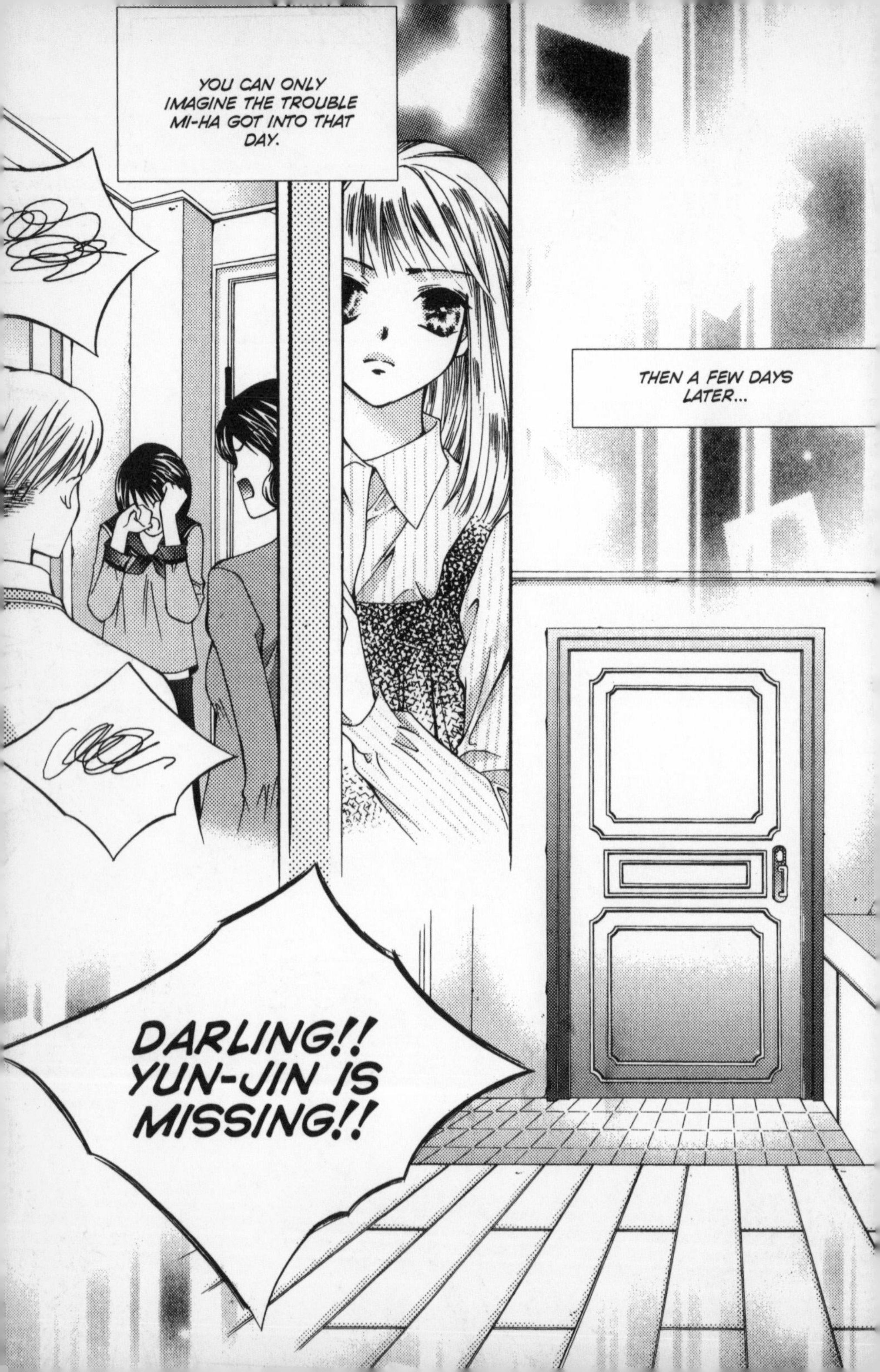
YOU CAN ONLY IMAGINE THE TROUBLE MI-HA GOT INTO THAT DAY.
THEN A FEW DAYS LATER...
DARLING!! YUN-JIN IS MISSING!!

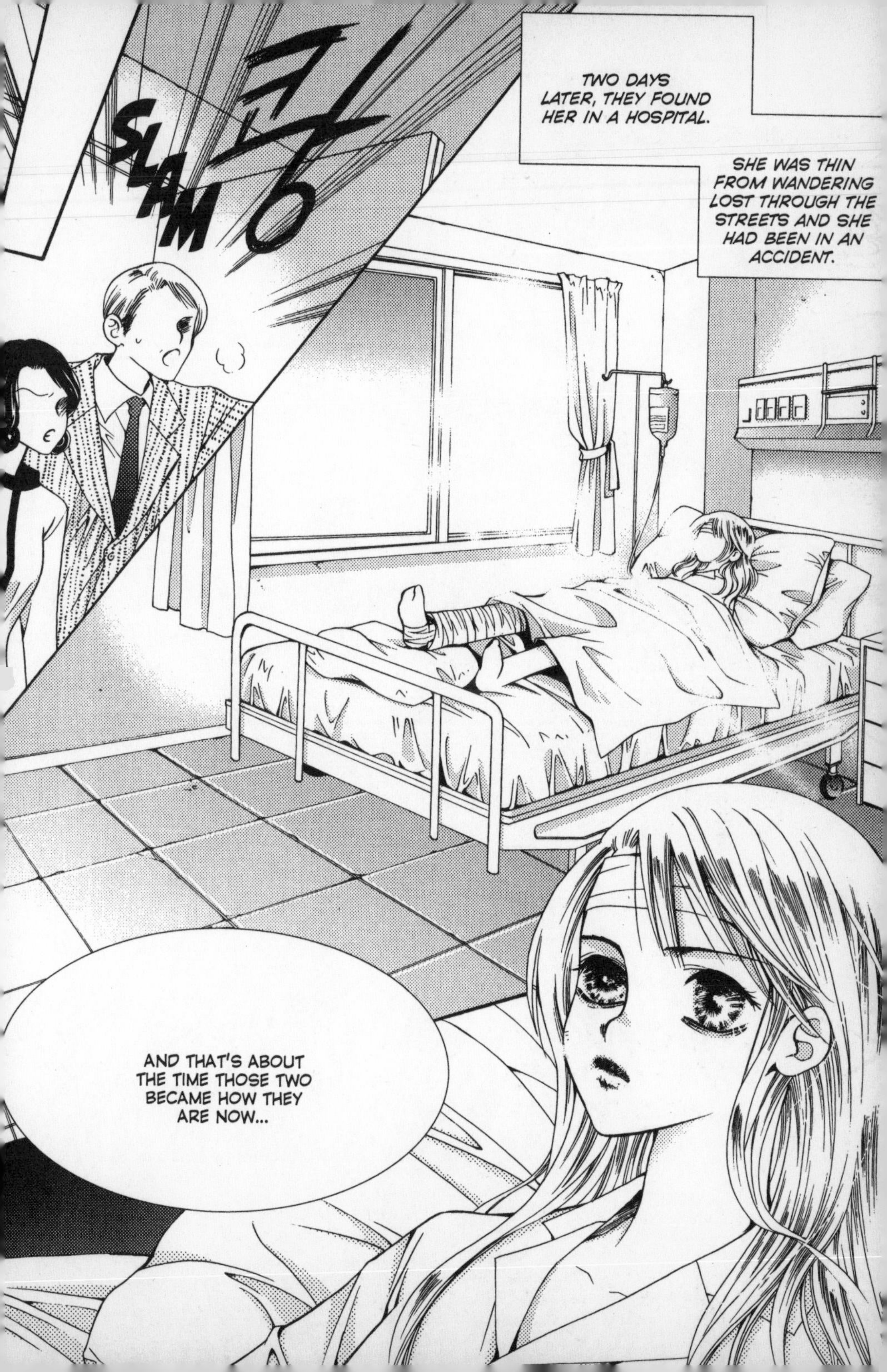
SLAM
TWO DAYS LATER, THEY FOUND HER IN A HOSPITAL.
SHE WAS THIN FROM WANDERING LOST THROUGH THE STREETS AND SHE HAD BEEN IN AN ACCIDENT.
AND THAT'S ABOUT THE TIME THOSE TWO BECAME HOW THEY ARE NOW...

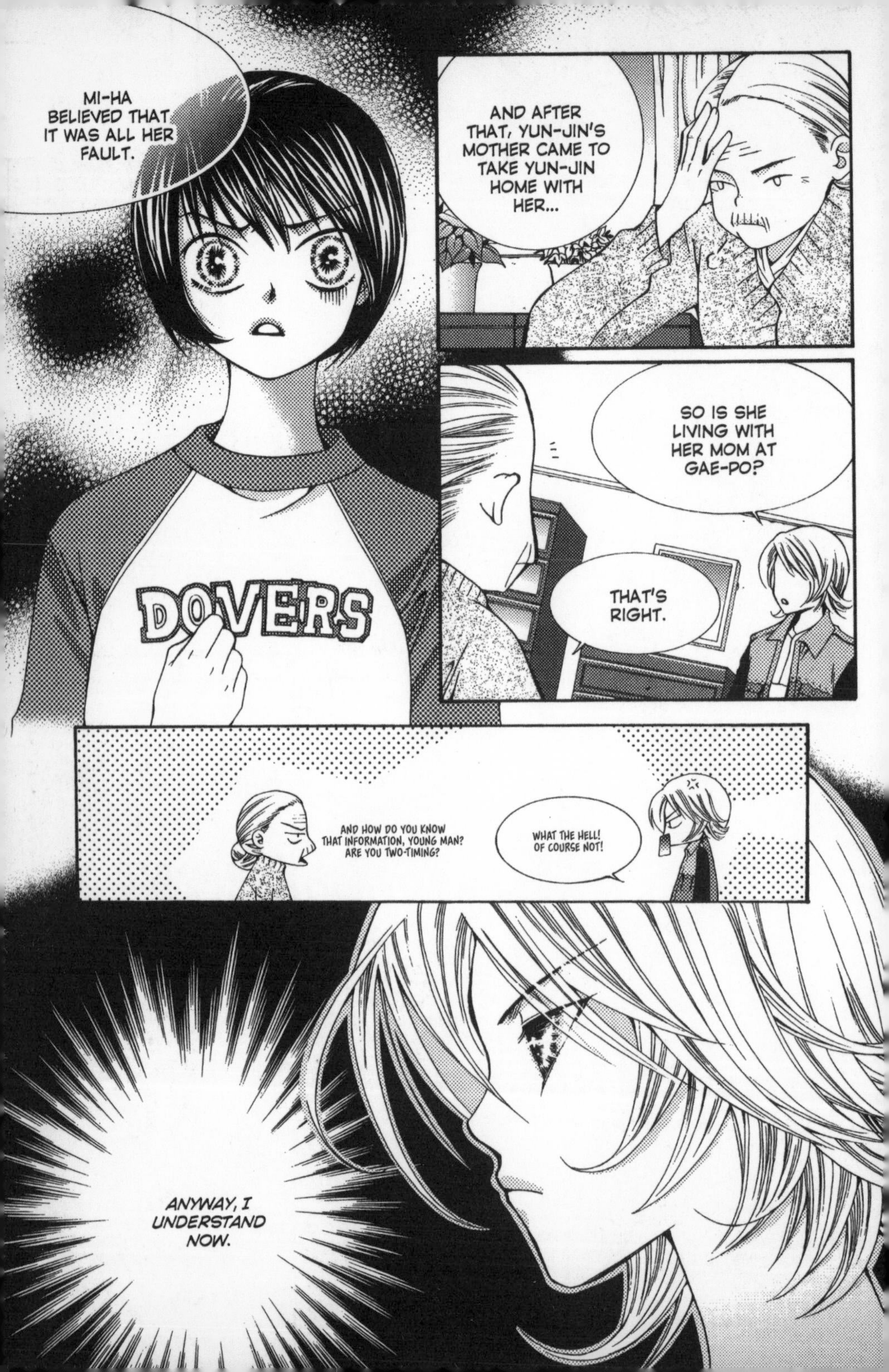
MI-HA BELIEVED THAT IT WAS ALL HER FAULT.
AND AFTER THAT, YUN-JIN'S MOTHER CAME TO TAKE YUN-JIN HOME WITH HER...
SO IS SHE LIVING WITH HER MOM AT GAE-PO?
THAT'S RIGHT.
AND HOW DO YOU KNOW THAT INFORMATION, YOUNG MAN? ARE YOU TWO-TIMING?
WHAT THE HELL! OF COURSE NOT!
ANYWAY, I UNDERSTAND NOW.
DOVERS

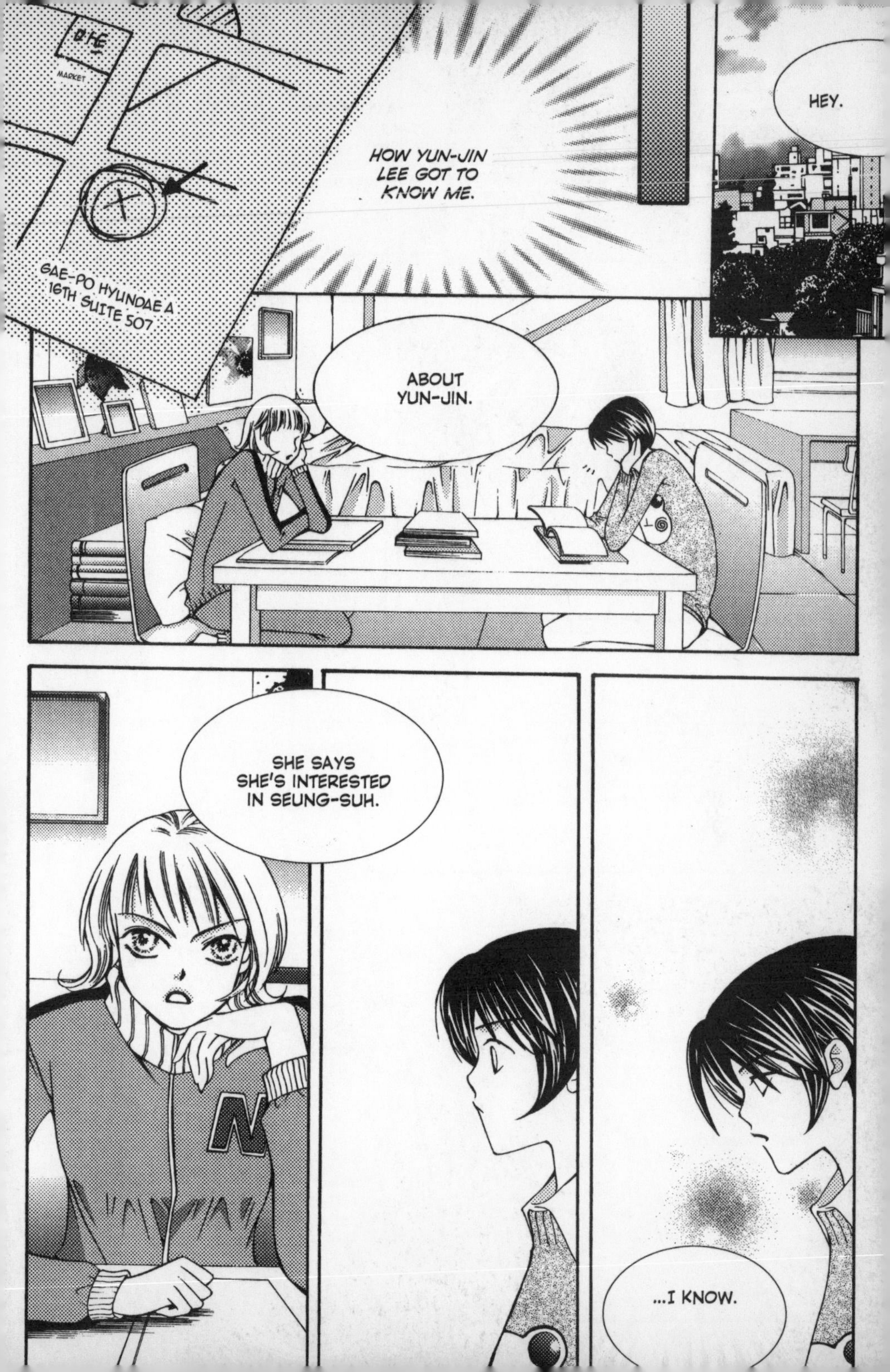
MARKET
GAE-PO HYUNDAE A 16TH SUITE 507
HOW YUN-JIN LEE GOT TO KNOW ME.
HEY.
ABOUT YUN-JIN.
SHE SAYS SHE'S INTERESTED IN SEUNG-SUH.
...I KNOW.

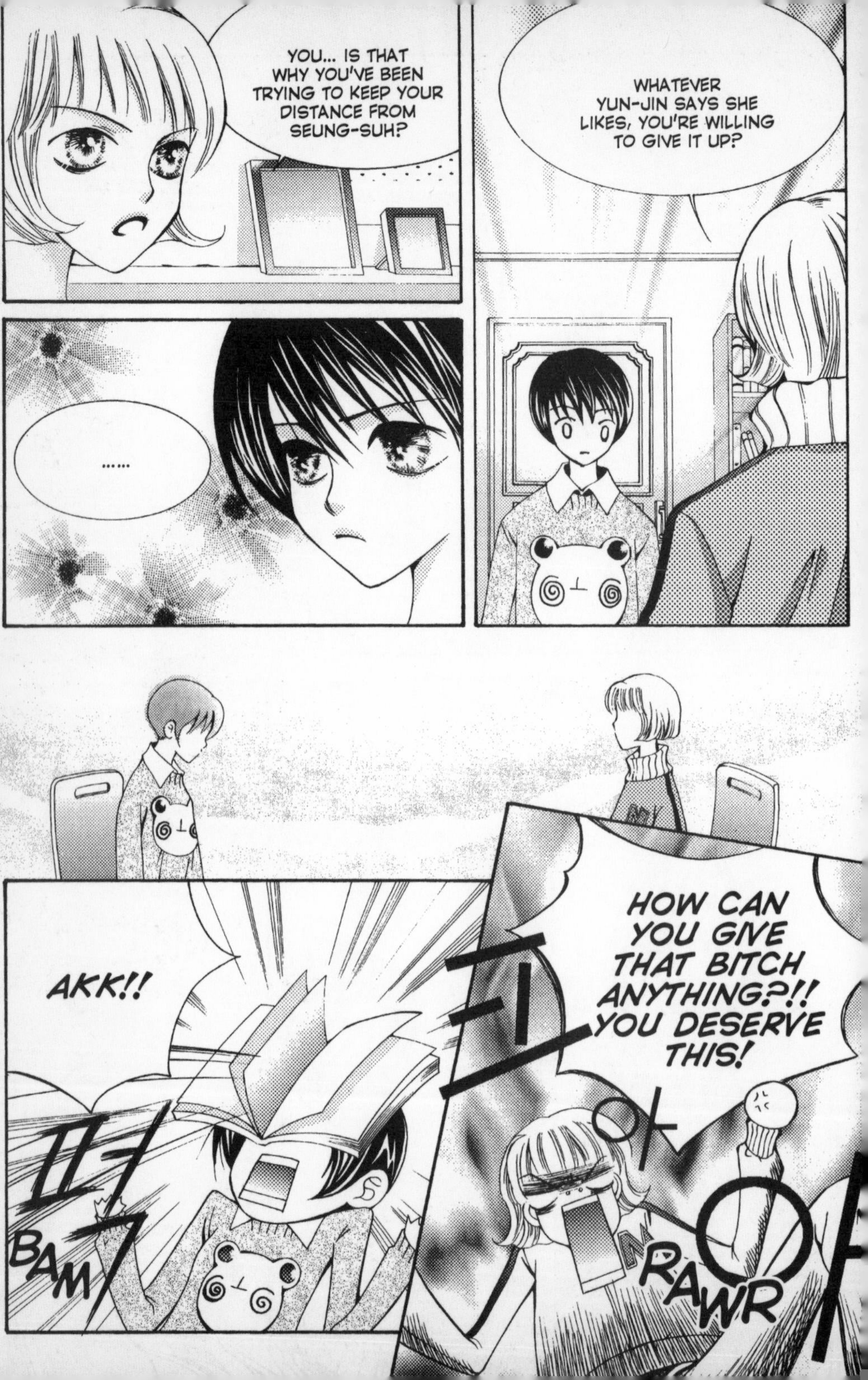
YOU... IS THAT WHY YOU'VE BEEN TRYING TO KEEP YOUR DISTANCE FROM SEUNG-SUH?
WHATEVER YUN-JIN SAYS SHE LIKES, YOU'RE WILLING TO GIVE IT UP?
......
AKK!!
BAM
HOW CAN YOU GIVE THAT BITCH ANYTHING?!! YOU DESERVE THIS!
RAWR

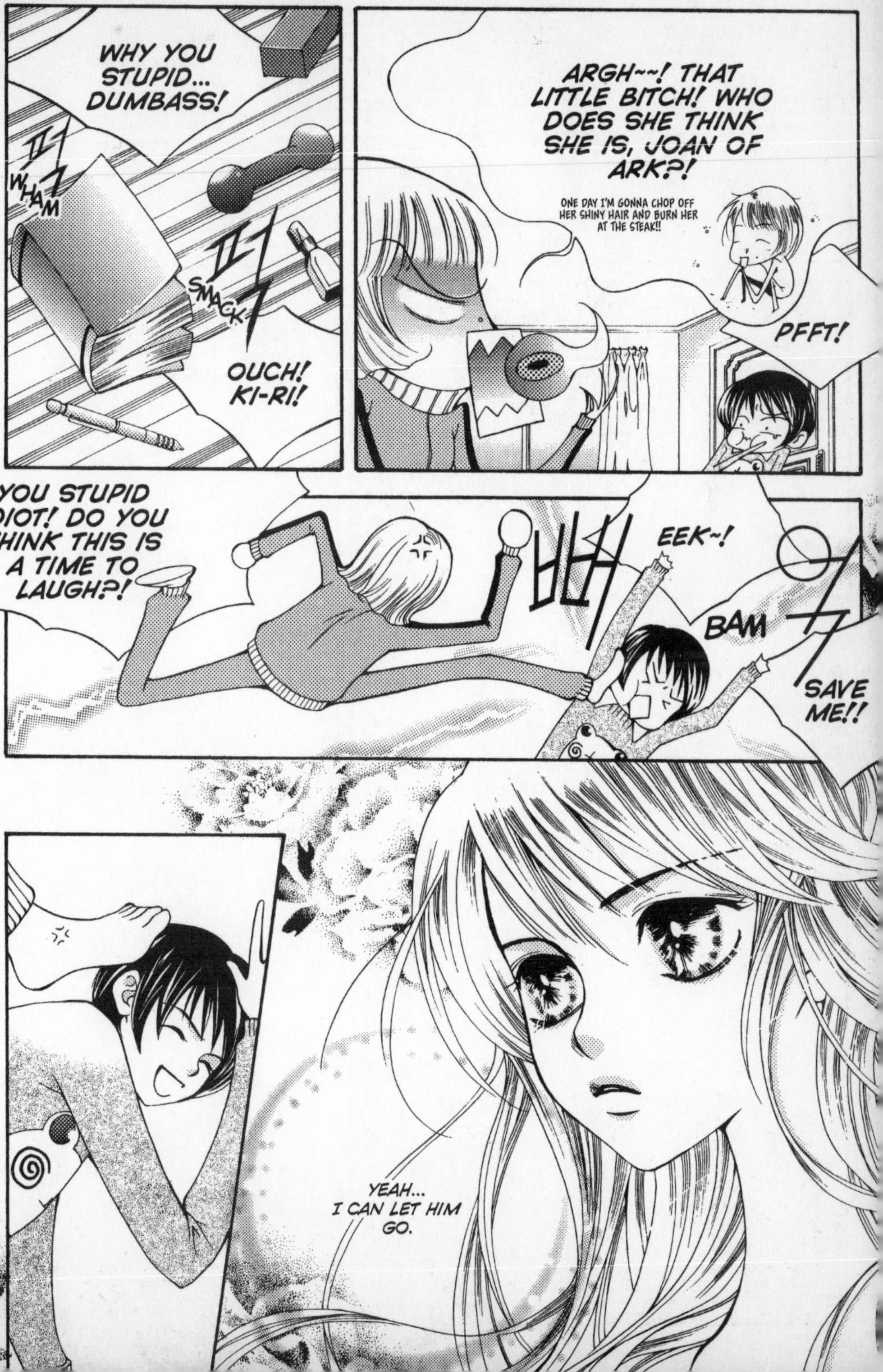
WHY YOU STUPID... DUMBASS!
WHAM
SMACK
OUCH! KI-RI!
ARGH~~! THAT LITTLE BITCH! WHO DOES SHE THINK SHE IS, JOAN OF ARK?!
ONE DAY I'M GONNA CHOP OFF HER SHINY HAIR AND BURN HER AT THE STEAK!!
PFFT!
YOU STUPID IDIOT! DO YOU THINK THIS IS A TIME TO LAUGH?!
EEK~!
BAM
SAVE ME!!
YEAH... I CAN LET HIM GO.

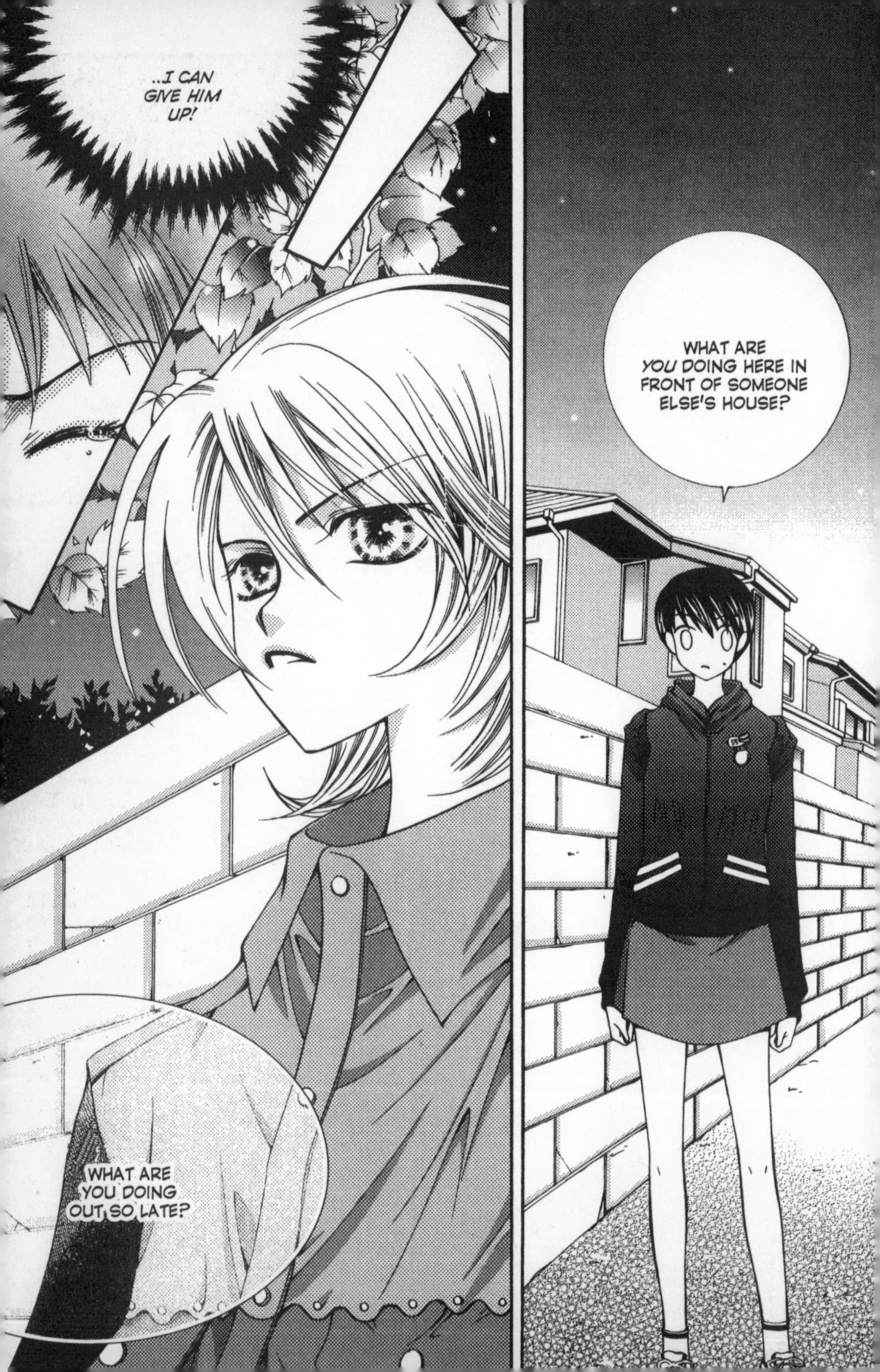
..I CAN GIVE HIM UP!
WHAT ARE YOU DOING OUT SO LATE?
WHAT ARE *YOU* DOING HERE IN FRONT OF SOMEONE ELSE'S HOUSE?

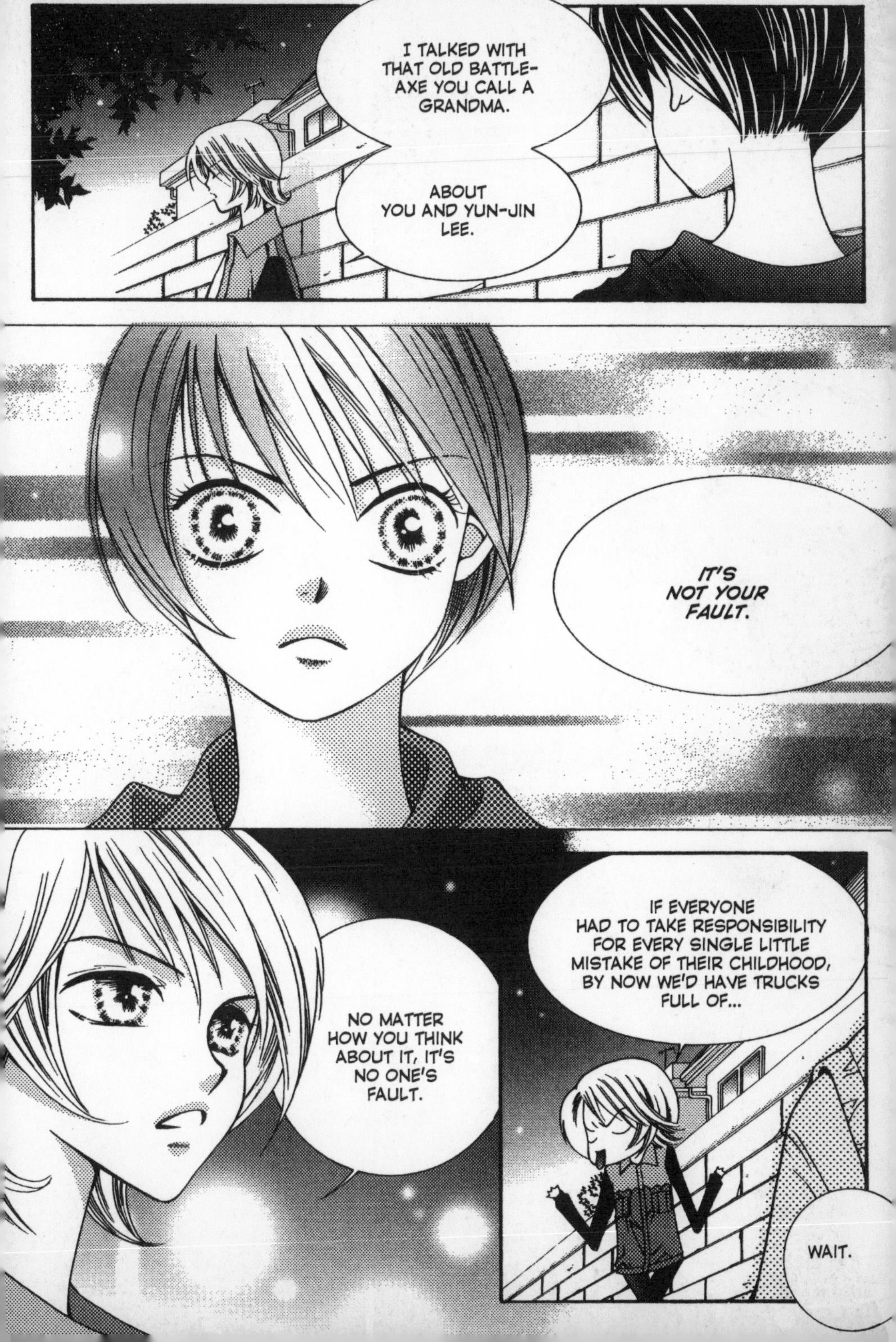
I TALKED WITH THAT OLD BATTLE-AXE YOU CALL A GRANDMA.
ABOUT YOU AND YUN-JIN LEE.
IT'S NOT YOUR FAULT.
NO MATTER HOW YOU THINK ABOUT IT, IT'S NO ONE'S FAULT.
IF EVERYONE HAD TO TAKE RESPONSIBILITY FOR EVERY SINGLE LITTLE MISTAKE OF THEIR CHILDHOOD, BY NOW WE'D HAVE TRUCKS FULL OF...
WAIT.

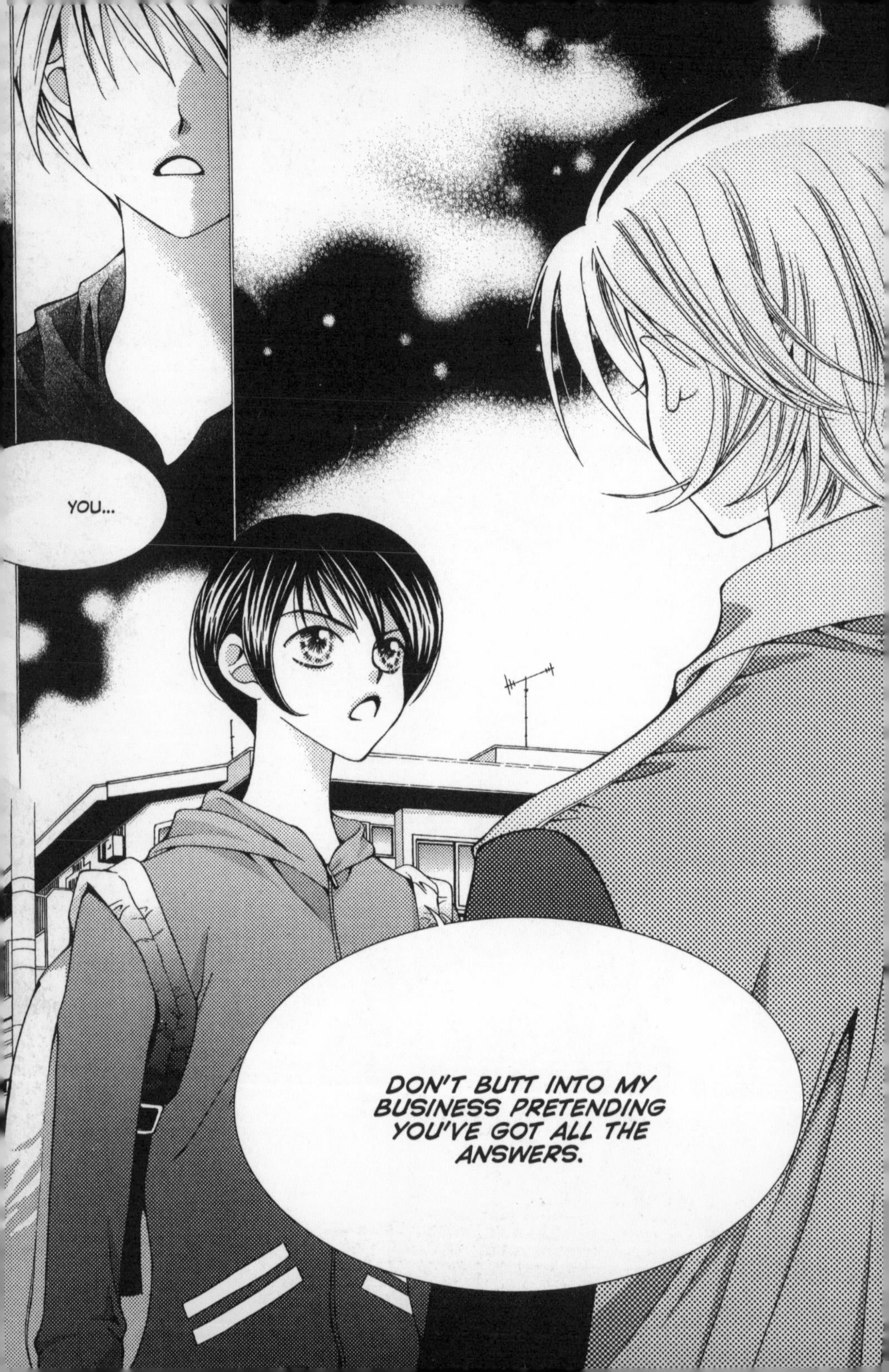
YOU...
DON'T BUTT INTO MY BUSINESS PRETENDING YOU'VE GOT ALL THE ANSWERS.

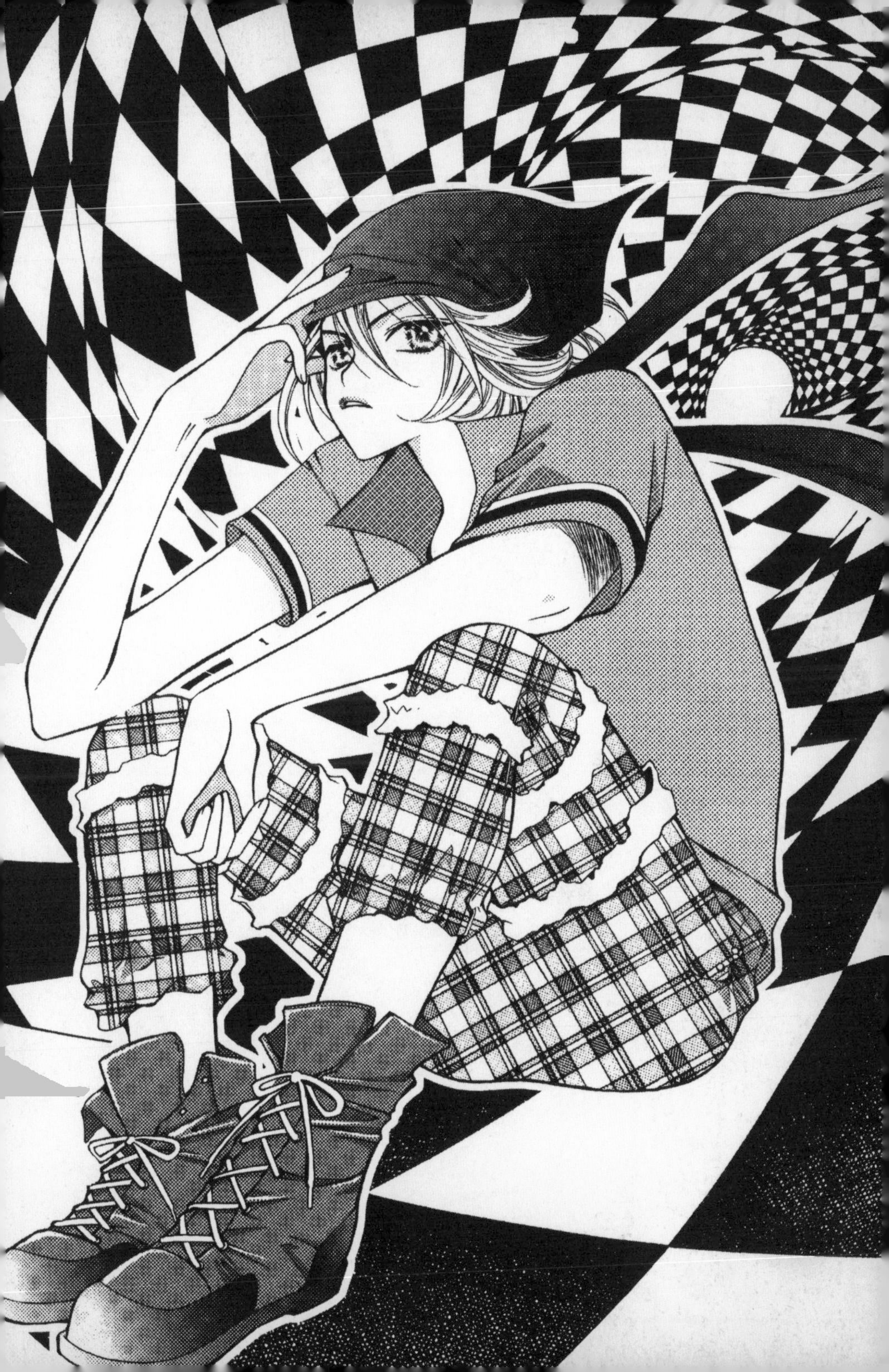

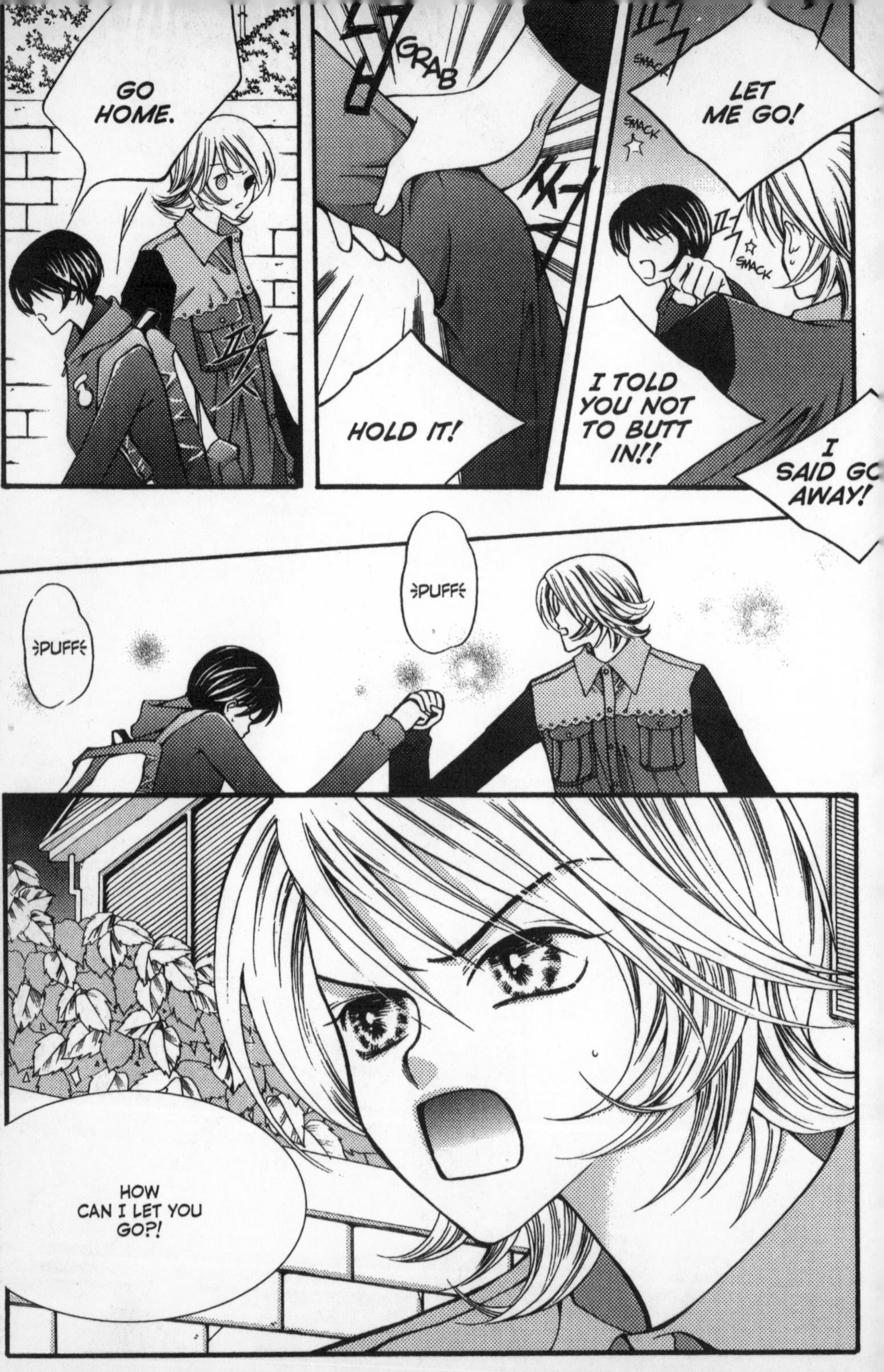
GO HOME.
GRAB
HOLD IT!
SMACK
LET ME GO!
SMACK
SMACK
I TOLD YOU NOT TO BUTT IN!!
I SAID GO AWAY!
PUFF
PUFF
HOW CAN I LET YOU GO?!

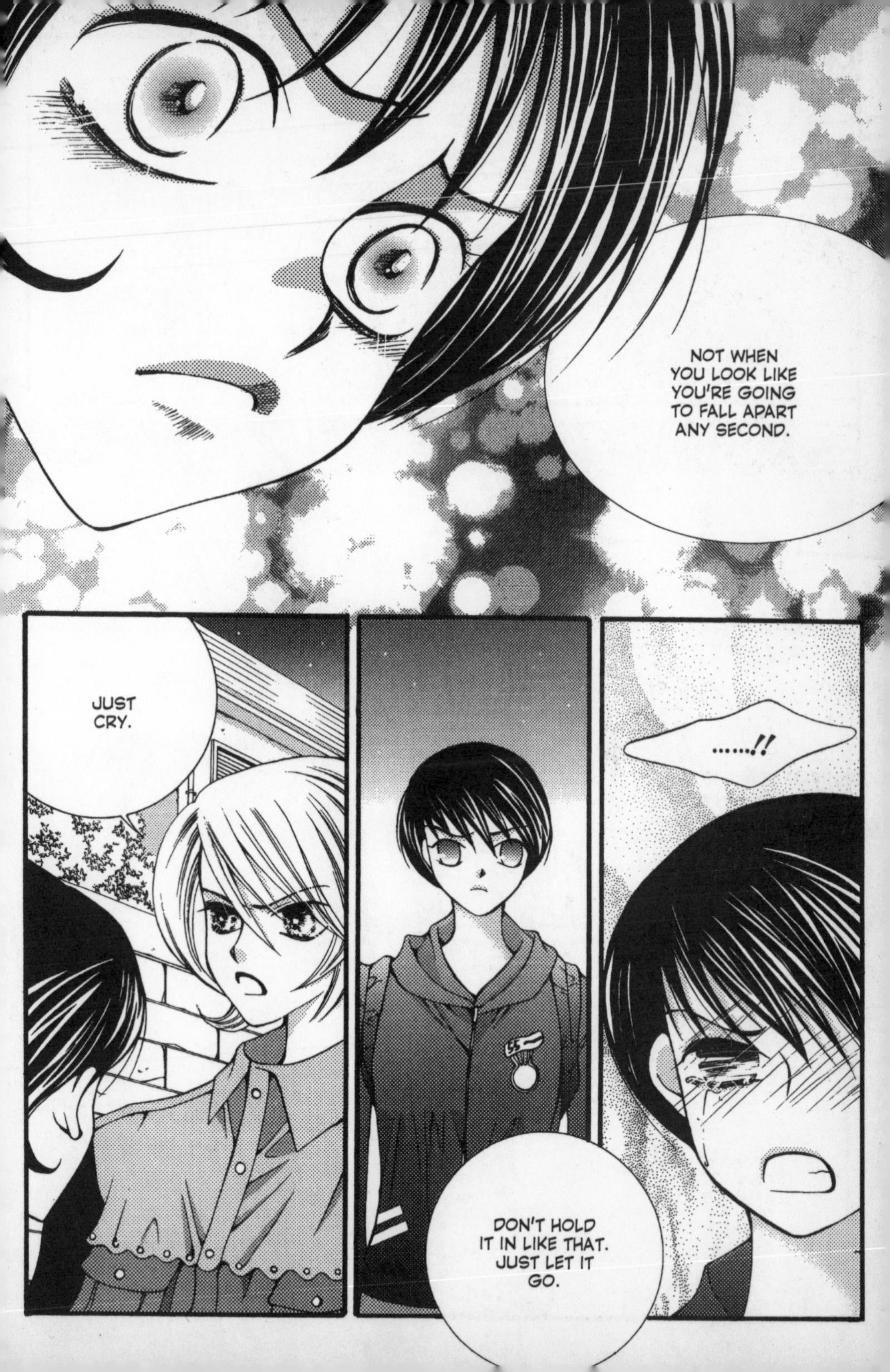
NOT WHEN YOU LOOK LIKE YOU'RE GOING TO FALL APART ANY SECOND.
JUST CRY.
DON'T HOLD IT IN LIKE THAT. JUST LET IT GO.
......!!

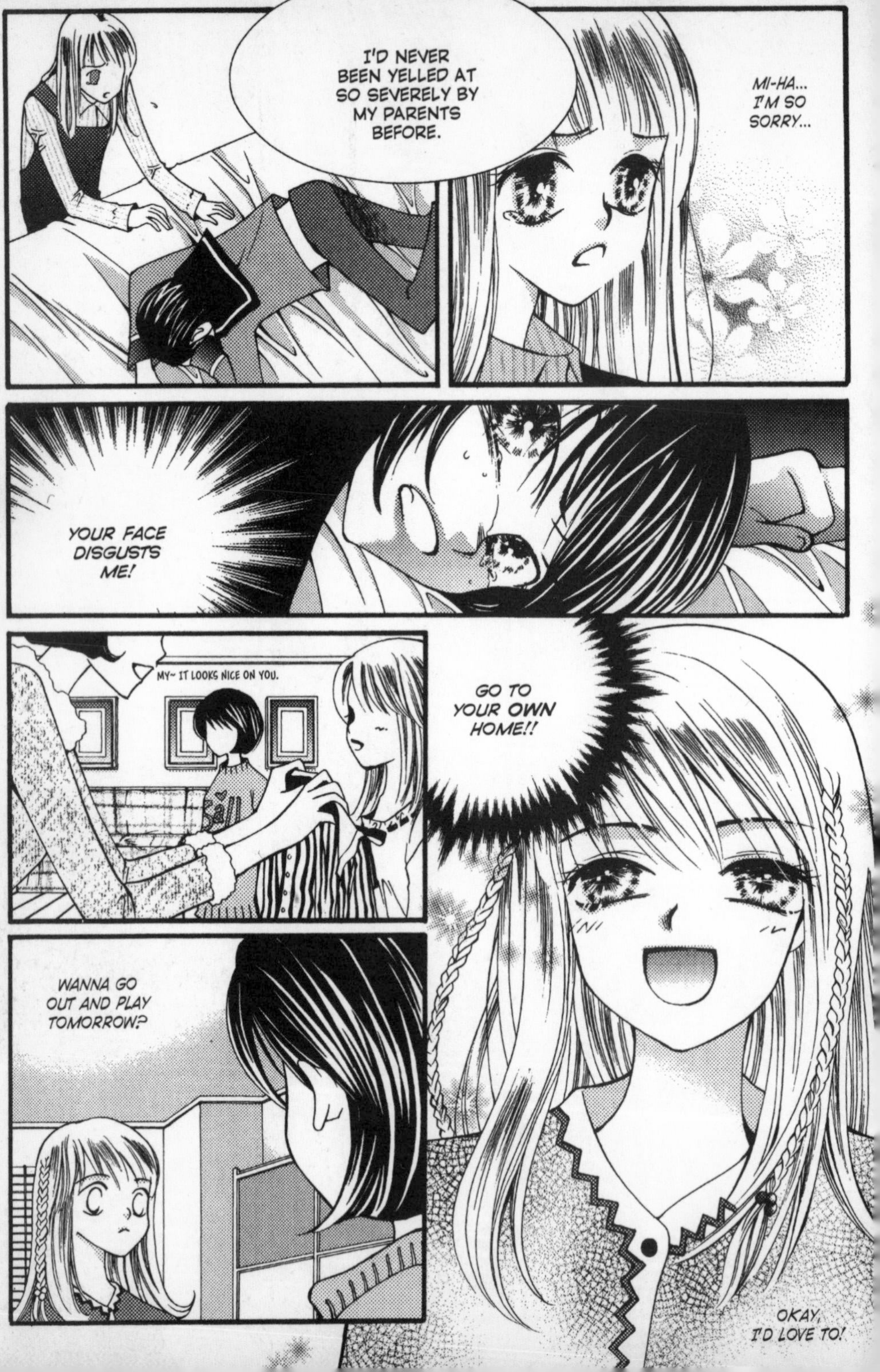
I'D NEVER BEEN YELLED AT SO SEVERELY BY MY PARENTS BEFORE.
MI-HA... I'M SO SORRY...
YOUR FACE DISGUSTS ME!
MY~ IT LOOKS NICE ON YOU.
GO TO YOUR OWN HOME!!
WANNA GO OUT AND PLAY TOMORROW?
OKAY, I'D LOVE TO!

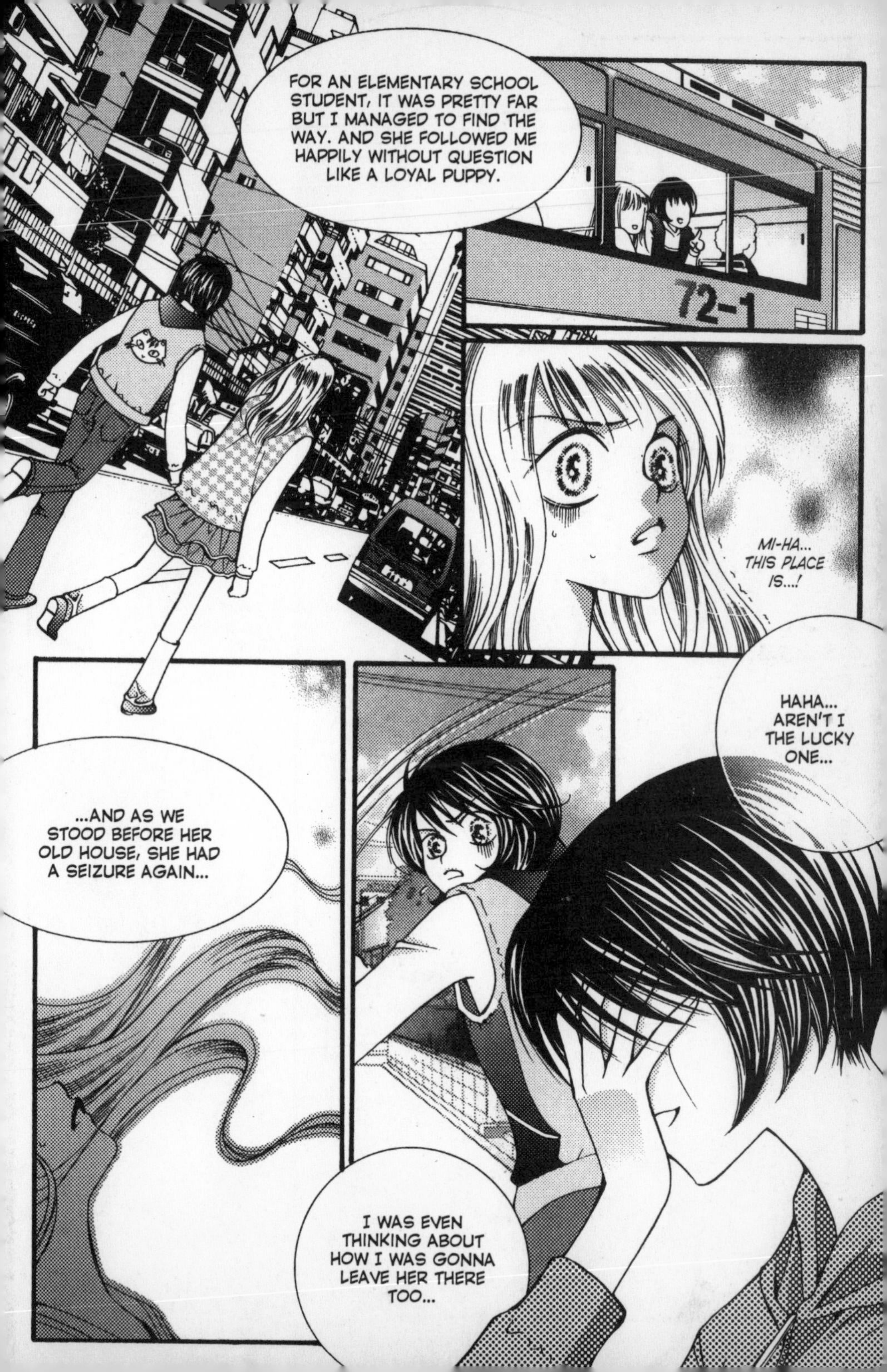
FOR AN ELEMENTARY SCHOOL STUDENT, IT WAS PRETTY FAR BUT I MANAGED TO FIND THE WAY. AND SHE FOLLOWED ME HAPPILY WITHOUT QUESTION LIKE A LOYAL PUPPY.
72-1
MI-HA... THIS PLACE IS...!
...AND AS WE STOOD BEFORE HER OLD HOUSE, SHE HAD A SEIZURE AGAIN...
HAHA... AREN'T I THE LUCKY ONE...
I WAS EVEN THINKING ABOUT HOW I WAS GONNA LEAVE HER THERE TOO...

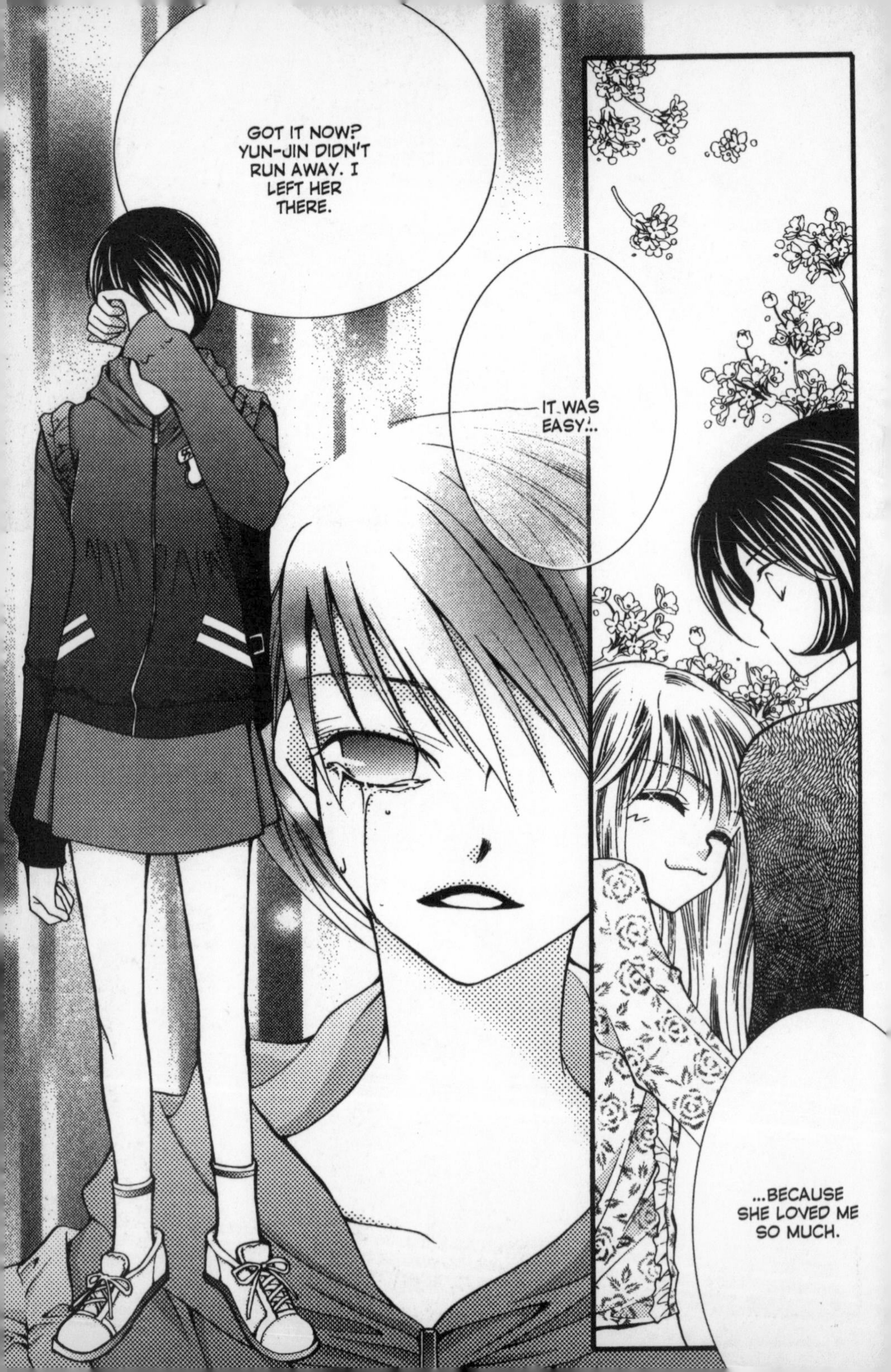
GOT IT NOW? YUN-JIN DIDN'T RUN AWAY. I LEFT HER THERE.
IT WAS EASY...
...BECAUSE SHE LOVED ME SO MUCH.

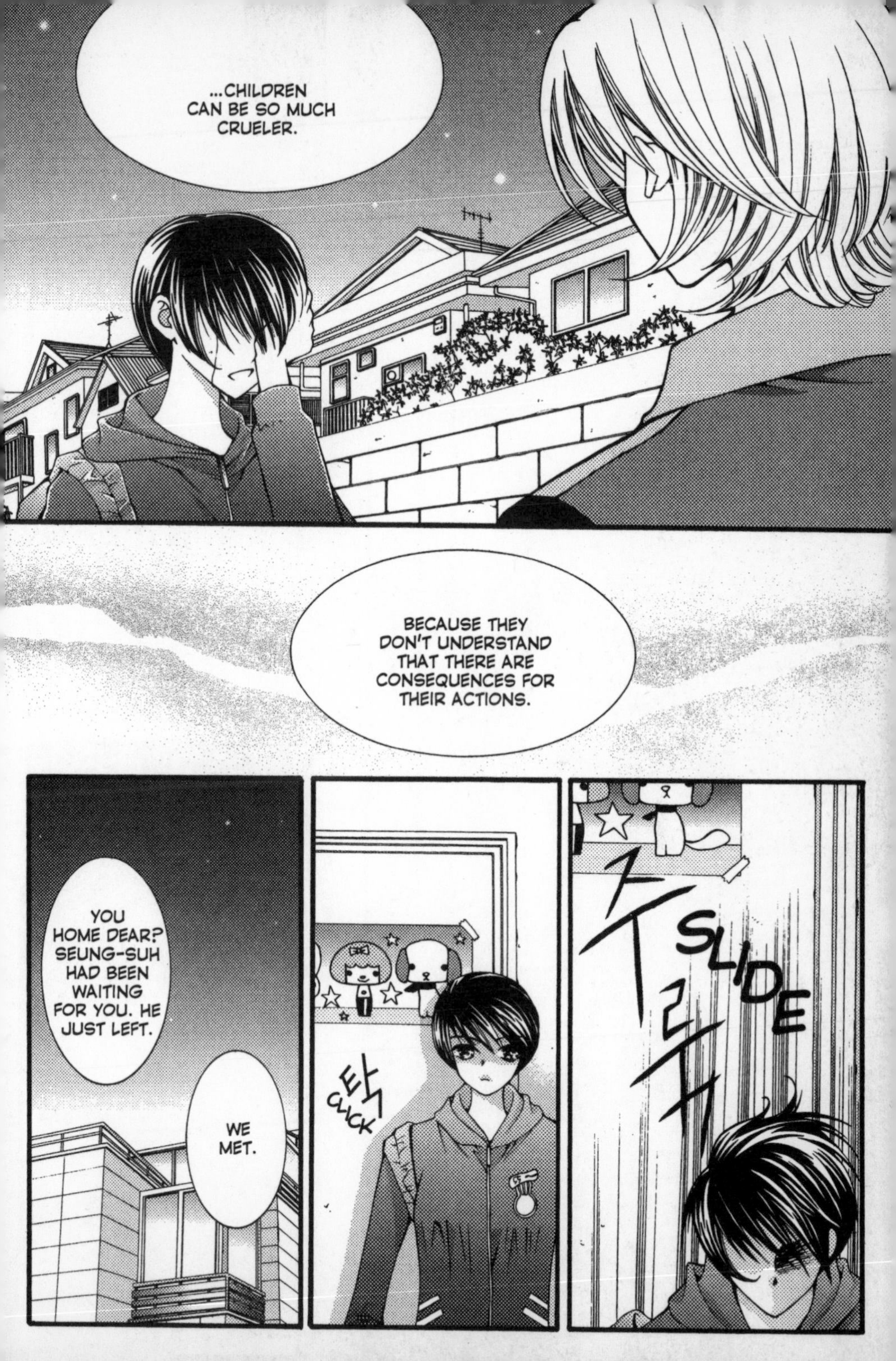
...CHILDREN CAN BE SO MUCH CRUELER.
BECAUSE THEY DON'T UNDERSTAND THAT THERE ARE CONSEQUENCES FOR THEIR ACTIONS.
YOU HOME DEAR? SEUNG-SUH HAD BEEN WAITING FOR YOU. HE JUST LEFT.
WE MET.
탁
CLICK
SLIDE

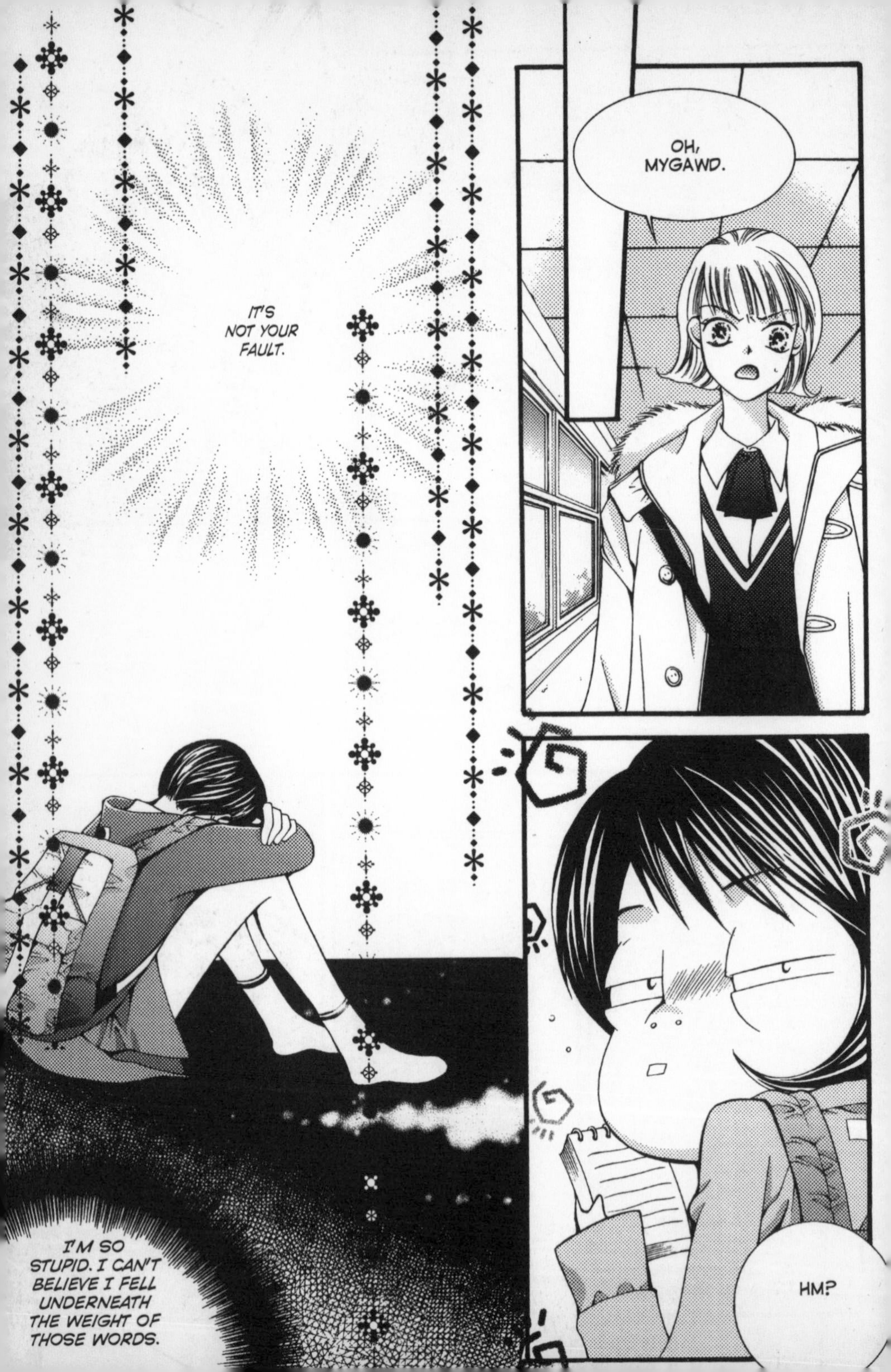
IT'S NOT YOUR FAULT.
I'M SO STUPID. I CAN'T BELIEVE I FELL UNDERNEATH THE WEIGHT OF THOSE WORDS.
OH, MYGAWD.
HM?

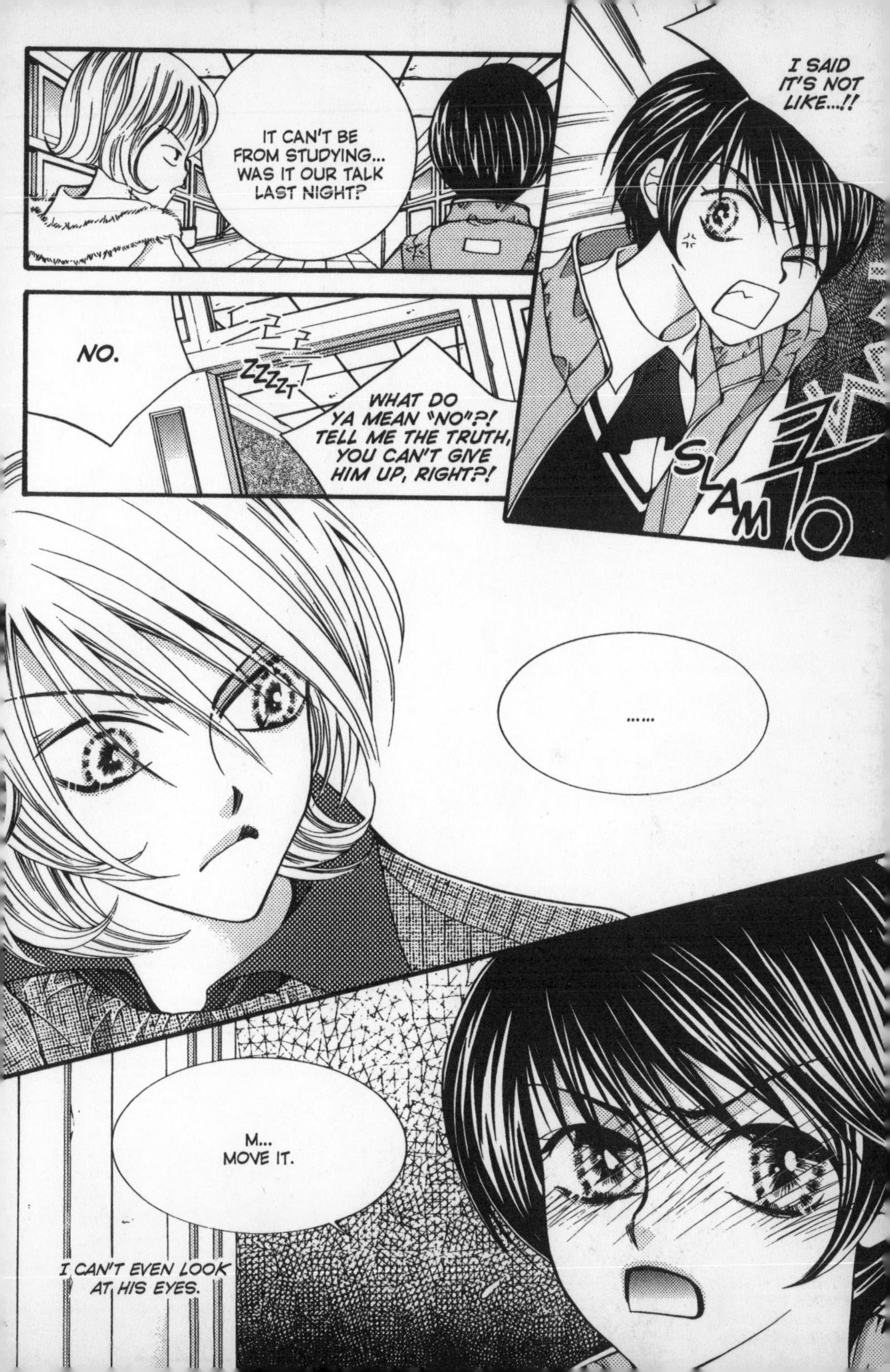

IT CAN'T BE FROM STUDYING... WAS IT OUR TALK LAST NIGHT?
NO.
ZZZZZT
WHAT DO YA MEAN "NO"?! TELL ME THE TRUTH, YOU CAN'T GIVE HIM UP, RIGHT?!
I SAID IT'S NOT LIKE...!!
SLAM
......
M... MOVE IT.
I CAN'T EVEN LOOK AT HIS EYES.

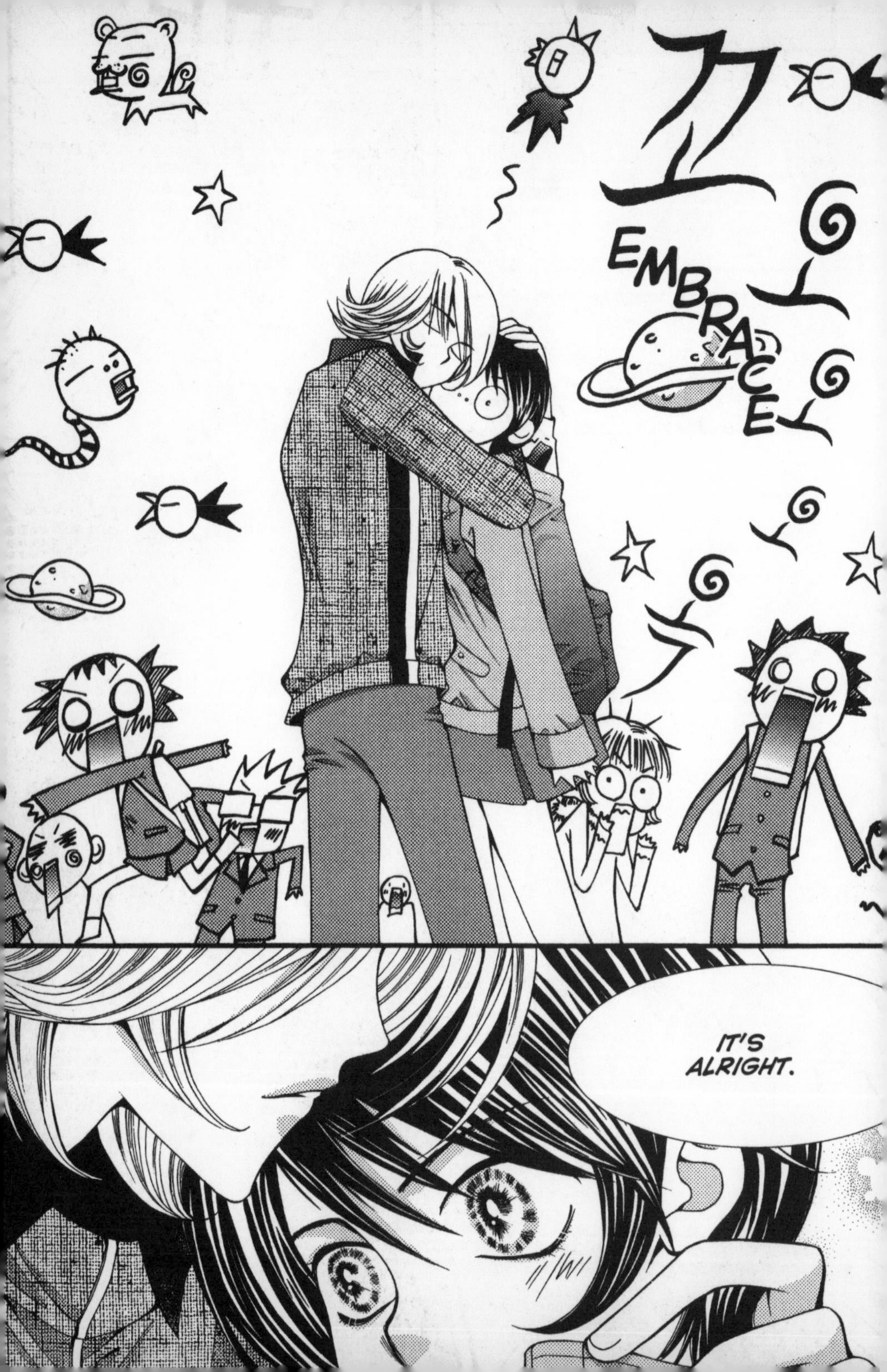
EMBRACE
IT'S ALRIGHT.

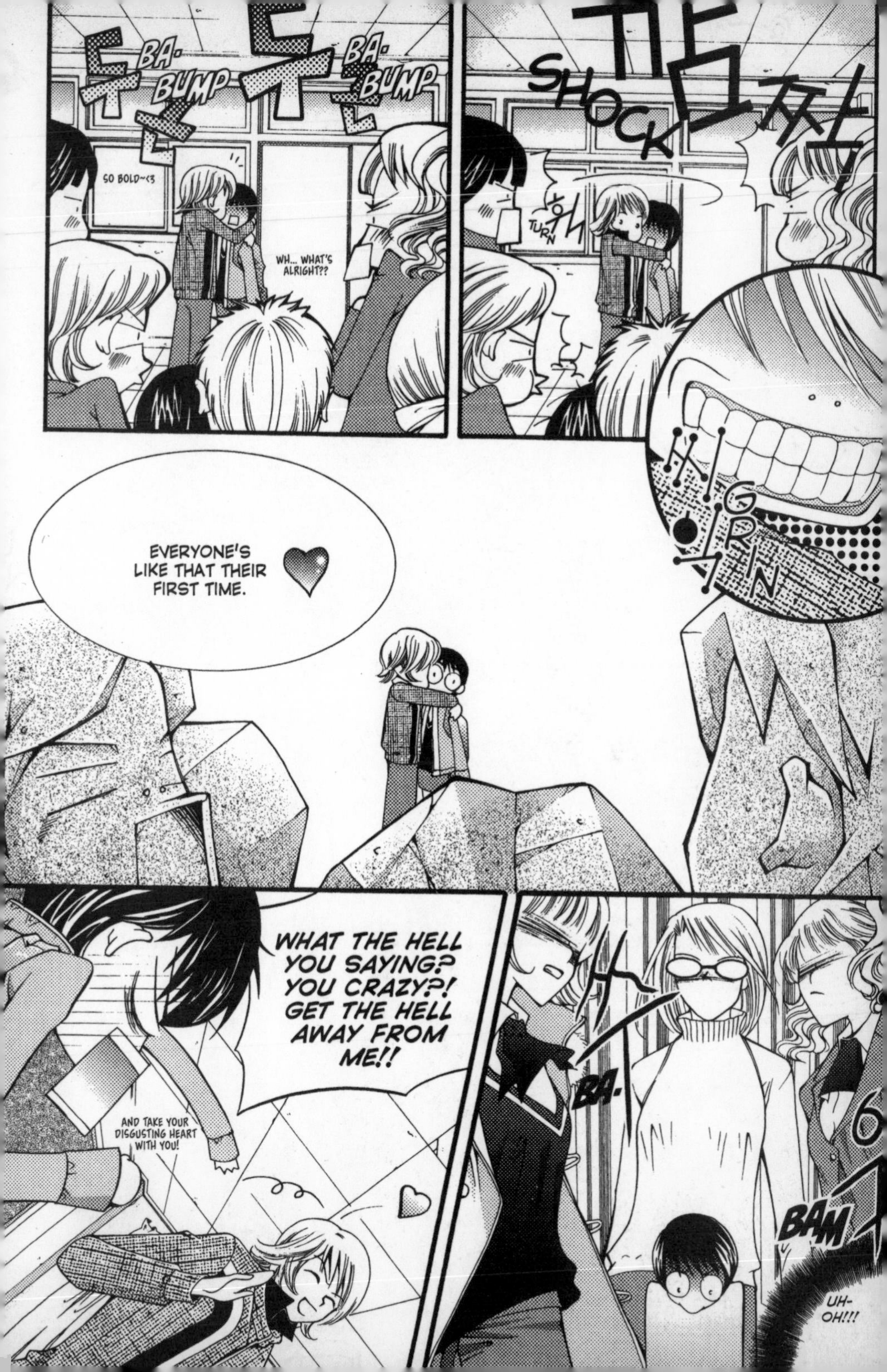
BA-BUMP
BA-BUMP
SO BOLD~<3
WH... WHAT'S ALRIGHT??
THE SHOCK
TURN
EVERYONE'S LIKE THAT THEIR FIRST TIME.
GRIN
WHAT THE HELL YOU SAYING? YOU CRAZY?! GET THE HELL AWAY FROM ME!!
AND TAKE YOUR DISGUSTING HEART WITH YOU!
BA-
BAM
UH-OH!!!

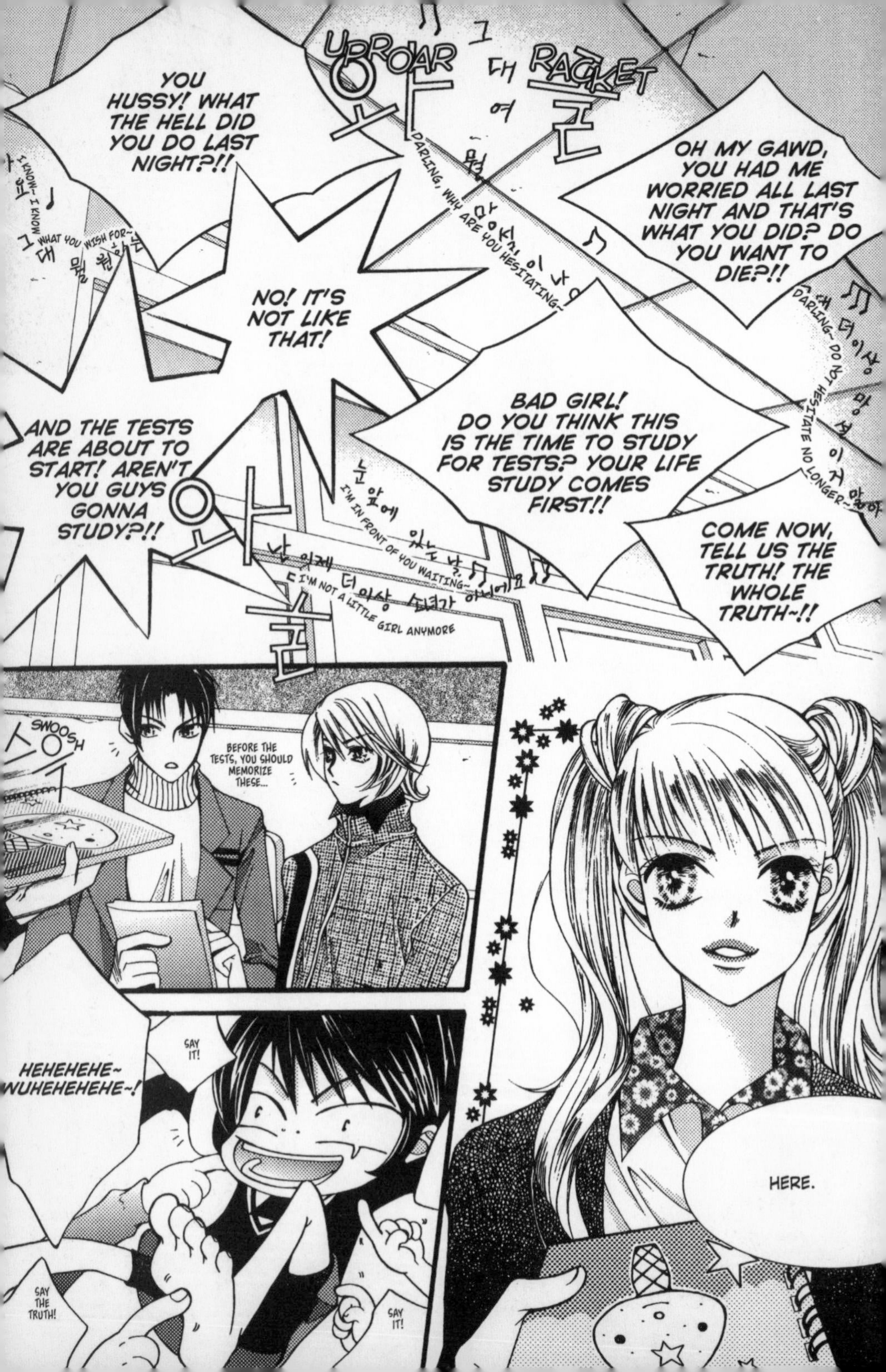
YOU HUSSY! WHAT THE HELL DID YOU DO LAST NIGHT?!!
UPROAR
RACKET
OH MY GAWD, YOU HAD ME WORRIED ALL LAST NIGHT AND THAT'S WHAT YOU DID? DO YOU WANT TO DIE?!!
I KNOW~ I KNOW~ WHAT YOU WISH FOR~
DARLING, WHY ARE YOU HESITATING~
NO! IT'S NOT LIKE THAT!
AND THE TESTS ARE ABOUT TO START! AREN'T YOU GUYS GONNA STUDY?!!
BAD GIRL! DO YOU THINK THIS IS THE TIME TO STUDY FOR TESTS? YOUR LIFE STUDY COMES FIRST!!
DARLING~ DO NOT HESITATE NO LONGER~
I'M IN FRONT OF YOU WAITING~
I'M NOT A LITTLE GIRL ANYMORE
COME NOW, TELL US THE TRUTH! THE WHOLE TRUTH~!!
SWOOSH
BEFORE THE TESTS, YOU SHOULD MEMORIZE THESE...
SAY IT!
HEHEHEHE~ WUHEHEHEHE~!
SAY THE TRUTH!
SAY IT!
HERE.

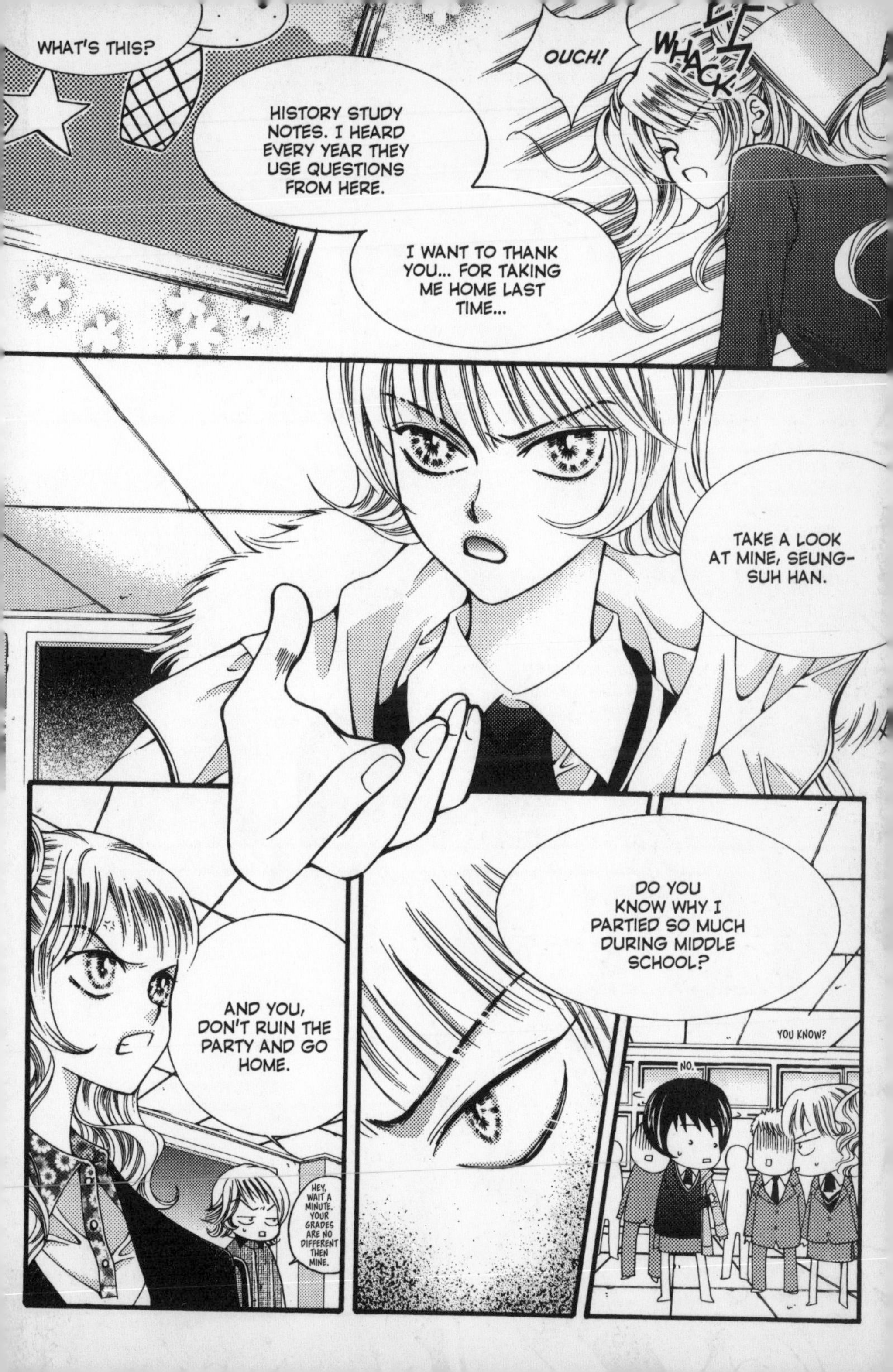
WHAT'S THIS?
HISTORY STUDY NOTES. I HEARD EVERY YEAR THEY USE QUESTIONS FROM HERE.
I WANT TO THANK YOU... FOR TAKING ME HOME LAST TIME...
OUCH!
WHACK
TAKE A LOOK AT MINE, SEUNG-SUH HAN.
AND YOU, DON'T RUIN THE PARTY AND GO HOME.
HEY, WAIT A MINUTE. YOUR GRADES ARE NO DIFFERENT THEN MINE.
DO YOU KNOW WHY I PARTIED SO MUCH DURING MIDDLE SCHOOL?
YOU KNOW?
NO.

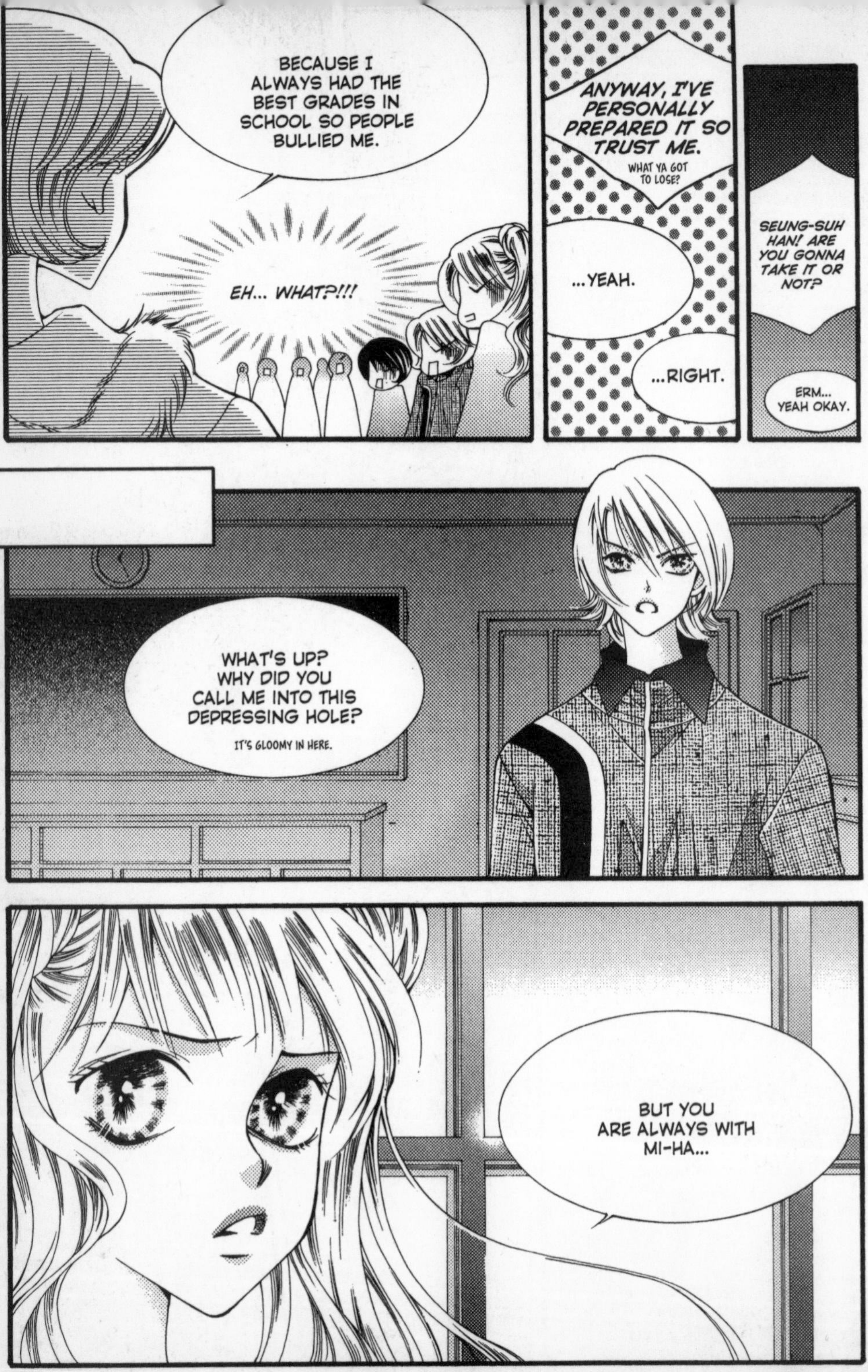
BECAUSE I ALWAYS HAD THE BEST GRADES IN SCHOOL SO PEOPLE BULLIED ME.
EH... WHAT?!!!
ANYWAY, I'VE PERSONALLY PREPARED IT SO TRUST ME.
WHAT YA GOT TO LOSE?
...YEAH.
...RIGHT.
SEUNG-SUH HAN! ARE YOU GONNA TAKE IT OR NOT?
ERM... YEAH OKAY.
WHAT'S UP? WHY DID YOU CALL ME INTO THIS DEPRESSING HOLE?
IT'S GLOOMY IN HERE.
BUT YOU ARE ALWAYS WITH MI-HA...

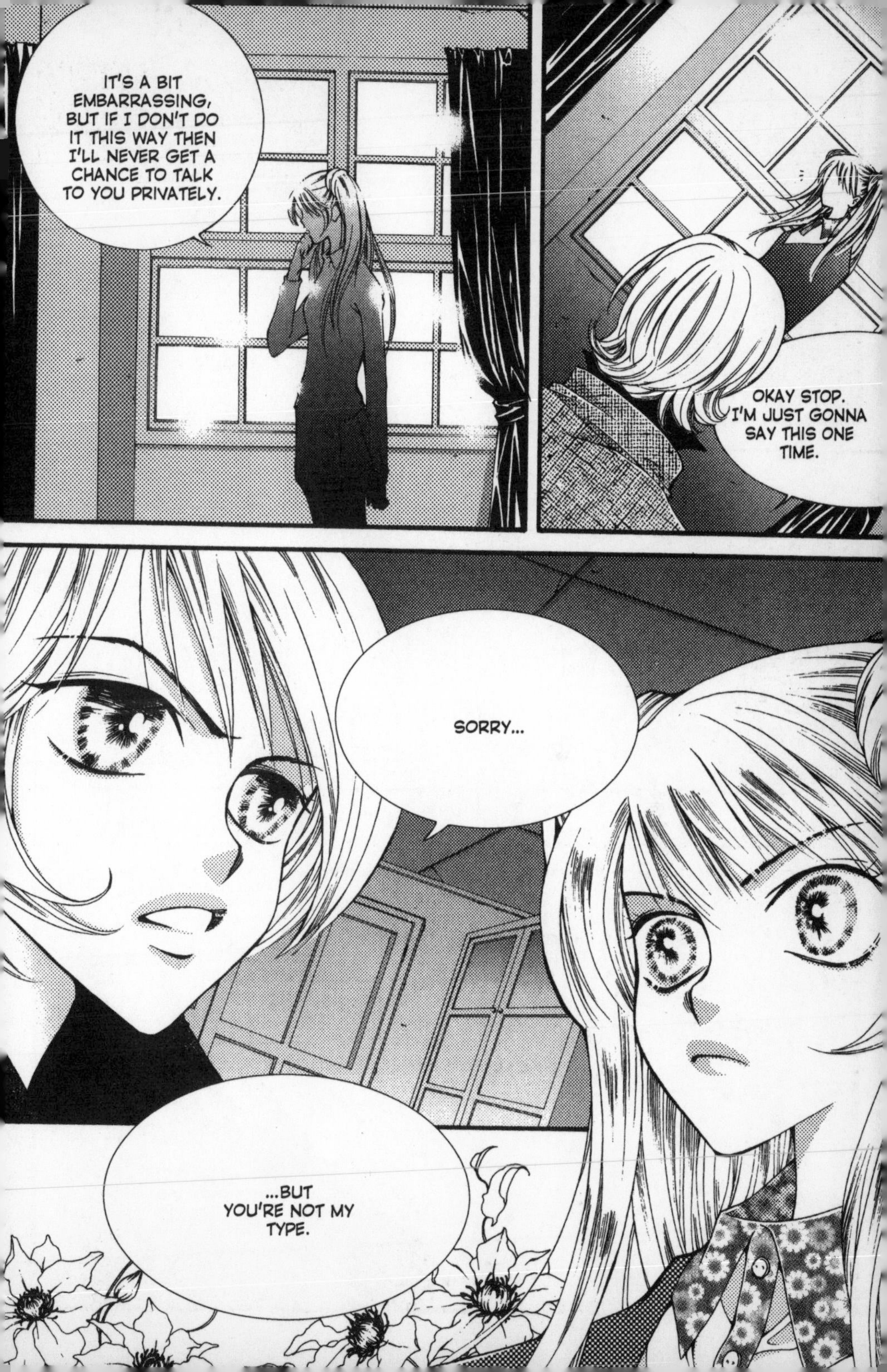
IT'S A BIT EMBARRASSING, BUT IF I DON'T DO IT THIS WAY THEN I'LL NEVER GET A CHANCE TO TALK TO YOU PRIVATELY.
OKAY STOP. I'M JUST GONNA SAY THIS ONE TIME.
SORRY...
...BUT YOU'RE NOT MY TYPE.

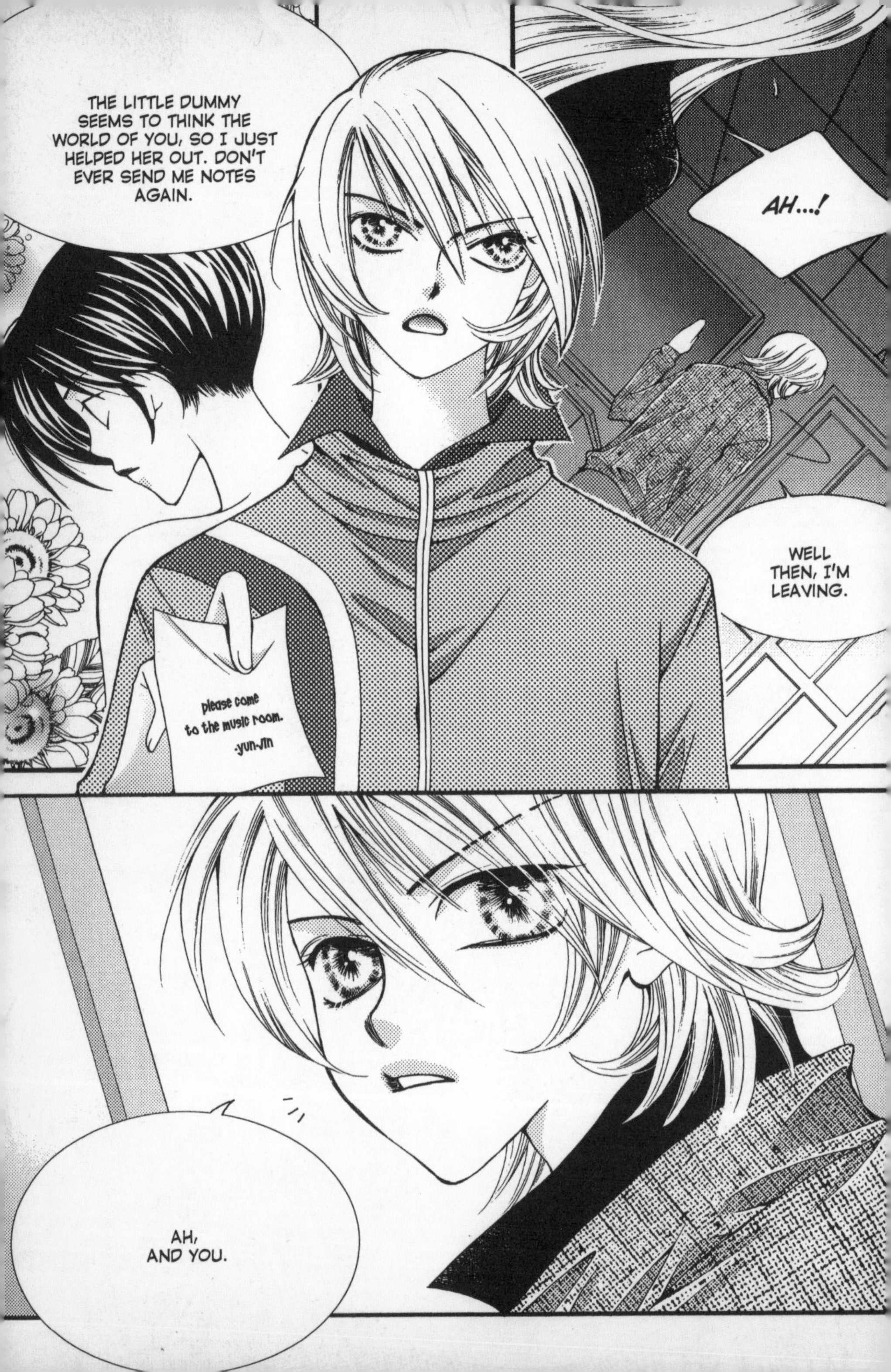
THE LITTLE DUMMY SEEMS TO THINK THE WORLD OF YOU, SO I JUST HELPED HER OUT. DON'T EVER SEND ME NOTES AGAIN.
please come to the music room. -yun-jin
AH...!
WELL THEN, I'M LEAVING.
AH, AND YOU.

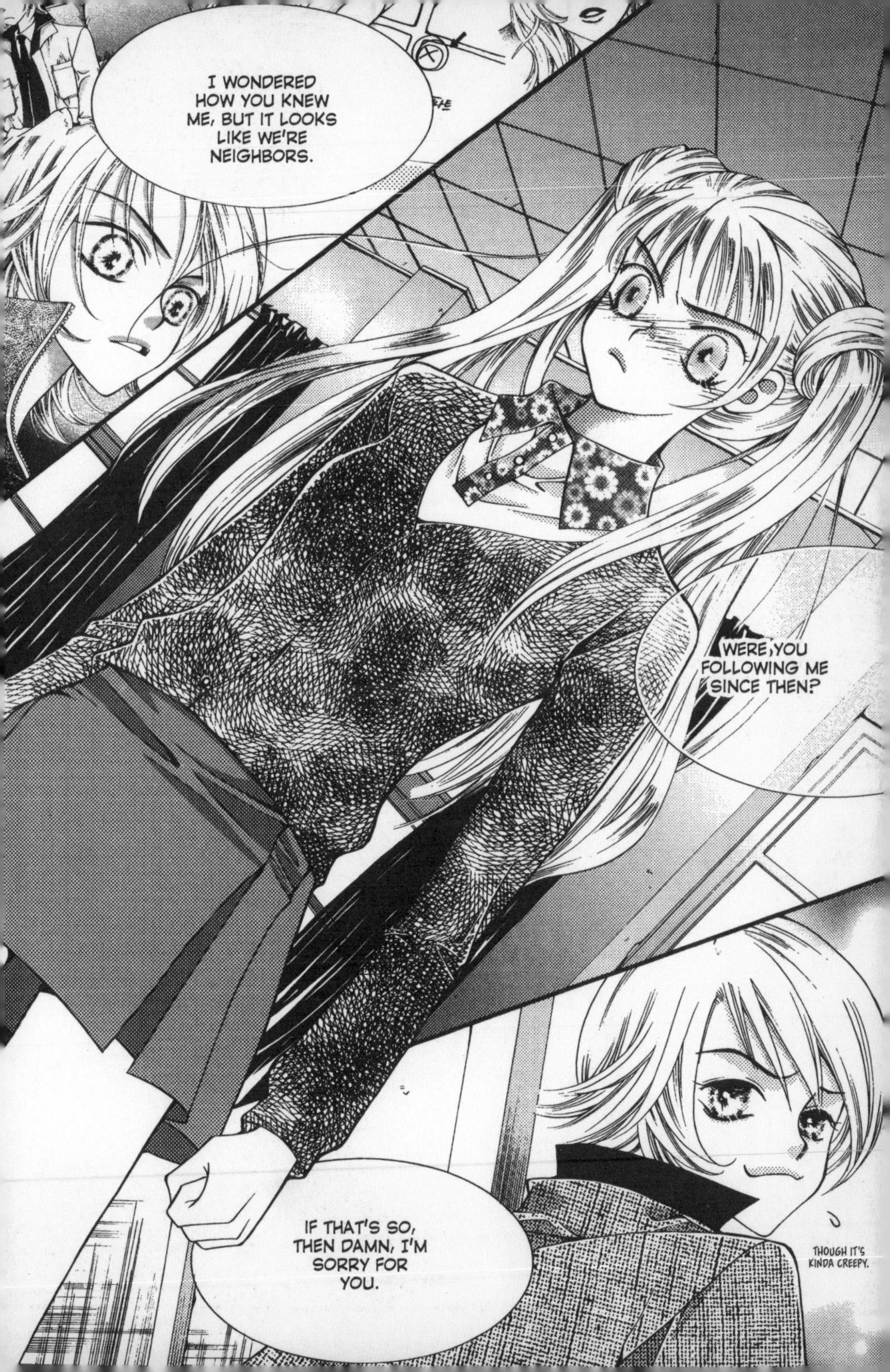
I WONDERED HOW YOU KNEW ME, BUT IT LOOKS LIKE WE'RE NEIGHBORS.
WERE YOU FOLLOWING ME SINCE THEN?
IF THAT'S SO, THEN DAMN, I'M SORRY FOR YOU.
THOUGH IT'S KINDA CREEPY.

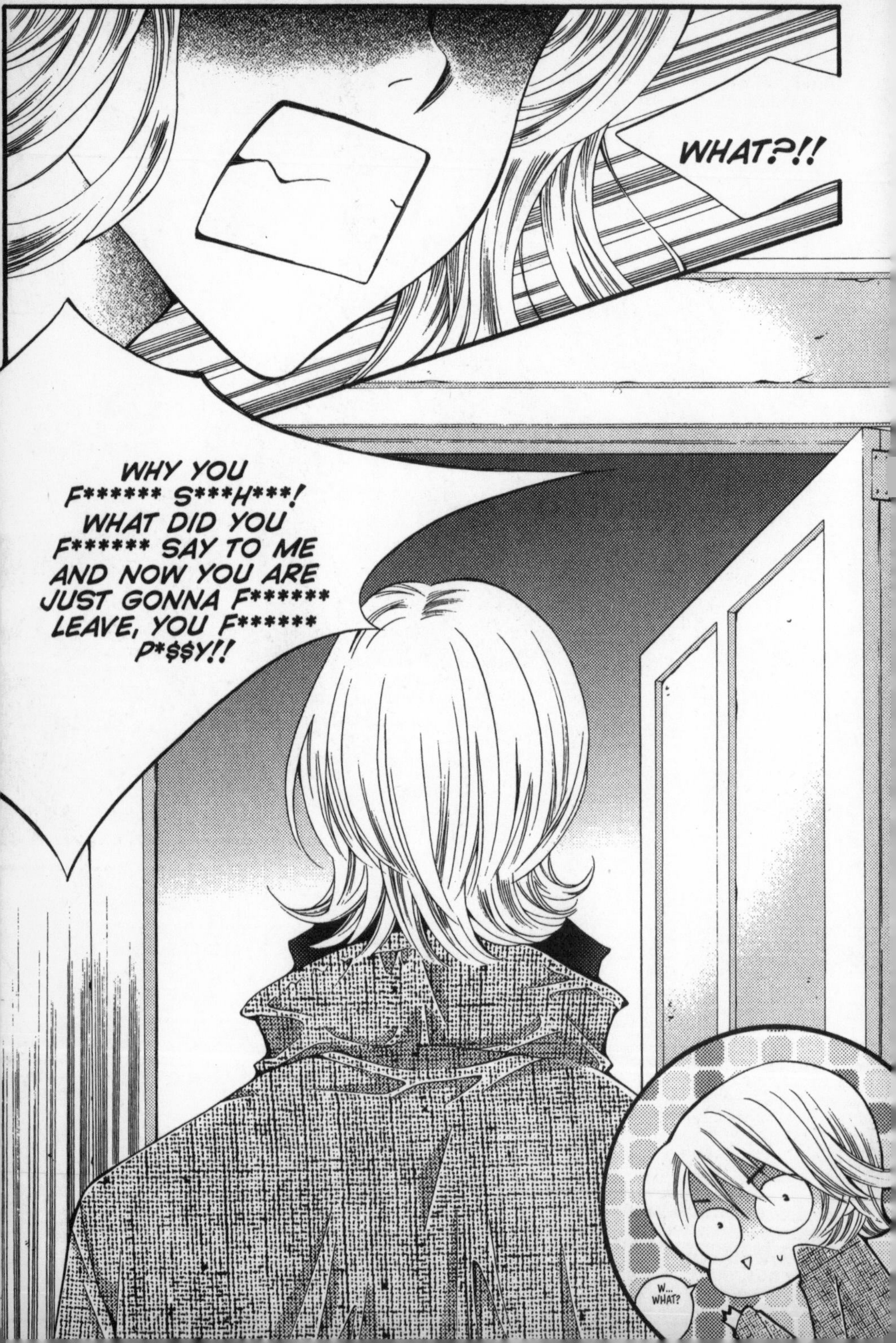
WHAT?!!
WHY YOU F****** S***H***! WHAT DID YOU F****** SAY TO ME AND NOW YOU ARE JUST GONNA F****** LEAVE, YOU F****** P*$$Y!!
W... WHAT?

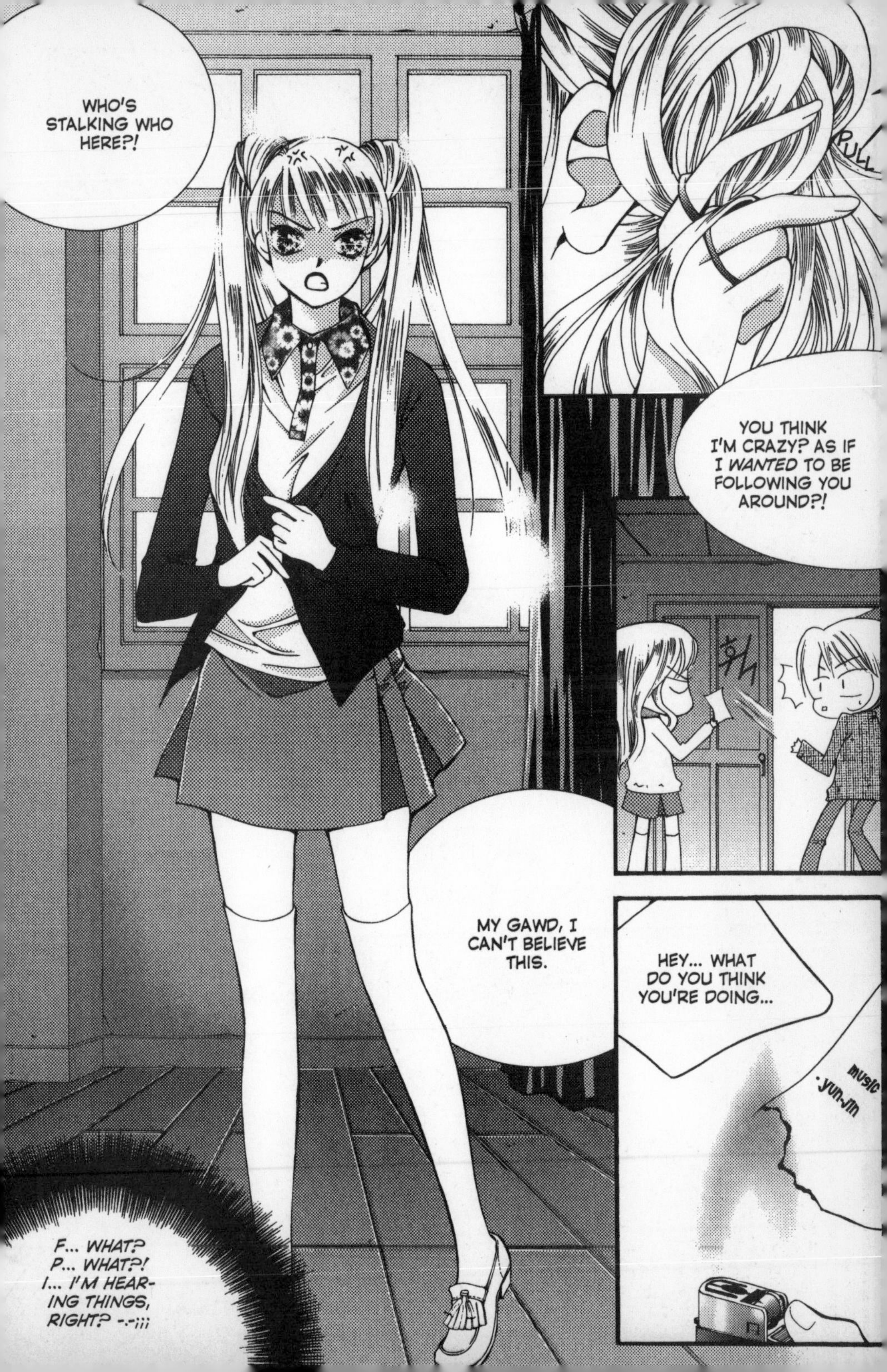
WHO'S STALKING WHO HERE?!
MY GAWD, I CAN'T BELIEVE THIS.
F... WHAT? P... WHAT?! I... I'M HEAR-ING THINGS, RIGHT? -.-;;;
PULL
YOU THINK I'M CRAZY? AS IF I *WANTED* TO BE FOLLOWING YOU AROUND?!
HEY... WHAT DO YOU THINK YOU'RE DOING...
music
·yun-jin

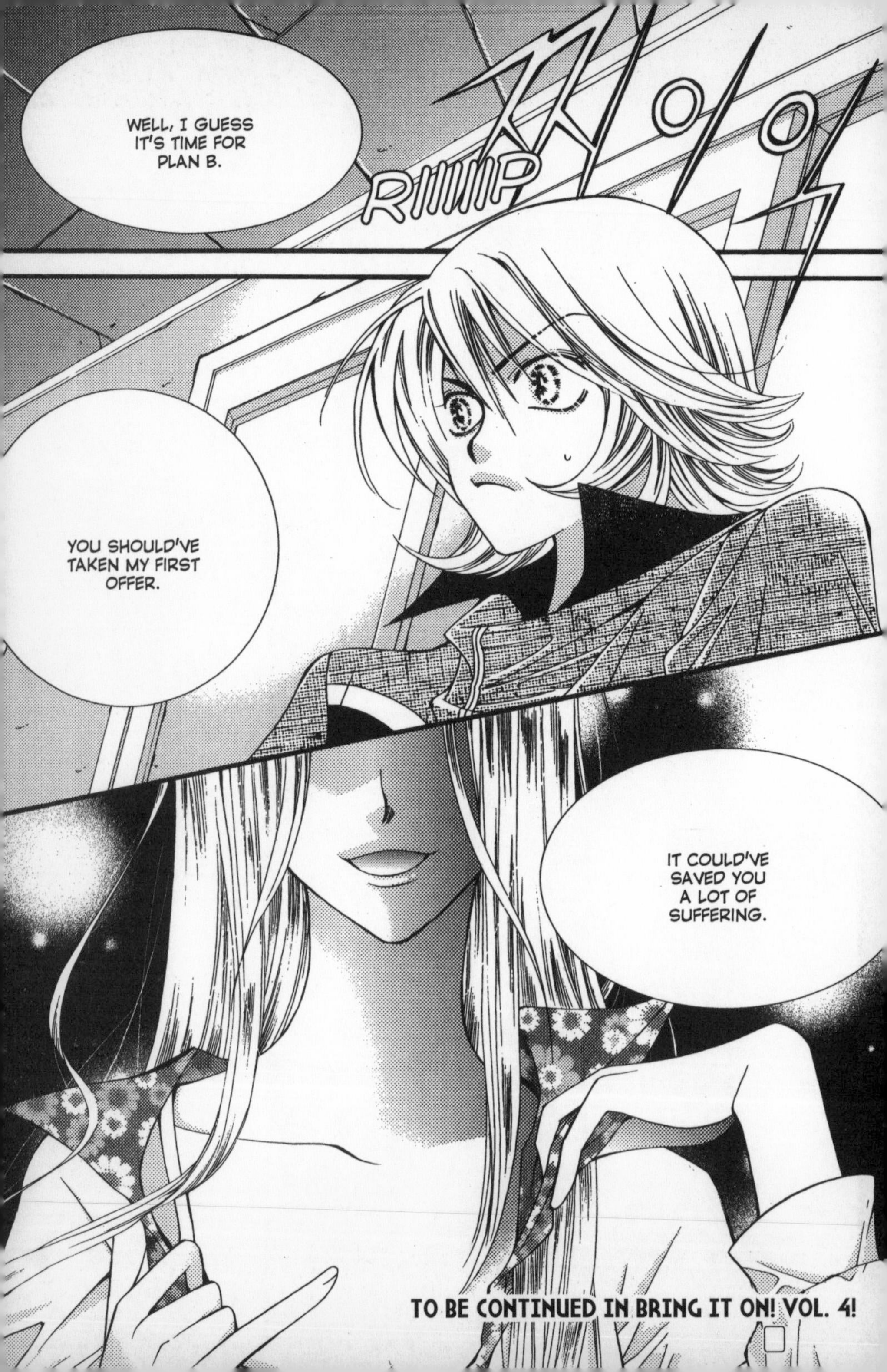
WELL, I GUESS IT'S TIME FOR PLAN B.
RIIIIIP
YOU SHOULD'VE TAKEN MY FIRST OFFER.
IT COULD'VE SAVED YOU A LOT OF SUFFERING.
TO BE CONTINUED IN BRING IT ON! VOL. 4!

Preview

Cynical Orange

vol.2

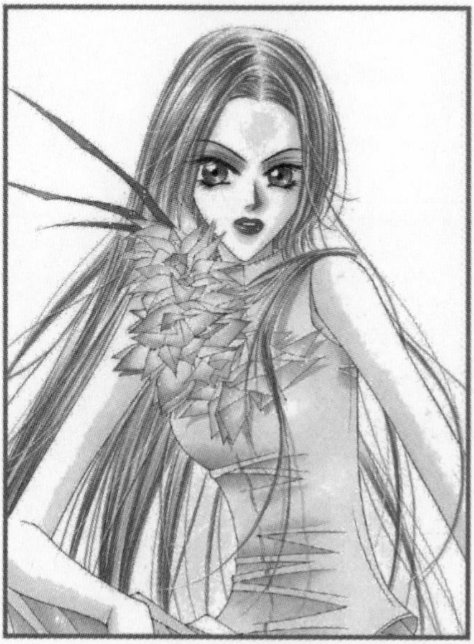

Yun JiUn

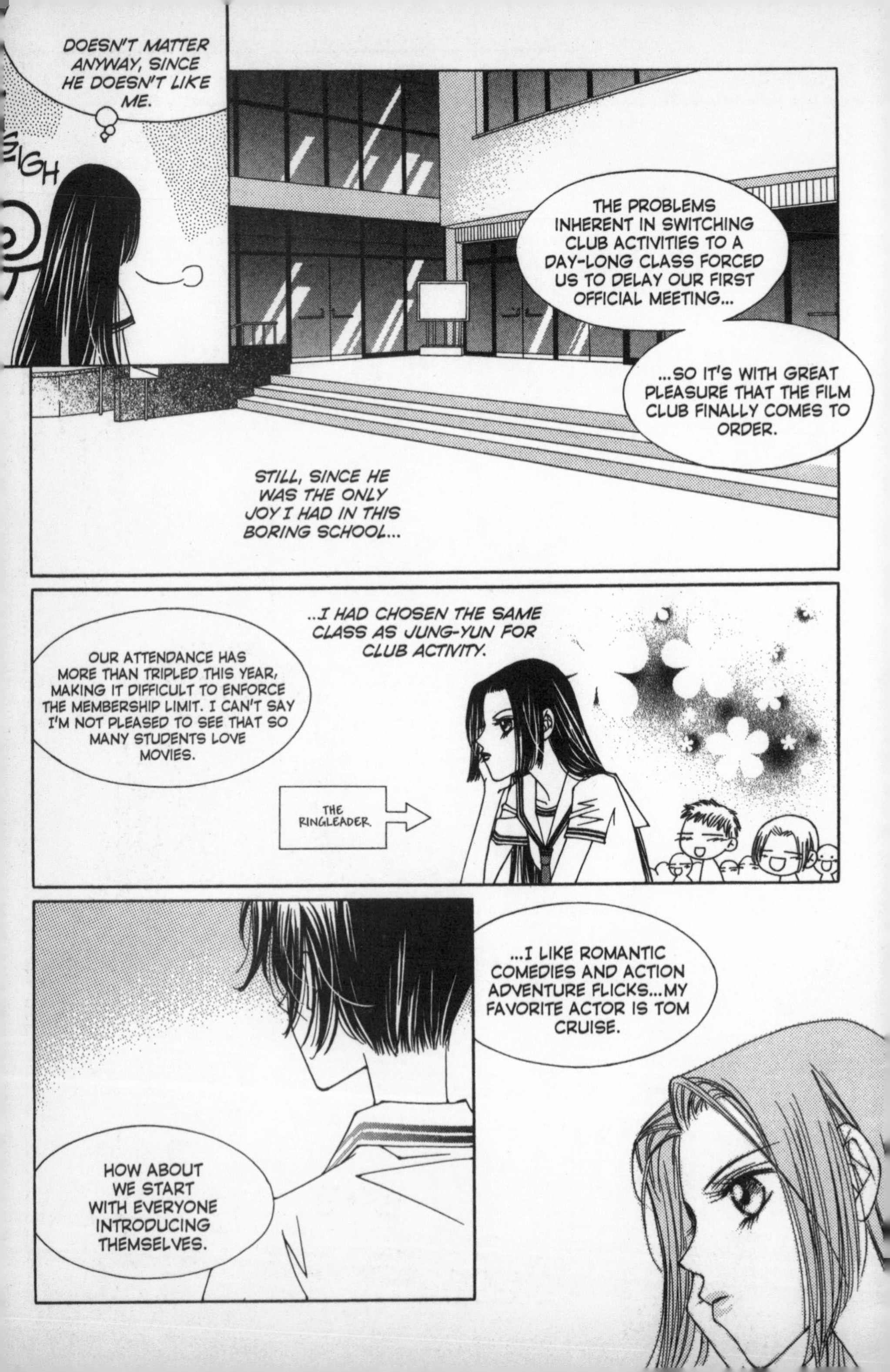
DOESN'T MATTER ANYWAY, SINCE HE DOESN'T LIKE ME.
SIGH
THE PROBLEMS INHERENT IN SWITCHING CLUB ACTIVITIES TO A DAY-LONG CLASS FORCED US TO DELAY OUR FIRST OFFICIAL MEETING...
...SO IT'S WITH GREAT PLEASURE THAT THE FILM CLUB FINALLY COMES TO ORDER.
STILL, SINCE HE WAS THE ONLY JOY I HAD IN THIS BORING SCHOOL...
..I HAD CHOSEN THE SAME CLASS AS JUNG-YUN FOR CLUB ACTIVITY.
OUR ATTENDANCE HAS MORE THAN TRIPLED THIS YEAR, MAKING IT DIFFICULT TO ENFORCE THE MEMBERSHIP LIMIT. I CAN'T SAY I'M NOT PLEASED TO SEE THAT SO MANY STUDENTS LOVE MOVIES.
THE RINGLEADER.
HOW ABOUT WE START WITH EVERYONE INTRODUCING THEMSELVES.
...I LIKE ROMANTIC COMEDIES AND ACTION ADVENTURE FLICKS...MY FAVORITE ACTOR IS TOM CRUISE.

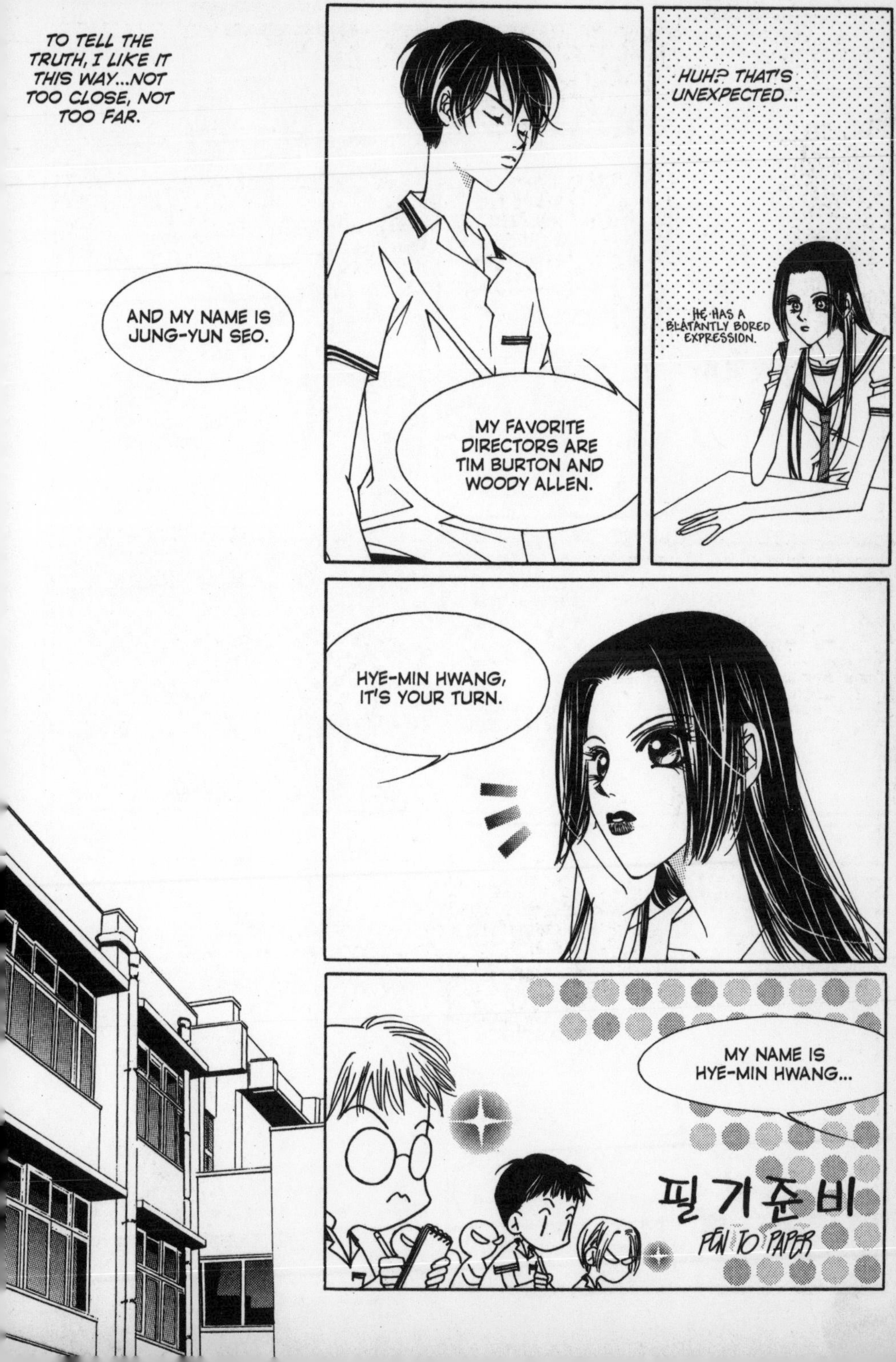
TO TELL THE TRUTH, I LIKE IT THIS WAY...NOT TOO CLOSE, NOT TOO FAR.
AND MY NAME IS JUNG-YUN SEO.
MY FAVORITE DIRECTORS ARE TIM BURTON AND WOODY ALLEN.
HUH? THAT'S UNEXPECTED...
HE HAS A BLATANTLY BORED EXPRESSION.
HYE-MIN HWANG, IT'S YOUR TURN.
MY NAME IS HYE-MIN HWANG...
필기준비
PEN TO PAPER

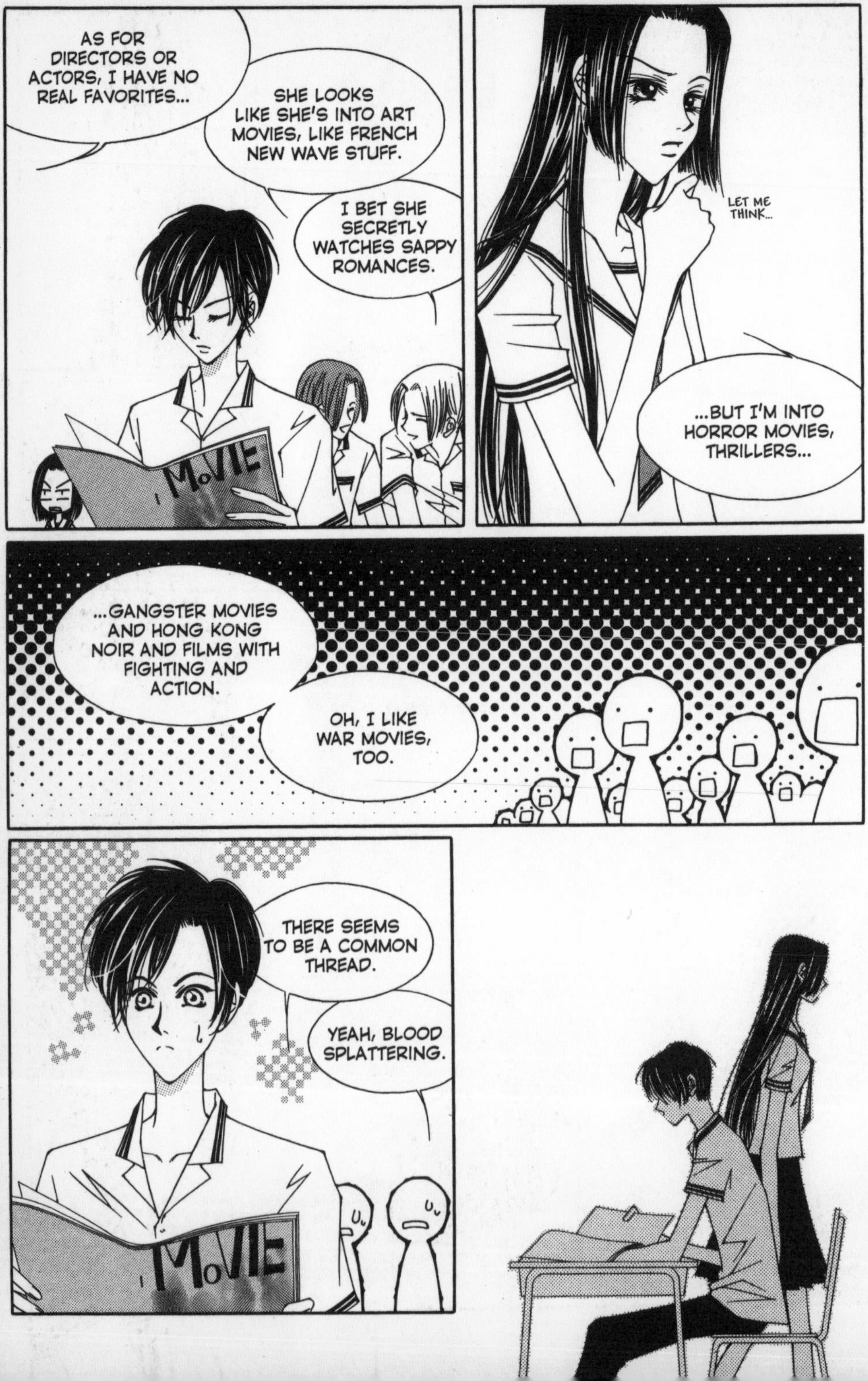
AS FOR DIRECTORS OR ACTORS, I HAVE NO REAL FAVORITES...
SHE LOOKS LIKE SHE'S INTO ART MOVIES, LIKE FRENCH NEW WAVE STUFF.
I BET SHE SECRETLY WATCHES SAPPY ROMANCES.
MOVIE
LET ME THINK...
...BUT I'M INTO HORROR MOVIES, THRILLERS...
...GANGSTER MOVIES AND HONG KONG NOIR AND FILMS WITH FIGHTING AND ACTION.
OH, I LIKE WAR MOVIES, TOO.
THERE SEEMS TO BE A COMMON THREAD.
YEAH, BLOOD SPLATTERING.
MOVIE

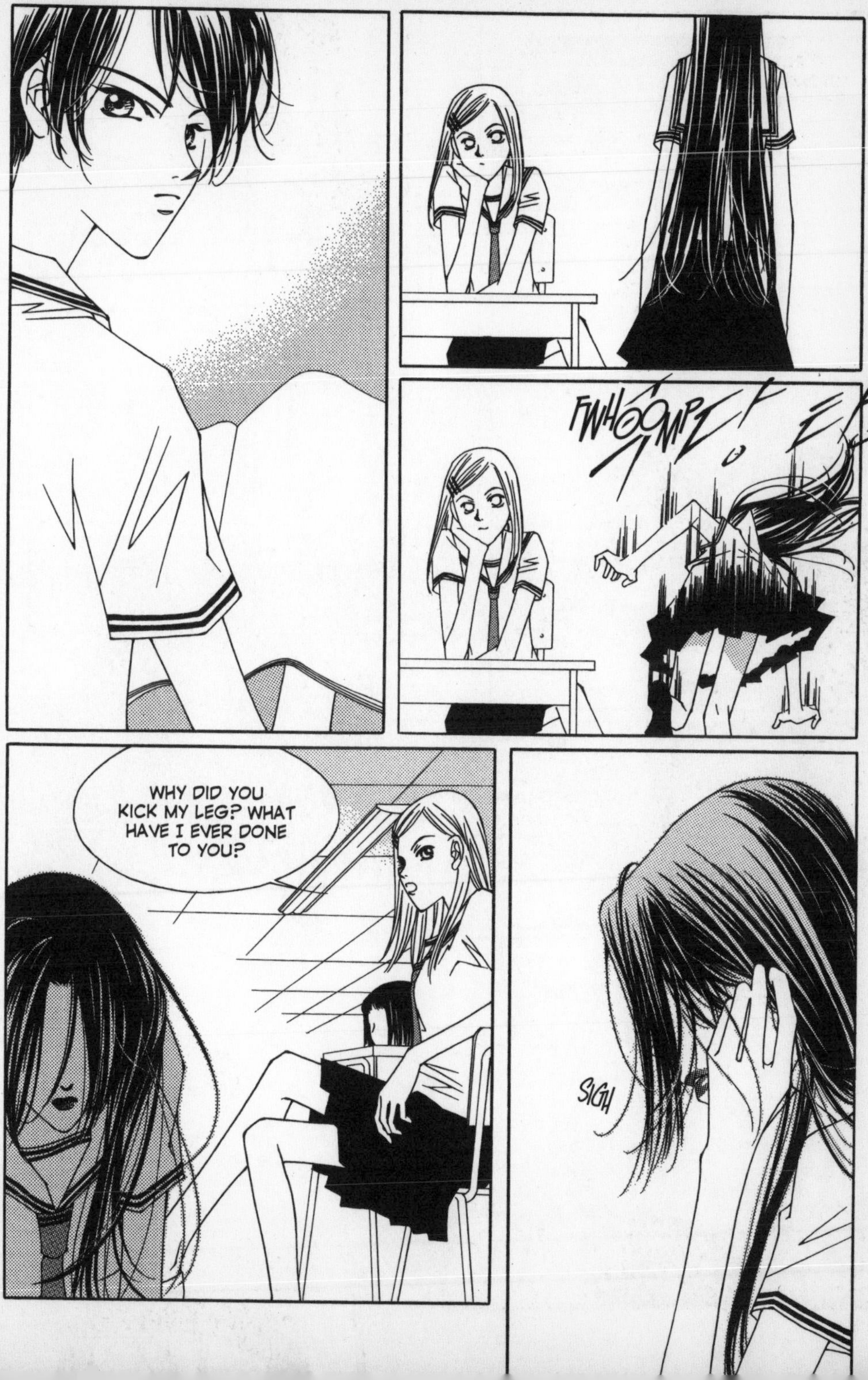
FWHOOMPF
WHY DID YOU KICK MY LEG? WHAT HAVE I EVER DONE TO YOU?
SIGH

I'M SORRY.

IT WAS TOTALLY MY FAULT.

I DIDN'T SEE YOUR LEG. I APOLOGIZE.

I DON'T KNOW HOW I COULD HAVE MISSED SUCH A THICK TREE TRUNK, WITH ALL THAT HAIR GROWING ON IT...

I MUST BE GETTING OLD.

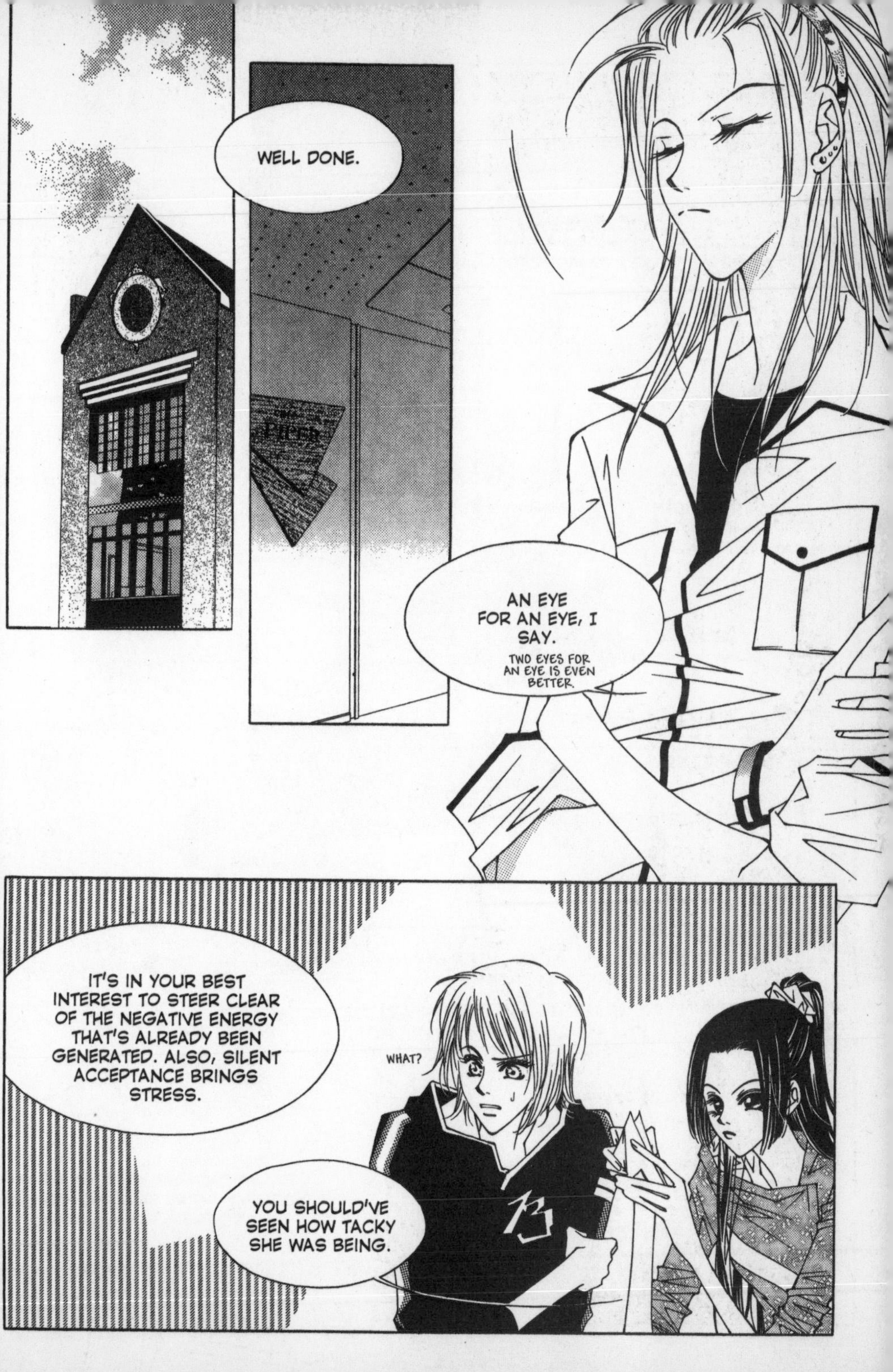
WELL DONE.
AN EYE FOR AN EYE, I SAY.
TWO EYES FOR AN EYE IS EVEN BETTER.
IT'S IN YOUR BEST INTEREST TO STEER CLEAR OF THE NEGATIVE ENERGY THAT'S ALREADY BEEN GENERATED. ALSO, SILENT ACCEPTANCE BRINGS STRESS.
WHAT?
YOU SHOULD'VE SEEN HOW TACKY SHE WAS BEING.

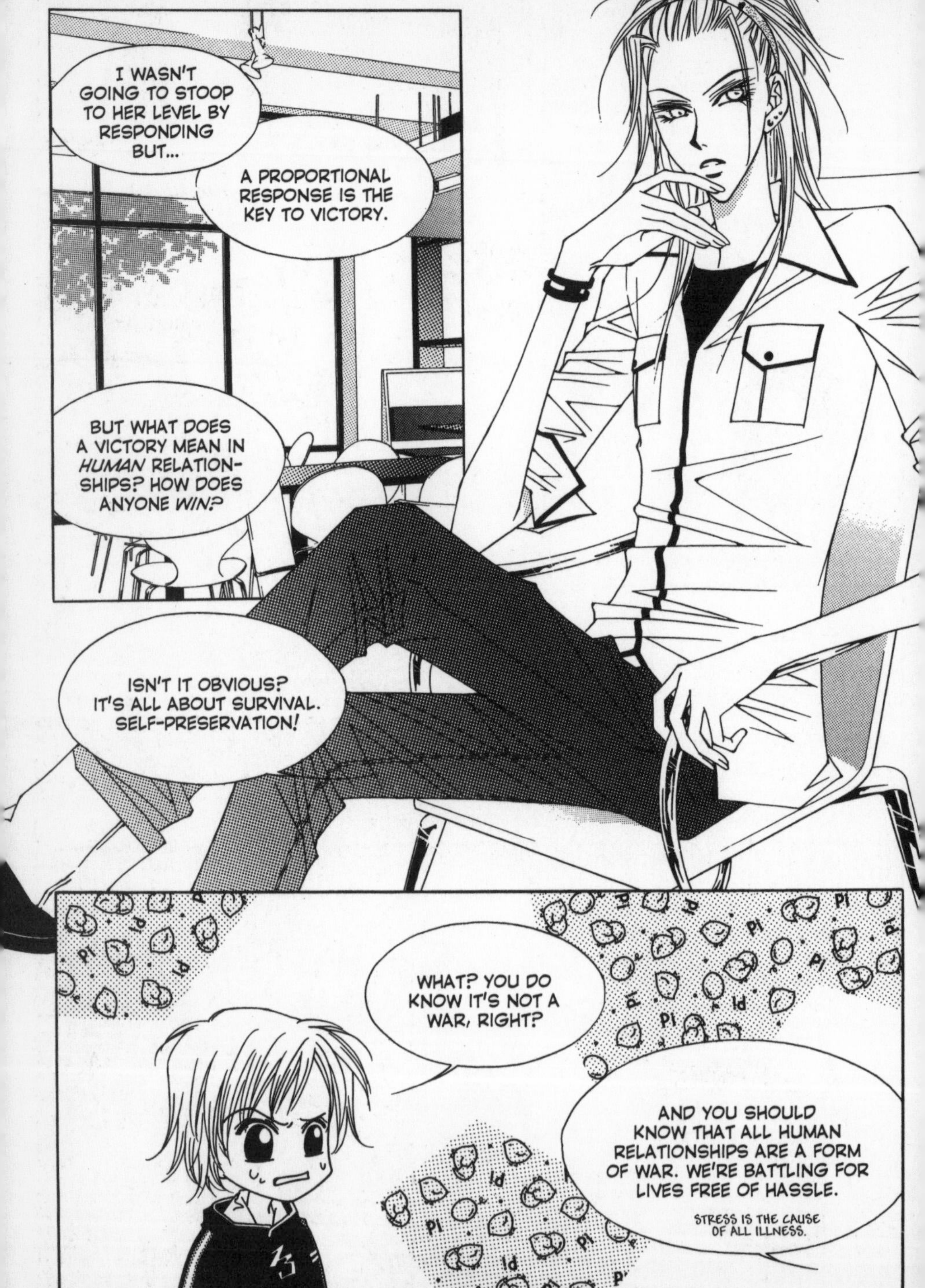
I WASN'T GOING TO STOOP TO HER LEVEL BY RESPONDING BUT...
A PROPORTIONAL RESPONSE IS THE KEY TO VICTORY.
BUT WHAT DOES A VICTORY MEAN IN *HUMAN* RELATIONSHIPS? HOW DOES ANYONE *WIN*?
ISN'T IT OBVIOUS? IT'S ALL ABOUT SURVIVAL. SELF-PRESERVATION!
WHAT? YOU DO KNOW IT'S NOT A WAR, RIGHT?
AND YOU SHOULD KNOW THAT ALL HUMAN RELATIONSHIPS ARE A FORM OF WAR. WE'RE BATTLING FOR LIVES FREE OF HASSLE.
STRESS IS THE CAUSE OF ALL ILLNESS.

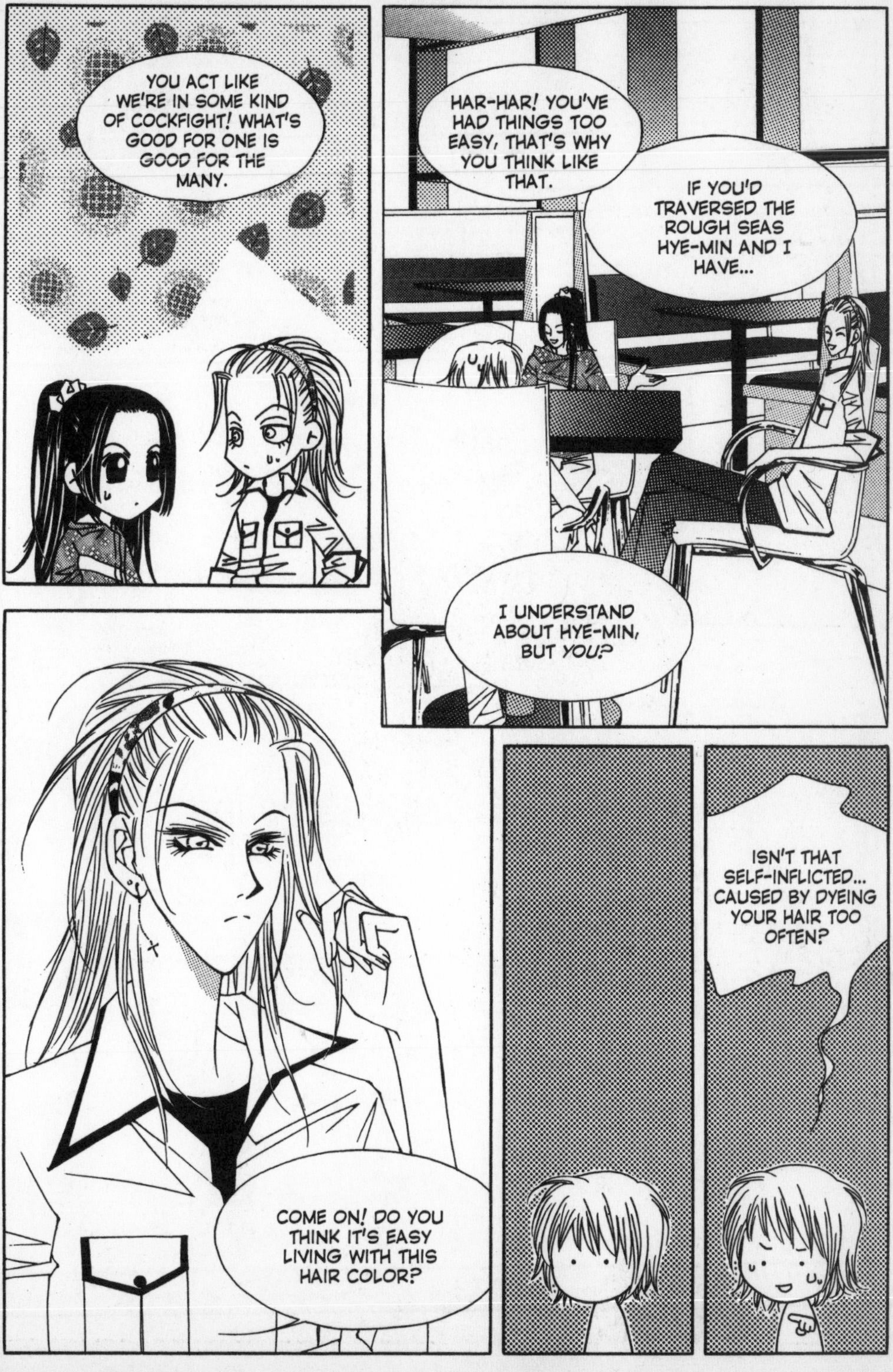
YOU ACT LIKE WE'RE IN SOME KIND OF COCKFIGHT! WHAT'S GOOD FOR ONE IS GOOD FOR THE MANY.
HAR-HAR! YOU'VE HAD THINGS TOO EASY, THAT'S WHY YOU THINK LIKE THAT.
IF YOU'D TRAVERSED THE ROUGH SEAS HYE-MIN AND I HAVE...
I UNDERSTAND ABOUT HYE-MIN, BUT *YOU?*
COME ON! DO YOU THINK IT'S EASY LIVING WITH THIS HAIR COLOR?
ISN'T THAT SELF-INFLICTED... CAUSED BY DYEING YOUR HAIR TOO OFTEN?

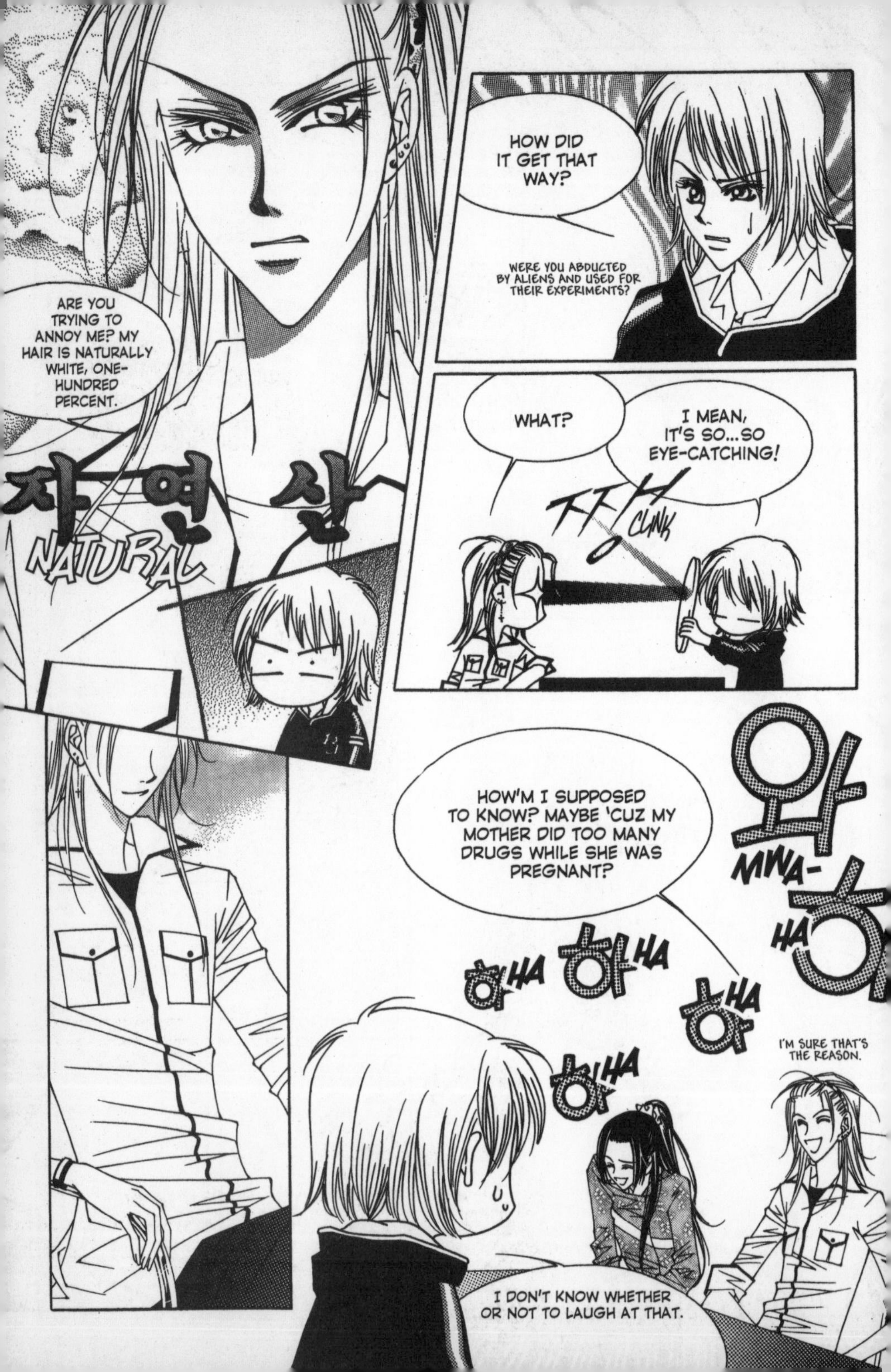
ARE YOU TRYING TO ANNOY ME? MY HAIR IS NATURALLY WHITE, ONE-HUNDRED PERCENT.
자연산
NATURAL
HOW DID IT GET THAT WAY?
WERE YOU ABDUCTED BY ALIENS AND USED FOR THEIR EXPERIMENTS?
WHAT?
I MEAN, IT'S SO...SO EYE-CATCHING!
CLINK
HOW'M I SUPPOSED TO KNOW? MAYBE 'CUZ MY MOTHER DID TOO MANY DRUGS WHILE SHE WAS PREGNANT?
와하
MWA-HA
하 HA
하 HA
하 HA
하 HA
I'M SURE THAT'S THE REASON.
I DON'T KNOW WHETHER OR NOT TO LAUGH AT THAT.

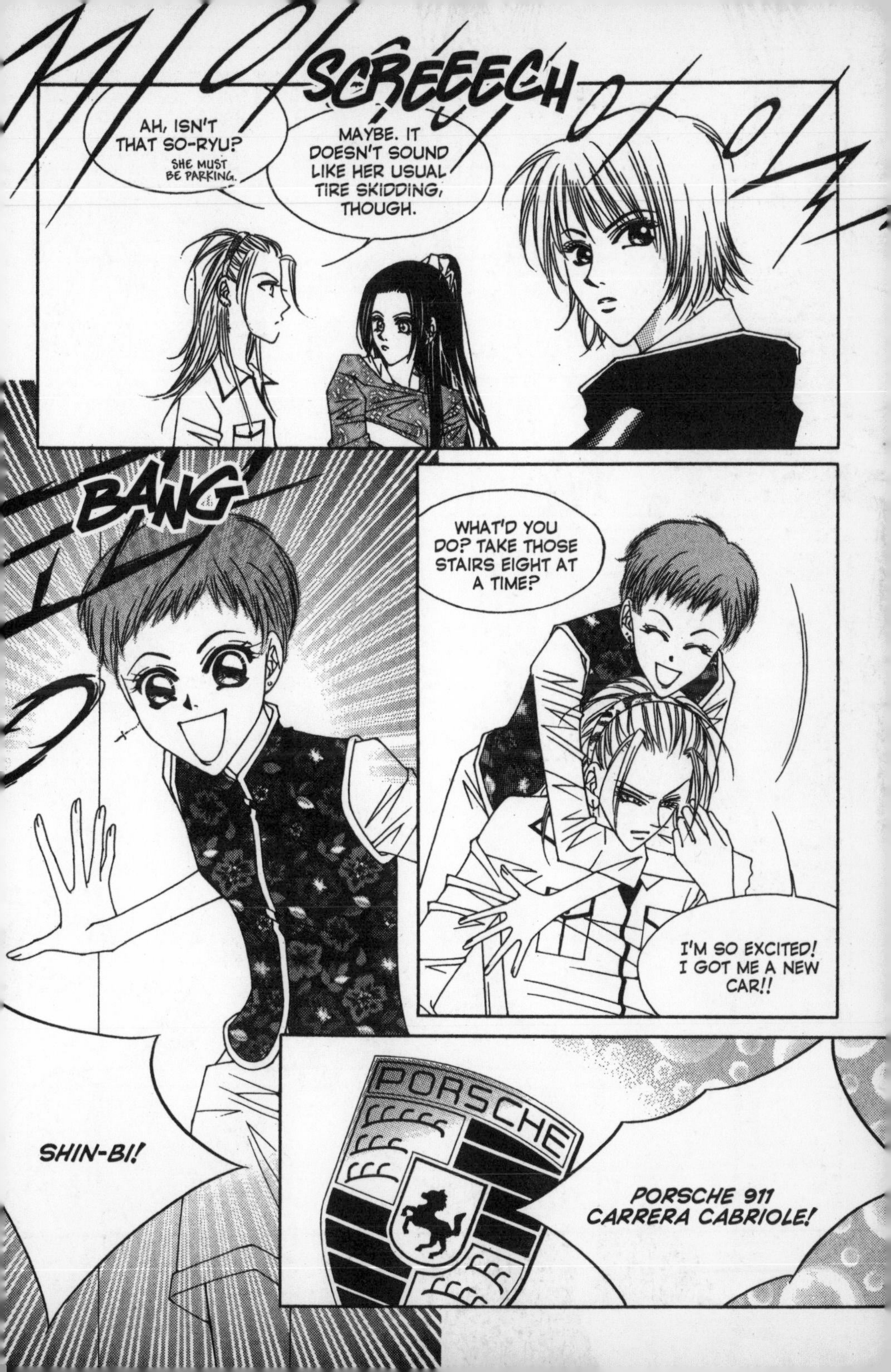
SCREEECH
AH, ISN'T THAT SO-RYU?
SHE MUST BE PARKING.
MAYBE. IT DOESN'T SOUND LIKE HER USUAL TIRE SKIDDING, THOUGH.
BANG
SHIN-BI!
WHAT'D YOU DO? TAKE THOSE STAIRS EIGHT AT A TIME?
I'M SO EXCITED! I GOT ME A NEW CAR!!
PORSCHE
PORSCHE 911 CARRERA CABRIOLE!

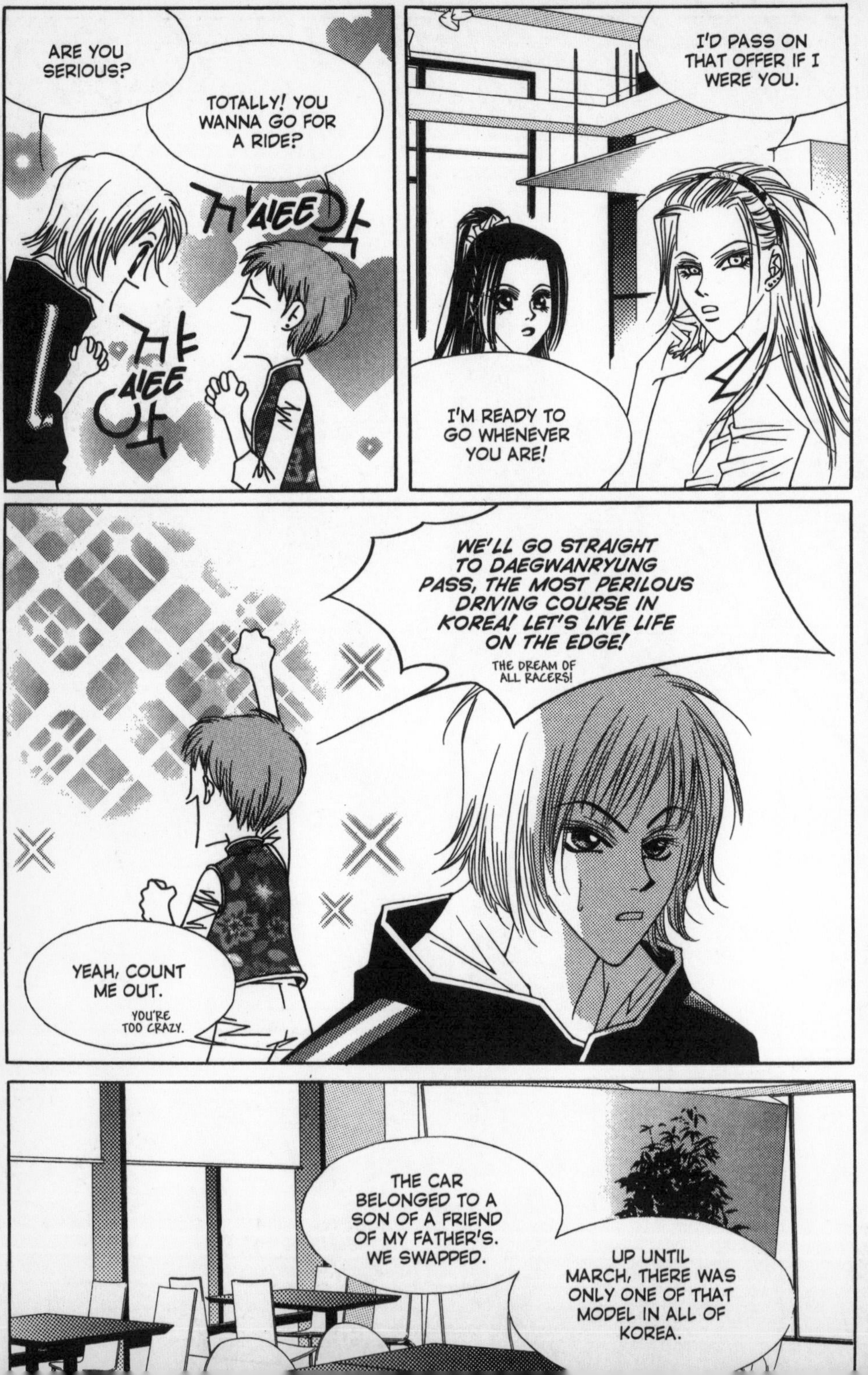

ARE YOU SERIOUS?
TOTALLY! YOU WANNA GO FOR A RIDE?
꺄 AIEE 악
꺄 AIEE 악
I'D PASS ON THAT OFFER IF I WERE YOU.
I'M READY TO GO WHENEVER YOU ARE!
WE'LL GO STRAIGHT TO DAEGWANRYUNG PASS, THE MOST PERILOUS DRIVING COURSE IN KOREA! LET'S LIVE LIFE ON THE EDGE!
THE DREAM OF ALL RACERS!
YEAH, COUNT ME OUT.
YOU'RE TOO CRAZY.
THE CAR BELONGED TO A SON OF A FRIEND OF MY FATHER'S. WE SWAPPED.
UP UNTIL MARCH, THERE WAS ONLY ONE OF THAT MODEL IN ALL OF KOREA.

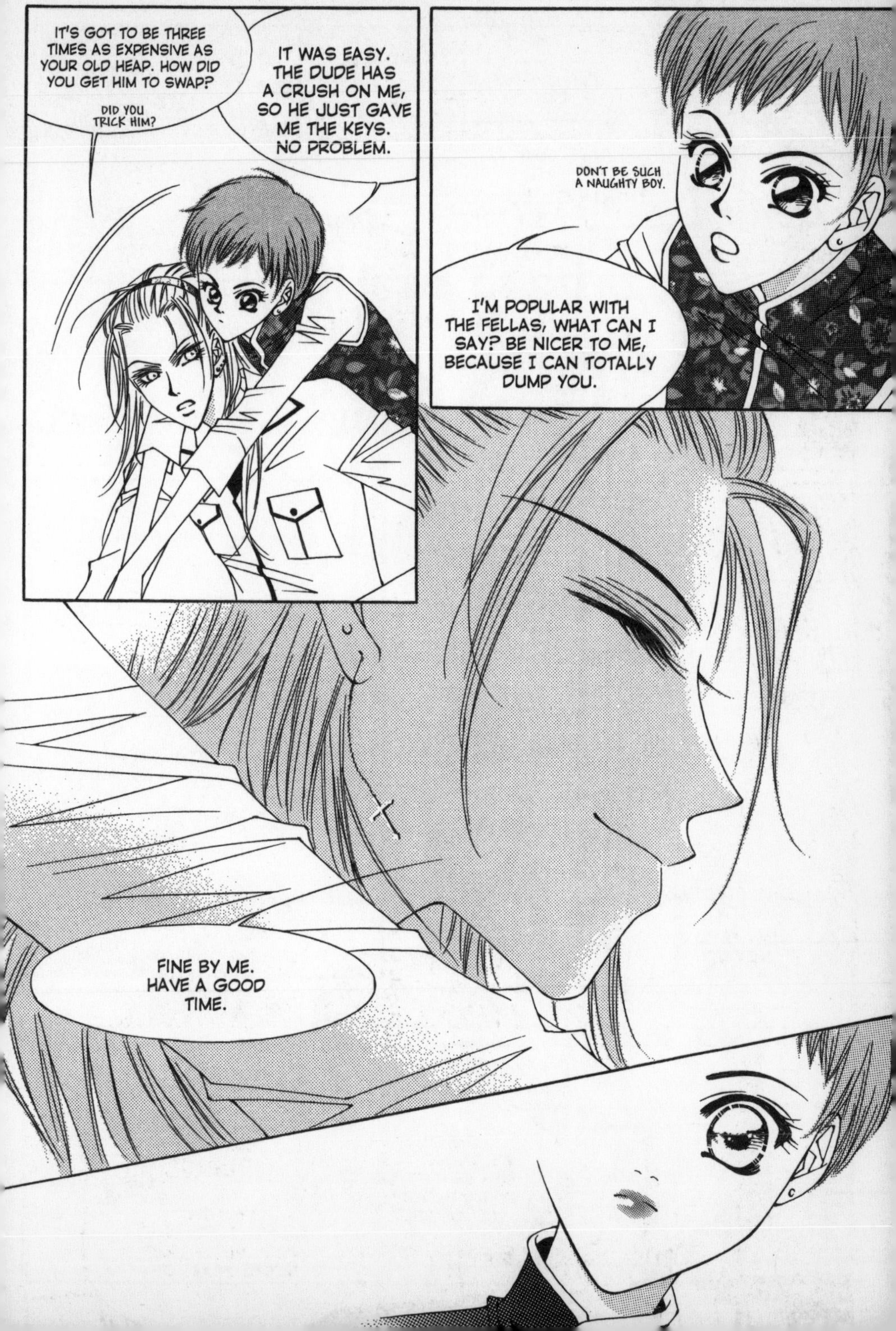
IT'S GOT TO BE THREE TIMES AS EXPENSIVE AS YOUR OLD HEAP. HOW DID YOU GET HIM TO SWAP?
DID YOU TRICK HIM?
IT WAS EASY. THE DUDE HAS A CRUSH ON ME, SO HE JUST GAVE ME THE KEYS. NO PROBLEM.
DON'T BE SUCH A NAUGHTY BOY.
I'M POPULAR WITH THE FELLAS, WHAT CAN I SAY? BE NICER TO ME, BECAUSE I CAN TOTALLY DUMP YOU.
FINE BY ME. HAVE A GOOD TIME.

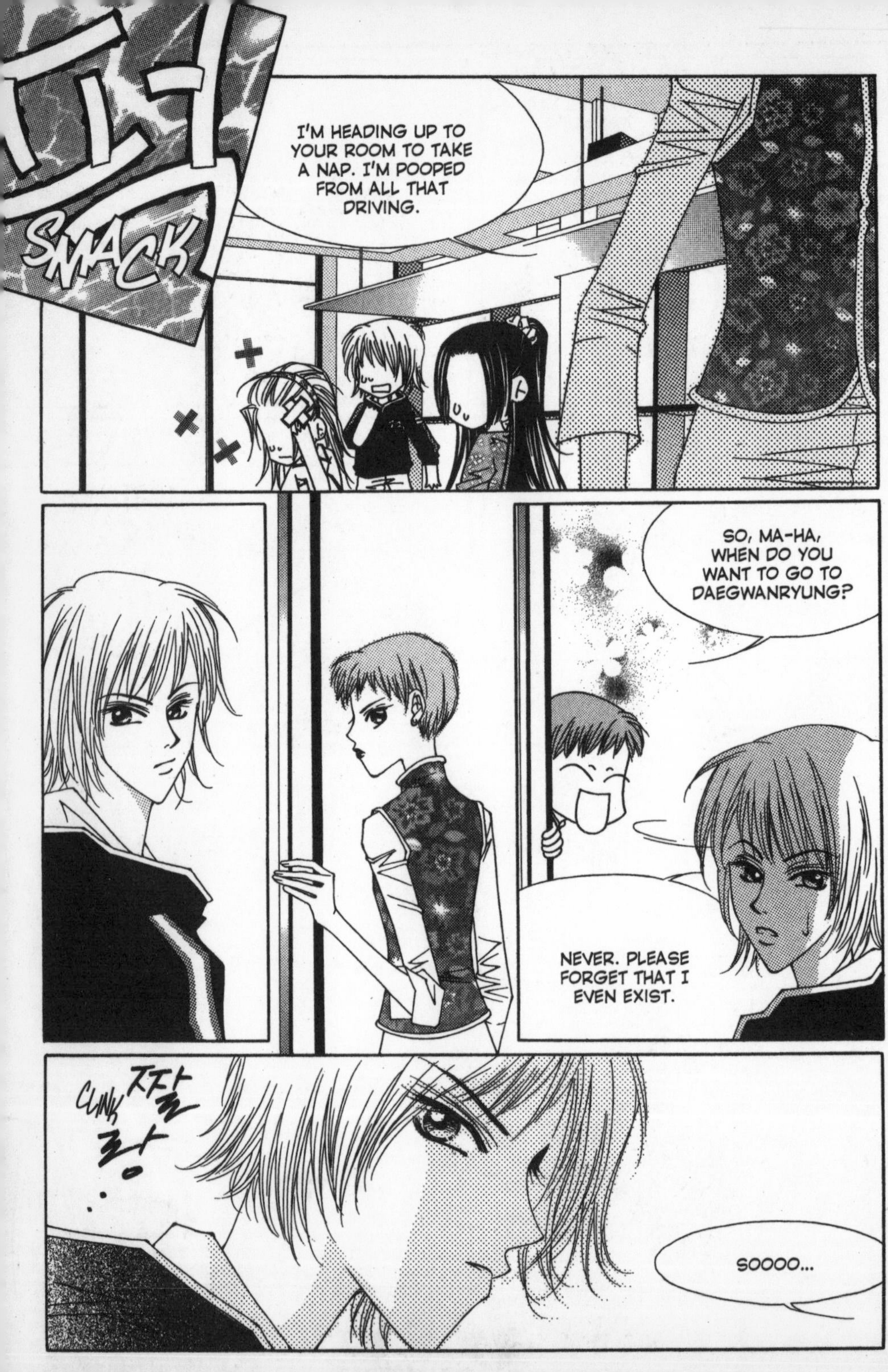
SMACK
I'M HEADING UP TO YOUR ROOM TO TAKE A NAP. I'M POOPED FROM ALL THAT DRIVING.
SO, MA-HA, WHEN DO YOU WANT TO GO TO DAEGWANRYUNG?
NEVER. PLEASE FORGET THAT I EVEN EXIST.
CLINK
SOOOO...

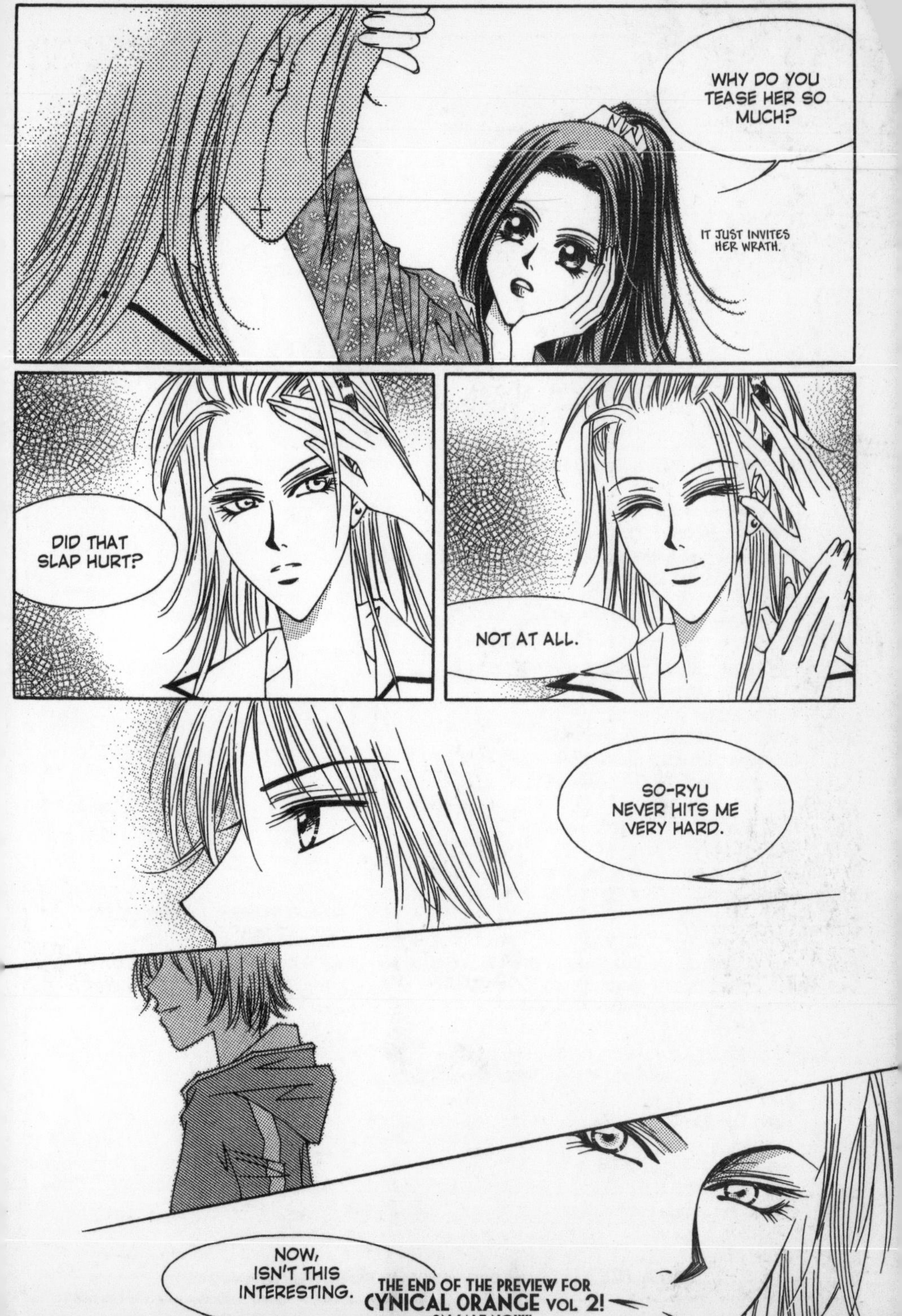
WHY DO YOU TEASE HER SO MUCH?
IT JUST INVITES HER WRATH.
DID THAT SLAP HURT?
NOT AT ALL.
SO-RYU NEVER HITS ME VERY HARD.
NOW, ISN'T THIS INTERESTING.
THE END OF THE PREVIEW FOR CYNICAL ORANGE VOL 2! ON SALE NOW!

Danbi Original

Bring it on! vol.3

Story and art by HyeKyung Baek

Translation Jackie Oh
English Adaptation Oliver Strong
Touch-up and Lettering Terri Delgado · Marshall Dillon
Graphic Design EunKyung Kim

ICE Kunion

Managing Editor Marshall Dillon
Marketing Manager Erik Ko
Senior Editor JuYoun Lee
Editorial Director MoonJung Kim
Managing Director Jackie Lee
Publisher and C.E.O. JaeKook Chun

Bring it on! © 2005 HyeKyung Baek
First published in Korea in 2002 by SIGONGSA Co., Ltd.
English text translation rights arranged by SIGONGSA Co., Ltd.
English text © 2005 ICE KUNION

Published by ICE Kunion.
SIGONGSA 2F Yeil Bldg. 1619-4, Seocho-dong, Seocho-gu, Seoul, 137-878, Korea

ISBN : 89-527-4479-9

First printing, August 2006
10 9 8 7 6 5 4 3 2 1
Printed in Canada

www.ICEkunion.com/www.koreanmanhwa.com